ENTREPRENEURSHIP

RESEARCH IN THE SOCIOLOGY OF WORK

Series Editor: Randy Hodson
http://www.sociology.ohio-state.edu/work

RESEARCH IN THE SOCIOLOGY OF WORK   VOLUME 15

ENTREPRENEURSHIP

EDITED BY

LISA A. KEISTER

Department of Sociology, The Ohio State University, Columbus, USA

United Kingdom – North America – Japan
India – Malaysia – China

Emerald Group Publishing Limited
Howard House, Wagon Lane, Bingley BD16 1WA, UK

British Library Cataloguing in Publication Data
A catalogue record for this book is available from the British Library

ISBN: 978-0-7623-1191-0
ISSN: 0277-2833 (Series)

Awarded in recognition of
Emerald's production
department's adherence to
quality systems and processes
when preparing scholarly
journals for print

INVESTOR IN PEOPLE

CONTENTS

v

**PART III:
CONTEXT AND OPPORTUNITIES**

LIST OF CONTRIBUTORS

Howard E. Aldrich	Department of Sociology, University of North Carolina, USA
R. Saylor Breckenridge	Department of Sociology, Wake Forest University, USA
Louis Corsino	Department of Sociology, North Central College, USA
Amy Davis	Department of Sociology, University of North Carolina, USA
Yi Jiang	Fisher College of Business, The Ohio State University, USA
Lisa A. Keister	Department of Sociology, College of Social and Behavioral Sciences, Ohio State University, USA
Bruce A. Kirchhoff	New Jersey Institute of Technology, USA
Kevin T. Leicht	Department of Sociology, The University of Iowa, Iowa, USA
Stephen Lippmann	Department of Sociology, University of North Carolina, USA
Beverly Mizrachi	Department of Sociology and Anthropology, Ashkelon Academic College, Ashkelon, Israel
Mike W. Peng	Department of Management and Human Resources, Fisher College of Business, Ohio State University, USA
Yusheng Peng	Brooklyn College, City University of New York, USA
Linda A. Renzulli	Department of Sociology, University of Georgia, USA

Jeremy Reynolds   Department of Sociology, University of
                         Georgia, USA

Akos Rona-Tas   Department of Sociology, University of
                         California, USA

Martin Ruef   Stanford University, Department of
                         Sociology, Princeton University, USA

Matild Sagi   TARKI, Budapest, Hungary

Bruce C. Skaggs   Department of Management, Isenberg School
                         of Management, University of Massachusetts,
                         USA

Maricela Soto   Resurrection Behavioral Health (Procare
                         Center), USA

Ian M. Taplin   Department of Sociology, Wake Forest
                         University, USA

Noam Wasserman   Harvard Business School, USA

Shaker A. Zahra   Blank Center for Entrepreneurship, Babson
                         College, USA

INTRODUCTION

Entrepreneurship is an important part of the structure and functioning of organizations and economies. Entrepreneurship, or new business formation, can also shape social and economic stratification in an economy and may be an important vehicle for social mobility. In 1934, Schumpeter first identified entrepreneurs as distinct from business owners and managers, and he argued that entrepreneurship was essential for economic growth and development. Since then, the importance of entrepreneurs and entrepreneurship has been increasingly evident, and entrepreneurship has been accepted as a distinct field of study in the social sciences and business schools. Entrepreneurship has also become more pervasive. In the U.S., more adults are currently attempting to start new businesses than at any other time in the past century. Estimates suggest that nearly 8% of the adult population is actively engaged in starting a business. Including both those in the process of starting a business (i.e., nascent entrepreneurs) and those owning or managing firms started 3.5 years ago or less, approximately 11% of the U.S. adults can be considered entrepreneurs. In developing countries, prevalence rates are much higher (Reynolds 2004; Reynolds et al. 2002).

Yet defining entrepreneurship can be somewhat difficult. Entrepreneurship is typically considered synonymous with business start-up or the creation of new organizations. Although entrepreneurship research was originally part of the study of small business and there is still some overlap between entrepreneurial endeavors and small businesses, entrepreneurs and small business owners are now typically considered separate entities (Carland et al. 1994). At the same time, researchers have become increasingly willing to accept some degree of uncertainty regarding when a business has begun, and thus, some ambiguity in who qualifies as an entrepreneur is typical in the literature. Finally, it is possible to distinguish entrepreneurs from the broader category of self-employed people, but there is considerable overlap between these two groups as well.

The chapters that are included in this volume highlight many of the issues that are central to the study of entrepreneurship today and also break new ground in the field. The chapters explore the importance of entrepreneurship, the process by which entrepreneurship occurs, and the way both meaning and process vary with context and opportunity structures. These chapters address long-standing controversies in the study of entrepreneurship, and they also identify new, innovative questions and approaches. As a result, both seasoned entrepreneurship researchers and those who are new to the field will find the chapters interesting and useful.

PART I. WHY STUDY ENTREPRENEURSHIP?

The chapters in Part I highlight some of the central reasons for studying entrepreneurship at the aggregate, family, and individual levels. Lippmann, Davis, and Aldrich develop society level propositions about the relationship between inequality and entrepreneurship. They define entrepreneurship for both individuals and societies, and they argue that factors such as development, state policies, sector shifts, and changing labor market conditions affect levels of inequality and also increase incentives for entrepreneurship. The authors distinguish entrepreneurship undertaken out of necessity and entrepreneurship that takes advantage of market opportunities, and they propose that changing social and economic conditions affect entry into each type of entrepreneurship. The arguments presented in this chapter are well-grounded in previous theoretical and empirical research, but they ask about the relationship between entrepreneurship and inequality in a fresh, new way. Not only does this chapter clarify the factors that lead to entrepreneurship, but it also identifies new relationships between business start-ups and stratification that have not been explored previously.

The second chapter in Part I focuses on the implications of self-employment at the individual and family levels. Jeremy Reynolds and Linda Renzulli examine how self-employment may prevent work and life roles from interfering with each other. They argue that self-employment can prevent work from interfering with life roles, particularly for women. However, they also propose that self-employment increases the likelihood that life will interfere with work. Reynolds and Renzulli then use a unique set of analyses of nationally representative data to explore work-life conflict among the self-employed. The findings suggest additional reasons that research on entrepreneurship and self-employment has important implications that extend beyond understanding business and the functioning of complex organizations. Indeed, as this chapter shows, the effect of self-employment extends well beyond economics and finances and shapes outcomes that are typically studied in research on the family. Again, this chapter draws on previous approaches in studying both the self-employed and families, but the authors ask their questions in a unique way and are, therefore, able to deliver an innovative set of propositions and corresponding findings.

PART II. THE ENTREPRENEURSHIP PROCESS

The chapters in Part II investigate the entrepreneurship process. In the first chapter, Martin Ruef explores the process by which organizations are founded. Ruef underscores the importance of the dynamics of the entrepreneurial process and stresses that research that considers business start-ups as discrete events overlooks much of what is interesting and important about the process. He proposes that organizational founding is the result of a series of potential entrepreneurial activities such as initiation, resource mobilization, legal establishment, social organization, and operational start-up. He then shows empirically that social context has a rather consistent effect on the occurrence and sequencing of the founding process.

Shaker Zahra and Bruce Kirchhoff explore the next part of the process: the determinants of new venture growth. They point out that unlimited growth is not necessarily the goal of all new ventures, but they also note that some growth is critical for survival. Although access to many types of resources affects growth, the availability of technological resources is particularly important in recent decades. Zahra and Kirchhof argue that young start-up firms, those 5 years or less, benefit from using a different set of technological resources than adolescent firms, those 6–8 years old. They also argue that different technological resources propel domestic and international growth.

Bruce Skaggs and Kevin Leicht explore the process by which management–labor relations change over time within established organizations. They provide a model of the evolution of the ideological paradigm governing management–labor relations, and they argue that managers' desire for autonomy and their responses to environmental shocks and stakeholder actions drive changes in their approach to labor. Skaggs and Leicht trace historic shifts to and from five paradigms: entrepreneurialism, scientific management, human relations management, and a paradigm they call neo-entrepreneurialism. Although this chapter does not fit the typical mold of an article about entrepreneurship, it does underscore – in a unique and inventive way – the role the entrepreneurialism plays in the process of organizational transformation.

Noam Wasserman also focuses on changes within organizations in his study of a transformation that is underway in the structure of venture capital firms. Wasserman's chapter begins with the observation that nonpyramidal firms have dominated the venture capital industry for decades, but many are now attempting to transition to pyramidal organization structures. He then investigates the factors that encourage venture capital firms to undertake this type of change, the hurdles firms face in making this sort of change, and organizational traits that might impede or aid the transformation. Previous research that explored similar transitions in other industries relied on retrospective data, but Wasserman studies the process as it happens. As a result, his findings provide insight into entrepreneurial dynamics about which previous studies were only able to speculate.

In another chapter that takes advantage of a change while it is in process, Saylor Breckenridge and Ian Taplin present a case study of the emerging wine industry in North Carolina. Their chapter explores the growth of retail wineries and commercial wine production that are beginning to fill the growing void left by North Carolina's struggling tobacco industry. Breckenridge and Taplin examine how changes in the availability of land and capital interacted with an entrepreneurial climate that encouraged interest in winemaking. They draw on a conceptual model of small business growth and argue that firms gained credibility by associating with clusters, and they follow the growth of key wineries in the area. This chapter highlights the importance of the social side of entrepreneurship: the authors emphasize the centrality of association with other firms and information sharing among wineries during inception.

PART III. CONTEXT AND OPPORTUNITIES

As Patricia Thornton (1999) pointed out in her review of the entrepreneurship literature in sociology, entrepreneurship research no longer focuses only on the supply side or individual traits that motivate business formation. Rather there is an increasing awareness of the importance of the demand side of the process, that is the environment and interactions between individual entrepreneurs, groups of entrepreneurs, and other organizations that create incentives and opportunities for business start-ups. The context within which entrepreneurship occurs affects the likelihood of business start-ups, the process by which the businesses begin, and the success of the business. The chapters in the final section of this volume analyze the role that context and opportunity play in the entrepreneurship process.

Louis Corsino and Maricella Soto provide a case study of ethnic strategies among Mexican-American entrepreneurs. They start by demonstrating that entrepreneurship among Mexican-Americans was low historically, but it has increased in recent years. Corsino and Soto then use in-depth interviews with Mexican-American entrepreneurs to explore the unique strategies these individuals used to become self-employed. They argue that changes in opportunities and changes in capacities for resource mobilization in the Mexican-American community have increased the attractiveness of entrepreneurship and have made it possible for increasing numbers of Mexican-Americans to become entrepreneurs.

Beverly Mizrachi uses a case study of a Moroccan immigrant woman entrepreneur to explore the factors that encourage immigrants to become entrepreneurs. Mizrachi's focus is on the personality traits that shape entry into self-employment for the woman whose life history she presents. In particular, Mizrachi highlights the importance of a need for achievement, a willingness to take risks, innovativeness, and a desire to accumulate wealth in the process of becoming an entrepreneur. She shows that the woman she studied used these skills and took advantage of an ethnic revival in Morocco to create a successful business, create financial security for herself, and become upwardly mobile.

The final three chapters explore a unique and currently very important context: transition economies. Akos Rona-Tas and Matild Sagi explore what has been described as an extremely rapid growth of entrepreneurship in Eastern Europe following the end of Communism. Rona-Tas and Sagi argue that many descriptions of the miracle in Eastern Europe were overly optimistic because they conflated entrepreneurship with self-employment. This chapter makes an important plea to disaggregate various forms of independent business sector activity in transition economies and in other contexts.

Mike Peng and Yi Jiang explore changes in entrepreneurship during transition in order to ask how entrepreneurs strategize during institutional transition and how these strategies affect their behavior as entrepreneurs. This chapter is unique in at least a couple of very important ways. First, Peng and Jiang focus on the factors that motivate the behavior of the entrepreneur, and second, they look broadly at transition economies including contexts as broad-ranging as China, Poland, and Russia. They argue that entrepreneurs are best able to navigate the unique conditions that characterize institutional change by adopting aggressive strategies, networking widely, and blurring boundaries.

In the final chapter, Yusheng Peng focuses on entrepreneurship in rural China during transition. He explores competing arguments about the role that unique rural family patterns and kinship ties play in facilitating or impeding entrepreneurial activity in this context. Peng explores the formation of rural enterprises and uses village-level data to argue that close-knit kinship networks are positively related to the proliferation of independent business endeavors during this crucial stage of rural development in China. This chapter underscores the importance of social networks in the entrepreneurial process, but it also highlights the fact that important inputs such as social networks may have unique cultural incarnations in developing economies or transition economies.

The chapters in this volume draw attention to many of the areas of research on entrepreneurship that are currently attracting scholarly attention. They highlight the broad range of questions that researchers ask, and they demonstrate that understanding of entrepreneurship is improving rapidly. Yet, these papers can also be seen as an invitation to readers to participate in an area of scholarly inquiry that continues to offer rich opportunities to understand a form of social and economic behavior that is both wonderfully interesting and of critical importance. As increasing numbers of people enter entrepreneurship, it will undoubtedly become a more important part of economic and social life. At the same time, data on entrepreneurship are improving and, as a result, researchers are able to ask increasingly provocative questions. As data and empirical work expand and improve, so does theoretical and conceptual work on the determinants of entrepreneurship, the process by which businesses are formed, the reasons that businesses fail or succeed, the implications of business formation for other outcomes, and related questions. I hope that these chapters will inspire you to join us in taking advantage of this unique set of opportunities to explore questions related to entrepreneurship.

REFERENCES

Carland, James W., Hoy Frank, William R. Boulton, and Jo Ann C. Carland. 1994. "Differentiating Entrepreneurs from Small Business Owners: A Conceptualization." *Academy of Management Review* 9:354–359.

Reynolds, Paul D. 2004. "Entrepreneurship over Time: Measures of Activity and Recent Changes in the US: 1993–2002." Working paper.

Reynolds, Paul D., William D. Bygrave, Erkko Autio, and Michael Hay. 2002. *GEM Global 2002 Summary Report*. Arthur M. Blank Center for Entrepreneurship, Babson College, Babson Park, MA: Global Entrepreneurship Monitor.

Schumpeter, Joseph A. 1934. *The Theory of Economic Development*. Cambridge, MA: Harvard University Press.
Thornton, Patricia. 1999. "The Sociology of Entrepreneurship." *Annual Review of Sociology* 25:19–46.

Lisa A. Keister
Editor

PART I:
WHY STUDY
ENTREPRENEURSHIP?

ENTREPRENEURSHIP AND INEQUALITY

Stephen Lippmann, Amy Davis and Howard
E. Aldrich

ABSTRACT

Nations with high levels of economic inequality tend to have high rates of entrepreneurial activity. In this paper, we develop propositions about this relationship, based upon current research. Although we provide some descriptive analyses to support our propositions, our paper is not an empirical test but rather a theoretical exploration of new ideas related to this topic. We first define entrepreneurship at the individual and societal level and distinguish between entrepreneurship undertaken out of necessity and entrepreneurship that takes advantage of market opportunities. We then explore the roles that various causes of economic inequality play in increasing entrepreneurial activity, including economic development, state policies, foreign investment, sector shifts, labor market and employment characteristics, and class structures. The relationship between inequality and entrepreneurship poses a potentially disturbing message for countries with strong egalitarian norms and political and social policies that also wish to increase entrepreneurial activity. We conclude by noting the conditions under which entrepreneurship can be a source of upward social and economic mobility for individuals.

Entrepreneurship
Research in the Sociology of Work, Volume 15, 3–31
Copyright © 2005 by Elsevier Ltd.
All rights of reproduction in any form reserved
ISSN: 0277-2833/doi:10.1016/S0277-2833(05)15002-X

INTRODUCTION

Nations vary widely in their levels of entrepreneurial activity, ranging from countries in which large employers and the state dominate labor markets to countries in which small firms and self-employed craft workers play much the same role they did a century ago. Nations also vary widely in their levels of economic inequality, ranging from countries in which wealthy families dominate the economic scene to countries in which wealth is widely shared and ostentatious displays of wealth are frowned upon. We have reason to believe that these two phenomena are linked. The same social and economic dynamics that increase societal levels of economic inequality – the uneven distribution of a society's financial resources within its population – may also lead to increases in rates of entrepreneurial activity. In addition, institutional factors, such as wealth transfer and labor market policies, may strengthen the link between inequality and entrepreneurship.

In this paper, we offer two contributions. First, we review the existing literature on the relationships between societal level inequalities and entrepreneurship, and second, we develop theoretically based propositions to suggest future empirical projects. Although we provide some descriptive analyses to support our propositions, our paper is not an empirical test but rather a theoretical exploration of new ideas related to this topic. We draw on various research streams in what we believe is one of the first attempts to integrate the literature on societal level inequalities and entrepreneurship.

Our plan is as follows. We briefly note the historical importance of inequality and explore two sides of an argument concerning inequality's possible consequences for individual opportunities. We then offer a definition of entrepreneurship at the individual and societal levels, explaining the difference between necessity- and opportunity-based entrepreneurship. We incorporate that distinction into our propositions concerning cross-national differences in entrepreneurial activities. Next, we review sociological theories of how and why various social and economic structures, including economic development and inequality, affect the distribution of resources needed by entrepreneurs across societies. We draw on these literatures to develop propositions intended to provide theoretical linkages between the causes of inequality and the great variation in entrepreneurial activity among nations. If certain types of entrepreneurial activity require financial resources, then the unequal distribution of these resources and differential access to them could restrict entrepreneurship to certain groups and suppress entrepreneurial activity generally. Alternatively, if inequality limits individuals' opportunities to participate in the formal labor market, they may pursue self-employment as a last resort. We conclude by discussing the implications of our arguments for further research.

INEQUALITY

Concern with inequalities in access to power and valued resources has been central to sociological research since the discipline's inception (e.g. Marx 1852). On one side, some social theorists have emphasized the systematic reproduction of wealth and privilege inequalities that favor the well off at the expense of the less fortunate. On the other side, some theorists have emphasized the expanded opportunities available to people from humble origins as economies grow. Thus, both sides in this debate have argued that the extent to which resources are unequally distributed within and between societies has a profound impact on whether social and economic inequality increases or declines.

Conceptualizing Wealth Inequality

Although the distribution of wealth is understudied by sociologists, it is a crucial aspect of inequality in the United States and throughout the rest of the world. Most studies of economic inequality focus on income, but wealth and income are not highly correlated. In addition, for a variety of reasons, wealth inequality is much more severe than income inequality (Keister and Moller 2000). For our purposes, wealth is more relevant than income to the relationship between economic inequality and entrepreneurship. To the degree that financial resources are necessary for becoming an entrepreneur, wealth, in the form of real and financial assets, is more likely than income to be the resource that nascent entrepreneurs rely on.

Unfortunately, severe data limitations with regard to measuring actual household wealth have hampered attempts to clear up the relationship between wealth and entrepreneurship. Accordingly, previous research gives us little guidance concerning the impact of financial capital on new business formation (Dunn and Holtz–Eakin 2000; Reynolds and White 1997; Kim, Aldrich and Keister 2003). For example, research in the United States on the relationship between household wealth and new business formation has yielded mixed results (Reynolds and White 1997; Kim et al. 2003).[1] We are not aware of any research that has used the same definitions of inequality and entrepreneurship across nations, except for the Global Entrepreneurship Monitor project, described later in our paper. We offer propositions the testing of which would require such data and thus justify a new research thrust in the field of entrepreneurship.

Economic Inequality and Opportunity

Arguments concerning the *negative* consequences of inequality note that the social structures of modern societies severely inhibit mobility chances for some people (Blau and Duncan 1967; Fijiwara-Greve and Greve 2000). Through direct inheritance of wealth, privilege and status structures can be reproduced from one generation to the next (Keister and Moller 2000). People occupying advantageous levels in the occupational structure often manage to pass along educational opportunities to their offspring, as shown by the high rate at which children of self-employed professionals become professionals themselves (Blau and Duncan 1967; Sobel, Becker and Minick 1998).

The unequal distribution of resources often magnifies other disadvantages associated with the ascriptive characteristics of individuals, including race and gender (Blau 1977; Tilly 1998). People born into poor families and residing in impoverished areas face bleak prospects for upward mobility (Wilson 1996). If underrepresented and underprivileged groups are consistently excluded from sources of access to resources, then their life chances are damaged (Tomaskovic-Devey 1993).

When two social dimensions are highly correlated with other social distinctions, such as wealth with race or gender, theorists call them "consolidated" (Blau 1977). To the degree that inequality is consolidated and a lack of resources inhibits entrepreneurship, the founding of new businesses contributes to the reproduction of social and economic inequalities. In addition, by limiting entrepreneurial opportunities, persistent inequalities may narrow the range of startup types in a society, thus limiting organizational and industrial diversity.[2]

Arguments concerning the *positive* role of inequalities in wealth and income turn on the proposition that self-employment can be a source of social and economic mobility for individuals (Keister 2000). Since the industrial revolution spread from England to other western capitalist societies in the 19th century, one widespread socio-political ideology has encouraged a "belief in success among the unsuccessful" (Bendix 1956). To be sure, when economies were growing rapidly, expanding opportunities allowed many immigrants and children of the working class to become prosperous business owners. The spurt of economic growth in the 1990s seems to have reawakened that dream. Indeed, some research suggests that entrepreneurship may be impervious to some of the posited constraints on business startups and therefore still represents an important source of mobility for entrepreneurs and their families.

ENTREPRENEURSHIP

Entrepreneurial activities are central to the evolution of capitalist societies because new businesses drive economic and employment growth. In capitalist societies, continued economic growth depends on the extent to which potential entrepreneurs can obtain and effectively utilize the social and economic resources they need. Moreover, new firms' foundings and disbandings generate a great deal of employment volatility through job creation and destruction. For example, between 1992 and 1996, newly founded organizations created about 28 million jobs in the United States (Birch 1997). In the first years of the 21st century, fewer new businesses were founded and the rate of job creation slowed.

Entrepreneurship at the Level of Individuals and Teams

"Entrepreneur" and "entrepreneurship" constitute somewhat contested terms, especially outside of the community of scholars who regularly publish in entrepreneurship journals (Gartner 1985). Debates over the meaning of the terms became a regular feature of conference presentations and journal articles in the 1970s, as the field struggled for academic legitimacy. Some of the debates reflected the field's attempt to distinguish the field of "entrepreneurship" from the field of "small business studies," which had been the traditional home of people studying business startups. The debate also reflected disciplinary disputes over units and levels of analysis, period, methods, and theoretical perspectives (Aldrich 2004).

Over the past decade, several teams of researchers have used a scheme developed by Katz and Gartner (1985) to study the emergence of new organizations, with the largest project being the Panel Study of Entrepreneurial Dynamics, or PSED. Their investigations have shown that researchers must accept some degree of imprecision and ambiguity in deciding when entrepreneurs have truly "created" an organization. Working within this perspective, researchers do not sharply delimit the concepts of "self-employment" from "creating an organization," or make someone's status as an entrepreneur dependent on whether he or she employs others. Sociologically, an "organization" exists to the extent that a socially recognized bounded entity exists that is engaged in exchanges with its environment. In the remainder of this chapter, we focus on the study of entrepreneurship as the creation of new organizations and we will label the people who create organizations and manage them during their early years as "entrepreneurs," in keeping with the way sociological research on entrepreneurship is characteristically framed.

Entrepreneurship at the Level of the Nation-state

Theorizing cross nationally requires a generic conceptualization of entrepreneurship. Most entrepreneurship research has been conducted within single countries and thus has not been concerned with societal level rates. Investigators doing cross-national research have mainly studied differences in individual entrepreneurs across countries, rather than differences in societal level rates. In response to this lack of truly comparative national level data, the Global Entrepreneurship Monitor (GEM) project set out to provide internationally comparable data from multiple countries concerning entrepreneurial activity (Reynolds et al. 2002). GEM, which began in 1999, conducts surveys of at least 2,000 adults in each nation studied, as well as a smaller number with national experts.

GEM reports the level of total entrepreneurial activity (TEA) for a nation based on two indicators. The first indicator is the percentage of the labor force actively involved in starting a new venture that has not yet become an operating business. The second indicator is the percentage of individuals in the labor force who either own or manage a business that is less than 42 months old. Taken together, the TEA indicators provide a reasonable estimate of the level of entrepreneurial activity in a nations labor force. In 2001, its values ranged from 1.8 in Japan to 18.9 in Thailand.

Types of Entrepreneurship

Ambitions to start a business are widespread in the populations of many capitalist societies, but resources are not. Researchers have debated the role that *financial resources* play in influencing an individual's likelihood of becoming a nascent entrepreneur. Financial resources refers to property, stocks and bonds, tangible goods, and other assets that can be pledged in exchange for credit or actually turned into a liquid form, such as money used in leasing or purchasing resources.

Some researchers have asserted that financial resources are critical for entrepreneurship and that liquidity constraints inhibit start-ups (Evans and Jovanovic 1989; Bates 1997; Blanchflower and Oswald 1998; Fischer and Massey 2000). They reason that business start-ups often require a substantial sum of money and that entrepreneurs' access to credit markets will be constrained due to the risks associated with a new venture. This viewpoint emphasizes that equity, particularly from family wealth holdings, allows entrepreneurs to obtain credit, and those with little personal wealth simply will not secure necessary start-up loans and capital (Bates 1997). Thus, we would expect those with high net-worth to be more likely than others to become self-employed (Evans and Leighton 1989; Fischer and Massey 2000).

Researchers who disagree with the emphasis on financial resources argue that economists and others have placed too much importance on the availability of monetary assets (Aldrich 1999). Many small businesses do not require large amounts of financial capital in their start-up phase and most founders begin their businesses with little or no capital. In the U.S., well over half of all owners in the mid-1990s required less than $5,000 dollars to start their businesses (U.S. Census 1997). Home-based businesses, for instance, which accounted for half of all new businesses in 1992, often require little capital up front.

Even though most small businesses start very small and with low levels of capital investment, financial resources have nonetheless been linked to the subsequent success of new business ventures (Fichman and Levinthal 1991). Newly founded organizations face severe obstacles to their survival (Aldrich and Auster 1986). Starting a new business requires human and physical resources, and financial reserves can help struggling new businesses acquire relevant competencies and market share (Aldrich and Auster 1986; Aldrich and Fiol 1994). Entrepreneurs starting with more assets survive the liabilities associated with newness more readily than entrepreneurs with fewer assets (Stinchcombe 1965).

Whereas financial resources may play a critical factor in the *success* of a newly formed business, its role in determining whether a person *becomes* a nascent entrepreneur is unclear. We feel that some clarity can be brought to this debate by distinguishing between two broad types of entrepreneurial activities: *opportunity* entrepreneurship and *necessity* entrepreneurship

Table 1.   Necessity and Opportunity Entrepreneurship and Their
Relationships to Social, Human, and Financial Capital.

Necessity Entrepreneurship: Undertaken when there are few or no other opportunities for
gainful labor market participation
• Typically relies on little or no financial capital
• Once decision is made, success partially dependent upon social and human capital

Opportunity Entrepreneurship: Undertaken to take advantage of perceived market opportunities
• Recognition of such opportunities is positively related to social and human capital
• Once decision is made, financial capital becomes relevant to success

(Reynolds et al. 2002), as defined in Table 1. This distinction is an important
one, we argue, because it helps to explain the conditions under which financial resources affect entrepreneurial decisions. We summarize the relationships between types of entrepreneurship and resources in Table 1.

Necessity Entrepreneurship
People undertake necessity entrepreneurship when there are few, if any,
other options for finding suitable work. We believe that entrepreneurs often
undertake this type of entrepreneurial activity with little or no financial
capital because it constitutes a final effort to secure an income when other
employment options fail. In short, it represents a failure of labor markets to
provide opportunities that are more attractive than self-employment. One
can easily imagine that this type of entrepreneurship will be more prevalent
in certain economic and social contexts than others, as we discuss below. In
addition, one might reasonably expect that this type of activity will provide,
on average, substantially fewer opportunities for individual upward mobility and organizational and economic growth than the second type of entrepreneurial activity.

Opportunity Entrepreneurship
People undertake opportunity entrepreneurship when they perceive an opportunity in the market, which can include underserved, poorly served, or
newly emerging niches. Knowledge of these niches can be considered a form
of human capital, typically gained from industry experience (Burton et al.
2002). In addition, people embedded in wide-ranging and diverse social
networks have greater access to such knowledge. Opportunity entrepreneurship probably depends more than necessity entrepreneurship on the
possession of human capital. If so, then opportunity-based endeavors

provide the greatest potential for individual mobility, organizational growth, and job creation. Therefore, opportunity entrepreneurship will be, on average, more beneficial to economies and societies than that arising out of necessity.

SOCIETAL LEVEL ECONOMIC INEQUALITY AND ENTREPRENEURSHIP

Countries with higher levels of wealth inequality tend to have higher rates of entrepreneurship. The GEM project found that the greater the level of wealth inequality in a society, the higher its level of total entrepreneurial activity, necessity entrepreneurship, and opportunity entrepreneurship. The GEM measured wealth inequality using the Gini index, which assesses the extent to which the population of a country shares unequally in a nation's total wealth. It is calculated as the extent to which the distribution departs from perfect equality, and is scaled from a minimum value of 0 to a maximum value of 1, with 0 representing no inequality and 1 representing complete inequality. For example, if every household had exactly the same wealth holdings, then there would be no inequality and the Gini index would be 0. At the other extreme, if a small fraction of all households held all the wealth in a nation, the Gini index would be almost one. Although it has some limitations, the Gini index is the most widely used measure for making cross-national comparisons of inequality.

In Fig. 1, we plot the relationship between economic inequality, as measured by the Gini index, and total entrepreneurial activity. This relationship is linear, with a correlation of 0.451, demonstrating that inequality and total entrepreneurial activity rise in tandem. However, when total entrepreneurial activity is broken down into its two component parts, the relationships between economic inequality and both necessity and opportunity entrepreneurship become nonlinear. For each of these bivariate relationships, a quadratic form provides the best fit, as represented by the following equation:

$$Y = X + X^2$$

where Y is the rate of entrepreneurial activity, and X is the Gini index of economic inequality. These quadratic relationships are presented in Figs. 2 and 3.[3] In Fig. 2, we see that increases in wealth inequality raise a nation's level of necessity entrepreneurship at an increasing rate, whereas Fig. 3

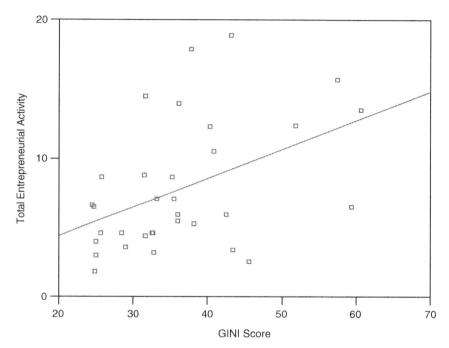

Fig. 1. Total Entrepreneurial Activity and Economic Inequality. *Source:* Reynolds et al. (2002). $R^2 = 0.415$.

shows that opportunity entrepreneurship has a curvilinear relationship with inequality. Opportunity entrepreneurship is highest at an intermediate level of wealth inequality.

What might account for these relationships? Based on other information in the GEM report, at least two complementary explanations appear plausible. First, countries with higher levels of wealth inequality have larger poor and low-income/wealth populations. For such groups, which also typically have low levels of education and few connections to sources of power and influence, necessity entrepreneurship might be the most readily available option for earning a living. Therefore, high levels of wealth inequality should be positively related to high levels of necessity entrepreneurship.

A second explanation, which focuses on wealth held by the most privileged groups in society, posits that higher levels of wealth inequality may be an indication that some segments of the population have surplus capital to invest in new ventures, and therefore increase opportunity entrepreneurial

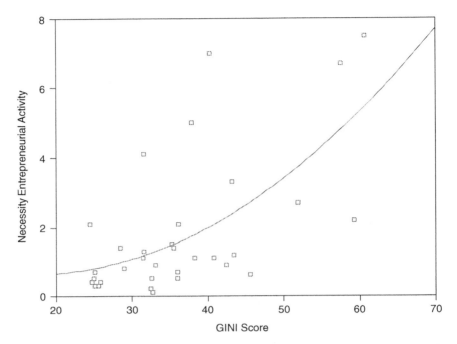

Fig. 2. Necessity Entrepreneurship and Economic Inequality. *Source:* Reynolds et al. (2002). $R^2 = 0.385$.

activity. They could either invest it in their own startups or act as angel investors for the startup activities of others. At moderate levels of inequality, "elite mobilization can activate the community field and encourage other groups to become involved – if cultural or financial capital of the elites and other residents is not so unequally distributed that inter-group trust is lacking" (Flora 1998: 500). Therefore, rising inequality indicates that elites have begun to accumulate a disproportionate share of resources that they can use to initiate economic development. By investing surplus capital in the pursuit of perceived market opportunities, elites increase the level of opportunity entrepreneurship. In addition, the improved life chances and luxurious life style associated with greater wealth serve as an incentive for potential entrepreneurs.

The four countries with the highest levels of inequality – Mexico, Chile, South Africa, and Brazil – have low-to-moderate levels of opportunity entrepreneurship. Rapid industrialization in Mexico may largely account for

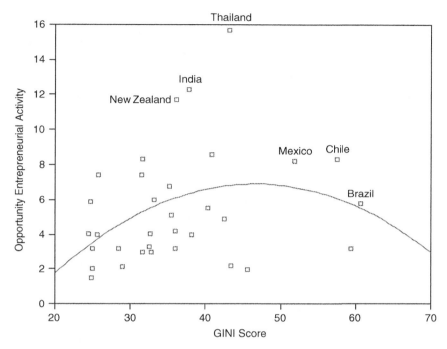

Fig. 3. Opportunity Entrepreneurship and Economic Inequality. *Source:* Reynolds et al. (2002). $R^2 = 0.127$.

its high level of inequality. Firms from advanced industrial nations, particularly the U.S., have found it attractive for its low labor costs and its proximity to domestic markets and infrastructure. This trajectory increased inequality as low-wage manufacturing work became an increasingly dominant part of Mexico's labor market. In addition, foreign firms have controlled much of the economic growth in Mexico in the past several decades, thus limiting opportunities for high-quality entrepreneurship among Mexico's citizenry.

The Chilean economy, while growing, remains primarily dependent on capital intensive extractive industries including mining, fishing, and forestry, which may explain its relatively limited opportunity in entrepreneurial activity. These industries provide relatively few opportunities for new business formation. In addition, the Chilean economy continues to feel the enduring effects of the coup of 1973, as the country struggles to find its footing after the repressive Pinochet regime. South Africa suffers from extremely high levels of unemployment and poverty, which account for its high Gini score. In addition, persistent crime and corruption, and the enduring legacy of apartheid, help to suppress opportunities for successful entrepreneurship among a large portion of the population. Chaotic fiscal policies, high inflation, and steadily rising foreign debt in Brazil have left it an unattractive place for foreign investment, thus limiting its opportunity in entrepreneurial activity. In addition, Brazil's stagnant economy has led to very high levels of inequality.

Thus, it appears that moderate levels of inequality do help *opportunity entrepreneurship* to flourish. Countries with high levels of inequality do not experience as much opportunity entrepreneurship because people lack the resources and information required to take advantage of opportunities essential for such activity.

Furthermore, as revealed in Fig. 3, the three countries with the highest levels of opportunity entrepreneurship, New Zealand, India, and Thailand, fall very close to the mean Gini score for the entire sample.[4] Thailand and India are known for having large populations of highly educated workers and high numbers of businesses engaged in outsourcing and subcontracting arrangements with foreign firms. The increasing prevalence of these arrangements continues to create many high-quality opportunities for entrepreneurs in a variety of industries. When we remove these nations from the analysis, the inverted-U shaped curve remains virtually unchanged. This result further supports our contention that *moderate* levels of economic inequality are favorable for opportunity entrepreneurship.

These proposed explanations for the positive association between economic inequality and entrepreneurship posit a direct effect of inequality on entrepreneurship. Recent theories of the causes of inequality suggest other forces that may indirectly strengthen the link between inequality and entrepreneurship because of their direct effects on one or both.

INEQUALITY AND ENTREPRENEURSHIP IN THEORETICAL PERSPECTIVE

Studies from a variety of theoretical backgrounds have found that the factors that affect countries' levels of income inequality also affect their labor market structures, dynamics, and outcomes. These studies have focused mainly on how a country's level of economic development (Kuznets 1953; Nielsen and Alderson 1995) or position in the world system (Wood 1994) affects the size and growth of various economic sectors, and how these sectoral dynamics affect income and wealth inequality and opportunities for social mobility. Typically, however, these studies ignore self-employment and entrepreneurial activity, even though they are an increasingly important part of labor markets across the globe (Aldrich 1999; but see Aronson 1991). In this section, we review the literature on economic and industrial development in order to develop a set of propositions about factors that may create a link between inequality and entrepreneurship.

We examine seven structures and processes linked with varying levels of entrepreneurship and inequality: economic development, government policies, foreign direct investment, growth in the service sector, increasing labor market flexibility, wealth transfer programs, and variation in the strength of the working class. We review each and explain how we feel it should be included in a comprehensive explanation of the linkage we identified. All seven are listed in Table 2.

Development and Economic Inequality

We begin with the pioneering work of Kuznets (1953, 1955), who argued that inequality follows an inverted U-shaped path coincident with economic and industrial development. According to his logic, as countries begin to develop an industrial infrastructure, newly created wealth becomes concentrated in the hands of those who control that infrastructure. In Marx's terms, others are forced to sell their labor power or engage in agriculture or small-scale production and thus do not share equally in the newly created wealth. However, as development continues, opportunities for increased income spread to more segments of the population; the agricultural sector shrinks and participation in the industrial economy becomes more widespread. Kuznets' theory has been supported for income inequality in a variety of settings (Lindert and Williamson 1985), and a similar trend has been documented for wealth inequality (Lampman 1962).

Since a country's level of economic development constitutes a major predictor of its level of inequality, we offer the following proposition:

Proposition 1. Developing nations experience higher rates of entrepreneurship.

Proposition 1 gains some support from the GEM data, as shown in Fig. 4. At low levels of development, as measured by energy consumption per capita, total entrepreneurial activity was high in 2001. According to the

Table 2. Explanations for the Positive Relationship Between
Entrepreneurship and Inequality.

Structure/Process	Effect on Inequality	Effect on Entrepreneurial Activity
Economic development	(+) U-shaped pattern (Kuznets 1953)	(+) Provides new markets for goods and services
Government policies favoring development	(+)Creates new class of industrial elite, new industrial working class	(+) Provides finances and market opportunities for nascent entrepreneurs
Foreign Direct investment	(+) Creates an elite managerial and financier class, increases the number of low wage, low skill manufacturing jobs	(+) Provides finances and market opportunities for nascent entrepreneurs
Rapid service sector growth	(+) Bifurcation of labor market into highly skilled, high-wage service jobs and low skill, low-wage service jobs	(+) Creates new market demands
Increasing employment flexibility	(+) Returns to skill through occupational labor markets, increasing employment insecurity	(+) Individuals less tied to particular firms, responses to employment insecurity through individual opportunity
Wealth transfer programs	(−) Redistributes wealth equitably across the population	(−) Reduces the need to rely on necessity entrepreneurship as a last resort
Strong working class	(−) Helps to encourage the redistribution of wealth, the formation of occupational labor markets, and protect their economic interests	(−) Reduces the need to rely on necessity entrepreneurship because jobs are more secure due to occupational labor markets

GEM, developing Latin American countries and developing countries in Asia had entrepreneurship rates over 10%, figures well above the average rate of 7% for all of the GEM countries.[5] As countries develop, more opportunities for entrepreneurship may emerge as underserved markets expand and more people move into self-employment because traditional sectors of the economy shrink. However, it appears, in the quadratic relationship shown in Fig. 4, that after development reaches a certain

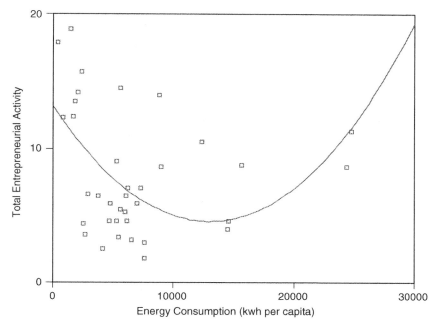

Fig. 4. Total Entrepreneurial Activity and Economic Development. *Source:* Reynolds et al. (2002) and World Bank Group (2004). $R^2 = 0.260$.

stage, entrepreneurial activity declines and then picks up again at higher levels of development.

Government Support for New Businesses

Several key factors associated with national economies in both developing and developed nations may account for variation in economic inequality and entrepreneurial activity. Clearly, development may be the result of an active strategy pursued by governments wishing to compete in the global economy. State agencies and programs in developing nations play a large role in industrial development through fiscal policies that favor business and entrepreneurial activity, including taxation, investments, loans, and other policies (Evans et al. 1985; Wade 1990). To compete in an increasingly global economy, developing nations may encourage the growth of certain targeted industries, which can create an industrial elite and increase economic inequality. These same policies may also provide the seeds for new businesses.

Similar processes can occur in developed nations, as well. In Ireland, for example, the Industrial Development Authority worked throughout the 1990s to recruit existing high-tech companies. Ireland also formed an organization called Enterprise Ireland to encourage and support entrepreneurship in similar industries (Florida 2002). As a result, Ireland has the second highest rate of opportunity entrepreneurial activity (7.8) among Western nations, behind only the United States. We therefore expect that countries actively pursuing such strategies generate favorable contexts for opportunity entrepreneurship.

Proposition 2. Governments whose policies and regulations favor the emergence of a market economy and industrial development will experience more opportunity entrepreneurship.

Rona-Tas (1994) provided support for this idea in his research on Hungary's transition from socialism to capitalism, which distinguished between countries experiencing an *erosion* of socialism versus countries experiencing a *transition* from socialism. The erosion of socialism was a passive process in which socialist institutions dissolved. The transition from socialism, on the other hand, has become an active strategy followed by governments to create a market economy. According to Rona-Tas, countries undergoing a transition provided many more opportunities for entrepreneurs and experienced greater levels of entrepreneurial activity.

Foreign Direct Investment

Industrial development may also be the result of foreign direct investment (FDI) in industrial infrastructure, with firms taking advantage of welcoming environments in many developing nations, including cheaper labor costs and more lax regulatory standards. FDI has been criticized by world-systems theory because of its role in developing countries (Bornschier and Chase-Dunn 1985). Critics argue that FDI creates long-term dependence of developing nations upon transnational corporations and contributes to inequality by creating a group of highly paid managers and professionals, in addition to low-wage manufacturing and other marginal jobs. However, recent research has shown that FDI might actually be of some benefit to the economies of developing nations (Alderson and Nielsen 1999; Soysa and Oneal 1999). As foreign firms invest money directly in their own operations or through subcontracting and other outsourcing arrangements, they also create opportunities for entrepreneurial activity by stimulating new markets and pumping new financial resources into the economy.

Proposition 3. Foreign investment in developing nations increases their opportunity entrepreneurship rates.

Sectoral Shifts

Developing nations often undergo a dramatic sectoral shift away from agriculture and into manufacturing and services. As agriculture shrinks, those individuals or families formerly engaged in agricultural activity must compete in a new economic order. Early on, this process disrupts traditional means of securing a living and leads to increased economic inequality. Although many make the adjustment by becoming employees of larger firms, many also turn to entrepreneurial activities (Rona-Tas 1994). For some, the decline of agriculture reduces traditional opportunities for securing a living. As the sectoral balance shifts away from agriculture, these individuals may have few opportunities in the new industrial sectors that emerge. Entrepreneurship may be their best or only option. At the same time, the growth of the service sector may create new economic opportunities that entrepreneurs can exploit.

Proposition 4. As developing countries' economies shift away from agriculture, both necessity and opportunity entrepreneurship increase.

Whereas developing nations industrialize and experience declines in agriculture and increases in their manufacturing activity, advanced industrialized nations suffer a concurrent decline in their manufacturing sector. This dual dynamic represents the essence of globalization, as firms in advanced countries move production abroad to take advantage of cheaper labor, production chains span political boundaries, and economies become global (Alderson 1997). A major outcome of the globalization of production has been a relative decline in the size of the manufacturing sector in advanced industrial economies, and an overall shift in labor market demands in these nations, as highlighted by the U.S. case. Labor market restructuring has created an increasingly bifurcated labor force of high-skill, high-wage and low-skill, low-wage service work (Harrison and Bluestone 1988). For this reason, the dynamics of globalization have allegedly increased inequality among advanced industrial and post-industrial nations, leading to "the great U-turn" in the Kuznets curve (Alderson and Nielsen 2002; Harrison

Table 3. Entrepreneurial Activity in the United States and Other Developed Nations in 2002.

	Total Entrepreneurial Activity[a]	Opportunity Entrepreneurship[b]
All nations	8.08	5.63
Developed nations	6.52	5.20
United States	10.5	8.6

Source: Reynolds et al. (2002).
[a]Percent of labor force either actively involved in starting a new venture or the owner/manager of a business that is less than 42 months old.
[b]Percent of labor force electing to start a business as one of several possible career options.

and Bluestone 1988). In addition, the labor market options facing workers in the "new" economy have changed dramatically.

According to the GEM reports, the U.S. rates of total entrepreneurship and opportunity entrepreneurship are well above the average for all countries included in the dataset, and remarkably above countries at similar levels of industrial development, as reported in Table 3. Models that focus on general characteristics of developing nations that might foster entrepreneurship fall well short of explaining the United States' unique level of entrepreneurial activity. Deindustrialization has had unique and significant effects on employment and labor market dynamics in the United States, which may account for its comparatively higher levels of entrepreneurial activity.

Why might deindustrialization in the U.S. lead to increases in entrepreneurial activity as well as inequality? Some have argued that deindustrialization constitutes a natural outcome of economic growth, and that as societies become affluent and productivity rises, the demand for services increases (Alderson 1999). A hallmark of economic maturity is a decline in the manufacturing sector and an increase in the service sector. Therefore, the rapid growth of the service sector may create more opportunities for engaging in entrepreneurial activity to serve new and underserved niches.

Proposition 5. The rapid growth of the service sector during deindustrialization leads to an increase in opportunity entrepreneurship.

Changing Employment Institutions

Others argue that deindustrialization, instead of being a natural outcome of the advanced stages of industrial development, constitutes one component of an active strategy by firms to move manufacturing overseas. According to Bluestone and Harrison (1982), deindustrialization is not simply the outcome of a natural evolutionary process, but rather part of a managerial strategy undertaken in the U.S. in response to increasing global competition. In addition to massive reductions in capital investment and development, a large part of this strategy involved reducing labor costs. Millions of workers lost their jobs in unprecedented numbers as employers dismantled the social contract that had governed employer–employee relations after World War II. Workers were no longer guaranteed employment security in return for their commitment and loyalty. Union-busting campaigns undercut the structural sources of labor's power and employment in the U.S. became increasingly unstable.

Early on, such instability generated a good deal of concern from labor market analysts (Bluestone and Harrison 1982; Harrison and Bluestone 1988; Osterman 1988) and policy makers (Reich 1983). However, as downsizing and employment instability became a regular occurrence in the U.S. labor market, these processes also became a more "institutionally regular" part of employment relations and career development (Osterman 1999). Employees have slowly developed adaptive responses to this instability by making new investments in education and taking a more pro-active role in identifying opportunities for career advancement and mobility.

Not only are firms becoming less committed to long-term relationships with their employees, but employees also feel less committed to specific firms over the course of their careers (Osterman 1999). Perhaps in response to the decline of firm internal labor markets and stable employment, many workers have taken on a more individualistic approach to career development (DiTomaso 2001). Often, this means taking on more self-directed work within firms. As employment instability and an emphasis on self-direction evolve in tandem, however, many workers opt out of binding relationships with firms and behave like independent contractors. In particular, workers with high levels of education and valuable skills are seeking new opportunities for themselves. People in the emerging "creative class" often seek these opportunities through business start-ups (Florida 2002).

Proposition 6. Increasing employment flexibility leads to an increase in opportunity entrepreneurship.

We are not making a deterministic argument. Dynamic relationships between development, inequality, and entrepreneurial activity create specific political and social structures at particular historical conjunctures. The political and social structures that affect economic inequality do so in large part by changing labor market structures and processes (Kalleberg and Berg 1987). Political policies influence the degree to which individuals must rely on the labor market to gain a living, and taxation policies determine how much wealth is transferred from those with large wealth holdings to those without. Class structures in societies depend upon the size of occupational and industrial groups and their degree of mobilization. When groups are highly mobilized and influential, they can protect their interests more effectively. These structures alter the choices individuals must make about their labor force participation. Therefore, as we explain below, they should have an effect on entrepreneurial activity.

Welfare State Structure

The policies and provisions provided by modern welfare states vary greatly from nation to nation. In his path-breaking work, Esping-Andersen (1990) categorized these structures into three regime types. The regime types differed in the level and type of provisions they guaranteed citizens and the effects they had on labor market dynamics. Esping-Andersen argued that the three regime-types – liberal, corporatist, and social democratic – differed in the degree of decommodification they allowed. The most generous social democratic welfare states go the furthest in allowing citizens to maintain a livelihood without reliance on the market, whereas liberal regimes tie benefit provision directly to market participation and stigmatize recipients, furthering dependence on the market for all except the most desperate citizens.

What effect does regime-type have on levels of income and wealth inequality? Nations with social democratic welfare state regimes often have a strong egalitarian ethic. Such nations bring down levels of wealth inequality by decommodifying labor and redistributing large amounts of wealth. On the opposite end of the spectrum, liberal regimes have high levels of wealth inequality and mechanisms to encourage participation in the labor market as a source of income and mobility. We propose that welfare state policies also affect entrepreneurial activity, reinforcing the relationship between inequality and entrepreneurial activity. If necessity entrepreneurship is, by definition, a final effort to secure a living when other labor market options fail, then strong welfare state policies in the form of unemployment insurance and job training programs should reduce the need to rely on necessity entrepreneurship.

Proposition 7. Nations with more generous welfare state policies have lower rates of necessity entrepreneurship.

Figs. 5 and 6 show the total and necessity entrepreneurial rates of countries categorized by Esping-Andersen's (1990) regime typology. As Fig. 5 makes clear, corporatist and social-democratic regimes, both of which decommodify labor and transfer more wealth than liberal states, have lower rates of total entrepreneurial activity. The relationship between regime type and necessity entrepreneurship is even more striking. Social democratic regimes have two-thirds the amount of necessity entrepreneurship of

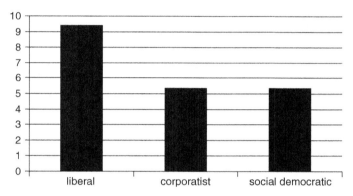

Fig. 5. Total Entrepreneurial Activity by Welfare State Regime Type. (Percentage of Labor Force involved in Nascent Entrepreneurship.) *Source:* Reynolds et al. (2002).

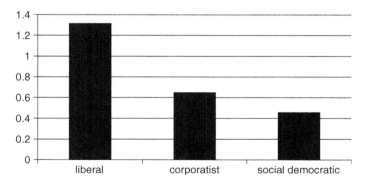

Fig. 6. Necessity Entrepreneurship by Welfare State Regime Type. (Percentage of Labor Force involved in Nascent Entrepreneurship.) *Source:* Reynolds et al. (2002).

corporatist regimes, and only one-third of that of liberal regimes. According to the GEM data, citizens of regimes that decommodify labor rely less on necessity entrepreneurship to secure a living than citizens of other regime types.

Strength of the Working Class

Some theorists have argued that the negative relationship between economic equality and entrepreneurial activity stems from the strength of a nation's working class. Nations with highly organized and influential working classes experience less inequality because unions and other working class organizations are able to exert their influence to gain a larger share of the economic and social fruits of their labor. In many industrially advanced European nations, labor parties after World War II were able to pursue policies of full employment, unemployment benefits, and related social benefits (Korpi 1989; Korpi and Palme 2000). In addition, many egalitarian countries have a strong working class (Esping-Andersen 1990, 1994). The presence of a strong working class curtails many of the negative effects of globalization and employment instability that we previously argued may cause an increase in entrepreneurial activity.

Proposition 8. The presence of a highly mobilized and influential working class will reduce necessity entrepreneurship rates.

McManus (2000) confirmed this association in her research on the quality of self-employment in Germany and the U.S. In Germany, the presence of influential union–employer associations and strong occupational labor market has contributed to more labor market stability and a higher earnings floor for many of the same occupations that are in decline in the U.S. These factors, in turn, have led to a lower rate of poor quality self-employment in Germany than in the U.S. Strong occupational labor markets and more labor market stability resulted in more stable, higher quality self-employment in Germany.

DISCUSSION AND CONCLUSION

We have focused on the way in which societal-level inequalities in resource distributions affect entrepreneurial activity. Interestingly, those countries with higher levels of wealth inequality have higher levels of entrepreneurial activity. High levels of wealth inequality might indicate that those in the upper end of the income distribution have surplus capital to invest in new business ventures. Conversely, in societies in which large segments of the population have few financial resources, self-employment may be the only viable form of employment for many people.

We outlined a perspective that focuses on cross-national comparisons of the factors that influence a country's level of economic inequality. We asked what effect economic inequality may have on labor markets and rates of entrepreneurship. Identifying the structural causes of this relationship will generate valuable information for all nations interested in business start-ups, job growth, and social and economic opportunity. Table 2 summarizes the seven factors we identified in our literature review. Note that all seven have similar effects on inequality and entrepreneurship and that many are inter-related. We suggest that states interested in policies favoring entre-preneurship could begin with any of the seven.

Policy Implications

Unequal possession of resources can hamper a social group's abilities to engage in entrepreneurial activity, but entrepreneurship can also disrupt patterns of inequality and may be a source of upward mobility for individuals (Stinchcombe 1965). In the U.S., entrepreneurship has been a significant source of upward mobility for minority and immigrant groups who are more likely to be excluded from opportunities for mobility in conventional labor markets. In formerly socialist nations, however, the human and social capital advantages that accrued to cadres seemed to persist during the transition to capitalism. In these societies, it appears that entrepreneurship is less likely to be a source of mobility. Nonetheless, the situation may change because capitalist institutions have yet to become fully developed and firmly entrenched in many countries still in transition.

Wealth and gender inequality are widespread and persistent in advanced capitalist societies. Even as women's labor force participation approaches that of men, they continue to be segregated into lower-paying, lower-status occupations. The inheritability of wealth ensures its unequal distribution from generation to generation. In fact, after years of stability, wealth in-equality in the United States has been increasing (Keister and Moller 2000). We have not addressed the role that the entrepreneurship might play in overcoming these structured and durable forms of inequality. However, we do know that starting a business appears to require very little financial capital and represents a possible source of mobility for individuals. Therefore, although entrepreneurship might not seriously erode the level of structured wealth inequality, it may provide individuals with the opportunities to move out of their current class locations. Gender, on the other hand, is highly consolidated with inequalities in access to human and social capital (Aldrich, Elam, and Reese 1996). Given the importance that these resources have in the founding process, prevailing patterns in gender inequality might do more to restrict entrepreneurial opportunities than entrepreneurship will do to upset gender inequality.

Schumpeter, a dominant voice in the entrepreneurship literature of the last century, emphasized the role that entrepreneurs play in introducing variation into organizational populations and societies (Becker and Knudsen 2002). Variation across social groups represents a potential source of diversity in organizational populations. When some groups are less likely to start new organizations than others, diversity suffers. Moreover, problems of social justice arise when social groups have unequal access to economic and social resources that are important in the process of entrepreneurship. When members of disadvantaged groups no longer believe in the possibilities of "success among the unsuccessful," they may turn to other, socially disruptive channels in the pursuit of economic advancement.

The positive relationship between economic inequality and entrepreneurial activity poses a disturbing message for those nations with strongly egalitarian norms that seek to increase business start up rates. We have argued that state policies encouraging social and economic equality may suppress entrepreneurial activity, while those favoring entrepreneurship may unintentionally lead to higher levels of economic inequality. Pursued unthinkingly, programs promoting entrepreneurship may thus cause unwanted consequences. However, once forewarned, policy makers can watch for unintended consequences and plan for them.

NOTES

1. Many entrepreneurs use various "boot strapping" methods to secure the finances required during the initial stages of new business formation. Borrowing money from family members, withholding their own wages, or using personal credit cards to purchase supplies and equipment are the primary ways that entrepreneurs can get around capital constraints (Winborg and Landstrom 2000).

2. Diversity is an important source of variation in organizational populations (Aldrich 1999), and variation across organizations increases the likelihood of innovations and the level of competitive intensity in industries (Kaufman 1991). It is

important, therefore, to understand the factors that encourage or inhibit such diversity.

3. For readability, we have suppressed case labels in all figures except in Fig. 3, where particular cases merit identification and further discussion.

4. The mean score on the Gini index for the entire sample is 36.32 (S.D. 10.00). The respective Gini scores for New Zealand, India, and Thailand are 36.17, 37.83, and 43.15.

5. Mexico – 12%, Brazil – 13%, Argentina – 14%, Chile – 16%, China – 12%, Korea – 14%, India – 18%, Thailand – 19%.

ACKNOWLEDGMENTS

We would like to thank Arthur Alderson, Clinton Key, Kammi Schmeer, and Steve Vaisey for their comments on earlier versions of this paper.

REFERENCES

Alderson, Arthur S. 1997. "Globalization and Deindustrialization: Direct Investment and the Decline in Manufacturing Employment in 17 OECD Nations." *Journal of World Systems Research* 3:1–34.

------. 1999. "Explaining Deindustrialization: Globalization, Failure, or Success?." *American Sociological Review* 64:701–721.

Alderson, Arthur S. and Francois Nielsen. 1999. "Income Inequality, Development, and Dependence: A Reconsideration." *American Sociological Review* 64:606–631.

Aldrich, Howard. 1999. *Organizations Evolving.* London: Sage.

------. 2004. "Entrepreneurship." Pp. 451–477 in *Handbook of Economic Sociology*, edited by R. Swedberg and N. Smelser. Princeton, NJ: Princeton University Press.

Aldrich, Howard E. and Ellen R. Auster. 1986. "Even Dwarfs Started Small." Pp. 165–198 in *Research in Organizational Behavior* Vol. 8, edited by B.M. Staw and L.L. Cummings. Greenwich, CT: JAI Press.

Aldrich, Howard E., Amanda B. Elam, and Pat R. Reese. 1996. "Strong Ties, Weak Ties, and Strangers: Do Women Business Owners Differ from Men in Their Use of Networking to Obtain Assistance?." Pp. 1–25 in *Entrepreneurship in a Global Context*, edited by S. Birley and I. MacMillan. London: Routledge Ltd.

Aldrich, Howard E. and Marlene C. Fiol. 1994. "Fools Rush In? The Institutional Context of Industry Creation." *Academy of Management Review* 19:645–670.

Aronson, Robert L. 1991. *Self-Employment: A Labor Market Perspective.* Ithaca, NY: ILR Press.

Bates, Timothy. 1997. *Race, Self-Employment, and Upward Mobility: An Illusive American Dream.* Washington, DC: Woodrow Wilson Center Press.

Becker, Markus C. and Knudsen Thorbjørn. 2003. "The Entrepreneur at a Crucial Juncture in Schumpeter's Work: Schumpeter's 1928 Handbook Entry Entrepreneur." *Advances in Australian Economics* 6:199–234.

Bendix, Reinhard. 1956. *Work and Authority in Industry: Ideologies of Management in the Course of Industrialization.* New York: Wiley.

Blanchflower, David G. and Andrew J. Oswald. 1998. "What Makes an Entrepreneur." *Journal of Labor Economics* 16:26–60.

Blau, Peter M. 1977. *Inequality and Heterogeneity: A Primitive Theory of Social Structure.* New York: Free Press.

Bluestone, Barry and Bennett Harrison. 1982. *The Deindustrialization of America: Plant Closings, Community Abandonment, and the Dismantling of Basic Industry.* New York: Basic Books.

Burton, M. Diane, Jesper Sorenson, and Christine Beckman. 2002. "Coming From Good Stock: Career Histories and New Venture Formation." in *Social Structure and Organizations Revisited,* edited by M. Lounsbury and M. Vantresca. Amsterdam: JAI/Elsevier.

DiTomaso, Nancy. 2001. "The Loose Coupling of Jobs: The Subcontracting of Everyone?." in *Sourcebook of Labor Markets: Evolving Structures and Processes,* edited by Ivar Berg and Arne L. Kalleberg. New York: Klewer Publishers.

Dunn, Thomas A. and Douglas Holtz-Eakin. 2000. "Financial Capital, Human Capital, and the Transition to Self-Employment: Evidence from Intergenerational Links." *Journal of Labor Economics* 18:282–304.

Esping-Andersen, Gosta. 1990. *The Three Worlds of Welfare Capitalism.* Princeton, NJ: Princeton University Press.

Evans, David S. and B. Jovanovic. 1989. "An Estimated Model of Entrepreneurial Choice Under Liquidity Constraints." *Journal of Political Economy* 7:808–827.

Evans, David S. and Linda S. Leighton. 1989. "Some Empirical Aspects of Entrepreneurship." *American Economic Review* 9:519–535.

Evans, Peter B., Rueschemeyer Dietrich, and Theda Skocpol, eds. 1985. *Bringing the State Back In.* Cambridge: Cambridge University Press.

Fichman, Mark and Daniel, A. Levinthal. 1991. "Honeymoons and the Liability of Adolescence: A New Perspective on Duration Dependence in Social and Organizational Relationships." *Academy of Management Review* 16:442–468.

Fischer, Mary and Douglas Massey. 2000. "Residential Segregation and Ethnic Enterprise in U.S. Metropolitan Areas." *Social Problems* 47:410–424.

Flora, Jan L. 1998. "Social Capital and Communities of Place." *Rural Sociology* 63:481–506.

Florida, Richard. 2002. *The Rise of the Creative Class: And How It's Transforming Work, Leisure, Community, and Everyday Life.* New York: Basic Books.

Fujiwara-Greve, Takako and Henrich R. Greve. 2000. "Organizational Ecology and Job Mobility." *Social Forces* 79:547–585.

Harrison, Bennett and Barry Bluestone. 1988. *The Great U-Turn: Corporate Restructuring and the Polarizing of America.* New York: Basic Books.

Kalleberg, Arne L. and Ivar Berg. 1987. *Work and Industry: Structures, Markets, and Processes.* New York: Plenum Press.

Keister, Lisa A. 2000. *Wealth in America.* New York: Cambridge University Press.

Keister, Lisa A. and Stephanie Moller. 2000. "Wealth Inequality in the Unites States." *Annual Review of Sociology* 26:63–81.

Kim, Phil H., Howard E. Aldrich, and Keister, Lisa A. 2003. "If I Were Rich? The Impact of Financial and Human Capital on Becoming a Nascent Entrepreneur" Paper presented at the annual meetings of the Academy of Management, Seattle, WA.

Korpi, Walter. 1989. "Power, Politics, and State Autonomy in the Development of Social Citizenship: Social Rights during Sickness in Eighteen OECD Countries since 1930." *American Sociological Review* 54:309–328.

Korpi, Walter and Joakim Palme. 1998. "The Paradox of Redistribution and the Strategy of Equality: Welfare State Institutions, Inequality and Poverty in the Western Countries." *American Sociological Review* 63:661–687.

Kuznets, Simon. 1953. *Shares of Upper Income Groups in Income and Savings.* New York: National Bureau of Economic Research.

------. 1955. "Economic Growth and Income Inequality." *The American Economic Review* 45:1–28.

Lampman, Robert J. 1962. *The Share of Top Wealth Holders in National Wealth, 1922–1956.* Princeton, NJ: Princeton University Press.

Lindert, Peter H. and Jeffrey, G. Williamson. 1985. "Growth, Equality, and History." *Explorations in Economic History* 22:341–377.

Marx, Karl. 1852. "The Eighteenth Brumaire of Louis Bonaparte."

McManus, Patricia A. 2000. "Market, State, and the Quality of New Self-Employment Jobs Among Men in the U.S. and Western Germany." *Social Forces* 78:865–905.

Nielsen, Francois and Arthur S. Alderson. 1995. "Income Inequality, Development, and Dualism: Results from an Unbalanced Cross-National Panel." *American Sociological Review* 60:674–701.

Osterman, Paul. 1988. *Employment Futures: Reorganization, Dislocation, and Public Policy.* New York: Oxford University Press.

------. 1999. *Securing Prosperity: The American Labor Market, How it has Changed, and What to Do About it.* Princeton, NJ: Princeton University Press.

Reich, Robert B. 1983. *The Next American Frontier.* New York: Times Books.

Reynolds, Paul D., Michael Hay, William D. Bygrave, Michael Camp and Autio, Erkko, 2002. "Global Entrepreneurship Monitor: Global Executive Report." *Kauffman Center for Entrepreneurial Leadership* Accessed on: November 20, 2003. http://www.gemconsortium.org/download/1080500608703/WebGlobalGEMReport11.12_1.pdf

Reynolds, Paul D. and Sammis B. White. 1997. *The Entrepreneurial Process: Economic Growth, Men, Women, and Minorities.* Westport, CT: Quorum Books.

Róna-Tas, A. 1994. "The First Shall Be Last? Entrepreneurship and Communist Cadres in the Transition from Socialism." *American Journal of Sociology* 100:40–69.

Sobel, Michael E., P. Mark Becker, and Susan M. Minick. 1998. "Origins Destinations and Association in Occupational Mobility." *American Journal of Sociology* 104:687–721.

Soysa, Indra and John R. Oneal. 1999. "Boon or Bane? Reassessing the Productivity of Foreign Direct Investment." *American Sociological Review* 64:766–782.

Stinchcombe, Arthur L. 1965. "Social Structure and Organizations." in *Handbook of Organizations*, edited by J.G. March. Chicago, IL: Rand McNally.

Tilly, Charles. 1998. *Durable Inequality.* Berkeley, CA: University of California Press.

Tomaskovic-Devey, Donald. 1993. *Gender and Racial Inequality at Work: The Sources and Consequences of Job Segregation.* Ithaca, NY: ILR Press.

U.S. Census Bureau. 1997. Characteristics of Business Owners, 1992 *Economic Census.* Washington, DC: U.S. Department of Commerce.

Wade, Robert. 1990. *Governing the Market: Economic Theory and the Role of Government in East Asian Industrialization.* Princeton, NJ: Princeton University Press.

Wilson, William J. 1996. *When Work Disappears: The World of the New Urban Poor.* New York: Alfred A. Knopf, Inc.

Winborg, Joakim and Hans Landstrom. 2000. "Financial Bootstrapping in Small Business: Examining Managers' Resource Acquisition Behaviors." *Journal of Business Venturing* 16:235–254.

Wood, Adrian. 1994. *North-South Trade, Employment, and Inequality.* New York: Oxford University Press.

World Bank Group. 2004. *Development Data Online.* Accessed March 9, 2004 http://devdata.worldbank.org/dataonline/

ECONOMIC FREEDOM OR SELF-IMPOSED STRIFE: WORK–LIFE CONFLICT, GENDER, AND SELF-EMPLOYMENT

Jeremy Reynolds and Linda A. Renzulli

ABSTRACT

This paper uses a representative sample of U.S. workers to examine how self-employment may reduce work-life conflict. We find that self-employment prevents work from interfering with life (WIL), especially among women, but it heightens the tendency for life to interfere with work (LIW). We show that self-employment is connected to WIL and LIW by different causal mechanisms. The self-employed experience less WIL because they have more autonomy and control over the duration and timing of work. Working at home is the most important reason the self-employed experience more LIW than wage and salary workers.

INTRODUCTION

Self-employment is sometimes regarded as the ultimate solution to workplace problems. It offers greater chances of upward mobility for those in

Entrepreneurship
Research in the Sociology of Work, Volume 15, 33–60
Copyright © 2005 by Elsevier Ltd.
ISSN: 0277-2833/doi:10.1016/S0277-2833(05)15003-1

lower income brackets (Holtz–Eakin, Rosen and Weathers 2000). It also provides workers, "a high degree of autonomy, in the sense of freedom from direct supervision, in the performance of their work tasks" (Goldthorpe 1980: 41). More generally, self-employment gives workers the chance to break free from bureaucratic control, the ability to decide when, where, and how to work, and the opportunity to "be their own boss." Self-employment may have special advantages for women (Arai 2000; Buttner and Moore 1997; Hughes 2003). In fact, many women start business ventures in the hopes of finding a sense of freedom and autonomy that their jobs did not provide (Brush 1992), or relief from the glass ceilings and patriarchal nature of existing organizations (Smeaton 2003). Clearly self-employment has much to offer, and many people seem quite happy to work for themselves (Smeaton 2003).

In this paper, we examine the extent to which self-employment lives up to its theoretical potential to solve one important employment problem men and women face: work-life conflict.[1] Although there is a growing literature on how work intersects with personal and family life, scant research is available on how self-employment may reduce or increase the conflict that arises when one has to balance work and life roles (for exceptions see Jurik 1998; Loscocco 1997; Parasuraman and Simmers 2001). In fact, Aldrich and Cliff have called attention to this gap and, "encouraged entrepreneurship researchers to incorporate family considerations in their conceptual models and empirical investigations" (2003: 574).[2] We answer this call with both theory and analysis. More specifically, we use boundary theory (Ashforth, Kreiner and Fugate 2000) and work–family border theory (Clark 2000) to predict levels of work-life conflict among self-employed and wage and salary workers. Then, we make hypotheses about the mechanisms by which self-employment should affect work-life conflict and test our predictions using data from the 1997 National Study of the Changing Workforce (NSCW). Since gender has played such an important role in the literature on work–life conflict (Greenhaus and Parasuraman 1999), we also pay special attention to the possibility that self-employment may affect the experiences of men and women differently. In short, we examine whether men and women who have pursued self-employment have found a solution to work–life conflict or simply misplaced their hope in an employment arrangement that leaves them no better off than the average wage and salary worker. As far as we know, this is the first study to examine the connection between self-employment and work–life conflict using a representative sample of workers and directional measures of work–life conflict.

Work–Life Conflict

Although holding both work and personal or family roles can improve psychological and physical health (Barnett 1999; Barnett and Hyde 2001), many people experience role conflict because the demands of their work and life roles are at least partially incompatible. This form of role conflict, which is called work–life conflict, is both widespread and harmful for workers and organizations (Allen et al. 2000; Galinsky, Bond and Friedman 1993; Galinsky, Kim and Bond 2001; Perry-Jenkins, Repetti and Crouter 2000). In some cases, work–life conflict is described as time-based because people do not have enough time to satisfy the demands of work and life roles (Greenhaus and Beutell 1985). An employee who misses a parent–teacher conference because of a business meeting, for instance, would experience time-based conflict. Work–life conflict can also be strain-based when people do not have enough energy to satisfy both work and family roles (Greenhaus and Beutell 1985). A mentally and physically exhausting day at work, for example, could make it difficult to be an attentive parent or spouse. Finally, people may experience behavior-based conflict when they have difficulty switching back and forth between behaviors that are appropriate for one role to behaviors that are appropriate for the other. Impersonal, bureaucratic styles of communication that are just fine at work, for instance, may raise eyebrows at home.

As the examples above suggest, work typically interferes with personal and family roles more than personal and family roles interfere with work (Greenhaus and Parasuraman 1999), but work–life conflict can originate in either the home or work environment (Carlson, Kacmar and Williams 2000; Frone, Russell and Cooper 1992). Consequently, many authors have begun using directional descriptions of work–life conflict (Allen et al. 2000; Greenhaus and Parasuraman 1999; Greenhaus and Powell 2003). Furthermore, research has shown that the determinants of the two types of conflict are different. In particular, work-related factors are the primary determinants of how much work will interfere with life roles, and family-related factors determine how much life roles will interfere with work (Frone, Yardley and Markel 1997; Greenhaus and Parasuraman 1999).

Consequently, we examine work–life conflict by examining how work interferes with life (WIL) and how life interferes with work (LIW). The few quantitative studies that have examined the connection between work–life conflict and self-employment have not used directional measures (see Parasuraman and Simmers 2001), therefore, our understanding of work–life conflict among the self-employed may be slightly misleading. Since self-employment is a characteristic of work, we expect it to be more closely related to WIL. Most of our hypotheses are about the factors that mediate the relationship between self-employment and WIL. Nevertheless, if self-employment alters the boundaries between work and life, it may also have an effect on LIW and our analyses also examine this possibility.

LITERATURE REVIEW AND HYPOTHESIS

Levels of Work–Life Conflict

Many authors suggest that organizations have played a crucial role in the spread of work–life conflict because they have been slow to accommodate the needs of a workforce in which families with one male breadwinner are increasingly rare (Clarkberg and Moen 2001; Jacobs and Gerson 1998). From this perspective, it appears that self-employed people should experience less WIL than wage and salary workers. Indeed, they do not face the same kinds of formal and informal organizational constraints and should be able to adjust their work roles to accommodate the demands of their personal and family lives. Some research indicates that the self-employed actually experience more work–life conflict than other workers (Parasuraman and Simmers 2001), but we suspect that distinguishing between WIL and LIW may reveal a more complex relationship. More specifically, although freedom from supervision and regulation may reduce WIL, it may also make work boundaries more permeable thus increasing LIW. Friends and family, for instance, may be more likely to contact people at work if there is no boss or regulation that prohibits such interruptions. As Clark suggests, border-keepers, such as bosses, help maintain borders, and when they are removed, more conflict may result (Clark 2000).

H1. The self-employed will have lower levels of WIL than wage and salary workers.

H2. The self-employed will have more LIW than wage and salary workers.

Mechanisms through which Self-Employment Affects Work–Life Conflict

As suggested above, we are particularly interested in identifying the specific mechanisms by which self-employment may affect work–life conflict. Work and personal or family roles often interfere with each other because we lack the time, energy, or psychological flexibility to accommodate both roles (Greenhaus and Beutell 1985), but certain forms of flexibility can help alleviate those types of interference. According to boundary theory and work/family border theory, workers should experience less conflict if they have autonomy and the ability to adjust the temporal and physical boundaries of work and life roles as needed. Temporal and physical flexibility and autonomy determine how permeable role boundaries are and thus the extent to which work and life activities will be integrated or segmented (Ashforth et al. 2000; Clark 2000). For a review of these theories, see Desrochers and Sargent (2003).

With nearly complete control over their workplaces and their own work efforts, the self-employed should be able to make these adjustments without too much trouble. Nevertheless, since making work more flexible may also make it harder to maintain desirable boundaries (Nippert-Eng 1996), self-employment may simply change the types of work–life conflict people experience. Below we draw on work/family border theory (Clark 2000) and boundary theory (Ashforth et al. 2000) to develop hypotheses about the mechanisms by which self-employment may affect how much work interferes with life and how much life interferes with work.

Temporal Control

Self-employed individuals should have less WIL than the average wage and salary worker to the extent that they have more control over the number and timing of the hours they work. That is, the self-employed will have temporal flexibility (Clark 2000). This is not to say that the self-employed will actually work fewer hours or change their schedules more often than other workers. We simply argue that the ability to *control* when and how long you work should reduce conflict by allowing people to make their work and personal schedules more compatible.

Many U.S. wage and salary workers have little control over how many hours they work, but the self-employed should have almost total control. Organizations are said to deny workers the option of exchanging pay for free time and have been accused of orchestrating a dramatic increase in the length of the work year (Schor 1991). Indeed, organizations may have explicit contracts that specify how many hours employees are required to work (Kahn and Lang 1992, 1995, 1996). Organizations may also restrict workers' choice of hours in more subtle or unintentional ways. They are more likely to offer fringe benefits to employees who work many hours (Averett and Hotchkiss 1995). They may also encourage many hours of work indirectly by emphasizing face time (Bailyn 1993; Fried 1998; Perlow 1995) or allowing bosses (Maume and Bellas 2001) and co-workers (Hochschild 1997; Kossek, Barber and Winters 1999) to establish and maintain a long-hour culture. Self-employed individuals, on the other hand, are their own bosses and can choose their co-workers. Since work time commitments are one of the major causes of WIL (Frone et al. 1997), the self-employed should experience less WIL because they are better able to control how many hours they work.

The self-employed should also enjoy temporal flexibility in the sense that they can control when they work. Flexible hours are not a guaranteed solution to work–life conflict (Christensen and Staines 1990). Nevertheless, the ability to control the timing of work hours should help eliminate scheduling conflicts (Hamermesh 1998) and may provide flexibility without blurring the boundaries between work and home (Desrochers and Sargent 2003). In fact, evidence suggests that the ability to control when you work weakens the positive association between work hours and work–life conflict (Hill et al. 2001). Flexible work hours should also help workers fulfill their desires for time with family members. Some couples synchronize their work schedules so that they can spend time together (Hamermesh 2002). Other employees adjust their work hours to accommodate childcare needs (Presser 1989, 1995). Flexible hours can make it easier to pick up children from daycare or work when another family member can be at home to care for young children. These advantages help explain why some studies found that flexible schedules are linked directly (Hill et al. 2001) or indirectly (Thomas and Ganster 1995) to lower levels of work–family conflict. Self-employment may not always provide this type of flexibility, especially when people work in retail sales or other industries that have fairly rigid hours (Arai 2000). However, since the likelihood of having flexible hours is greater for the self-employed (Golden 2001), it is reasonable to expect that the self-employed will be in a good position to avoid the inflexible schedules that cause WIL for other employees. Given these arguments, we make the following predictions:

H3a. Self-employment will reduce WIL by providing control over the duration of work.

H3b. Self-employment will reduce WIL by providing control over the timing of work.

Autonomy

Control over the operations or tasks at work may also affect levels of conflict. Some research indicates that when people have autonomy, they experience less conflict between work and life roles (Galinsky, Bond and Friedman 1996; Parasuraman and Simmers 2001). These findings fit nicely with Clark's suggestion that people who have more autonomy and thus more influence in their work domain may have more control over the borders of both work and life (2000). We therefore predict that autonomy at work will have an effect above and beyond that of temporal control. Since it is a characteristic of work, we expect that it will primarily affect WIL.

H4. Self-employment will decrease WIL by providing workplace autonomy.

Physical Location

Finally, the self-employed may be in a better position to control where they work and may often choose to work at home as a way of coping with the dual demands of life and work. The ability to work at home can be beneficial. Working at home eliminates commuting time and thus increases the amount of time people have for other activities. Working at home should also make the transition from work to personal and family roles easier and less costly (Ashforth et al. 2000) and allow people to respond more quickly to emergencies at home. It may also allow the blending of life and work spaces and activities (Clark 2000) and eliminate the need for special child-care arrangements. Perhaps this is why some researchers have found that working from home is associated with greater work–life balance (Hill, Ferris and Martinson 2003).

However, when people work from home they are also making the work–life border more permeable, thus leading to a blurring of the borders between work and life roles (Ashforth et al. 2000; Clark 2000). Family and friends, for instance, may think that work done at home is unimportant or free from deadlines, and as a result they may not hesitate to interrupt it with personal phone calls. Since people who work at home are often physically closer to family, friends, and other people who might interrupt their work, phone calls may even be supplemented with unannounced visits. Parents who work at home while their children are present are likely to face the largest number of interruptions. Furthermore, a permeable boundary also allows work roles to interfere with personal or family roles. Since the workplace is always only a step away, work-related phone calls, faxes, messes, deliveries, and other byproducts of work may interfere with personal conversations, meals, and other aspects of life.

Ultimately, when self-employed people work at home, they are likely to create an environment where *family space* and *work space* are not always distinct, and without bosses and other border keepers who help maintain work–life boundaries, any borders that they construct are likely to be rather permeable (see Clark 2000). Indeed, working at home leads to new challenges for people as they try to maintain their preferred boundaries (Berke 2003; Green and Cohen 1995), and it may even lead to greater work–life conflict (Nippert-Eng 1996).[3] Therefore, despite its potential benefits, working at home should increase work–life conflict, and the self-employed should have more WIL and LIW to the extent that they are more likely to work at home.[4]

H5. Self-employment will increase WIL and LIW by increasing the amount of work done at home.

Gender, Self-employment, and Work Life Conflict

Whether or not hypotheses 1–5 are supported, self-employment is unlikely to be a perfect solution to work–life conflict because it does not alter the gendered nature of the home or release people from self-imposed constrains. Consequently, self-employment may not be an equally effective solution to WIL and LIW for men and women. Some authors have suggested that part of the reason self-employed women earn less than self-employed men is that women do a greater share of household labor and thus are unable to work as many hours for themselves (Hundley 2001). Some evidence even suggests that self-employed people have gendered patterns of work–family conflict. Among women, family interferes more with work, and among men, work interferes more with family (Loscocco 1997). In fact, some authors have even argued that the switch to self-employment is a hegemonic process that encourages women to continue carrying the dual burden of paid and unpaid work (Green and Cohen 1995). Furthermore, self-employed people often re-create the same restrictive work arrangements that cause work–life conflict in other employment relationships (Jurik 1998). In many European countries, for example, self-employed women do not spend more time caring for their children than other employees, and self-employed men actually spend less time caring for their children (Hildebrand and Williams 2003). All these evidence suggests that although self-employment may offer the promise of flexibility, men and women may not always be able to make the most of that opportunity.

In particular, we expect self-employment to create less WIL and more LIW for women than for men. In part, this expectation is based on the idea that women tend to bear a larger share of the household labor than men (Coltrane 2000; Shelton and John 1996). However, gender may also moderate the effect of self-employment through its influence on attitudes about the appropriate roles of men and women at work and home. Many men and women still support traditional gender roles (Brewster and Padavic 2000), and despite more liberal attitudes, evidence suggests that women were just as committed to housework in 1995 as they were in 1975 (Robinson and Milkie 1998). Men, on the other hand, are more likely than women to prefer full-time paid work (Hakim 2000; Reynolds 2003). Perhaps this is because departing from gender norms can intensify time-based conflict (Gutek, Searle and Klepa 1991). In light of these considerations, we expect that women will take greater advantage of the flexibility of self-employment than men in order to reduce WIL. On the other hand, we also expect that the permeability that self-employment brings will do more to increase LIW among women than among men. In other words, self-employment may not free women from the demands of home, but it may place them in a situation where the demands of life roles are more likely to intrude.

H6a. Self-employment will decrease WIL more among women than among men.

H6b. Self-employment will increase LIW more among women than among men.

Data and Measures

In order to test our hypotheses, we use data from the 1997 National Study of the Changing Workforce (NSCW), a nationally representative sample of U.S. workers. These data are particularly valuable for our analysis because they contain detailed information about work–life conflict, time-use, family characteristics, and a representative sample of self-employed people. For a more complete description of the data, see Bond et al. (1998). After accounting for missing data, we have a final sample of 2,153 respondents.

Since work–life conflict is often described as having a direction (Carlson et al. 2000), and since we expect self-employment to have a greater impact on the nature of work than on the nature of home life, this analysis uses two dependent variables. While one measures the extent to which life interferes with work (LIW), the other measures the extent to which work interferes with life (WIL). Both measures were created by averaging five questions that ask about various sources of conflict. The measure of WIL, for instance, is based on the questions below, each of which offers the same answer choices: very often = 5, often = 4, sometimes = 3, rarely = 2, and never = 1.

In the past three months, how often have you not _____ because of your job?

(1) had enough time for yourself
(2) had enough time for your family or other important people in your life
(3) had the energy to do things with your family or other important people in your life
(4) been able to get everything done at home each day
(5) been in as good a mood as you would like to be at home

If more than one of the five questions was missing, respondents were assigned a missing value. In our final sample, the alpha for the measure of WIL is 0.85. The measure of LIW is constructed in the same manner from very similar questions that ask about the ways personal and family life can make it difficult to fulfill work roles.

In the past three months, how often has your family or personal life _____?

(1) kept you from getting work done on time at your job
(2) kept you from taking on extra work at your job
(3) kept you from doing as good a job at work as you could
(4) drained you of the energy you needed to do your job
(5) kept you from concentrating on your job

The index of LIW has an alpha of 0.79. In regression analyses, we control for LIW when WIL is the dependent variable and vice versa, because of the reciprocal relationship between the two (Frone et al. 1997).

The primary explanatory variables are designed to measure the mechanisms that may account for the effects of self-employment. We do not have a direct measure of control over the duration of work. Nevertheless, people who are working more or fewer hours than they prefer are unlikely to have control over the number of hours they work, therefore we use mismatches between the number of actual and preferred hours of work as a proxy for control over the duration of work. We measure control over the timing of work with a question that asks, "Overall, how much control would you say you have in scheduling your work hours – complete control, a lot, some, very little, or none?'' Autonomy is measured by averaging the three items below, which are coded 4 = strongly agree, to 1 = strongly disagree. The resulting index ranges from 1 to 4, and higher numbers indicate more autonomy.

(1) I have the freedom to decide what I do on my job.
(2) It is basically my own responsibility to decide how my job gets done.
(3) I have a lot of say about what happens on my job.

The alpha for the index of autonomy is 0.70. Finally, we measure the location of work by identifying respondents who work at least some regularly scheduled, non-overtime hours at home. See Table 1 for variable definitions and descriptive statistics for these variables and as well as variables that account for the demands that respondents face at work and home.[5]

In order to test our hypotheses, we also distinguish between self-employed and wage and salary workers. According to the Internal Revenue Service (IRS), people are self-employed if they carry on a trade or business as a sole proprietor or if they are an independent contractor, member of a partnership, or are otherwise in business for themselves. The NSCW identified respondents who are self-employed in their main job by asking a series of questions. First, respondents were asked if they were self-employed. Anyone who answered yes to this question was classified as self-employed. If respondents were unsure, they were prompted with the explanation that people are generally considered self-employed if they report income from their main job on schedule C of their IRS tax forms. Second, respondents were asked if social security or taxes were taken out of their pay. This helps identify other people who are classified as self-employed for legal purposes. Sometimes, people who do not have social security taken out of their pay are classified as independent contractors, a special form of self-employment. For this analysis, we simply classify them as self-employed because they do not have the same organizational constraints as wage and salary workers. Our final sample contains 358 respondents who are self-employed.

Analytic Strategy

In order to determine how and why self-employment affects work–life conflict, we conduct several multivariate analyses. We begin by examining the levels of WIL and LIW reported by self-employed and wage and salary workers. We also examine the amount of control each group has over the duration and timing of their work, the location of their work, the level of

Table 1. Means and Proportions by Employment Status[a].

	Variable	Description	Wage and Salary N = 1,795	Self-employed N = 358
Dependent Variables	Work interference with life (WIL)	Avg. of 5 items 1 = little 5 = much	2.97	2.86Δ
	Life interference with work (LIW)	Avg. of 5 items 1 = little 5 = much	1.96	2.05Δ
Mechanisms	Works preferred number of hours	1 = yes 0 = no	0.21	0.28Δ
	Amount of control over schedule	1 = none 2 = very little 3 = some 4 = a lot 5 = complete	2.94	4.07Δ
	Autonomy	Avg. of three items 1 = low 4 = high	3.04	3.62Δ
	Works some regular hours at home	Works some non-overtime hours at home 1 = yes 0 = no	0.20	0.56Δ
Work Characteristics	Weekly hours	Hours worked at all jobs	46.50	47.29
	Nights not home in last 3 mo.	Nights spent away from home due to work	2.31	2.41
	Work distress	Burned out or stressed by work (last 3 months) 1 = never 2 = rarely 3 = sometimes 4 = often 5 = very often	2.83	2.63Δ
	Work overload	Enough time to get everything done on job 1 = strongly agree 4 = strongly disagree	2.76	2.94Δ
	Personal earned income quintile	1 = lowest 5 = highest	3.00	3.29Δ

Personal and Family Characteristics			
Hours spent on chores	Hours spent on chores on average workday	2.44	2.50
Hours spent on childcare	Hours spent on childcare on average workday (those who do not have children are coded zero)	1.59	1.98Δ
Hours spent on eldercare	Hours spent on elder care on average workday (those who do not provide such care are coded zero)	0.15	0.14
Dissatisfaction with family life	How satisfied with family life 1 = extremely 2 = very 3 = somewhat 4 = not too satisfied	2.05	1.95Δ
White	1 = white 0 = non – white	0.80	0.85Δ
Female	1 = female 0 = male	0.47	0.39Δ
Lives with spouse/partner	1 = yes 0 = no	0.77	0.84Δ
Dual earner couple	Member of a dual-earner couple 1 = yes 0 = no	0.61	0.61
Number of children under 18	Continuous variable	1.09	1.16
Youngest child age 0–5	1 = yes 0 = no	0.25	0.25
Youngest child age 6–12	1 = yes 0 = no	0.21	0.21
Youngest child age 13–17	1 = yes 0 = no	0.13	0.12
Cares for elderly relative	1 = yes 0 = no	0.05	0.06
Family income quintile	1 = lowest 5 = highest	3.24	3.55Δ

[a]Note: Δ = differences between wage and salary and self-employed workers are statistically significant at the 0.05 level.

autonomy they enjoy, and how they may differ in terms of other work, personal, and family characteristics (Table 1). These analyses help us evaluate the hypotheses that the self-employed will have lower levels of WIL and higher levels of LIW than wage and salary workers, and they provide a way to assess our assumptions about the levels of flexibility that the self-employed should enjoy. We also conduct a bivariate analysis to provide preliminary tests of our hypotheses that autonomy and control over the duration and timing of work will decrease WIL, while working at home will increase both WIL and LIW (Table 2).

Next, we re-evaluate the mechanisms by which self-employment affects work–family conflict by estimating a series of nested OLS regressions. In particular, we examine how self-employment is related to WIL and LIW and how those relationships change as we control for the factors that should explain why self-employment affects work–life conflict. Guided by theory, the analyses for WIL emphasize work characteristics, and the analyses for LIW emphasize personal and family characteristics. The full models in both analyses, however, include the mechanisms that should mediate the effects of self-employment and thus allow for the possibility that the same mechanisms that affect WIL may affect LIW. These regressions also allow us to examine the hypotheses that self-employment will do more to decrease WIL and increase LIW among women than among men (Tables 3 and 4). Finally, in order to assess the importance of life demands that are only encountered

Table 2. Correlations between Conflict and Measures of Control by Employment Status.

Type of Conflict	Measures of Control	Correlation Between Conflict and Type of Control	
		Self-employed	Wage and Salary
WIL	Works preferred number of hours	−0.29*	−0.20*
	Amount of control over schedule	−0.19*	−0.18*
	Autonomy	−0.13*	−0.17*
	Works some regular hours at home	−0.05	0.03
LIW	Works preferred number of hours	−0.19*	−0.11*
	Amount of control over schedule	0.04	−0.02
	Autonomy	0.00	−0.04
	Works some regular hours at home	0.04	0.13*

*$p < 0.05$.

Table 3. OLS Regression of Work Interference with Life (WIL) on Explanatory Variables[a].

		Model 1	Model 2	Model 3
	Self-employed	-0.04^{**}	0.00	$0.04^{\dagger}$
Work Characteristics	Weekly hours	0.15^{**}	0.14^{**}	0.14^{**}
	Nights not home in last 3 mo.	0.05^{**}	0.06^{**}	0.06^{**}
	Work distress	0.42^{**}	0.38^{**}	0.38^{**}
	Work overload	0.13^{**}	0.14^{**}	0.14^{**}
	Personal earned income quintile	-0.02	-0.01	-0.01
Personal and Family Characteristics	White	0.03^{*}	0.04^{*}	0.04^{*}
	Female	0.06^{**}	0.05^{**}	0.07^{**}
	Lives with spouse/partner	0.02	0.03	$0.03^{\dagger}$
	Number of children under 18	0.08^{**}	0.07^{**}	0.07^{**}
	Cares for elderly relative	-0.03	-0.02	-0.02
	Life interference with work	0.25^{**}	0.26^{**}	0.26^{**}
Mechanisms	Works preferred number of hours		-0.05^{**}	-0.05^{**}
	Amount of control over schedule		-0.07^{**}	-0.07^{**}
	Autonomy		-0.07^{**}	-0.07^{**}
	Works some regular hours at home		-0.02	-0.02
	Female* self-employed			-0.05^{*}
	R^2	0.446	0.462	0.463
	R^2 Change		0.016^{*}	0.001^{*}
	N	2,153	2,153	2,153

[a]The numbers in the table are standardized coefficients.
$^{*}p<0.05.$
$^{**}p<0.01.$
$^{\dagger}p<0.1.$

by workers with young children, we estimate one set of regressions for respondents who have children less than 13 years of age (Table 5).

RESULTS

Simple univariate statistics provide some support for the hypotheses that the self-employed will have less WIL (H1) and more LIW (H2) than wage and

Table 4. OLS Regression of Life Interference with Work (LIW) on
Explanatory Variables[a].

		Model 1	Model 2
	Self-employed	0.06**	0.01
Life Characteristics	Hours spent on chores	0.02	0.02
	Hours spent on childcare	0.04	0.03
	Hours spent on eldercare	0.02	0.02
	Dissatisfaction with family life	0.13**	0.13**
Personal and Family	White	0.00	0.00
Characteristics	Female	0.02	0.03
	Lives with spouse/partner	0.00	0.00
	Dual earner couple	−0.03	−0.03
	Youngest child age 0–5	0.07**	0.07*
	Youngest child age 6–12	0.04[†]	0.04
	Youngest child age 13–17	0.02	0.02
	Family earned income quintile	0.05*	0.03
	Work interference with life	0.39**	0.40**
Mechanisms	Works preferred number of hours		−0.03
	Amount of control over schedule		0.05*
	Autonomy		0.02
	Works some regular hours at home		0.10**
	R^2	0.22	0.24
	R^2 Change		0.01*
	N	2,153	2,153

[a]The numbers in the table are standardized coefficients.
*$p < 0.05$.
**$p < 0.01$.
[†]$p < 0.1$.

salary workers (see Table 1). Admittedly, the observed differences in means
are not large, but they are statistically significant and in the expected directions. It is also apparent that the self-employed enjoy more control over
the duration and timing of their work, are more likely to work at home, and
have more autonomy than wage and salary workers. As indicated by other
comparisons in Table 1, the self-employed also differ from wage and salary
workers in a number of other ways. The self-employed, for instance, earn
more money and are less likely to feel burned out or stressed by their work,
but they are more likely to feel overloaded with work. The self-employed are
also more likely than other workers to be white, male, and have a partner or

Table 5. OLS Regression of Life Interference with Work (LIW) on Job, Personal, and Family Characteristics.[a] (Sample limited to respondents with children under 13 years of age).

		Model 1	Model 2
	Self-employed	0.06^*	0.01
Life Characteristics	Hours spent on chores on weekdays	0.01	0.01
	Hours spent on childcare on weekdays	0.05	0.05
	Hours spent on eldercare on weekdays	0.04	0.04
	Dissatisfaction with family life	0.11^{**}	0.12^{**}
Personal & Family Characteristics	White	0.00	0.00
	Female	0.10^{**}	0.10^{**}
	Lives with spouse/partner	0.07	$0.07^{\dagger}$
	Dual earner couple	-0.11^{**}	-0.11^{**}
	Youngest child age 0–5	0.02	0.02
	Satisfaction with child care	-0.14^{**}	-0.14^{**}
	Child care failures (last 3 months)	0.07^*	0.07^*
	Family earned income quintile	0.12^{**}	0.10^{**}
	Work interference with life	0.34^{**}	0.35^{**}
Mechanisms	Works preferred number of hours		-0.01
	Amount of control over schedule		0.04
	Autonomy		0.03
	Works some regular hours at home		0.09^{**}
	R^2	0.24	0.25
	R^2 Change		0.01^*
	N	1,023	1,023

[a]The numbers in the table are standardized coefficients.
$^*p < 0.05$.
$^{**}p < 0.01$.
$^{\dagger}p < 0.1$.

spouse. Finally, they spend more time on childcare and are less dissatisfied with their family lives than wage and salary workers.

Table 2 provides preliminary support for the hypothesized effects of control over the duration and timing of work and autonomy. As predicted by hypotheses H3a and H3b, respondents who can control how much and when they work have less WIL. It appears that these two forms of control benefit both the self-employed and the wage and salary workers. Although we did not predict that control over the number of work hours would affect LIW, the correlations indicate that among respondents who work the number of hours they prefer, life is less likely to interfere with work. Furthermore, hypothesis H4 predicted that autonomy would be associated with lower levels of WIL. The correlations clearly support this hypothesis.

Bivariate analyses provide mixed support for our predictions about the effects of working at home. In hypothesis H5, we predicted that working at home would be associated with higher levels of work–life conflict in both directions. The correlations, however, indicate that working at home is only associated with higher levels of LIW and only among wage and salary workers.

MECHANISMS AFFECTING WIL

Table 3 examines the relationship between WIL and self-employment in a multivariate context. Model 1 reveals that the self-employed do not simply report lower levels of WIL because they have different experiences at work or at home. The self-employed do have different experiences at work and home (see Table 1), but controlling for these factors barely changes the estimated effect of self-employment, which remains negative and statistically significant. In this sense, Model 1 does not improve our understanding of why the self-employed report less WIL than wage and salary workers. What we do learn from Model 1 is that our analysis is consistent with that of other authors who have found that work-related time commitments, distress, and feelings of overload are important predictors of how much work will interfere with life (Frone et al. 1997).

On the other hand, accounting for observed differences in autonomy, control over the duration and timing of work, and the ability to work at home makes the effect of self-employment disappear altogether (see Model 2). Together with the results in Model 1, this provides support for H3a and H3b and H4 by indicating that temporal flexibility and autonomy are the mechanisms through which self-employment reduces WIL. In other words, the self-employed experience lower levels of WIL because they tend to have more control over how long they work, when they work, and how they accomplish the tasks at hand. When wage and salary employees enjoy these same advantages, they experience virtually the same levels of WIL as the self-employed. The results for working at home, on the other hand, are not significant. We expected that working at home would increase WIL because it makes the boundary between work and life roles more permeable, but the data do not support this hypothesis (H5).

Finally, Model 3 shows that the effect of self-employment varies by gender. In hypothesis H6a, we predicted that self-employment would do more to prevent WIL among women than among men, and in order to examine this possibility, we tried interacting gender with self-employment and with each of the four mechanisms through which self-employment might affect WIL. Only the interaction with self-employment was significant, suggesting that self-employment affects WIL among men and women for the same reasons. Furthermore, after including the interaction between self-employment and gender, the main effect of self-employment is positive and marginally significant, while the interaction is negative and significant at the 0.05 level (see Table 3). In other words, after accounting for differences in autonomy and the ability to control the duration, timing, and location of work, it seems that self-employment may actually *increase* WIL among men. The more interesting question, however, is whether the gendered effects of self-employment will still be significant when our models do not control for differences in autonomy and control. We want to examine the net effect of self-employment, not the effect that remains after its most beneficial characteristics are held constant.

To clarify the *overall* effect of self-employment on WIL among men and women, we estimated a model that is mathematically equivalent to estimating Model 3 without the controls for the four mechanisms that mediate the effects of self-employment. More specifically, we removed the controls for the four mechanisms and then replaced the interaction as well as the main effects of gender and self-employment with indicator variables that represent the various combinations of gender and self-employment (i.e. wage and salary men, wage and salary women, self-employed men and, self-employed women). This modeling strategy provides a convenient way of estimating how these four groups of employees differ with regard to WIL, and even more importantly, it provides statistical tests of the overall group differences that the traditional interactions obscure. When wage and salary women are used as the reference category, we find that they experience significantly more WIL than the other three groups. When self-employed men are used as the reference category, we find that they report significantly less conflict than wage and salary women but that they experience similar levels of WIL as wage and salary men and self-employed women. Overall, these results indicate that self-employment has more advantages for women than for men. Men report similar levels of WIL whether they are self-employed or not, but since self-employed women have significantly less WIL than wage and salary women, gender differences in WIL are smaller among the self-employed.

MECHANISMS AFFECTING LIW

Table 4 examines whether self-employment also affects how often life interferes with work, and the results indicate that self-employment does have some disadvantages. In general, researchers have spent less time examining LIW than WIL (Perry-Jenkins et al. 2000), and the fairly small R^2 statistic for each of the three models indicates that we have much to learn. Nevertheless, Model 1 explains 22% of the variance in LIW, and it indicates that self-employment increases LIW. In fact, the indicator variable for self-employment is significant and positive even after controlling for personal, family, and life characteristics. These results support hypothesis H2, which predicted that the self-employed would have more LIW than other workers. The coefficient for female, on the other hand, is not significant, so there is little support for hypothesis H6b, which suggested that self-employment would increase LIW more among women than among men.

Model 2 sheds more light on the relationship between self-employment and LIW by examining the mechanisms that should mediate the effect of self-employment. In particular, since the coefficient for self-employment is not significant in Model 2, it appears that the effect of self-employment is mediated by working at home and the ability to control one's work schedule. More specifically, people who work at home or have control over their schedules report more LIW than other workers. This finding is consistent with hypothesis H5, boundary theory, and work/family border theory, which suggest that working at home can increase LIW because it makes the boundary between work and life roles more permeable. The effect of schedule control, however, is to a certain extent puzzling. Control over one's work schedule is generally considered to be advantageous, and we are surprised that it would significantly *increase* LIW. Nevertheless, boundary theory does suggest that flexible boundaries can increase role conflict if they require people to do more "boundary work" (Ashforth et al. 2000). Future research should do more to evaluate boundary theory and work/family border theory by testing their predictions regarding the circumstances under which permeability leads to conflict.

Table 5 takes a second look at LIW using the sample of respondents who have children under 13 years of age. Focusing on this group allows us to include information about childcare arrangements that is not available for other respondents, and we hoped that it would improve our understanding of how self-employment might affect LIW. The R^2 statistics are not much higher than they were in Table 4. Nevertheless, we find that women with children under 13 report more LIW than their male counterparts and that people experience less LIW when they have childcare arrangements that work well for them and are reliable. We also find that people who live with a partner or spouse report more LIW than the single parents who form the reference category. This suggests that although partners and spouses may help with childcare, living with a partner may also create additional life responsibilities that can interfere with work. We also find that being part of a dual-earner couple is associated with less LIW. We see this as an indication that stay-at-home partners may play an important role in reminding workers about their life responsibilities, and that working spouses may be less inclined or less able to interrupt each other at work. These interpretations are clearly ad-hoc, but they are consistent with Clark's discussion of boundary maintenance (Clark 2000), and we report our findings in the belief that they will be of interest to other researchers.

CONCLUSION

Empirical and theoretical research on work–life conflict is abundant and growing (Perry-Jenkins et al. 2000). At the same time, research on self-employment has proliferated in the last decade (Aldrich 2004). However, there is a paucity of research that examines the two phenomena together i.e. work–life conflict among the self-employed (for exceptions see Jurik 1998; Loscocco 1997; Parasuraman and Simmers 2001). Furthermore, when authors have examined work–life conflict among the self-employed, they have not used nationally representative samples or distinguished between conflict that arises from WIL and conflict that arises from LIW. We were able to fill this gap. First, we examined whether self-employment can reduce the extent to which work and life roles interfere with each other. Ultimately, we found that work interferes more with life among wage and salary workers than among the self-employed. On the other hand, we found that life interferes more with work among the self-employed.

Drawing on border theory (Ashforth et al. 2000) and work/life boundary theory (Clark 2000), we examined three types of control that help explain why self-employment helps prevent work from interfering with life. More specifically, we found that autonomy and temporal control help to prevent work from interfering with life and actually eliminate the observed effect of self-employment. In other words, control over the content, duration, and timing of work are crucial mechanisms by which self-employment prevents work roles from interfering with life roles. Put differently, when wage and

salary and self-employed workers have similar levels of control, they experience similar levels of work–life conflict.

In addition, gender plays an interesting role in determining how much
work will interfere with life. When trying to understand how self-employment
may help solve workplace problems, it is instructive to compare levels of
conflict among wage and salary workers and self-employed workers of the
same gender. It is also useful to look for gender differences in the levels of
conflict experienced by the self-employed. We find that self-employed men
and women experience similar levels of work interference, only because self-
employment reduces interference among women. In short, our analysis suggests that self-employment is more beneficial for women than for men.

These findings have two sets of implications. First, on average, self-
employment may have the potential to reduce (though not eliminate) the
tendency for work to interfere with life. This reduction, however, is because
of control. Therefore, when organizations provide their employees with
autonomy and control over the amount and timing of work and job
responsibilities, work should interfere with life responsibilities less often.
Second, these findings imply that it is not self-employment per se that
decreases conflict for women but rather the control they gain from it. Self-
employment has more benefits for women than for men, but this appears to
be because they experience a bigger increase in control. In fact, self-employed men report the same levels of work interference as wage and salary
men. When we control for the relative levels of control that the two groups
enjoy, self-employment itself actually leads to slightly higher levels of
interference from work. Ultimately, this means that control is the key. If
self-employed women do not have control, they will not have lowered levels
of work-life conflict. Similarly, if wage and salary women had more control,
they would have less conflict.

Nevertheless, as we said, WIL is only half the equation. Many U.S.
workers also find that life can interfere with work, and with respect to this
type of conflict, the self-employed are worse off than their wage and salary
counterparts. Ironically, the disadvantage is partially explained by the temporal flexibility that made the self-employed less prone to interference from
work. The other part of the explanation is that the self-employed are more
likely to work at home than wage and salary workers. We suspect that
people who work at home or have flexible schedules are more susceptible to
interruptions from friends and family, who may intentionally or unintentionally cross the temporal and physical boundaries of work. Without time
clocks, official schedules, telephone routing systems, or bosses to ward off
interruptions, the self-employed simply lack many of the structures and

people that shield wage and salary workers from life's interruptions. Clark (2000) discussed the permeability of home and work borders and suggested that permeability can in fact increase conflict. Our results show that permeability may indeed increase conflict – conflict that arises from the life sphere.

Our work has implications for future research in both the self-employment literature and the work–life conflict literature. First, our findings suggest a need for longitudinal studies that examine whether *switching* from wage and salary work to self-employment reduces or increases conflict in either direction. In our work, we can deduce that moving from a workplace that offers little control to self-employment (that offers a lot of control) will tend to decrease the extent to which work interferes with life. It is possible, however, that the self-employed are simply more inclined to report low levels of conflict than their wage and salary counterparts. Resolving this issue will require longitudinal data about workers who switch to self-employment or at least retrospective evaluations of the conflict that self-employed people had while they were wage and salary workers (see for instance Green and Cohen 1995). Nevertheless, we have shown that it is control that helps prevent WIL.

Second, although our results indicate that gender may moderate the effects of self-employment, more research will be needed to determine if gender differences in the nature of self-employment may be driving our results. Self-employment research has shown that men and women own different types of businesses in different industries (Baker, Aldrich and Liou 1997), work different hours, and have different sets of business networks (Renzulli, Aldrich and Moody 2000). In fact, women still lag behind men in their rates of ownership, profit, size, and success. Further research should evaluate these differences as a cause and consequence of the gendered relationship between self-employment and work–life conflict. It may be that the gender differences in our results reflect the types of businesses women own.

Third, our work examines control but not necessarily action. The next step for research in the area of work–life conflict is to study the effects of using the temporal and physical control workers may have. If having control over one's schedule is associated with life interfering with work, is that because the control itself causes the interference or because workers who have such control change their work schedules frequently?

So, is self-employment the answer? Is it a panacea for work–life conflict? As long as organizations remain inflexible and family unfriendly (see Clarkberg and Moen 2001; Glass and Estes 1997), self-employment may be an important path to workplace control that can help prevent work from interfering with life. Unfortunately, self-employed does nothing to reduce the extent to which life interferes with work – in fact, it seems like a trade off between the sources of conflict.

NOTES

1. Although many authors use the term work–family conflict, we prefer the more general term, work–life conflict because people who do not have traditional families also experience conflict between their work and personal or family roles. This change in terminology is consistent with the definition of "family" used by the Sloan Work and Family Research Network (see: http://www.bc.edu/bc_org/avp/wfnetwork/rft/mapping.html).

2. The definition of an entrepreneur is debated among scholars (see Gartner 1988), but for our purposes entrepreneurs and the self-employed are used synonymously.

3. Clark (1999) suggests that when the domains of home and work are similar, the blending of work and life roles (i.e. multitasking life and work activities) may reduce work–life conflict. Running an in-home day care center, for example, might allow a woman to work (by caring for other children) and attend to a life role (by caring for her own child) at the same time. Unfortunately, the 1997 NSCW data do not provide measures of domain similarity or the blending of work and life activities.

4. In contrast to most of our other hypotheses, this one mentions both WIL and LIW because unlike temporal flexibility and autonomy, working at home should affect the permeability of the boundary between work and life domains.

5. Since we are interested in the interplay between work and life roles, we would prefer to conduct an analysis that includes people who live alone but still have family and personal responsibilities. Unfortunately, the NSCW did not ask people who live alone how satisfied they are with their personal or family lives. Therefore, our analysis only includes people who lives with a spouse, partner, or at least one person to whom they are related by blood or adoption.

ACKNOWLEDGMENTS

An earlier version of this paper was presented at the Southern Sociological Society Annual Meetings in Atlanta, GA, 2004. We would like to thank participants at the sessions and Amy Davis for their comments on earlier drafts of this paper.

REFERENCES

Aldrich, Howard E. 2005. "Entrepreneurship." Pp. 451–457 in *Handbook of Economic Sociology*, edited by N. Smelser and R. Swedberg. Princeton, NJ: Princeton University Press.

Aldrich, Howard E. and Jennifer E. Cliff. 2003. "The Pervasive Effects of Family on Entrepreneurship: Toward a Family Embeddedness Perspective." *Journal of Business Venturing* 18:573–596.

Allen, T.D., D. Herst, C.S. Bruck, and M. Sutton. 2000. "Consequences Associated with Work to Family Conflict: A Review and Agenda for Future Research." *Journal of Occupational Health Psychology* 5:278–308.

Arai, A. Bruce. 2000. "Self-Employment as a Response to the Double Day for Women and Men in Canada." *Canadian Review of Sociology and Anthropology-Revue Canadienne De Sociologie Et D Anthropologie* 37:125–142.

Ashforth, Blake E., Glen E. Kreiner, and Mel Fugate. 2000. "All in a Day's Work: Boundaries and Micro Role Transitions." *Academy of Management Review* 25:472–491.

Averett, Susan L. and Julie L. Hotchkiss. 1995. "The Probability of Receiving Benefits at Different Hours of Work." *American Economic Review* 85:276–280.

Bailyn, Lotte. 1993. *Breaking the Mold.* New York: Free Press.

Baker, Ted, Howard E. Aldrich, and Nina Liou. 1997. "Invisible Entrepreneurs: The Neglect of Women Business Owners by Mass Media and Scholarly Journals in the United States." *Entrepreneurship and Regional Development* 9:221–238.

Barnett, Rosalind Chait. 1999. "A New Work–Life Model for the Twenty-First Century." *Annals of the American Academy of Political and Social Science* 562:143–158.

Barnett, Rosalind Chait and Janet Shibley Hyde. 2001. "Women, Men, Work, and Family – An Expansionist Theory." *American Psychologist* 56:781–796.

Berke, Debra L. 2003. "Coming Home Again – The Challenges and Rewards of Home-Based Self-Employment." *Journal of Family Issues* 24:513–546.

Bond, James T., Ellen Galinsky, and Jennifer E. Swansberg. 1998. *The 1997 National Study of the Changing Workforce.* New York: Families and Work Institute.

Brewster, Karim L. and Irene Padavic. 2000. "Change in Gender-Ideology, 1977–1996: The Contributions of Intracohort Change and Population Turnover." *Journal of Marriage and the Family* 62:477–487.

Brush, Candida G. 1992. "Research on Women Business Owners: Past Trends a New Perspective and Future Direction." *Entrepreneurship Theory and Practice* (Summer): 5–30

Buttner, E. Holly and Dorothy P. Moore. 1997. "Women's Organizational Exodus to Entrepreneurship: Self-Reported Motivations and Correlates with Success." *Journal of Small Business Management* 35:34–46.

Carlson, Dawn S., K. Michele Kacmar, and Larry J. Williams. 2000. "Construction and Initial Validation of a Multidimensional Measure of Work-Family Conflict." *Journal of Vocational Behavior* 56:249–276.

Christensen, Kathleen E. and Graham L. Staines. 1990. "Flextime: A Viable Solution to Work/Family Conflict?." *Journal of Family Issues* 11:455–476.

Clark, Sue Campbell. 2000. "Work/Family Border Theory: A New Theory of Work/Family Balance." *Human Relations* 53:747–770.

Clarkberg, Marin and Phyllis Moen. 2001. "Understanding the Time-Squeeze: Married Couples Preferred and Actual Work-Hour Strategies." *American Behavioral Scientist* 44:1115–1136.

Coltrane, S. 2000. "Research on Household Labor: Modeling and Measuring the Social Embeddedness of Routine Family Work." *Journal of Marriage and the Family* 62:1208–1233.

Desrochers, Stephan and Leisa D. Sargent. 2003. "Boundary/Border Theory and Work–Family Integration (a Sloan Work and Family Encyclopedia entry)." Vol. 2004: Sloan Work and Family Research Network.

Fried, Mindy. 1998. *Taking Time: Parental Leave Policy and Corporate Culture*. Philadelphia, PA: Temple University Press.

Frone, Michael R., Marcia Russell, and M. Lynne Cooper. 1992. "Antecedents and Outcomes of Work Family Conflict – Testing a Model of the Work Family Interface." *Journal of Applied Psychology* 77:65–78.

Frone, Michael R., John K. Yardley, and Karen S. Markel. 1997. "Developing and Testing an Integrative Model of the Work–Family Interface." *Journal of Vocational Behavior* 50:145–167.

Galinsky, Ellen, James T. Bond, and Dana E. Friedman. 1996. "The Role of Employers in Addressing the Needs of Employed Parents." *Journal of Social Issues* 52:111–136.

------. 1993. *The Changing Workforce: Highlights of the National Study*. New York: Families and Work Institute.

Galinsky, Ellen, Stacy S. Kim, and James T. Bond. 2001. *Feeling Overworked: When Work Becomes Too Much*. New York: Families and Work Institute.

Gartner, William B. 1988. "Who is an Entrepreneur? is the Wrong Question." *American Journal of Small Business* 12:11–32.

Glass, Jennifer L. and Sarah Beth Estes. 1997. "The Family Responsive Workplace." *Annual Review of Sociology* 23:289–313.

Golden, Lonnie. 2001. "Flexible Work Schedules – Which workers get them?." *American Behavioral Scientist* 44:1157–1178.

Goldthorpe, John H. 1980. *Social Mobility and Class Structure in Modern Britain*. Oxford: Clarendon Press.

Green, Eillen and Laurie Cohen. 1995. "'Women's Business': Are Women Entrepreneurs Breaking New Ground or Simply Balancing the Demands of 'Women's Work' in a New Way?." *Journal of Gender Studies* 4:297–314.

Greenhaus, Jeffrey H. and Nicholas J. Beutell. 1985. "Sources of Conflict between Work and Family Roles." *Academy of Management Review* 10:76–88.

Greenhaus, Jeffrey H. and Saroj Parasuraman. 1999. "Research on Work, Family, and Gender: Current Status and Future Directions." Pp. 391–412 in *Handbook of Gender and Work*, edited by G.N. Powell. Thousand Oaks, CA: Sage Publications.

Greenhaus, Jeffrey H. and Gary N. Powell. 2003. "When Work and Family Collide: Deciding Between Competing Role Demands." *Organizational Behavior and Human Decision Processes* 90:291–303.

Gutek, Barbara A., Sabrina Searle, and Lilian Klepa. 1991. "Rational Versus Gender-Role Explanations for Work Family Conflict." *Journal of Applied Psychology* 76:560–568.

Hakim, Catherine. 2000. *Work-Lifestyle Choices in the 21st Century: Preference Theory*. Oxford; New York: Oxford University Press.

Hamermesh, Daniel S. 1998. "When We Work." *American Economic Review* 88:May321–325.

------. 2002. "Timing, Togetherness and Time Windfalls." *Journal of Population Economics* 15:601–623.

Hildebrand, Vincent and Donald R. Williams. 2003. "Self-employment and Caring for Children: Evidence from Europe." in *IRISS Working Paper Series*. Luxembourg.

Hill, E. Jeffery, Maria Ferris, and Vjollca Märtinson. 2003. "Does it Matter Where You Work? A Comparison of How Three Work Venues (Traditional Office, Virtual Office, and

Home Office) Influence aspects of Work and Personal/Family Life." *Journal of Vocational Behavior* 63:220–241.

Hill, E. Jeffery, Alan J. Hawkins, Maria Ferris, and Michelle Weitzman. 2001. "Finding an Extra Day a Week: The Positive Influence of Perceived Job Flexibility on Work and Family Life Balance." *Family Relations* 50:49–58.

Hochschild, Arlie Russell. 1997. *The Time Bind: When Work Becomes Home & Home Becomes Work*. New York: Metropolitan Books.

Holtz-Eakin, Douglas, Harvey S. Rosen, and Robert Weathers. 2000. "Horatio Alger Meets the Mobility Tables." *Small Business Economics* 14:243–274.

Hughes, K.D. 2003. "Pushed or Pulled? Women's Entry into Self-Employment and Small Business Ownership." *Gender Work and Organization* 10:433–454.

Hundley, Greg. 2001. "Why Women Earn Less than Men in Self-Employment." *Journal of Labor Research* 22:817–829.

Jacobs, Jerry A. and Kathleen Gerson. 1998. "Toward a Family-Friendly, Gender Equitable Work Week." *University of Pennsylvania Journal of Labor and Employment Law* 1:457–472.

Jurik, Nancy Carol. 1998. "Getting Away and Getting by – The Experiences of Self-Employed Homeworkers." *Work and Occupations* 25:7–35.

Kahn, Shulamit and Kevin Lang. 1992. "Constraints on the Choice of Work Hours: Agency versus Specific-Capital." *The Journal of Human Resources* 27:661–678.

------. 1995. "The Causes of Hours Constraints: Evidence from Canada." *Canadian Journal of Economics* 28:914–928.

------. 1996. "Hours Constraints and the Wage/Hours Locus." *Canadian Journal of Economics* 29:S71–S75.

Kossek, Ellen Ernst, Alison E. Barber, and Deborah Winters. 1999. "Using Flexible Schedules in the Managerial World: The Power of Peers." *Human Resource Management* 38:33–46.

Loscocco, Karyn A. 1997. "Work-Family Linkages among Self-Employed Women and Men." *Journal of Vocational Behavior* 50:204–226.

Maume, David J.Jr. and Marcia L. Bellas. 2001. "The Overworked American or the Time Bind? Assessing Competing Explanations for Time Spent in Paid Labor." *American Behavioral Scientist* 44:1137–1156.

Nippert-Eng, Christena E. 1996. *Home and Work : Negotiating Boundaries Through Everyday Life*. Chicago, IL: University of Chicago Press.

Parasuraman, Saroj and C.A. Simmers. 2001. "Type of Employment, Work–Family Conflict and Well–Being: A Comparative Study." *Journal of Organizational Behavior* 22:551–568.

Perlow, Leslie A. 1995. "Putting the Work Back into Work/Family." *Group and Organization Management* 20:227–239.

Perry-Jenkins, M., R.L. Repetti, and A.C. Crouter. 2000. "Work and Family in the 1990s." *Journal of Marriage and the Family* 62:981–998.

Presser, Harriet B. 1989. "Can We make Time for Children? The Economy, Work Schedules, and Child Care." *Demography* 26:523–542.

------. 1995. "Job Family, and Gender: Determinants of Nonstandard Work Schedules Among Employed Americans in 1991." *Demography* 32:577–598.

Renzulli, Linda, Howard Aldrich, and James Moody. 2000. "Family Matters: Gender, Networks, and Entrepreneurial Outcomes." *Social Forces* 79:523–546.

Reynolds, Jeremy. 2003. "You Can't Always Get the Hours You Want: Mismatches between Actual and Preferred Work Hours in the United States." *Social Forces* 81:1171–1199.

Robinson, John P. and Melissa A. Milkie. 1998. "Back to the Basics: Trends in and Role Determinants of Women's Attitudes toward Housework." *Journal of Marriage and the Family* 60:205–218.

Schor, Juliet B. 1991. *The Overworked American: The Unexpected Decline of Leisure.* New York: Basic Books.

Shelton, Beth Anne and Daphne John. 1996. "The Division of Household Labor." *Annual Review of Sociology* 22:299–322.

Smeaton, Deborah. 2003. "Self-employed workers: Calling the Shots or Hesitant Independents? A Consideration of the Trends." *Work Employment and Society* 17:379–391.

Thomas, Linda Thieda and Daniel C. Ganster. 1995. "Impact of Family-Supportive Work Variables on Work Family Conflict and Strain – a Control Perspective." *Journal of Applied Psychology* 80:6–15.

PART II:
THE ENTREPRENEURSHIP
PROCESS

ORIGINS OF ORGANIZATIONS:
THE ENTREPRENEURIAL PROCESS

Martin Ruef

ABSTRACT

This chapter combines insights from organizational theory and the entre-preneurship literature to inform a process-based conception of organiza-tional founding. In contrast to previous discrete-event approaches, the conception argues that founding be viewed as a series of potential entre-preneurial activities – including initiation, resource mobilization, legal establishment, social organization, and operational startup. Drawing on an original data set of 591 entrepreneurs, the study examines the effect of structural, strategic, and environmental contingencies on the relative rates with which different founding activities are pursued. Results demonstrate that social context has a fairly pervasive impact on the occurrence and sequencing of founding processes, with one possible exception being the timing of legal establishment.

INTRODUCTION

The process whereby formal organizations emerge from the actions and interactions of individuals has long held a privileged place in social theory. Weber turned his attention to the origins of organizations in his J.D. dis-

Entrepreneurship
Research in the Sociology of Work, Volume 15, 63–100
Copyright © 2005 by Elsevier Ltd.
All rights of reproduction in any form reserved
ISSN: 0277-2833/doi:10.1016/S0277-2833(05)15004-3

sertation (1889), which involved a comparative analysis of property rights and the capacity of those rights to yield organizations that are legally separate from the individual entrepreneurs that found them. For Joseph Schumpeter (1947), the origin of formal organizations lay less in the development of distinctive juristic actors and more in the development of new production functions within a society – that is, in the operational and innovative rather than legal development of organizations. Both Weber's legal and Schumpeter's operational criterion can be contrasted with a third perspective in which *social* organization is the defining hallmark of collective actors; thus, Homans (1950: 456–459) considered individuals' efforts to combat isolation to be a key motivation in the emergence of new formal groups (see also Ruef, Aldrich and Carter 2003). Meanwhile, social movement analysts (Olson 1968; Oberschall 1973: Chapter 4) called attention to resource mobilization as yet another facet of the formation of goal-oriented collectivities.

While early scholars framed the emergence of formal organizations primarily in theoretical and qualitative terms, considerable analytical leverage was introduced during the 1980s by researchers using quantitative accounts of organizational founding (e.g. Delacroix and Carroll 1983; Hannan and Freeman 1987, 1989; Aldrich and Staber 1988). Inspired by an evolutionary perspective (Hannan and Freeman 1977; Aldrich, 1979; Kimberly 1979), these models placed emphasis on the ecological conditions tying the origins of new organizations to the broader development of organizational populations and societal sectors. For the sake of analytic simplification, quantitative models typically relied on the convenient fiction that organizational foundings could be treated as discrete events. At the same time, both entrepreneurship scholars (Katz and Gartner 1988) and organizational sociologists (Hannan and Freeman 1989: 148–149) recognized the fiction and called for further research on the origins of organizations as a social *process* rather than event. Paralleling the varied interests of classical scholars, these researchers noted that organizational emergence might involve a number of potential stages, such as initiation, resource mobilization, legal establishment, social organization, and operational startup. More generally, bringing these activities back into the analysis of founding held the promise of connecting macro-level organizational theory with the more traditional micro-level emphasis of the sociology of work.

Despite such calls to arms, quantitative treatments of organizational founding have often remained silent on the issue of process. Studies that do consider the distinctive – and sometimes prolonged – stages of organizational founding have appeared outside the mainstream of organizational theory, primarily in the entrepreneurship literature (see Aldrich 1999: Chapter 4, for a review). Reynolds and White (1997) summarize the results of two surveys tracking organizations from conception to adolescence, with each survey addressing no less than 17 potential startup activities.[1] The survey data suggest considerable diversity in the number of startup activities undertaken by entrepreneurs, the sequencing of activities, and the rates with which these activities are accomplished. Given this diversity, the ostensible pattern whereby organizations emerge has been justifiably referred to as "chaotic and disorderly" by some commentators (Aldrich 1999: 77). Indeed, the only consistent patterns identified thus far in the entrepreneurship literature are tied to *outcomes* that distinguish entrepreneurs who have successfully founded an organization from those who are still trying or have given up (Carter et al. 1996).

This chapter is motivated by the paucity of empirical findings in the entrepreneurship literature and a proposal for a process-based formulation of organizational founding. The motivation entails a set of theoretical and methodological considerations. First, with some exceptions (e.g. Van de Ven et al. 1999), process-based studies of organizational founding have not attended to the structural, strategic, and environmental context within which startup activities are pursued. To some extent, this inattention may have resulted from the tendency of scholars to focus on lifecycle metaphors of organizational emergence, which consider parallels between immanent human development processes and organizational creation (Miles and Randolph 1980). Contingency theorists have argued persuasively against such metaphors, noting that entrepreneurial processes are likely to be affected significantly by social context: e.g. organizational form and environment (Lawrence 1993; Amburgey and Rao 1996).

A second concern derives from the diversity of human capital that underlies empirical research on founding processes in the entrepreneurship literature. By taking samples of entrepreneurs from the general population, entrepreneurship researchers aspire to be representative in their conclusions. At the same time, however, they also increase the variance of individual characteristics that must be factored into an explanation of the founding process (see Reynolds and White 1997: Chapter 4). Given the relatively small samples of entrepreneurs obtained in existing surveys, controlling for these individual factors has proven difficult, and, moreover, tangential to a research tradition that has departed from the once-popular emphasis on talents and traits of individual entrepreneurs (Gartner 1988; Aldrich 1999). From the perspective of a sociology of work, an alternative research design can be developed that samples from specific sub-populations (in which human capital is largely controlled for) and draws primary attention to the contextual features of entrepreneurial activities.

While it is impossible to address these issues definitively in one sitting, this chapter starts to unpack the process surrounding the creation of formal organizations. It begins with an analytical motivation for sorting founding events into a small number of startup stages and summarizes the use of these stages in existing research on organizational founding. Next, I draw theoretical connections between aspects of the entrepreneurial context – including organizational structure, strategy, and environment – and the rates with which startup stages are pursued. Event history models are applied to test the resulting hypotheses on a data set of startup efforts among 591 nascent entrepreneurs, active between 1945 and 1999. A concluding discussion addresses implications for current discrete-event approaches to modeling entrepreneurial activities.

THE PROCESS OF ORGANIZATIONAL FOUNDING

The organization literature points to two distinct research strategies employed in identifying events in the process of organizational founding. One, employed primarily by entrepreneurship researchers, is inductive and emphasizes the specific activities undertaken by nascent entrepreneurs in creating businesses and nonprofits: e.g. looking for physical facilities, investing personal funds in an organization, writing a business plan, etc. (see Reynolds and White 1997). Another strategy, employed primarily by organizational sociologists, is deductive and emphasizes theoretical ideal-types as sub-processes in the creation of organizations. For instance, organizational ecologists have identified initiation, resource mobilization, legal establishment, social organization, and operational startup as crucial startup activities (Hannan and Freeman 1989). Viewing startup activities as steps toward institutionalization, scholars in the institutional tradition have identified innovation, habitualization, objectification, and sedimentation as critical stages (Tolbert and Zucker 1996).

Both inductive and deductive strategies have their merits: the inductive approach lends itself to immediate operationalization by considering the concrete startup activities observed in empirical contexts; the deductive approach lends itself to theoretical generalization. In the following discussion, I combine both strategies by mapping operationalizations of organizational founding within the existing literature to the ideal-type processes noted in Hannan and Freeman's (1989) influential statement on organizational ecology.

Initiation

The process of initiation refers to a declared intention on the part of one or more nascent entrepreneurs to found an organization. Specific activities linked to initiation can include: serious discussion about starting a new organization, the formation of a founding team, public announcements regarding the intention to organize, and the public naming of a new collective identity. Initiation events provide the weakest criteria whereby a formal organization can be said to exist. Insofar as formal organizations are defined to be goal-directed, boundary-maintaining activity systems (see Aldrich 1999), the process of initiation merely provides a general specification of collective goals and draws a boundary around one or more members (e.g. nascent entrepreneurs) committed to achieving those goals.

Not surprisingly, the use of initiation activities to mark the founding of organizations is rare in the empirical literature. Some notable exceptions appear to involve the creation of so-called "minimalist" organizations (Aldrich et al. 1994; Halliday, Powell and Granfors 1987). For instance, Aldrich and Staber examined the founding patterns of trade associations by treating the appearance of a new association name in one or more data sources as indicative of a founding event (1988: 118–119). The mere appearance of a name does not necessarily mean that the association in question is legally established or has hired permanent staff or even operates on a day-to-day basis. However, this operationalization of organizational founding is entirely consistent with the minimalist nature of trade associations, which require few resources or ongoing activities for their existence (Aldrich et al. 1994).

Initiation activities are also relevant when researchers wish to examine the social structure linking entrepreneurs (or other helpers) at the inception of a new organization. Research interest may hinge on the network sources of ideas triggering the creation of an organization (Ruef 2002a) or the mechanisms bringing founders together (Ruef et al. 2003). To avoid success bias, researchers examining such early initiation processes tend to employ research designs that sample nascent entrepreneurs – individuals who are beginning to take serious steps toward starting a venture but need not have an operational venture in any sense of the word. The PSED represents one of the most ambitious efforts to sample entrepreneurs with this type of research design (see Reynolds 2000).

Resource Mobilization

As a startup stage, resource mobilization includes activities such as looking for permanent facilities and equipment, buying or leasing permanent facilities and equipment, and seeking or receiving external financial support. Aside from these more obvious aspects of resource mobilization, nascent entrepreneurs also tend to prepare documents at this founding stage that permit them to seek support from funders, philanthropists, or potential members. In the case of growth oriented for-profit organizations, the writing of a business plan is seen as a major step in the process of resource mobilization. Historically, organizations such as hospitals, labor unions, and professional associations have also developed charters that are critical in mobilizing support around a set of common goals.

Given the implicit connection between resource mobilization and the broader literature on collective action (Oberschall 1973), it is not surprising that operationalizations emphasizing this stage of organizational founding are often directed toward formalized social movements (see Hannan and Freeman 1987; McCarthy et al. 1988). Hannan and Freeman's study of the emergence of national labor unions is a case in point. They focus on foundings as a joint effort among a set of workers or local unions to create a national union that will protect their interests. In particular, foundings are delineated by the "date of a national convention that writes a charter for a new union or the date on which a merger between unions is ratified at national conventions" (1989: 149). These events, which entail resource mobilization occasioned by a key organizational document, can be distinguished from both legal establishment and initiation. With respect to the former, it can be noted that union charters are not necessarily *legal* documents in the eyes of the state and that a national union mobilized in this fashion may in fact be an illegal entity. With respect to the latter, a comparison with the operationalization applied to a minimalist organization, state bar associations (Halliday, Powell and Granfors 1987), suggests the following difference: for bar associations, members simply meet under the auspices of a collective identity; for labor unions, the conventions studied have the specific outcome of mobilizing support around (and ratifying) an organizational charter.

While conventional economic wisdom suggests that successful attempts at resource mobilization are crucial to the survival of new organizations, existing research provides only limited support for this contention, even among for-profit organizations. For instance, a study of bankruptcy and dissolution events among several hundred business startups revealed that the mobilization of external financing (either debt or equity-based) actually *increased* disbanding rates (Ruef 2002b). When entrepreneurs accept funding from stockholders, investment banks, venture capitalists, wealthy individuals, and the like, they may also expose themselves to the whims and fickle attachments of the investors. More generally, large-scale capitalization from external sources commonly imposes the risk of external control rather than the fruits of resource infusion.

Legal Establishment

The legal establishment of an organization involves formal recognition by the state that it operates as a legitimate collective entity. Activities involved in legal establishment may include: filing letters of incorporation or partnership, applying for a license to operate, receiving a legislative mandate, and seeking trademark or patent protection for core ideas associated with the enterprise. Weber's (1889) pathbreaking work defined the legal concept of joint liability as particularly important in the origins of modern organizations. With the full development of joint liability in contemporary systems of law, formal organizations could be fully separated from their founders and stakeholders in a manner that effectively hypostatized vital events (e.g. foundings, mergers, etc.) at the organizational level (see Coleman 1974).

Macro-level studies of organizations evidence considerable reliance on legal delineations of organizational founding, perhaps owing to the readiness with which these are identified in archival data sources. However, there also appears to be a substantive pattern linking the use of legal founding events with particular types of organizational forms. In particular, many of the forms that can be studied most readily with legal markers – government bureaus (Kaufman 1976), life insurance companies (Budros 1993), railroads (Dobbin 1995), day care centers (Baum and Oliver 1992), and voluntary social service organizations (Singh, Tucker and Meinhard 1991) – are located in highly institutionalized environments. These environments are defined by the importance of regulative and normative controls operating within them (see Scott 2002) and thus resonate with a legal-rational conception of organizational founding.

In the sociology of work, little micro-level research exists to reveal how entrepreneurs actually go about choosing one legal structure for their ventures as opposed to another. Although practical advice on legal strategy is plentiful (e.g. Khandekar and Young 1985), there is no descriptive evidence to suggest how quickly legal status tends to be pursued, what goals influence the choice of legal structure, and what constraints this choice subsequently imposes on founding activities. Consequently, my examination of this start-up stage will be largely exploratory in character.

Social Organization

As a startup stage, social organization entails such activities as the initial hiring or recruiting of permanent participants, the creation of authority systems, the development of motivational inducements or monitoring structures, and the emergence of social roles (Aldrich 1999: Chapter 5 and 6). Given my definition of initiation processes, such social organization applies explicitly to individuals *outside* the team of nascent entrepreneurs.

Recent scholarship has sought to clarify the effects of founder choices with respect to models of social organization. Examining a unique sample of interviews from Silicon Valley startups, Baron, Hannan and Burton (1999) distinguish founders' human resource models by (a) their source of employee attachment (pecuniary versus nonpecuniary benefits); (b) their bases of coordination and control (e.g. formal oversight versus peer culture); and (c) their mechanisms of employee selection (e.g. skill-based versus cultural fit). Although the cross-tabulation of these dimensions yields a large number of possible combinations, only five employment models were identified with considerable frequency in the sample of business startups. These include the classic Weberian model of bureaucracy, a Taylorist model of autocracy, and three other employment models – which stress collective commitment, employee "star" potential, and a meritocratic engineering culture, respectively.

In a separate analysis, Baron et al. (1996) study how different human resource (HR) practices emerge to support the social organization of new ventures. Among the Silicon Valley firms in their study, these practices include the development of employee orientation programs, organization charts, written performance evaluations, and the like. Because my interests in this chapter hinge on more generic patterns of organizational creation, I focus on the founding activity that serves as a precondition for the development of these more sophisticated HR practices – the hiring of a new organization's first non-founding member.

Operational Startup

The operational stage of organizational founding may include such events as announcing a service or product, developing an initial prototype for a service or product, and successfully completing the delivery of a service or product to external stakeholders. Among the various processes of organizational founding, social theorists have often viewed the operational stage of founding as having the most telling effects for society as a whole (Schumpeter 1947). This fact alone may account for the popularity of operational startup in studies of founding.

Considering the particular populations in which an operational criterion has been applied, another pattern becomes evident which parallels that noted for legal establishment above. One finds that much research emphasizing operational startup – Hannan and Freeman's (1989) study of semiconductor manufacturers (see also Schoonhoven et al. 1990); the Baum, Korn and Kotha (1995) study of fax transmission services; the Delacroix and Solt (1988) study of wineries; and the Hannan et al. (1995) study of automobile producers – examines forms that are embedded in environments with high technical complexity. Two general exceptions should, however, be noted. First, operationalizations considering operational startup are often applied when data is unavailable on the principal founding events of interest—as for some organizations in the Ranger–Moore, Banaszak-Holl and Hannan (1991) study of two heavily regulated forms, banks and life insurance companies. Second, operational startup appears to be the customary event type analyzed when organizational forms do not fall within one of the theoretical rubrics associated with other founding processes: including minimalist forms (initiation), collective action forms (resource mobilization), and forms in highly institutionalized arenas (legal establishment). Thus, research on hotels (Ingram and Inman 1996) and newspapers (Hannan and Freeman 1989; Delacroix and Carroll 1983) has employed operational startup as an indicator of organizational founding.

Micro-level analyses of operational startup have appeared primarily under the guise of time-to-market studies. For instance, Schoonhoven et al. (1990) considered the factors affecting operational startup among a sample of semiconductor manufacturers. They found that having a functionally diverse founding team (e.g. one that includes both marketing and manufacturing expertise) increased the rate with which operational startup was achieved, while attempts at technical innovation among entrepreneurs tended to reduce the rate of operational startup. The latter finding may, however, be sensitive to how innovation is defined. When "innovation" simply implies deviance from a dominant organizational form, such deviation can remove constraints from an otherwise rigid process of operational startup. For example, in a study of U.S. medical schools, I found that the orthodox, university-affiliated medical schools took significantly *longer* to achieve operational status than those organizations that adopted irregular medical philosophies (e.g. homeopathic schools) or those that were organized independently from a university (Ruef 2004). The difference between these findings and those of Schoonhoven and colleagues hinge on the nature of innovation in each context. Schoonhoven et al. (1990) consider how attempts to create new knowledge (or synthesize existing knowledge in new products) can delay operational entry. On the other hand, my study of medical schools suggests that deviations from a dominant organizational model that employ an alternative, *preexisting* template can actually increase the rate of operational startup.

CONTEXTUAL INFLUENCES ON FOUNDING STAGES

The preceding literature review suggests that there is often a pattern linking discrete operationalizations of founding events with the theoretical inclinations of a researcher and/or the types of organizations being analyzed. When consideration is limited to individual organizational populations, such patterns may have substantial justification: e.g. tracking the emergence of social protest organizations via instances of legal recognition seems less sensible than identifying instances of initiation or resource mobilization (the legal aspect of emergence could be seen instead as a marker of cooptation). For many types of organizations, though, it is not immediately evident that one founding stage should be favored over another as an indicator of organizational emergence. Thus, initiation, resource mobilization, legal establishment, social organization, and operational startup are all valid objects of study for populations of business enterprises.

This consideration calls for a comparative analysis of influences on various stages of organizational founding. In the following discussion, I analyze contextual influences – aspects of organizational structure, strategy, and environment – that have proven to be significant in scholarship on organizational founding processes. Given previous research in the sociology of organizations and work, six contextual influences are considered to be of particular interest. Competition, legitimacy, and regulation are the environmental factors that have received the greatest attention in organizational ecology and institutional analysis (Carroll and Hannan 2000; Scott 2001). Both organizational ecologists and management theorists have also examined the relation of strategic factors to founding processes, including the niche width of emerging organizations (Carroll and Swaminathan 1992) and the extent to which innovator or reproducer strategies are pursued (Aldrich 1999; Schoonhoven et al. 1990). Finally, recent attention has turned to the way that founding processes are affected by the structure of new organizations – in particular, their level of independence from existing formal organizations.

While drawing substantive parallels with population-level processes, the following discussion formulates its measures and hypotheses at the level of the emerging organization and the work activities undertaken by entrepreneurs. This involves some rethinking of the way that contextual influences on startup activities are conceptualized. For example, the well-known density-dependence argument of population dynamics suggests that founding rates are affected by the levels of legitimation and competition evidenced for a particular organizational population (Carroll and Hannan 2000). At the micro-level, this involves two separate processes: (a) to what extent do competition and legitimation affect the decision of individuals to become entrepreneurs in a given population or industry; and (b) to what extent do competition and legitimation affect the rate with which various startup activities are successfully pursued? The present analysis is concerned exclusively with the second micro-dynamic (the process of entrepreneurship) and thus tailors its measures to the vantage point of the entrepreneur.

Structural Independence

Sociologists have distinguished between a number of basic types of entrepreneurial entry into populations or industries, including *de novo* entries, *de alio* entries, and spin-offs (Carroll et al. 1996; see also Aldrich 1999: 275–276). *De novo* starting events involve the development of an independent venture that has no pre-existing formal linkages to another organization. Spin-offs and *de alio* starting events represent sponsored and lateral entries of established organizations into new niches, respectively.

Whether an emerging organization is structurally independent or linked in one fashion or another to pre-existing arrangements is likely to have a substantial impact on its startup process. First, the structural inertia of mature organizations (see Hannan and Freeman 1984) is likely to adversely affect rates of initiation for ventures that they sponsor. The preliminary phase of organizing, in which one or nascent entrepreneurs gather and declare their intention to create a new collective enterprise, is comparatively simple for autonomous startups. But when a startup is sponsored through existing organizational arrangements, the initiation stage often requires that a subset of members be dislodged from established roles in order to work with (or become) new organizational leaders. Given the habituation and oligarchical tendencies in many mature organizations (Michels 1968 [1915]; Barron et al. 1994), this process may be both cognitively difficult and politically contested.

Hypothesis 1. Independent startups are initiated more quickly than sponsored startups.

In other respects, sponsored entry can ameliorate the strains of starting a new venture. The established entity offers resource endowments, consisting of both financial and social capital, to a spin-off or franchise. Independently of the actual scale of these endowments, the mere existence of external ties to organizational sponsors conveys positional advantage (Hannan 1998): a sense of reliability and accountability, as seen by other stakeholders. As a result, the process of resource mobilization among sponsored starting events is expected to proceed more rapidly, and more successfully, than it does among *de novo* foundings.

Hypothesis 2. Independent startups are slower to mobilize resources than sponsored startups.

A second type of endowment involves taken-for-granted routines and competencies that are carried from an existing formal organization to a sponsored entrant. Some of these routines entail operational know-how directed at the development of services or products that are similar to those of the sponsoring entity. Other routines involve more basic principles of social organization, providing templates for authority systems, role relations, and incentives that can be adopted by a new venture from an existing organizational infrastructure. Given these stocks of existing routines, founding processes involving operational startup and social organization among structurally dependent entrants are likely to be accelerated.

Hypothesis 3. Independent startups are slower to hire or organize employees than sponsored startups.

Hypothesis 4. Independent startups are slower to become operational than sponsored startups.

Niche Generalism and Specialism

In addition to structural features, the pace and sequencing of startup processes in an emerging organization is likely to be affected by strategic "blueprints" maintained by its founders. While many of these blueprints evolve during the process of founding itself, two strategic dimensions are tied to an organizational idea in more primordial ways and may provide causal explanations for the character of the founding process: (1) niche *generalism* and *specialism*; and (2) *reproducer* versus *innovator* strategies (see Aldrich 1999).

The distinction of generalist and specialist strategies was introduced by Hannan and Freeman (1977, 1989), who noted that some formal organizations (*generalists*) occupy a wide niche that allows them to draw on resources and information in a variety of environments, while others (*specialists*) concentrate their efforts on a narrow niche that is focused within a more limited environmental context. The relative fitness of organizations conforming to these two strategies depends on the variability of environmental conditions. Specialist organizations are most viable when environmental conditions fluctuate within a narrow range; generalists perform better when environmental turbulence and uncertainty are high.

With respect to founding stages, niche-width strategies are likely to have their most pronounced impact on resource mobilization processes. Stinchcombe's (1965) argument on organizational imprinting noted that organizations tend to adapt to the environmental conditions prevailing around the time of their founding (see also Kimberly 1979). If so, specialist organizations may have an initial advantage in extracting resources, at least given the short-term stability in the environment. Entrepreneurs employing a specialist strategy are able to customize their organization's blueprint to the particular interests and cognitive assumptions of sponsors during the founding stage. Those with a generalist strategy, on the other hand, must appeal to a variety of audiences and environments. The generalist organizations are difficult to categorize and therefore will be slower to mobilize resources initially (Zuckerman 1999).

Hypothesis 5. Startups with a generalist strategy mobilize resources more slowly than specialists.

Reproducer and Innovator Strategies

Organizational scholars make a second strategic distinction in examining how organizations confront new, innovative opportunities in their social environment. Organizations with an *innovator* strategy, sometimes referred to as "first movers" (Brittain 1994), attempt to enter quickly into niches opened by technical or institutional change. Through their novel routines and technologies, they are able to take advantage of intrinsic growth rates in new organizational populations or to redefine environmental constraints in more mature industries. Organizations with a *reproducer* strategy, on the other hand, rely on more established routines and technologies; their key advantage is the efficient use of resources rather than the speed with which they confront innovative possibilities.

The differences in efficient resource use are likely to be most apparent in resource mobilization processes among emergent innovators and reproducers. The novelty of technologies and routines in innovative organizations demands both aggressive and rapid resource mobilization. The development of innovations imposes costs well beyond the mere reproduction of existing routines; moreover, innovators are forced to deploy resources rapidly in seeking first mover advantages in a market niche. Nascent entrepreneurs employing a reproducer strategy are able to offset resource requirements with the relative efficiency of established organizational routines, becoming more likely to attract resource support in a slow, methodical fashion.

Hypothesis 6. Startups with an innovator strategy mobilize resources more quickly than those employing a reproducer strategy.

The other impact on founding processes involves operational startup. As I have noted above, two opposing implications follow from the use of an innovator strategy. On the one hand, the creation of new knowledge (or synthesis of existing knowledge to create new products) can prolong operational entry (Schoonhoven et al. 1990). Entrepreneurs who are true first movers must deal with uncertainty that is readily avoided by those adopting a reproducer strategy. On the other hand, reproducers also face constraints when they adopt existing organizational templates that are specified relatively precisely. As a result, some entrepreneurs who are subject to strict normative guidelines (e.g. franchisees) may actually increase the delay until operational startup when employing a reproducer strategy.

Technical Environment

Emerging organizations encounter both technical and institutional pressures from their environment (Meyer and Scott 1983). Technical demands include such features as competing with existing organizations in a niche, attracting a qualified pool of labor, attracting investment capital, acquiring production inputs, and protecting intellectual property. Like organizational structure and strategy, an organization's technical environment is likely to have implications for its early life history – in particular, for those founding sub-processes that are oriented toward material-resource considerations. Technical demands on a new venture will increase the rate with which nascent entrepreneurs pursue resource mobilization efforts. Confronted with strong competition in input, output, and labor markets, entrepreneurs will be more inclined to turn to external actors for material support (although actual mobilization success may be more elusive). Meanwhile, operational startup, a second process oriented toward material-resource considerations, is likely to be constrained by competition and technical demands. As entrepreneurs encounter difficulties in securing inputs, technologies, or labor, organizational delivery of products and services will typically be delayed.

Hypothesis 7. Startups in highly competitive environments are quicker to attempt resource mobilization.

Hypothesis 8. Startups in highly competitive environments are slower to become operational.

The multidimensional nature of competitive pressures makes it difficult to tease out influences with respect to other startup activities. Competition over intellectual property can postpone legal establishment, but competition for skilled labor may encourage an organization to accelerate legal approval as a sign of stability to prospective members. Similarly, competition in the labor market often makes social organization more problematic, while competitive pressures in a product or service niche may stimulate recruitment of members early on. Given these opposing dynamics, no clear hypotheses can be offered for a general effect of competition on legal establishment or social organization.

Institutional Environment
Institutional demands represent a feature of the organizational environment that may be seen as orthogonal to technical demands (Meyer and Scott 1983). The institutional environment comprises cognitive rules concerning the recognizability of organizational structures and activities, normative rules concerning the appropriateness of structures and activities, and regulatory rules concerning the legality of structures and activities (Scott 2001). In ecological formulations, cognitive rules are assessed via the legitimation effect in density-dependence specifications (Carroll and Hannan 2000).

Normative and regulatory rules are typically represented jointly as historical period effects that influence rates of organizational founding within particular populations.

Neoinstitutional theory suggests that the effect of environmental demands on the founding process will reflect a certain homology between the types of institutional rules and the stage of founding being examined. Organizations confronting complex *regulatory* rules – e.g. employment law, product liability law, environmental law, etc. – will move more aggressively to establish themselves legally and limit liability on the part of owners. Those confronting systems of *normative* oversight – e.g. professional certification or accreditation (see Ruef and Scott 1998) – will incorporate formalized commitment to these systems in their founding rituals.[2]

Cognitive rules are more fundamental than those evidenced by normative and regulative frameworks, insofar as they suggest what types of emerging organizations are likely to be recognized by customers and competitors (Scott 2001). Recognizability of organizational form has perhaps its most determinate effects on operational startup. When the services or products of a new venture are readily compared to extant social artifacts, the announcement and delivery of such output to consumer markets is simplified considerably. Moreover, basic mimetic processes allow the emerging organization to copy operational routines from comparably situated corporate actors. When the template for a new venture is less conventional, these processes of social comparison and imitation are likely to be inhibited.[3]

Hypothesis 9. Startups facing strong regulatory environments are quicker to establish themselves legally than those facing weak regulation.

Hypothesis 10. Startups adopting a cognitively legitimated form are quicker to become operational than those adopting a form that is not widely recognized.

Summary of Contextual Influences

Fig. 1 summarizes my propositions concerning the effects of organizational structure, strategy, and environment on the relative pace of various stages in the founding process. Contrary to earlier research, these propositions suggest that there may be clear patterns to the founding process once contextual influences are taken into account. To use one example, an expected modal pattern of organizing for independent startups could feature an initiation stage, followed by resource mobilization, legal establishment, social organization, and operational startup. But sponsored foundings (involving

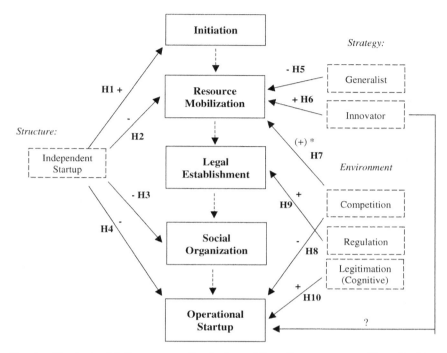

Fig. 1. Contextual influences on the timing of founding processes. *Note*: Positive signs (+) indicate that a characteristic increases the rate with which a founding process is completed by entrepreneurs. Negative signs (−) indicate that a characteristic decreases the rate.
*Competition is predicted to increase the rate with which resource mobilization is attempted, but not its successful completion.

ventures backed by a prior organizational infrastructure) may deviate from this sequence in predictable ways. Resource mobilization, social organization, and operational startup may occur earlier. Initiation activities – e.g. official declarations concerning a starting event or the creation of a founding team – may well be postponed until other stages are already under way.

More generally, the propositions suggest a general pattern in which the sequencing of startup activities and the salience of contextual influences interact with one another. While structural factors affect the timing of startup activities throughout the founding process, strategic factors are more relevant early in the ideal-type sequence (especially, with respect to resource mobilization) and environmental factors become more relevant later in the sequence. As entrepreneurs move from conception to established organization, the theory suggests that the flow of their activities becomes increasingly exposed to conditions outside the organization itself.

Aside from the impact of contextual factors on the timing of startup activities, the activities themselves can also affect the timing of one another. Operational startup may be more likely when successful resource mobilization brings financial capital into a new venture. Delayed legal incorporation could slow down operational startup rates. Current substantive evidence regarding such interdependencies is mixed (Schoonhoven et al. 1990) or nonexistent (Amburgey and Rao 1996: 1273), largely owing to the lack of models that incorporate transitions for multiple startup activities. As a result, specific hypotheses concerning activity interdependencies are not advanced here; instead, these dynamics are considered in an exploratory mode in the following empirical models.

DATA, MEASURES, AND METHODOLOGY

Data

Founding processes were examined empirically using an original data set on nascent entrepreneurs who attempted to start business organizations between 1945 and 1999.[4] Following previous research on nascent entrepreneurs, a two-stage sampling strategy was applied. In the first wave, an initial sample of 5,028 business professionals were surveyed. To reduce the variance of human capital, all professionals in the targeted sampling frame included alumni receiving MBA (masters of business administration) degrees from a graduate business program in the western United States. This sampling frame explicitly controls for the wide variety of educational experiences and business skills typically found among nascent entrepreneurs (see Reynolds and White 1997), but also limits the representativeness of the entrepreneurs studied. Given that the emphasis of the present study is on contextual factors affecting emerging organizations rather than individual-level factors, this trade-off appears to be justified.[5]

The business professionals were asked whether they had ever "*tried* to start a business" or spent some part of their career working as the founder of a startup. Those responding in the affirmative ($N = 1,786$) were included in the sampling frame of a more extensive survey of nascent entrepreneurs. These individuals were then asked to identify the nature of their most recent entrepreneurial effort, the steps involved in attempting to create the business, the types of innovations introduced, the environment of the organization during the period of founding, and various outcomes of the entrepreneurial process. Some 769 surveys were received, yielding a response rate of 43%.

As in any retrospective design, there were concerns about the ability of founders to accurately recall events in the founding process, particularly for serial entrepreneurs (those who had founded more than one venture during their careers). To improve recall, detailed information was only requested for the entrepreneurs' most recent attempted startup. Whenever possible, secondary data sources and surveys of multiple founding team members were used to confirm dates of startup activities. In general, recall accuracy appeared to be high due to the ability of entrepreneurs to consult written documentation (business plans, papers of incorporation, etc.) that provide an organizational memory of these events.

Dependent Measures

The process of entrepreneurship was characterized through an inventory of nine founding activities (see Table 1; Appendix, Q3). Three of the activities can be mapped in a one-to-one fashion onto the ideal-type startup stages reviewed earlier. Thus, the initiation stage is demarcated by the creation of a founding team, social organization by the hiring of the first employee, and legal establishment by either incorporation or the establishment of a proprietor- or partnership. Due to the typically prolonged nature of resource mobilization and operational startup, multiple activities were analyzed to consider these founding stages. Resource mobilization includes the preparation of a business plan, as well as obtaining (initial) external financing. Operational startup includes the announcement of a product or service, as well as the sale/delivery of a product or service.

The survey instrument asked respondents to indicate the month and year for each founding activity undertaken, as applicable. Among the 769 respondents, 74 omitted questions related to the process of entrepreneurship and another 104 only identified a single activity. Following previous research on nascent entrepreneurs (see Reynolds and White 1997), those individuals only performing a single startup activity were excluded from further analysis. The reasoning behind this exclusion is both methodological and substantive. Methodologically, the concept of a startup "sequence" is rendered vacuous by foundings that only involve a single activity.

Table 1. Frequency, Timing, and Sequencing of Organizational Founding Processes (total $N = 591$).

Process	Overall Frequency	Mean Time to Event (months)	First Stage	Second Stage	Third Stage	Fourth (+) Stage
Initiation						
Create founding team	591	3.1	439 (74%)[a]	99 (17%)	33 (6%)	20 (3%)
Resource Mobilization						
Prepare business plan	468	6.0	263 (56%)	134 (29%)	48 (10%)	23 (5%)
Obtain external financing	378	14.4	35 (9%)	110 (29%)	115 (30%)	118 (31%)
Legal Establishment						
Incorporate/establish	547	4.8	199 (36%)	232 (42%)	88 (16%)	28 (5%)
Partner- or proprietorship						
Social Organization						
Hire first employee	482	10.5	91 (19%)	123 (26%)	134 (28%)	134 (28%)
Operational Startup						
Announce product/service	404	11.0	72 (18%)	97 (24%)	108 (27%)	127 (31%)
Sell product/service	499	10.7	88 (18%)	104 (21%)	114 (23%)	193 (39%)

[a]Includes 167 "trivial" instances of initiation involving ventures formed by a single entrepreneur.

Substantively, there is an interest in focusing on entrepreneurs who are seriously pursuing the idea of founding a new organization. Many startups involving a single activity (e.g. organizing a founding team or writing a business plan) do not necessarily suggest a durable commitment by the entrepreneur.

The overall frequency of founding activities in the remaining 591 emergent organizations varies slightly. An initiation activity (e.g. the creation of a founding team) is implemented in all of these ventures at some point, while 82% hire an employee, and only 64% of the ventures obtain external funding during the founding process.[6] Further insights into the timing of founding activities can be gained by separating them into sequential stages, where a stage is defined to be a period of time where one or more of the activities in the inventory are begun. Seventy-four percent of the initiation events occur during the first stage of organizational founding, while a mere 18% of the events involving operational startup occur during that stage. More generally, the sequential distribution of activities conforms to a typical pattern of organizing that begins with initiation, proceeds to resource mobilization, legal establishment, and social organization, and concludes with operational startup. The one wrinkle in this general pattern is the culminating phase of resource mobilization (in the form of external financing), which often occurs at some length after preliminary mobilization efforts (e.g. the writing of a business plan) have been undertaken. As suggested earlier, this reflects the prolonged nature of mobilization activities during the founding process.

Independent Measures

Structure
The structure of an emerging organization is characterized by its dependence on a prior organizational infrastructure. When entrepreneurs found independent startups, these are classified as *de novo* foundings. Other types of startup events subsume purchases or takeovers of existing businesses, startups sponsored by existing businesses, and franchises (Appendix, Q1).

Strategy
I evaluated the niche-width strategy of a new venture in terms of the cumulative number of industries that the venture's founders sought to compete in. Niches were selected from a standardized list of 60 industries (Appendix, Q2). *Specialist* organizations are those seeking to compete in

relatively few industries, while *generalist* organizations seek to compete in a larger number of industries. A second dimension of organizational strategy was gleaned from founders' attitudes toward innovation. Innovative practices – introducing new types of products or services, introducing new methods of production, developing new supplier linkages, etc. – were grouped into eight analytical categories (Appendix, Q4; Ruef 2002a). *Reproducers* are represented by those entrepreneurs pursuing a relatively small number of these types of innovation; *innovators*, by contrast, attempt to take on a large number of innovative practices in founding their ventures. Rather than dichotomizing the variable, tendencies toward an innovator strategy were measured via the cumulative number of categorized innovations proposed for an emergent organization.

Environment
Entrepreneurs' perceptions concerning competition, regulation, and legitimacy at the time of founding serve as indicators of the organizational environment. Entrepreneurs were asked to rate pressures posed by five technical features of the environment, six regulatory features, and two features related to the cognitive legitimacy of their organizational form (Q5). These variables were then included in a confirmatory factor analysis (Bollen 1989) that tied the observed indicators to three latent variables (competition, regulation, legitimacy) and covariances among them. Factor scores for each of the latent variables were extracted using the estimated regression loadings from the CFA (see Ruef 2002b for further details).

Process
Time-varying covariates were included to capture the effects of different startup activities on one another, with each activity being represented by a dichotomous event variable (1 indicating that the event had occurred prior to a given spell, 0 indicating that it had not). To conserve degrees of freedom, only one event was used to represent the effects of resource mobilization (developing a business plan) and one was used to represent operational startup (announcing a product or service). The effects of legal establishment and social organization on other startup activities were also considered. Because initiation (the formation of a founding team) is a trivial startup event for emerging organizations that only have a single founder, it was not incorporated into the process specification.

Control Variables

The analysis of founding processes controls for entrepreneurs' perceptions of environmental munificence (the carrying capacity available to sustain organizations like their new ventures). Munificence is calculated as a weighted function of 14 economic, political, social, and technological conditions prevailing at the time of organizational founding (see Ruef 2002b, Table A1). Entrepreneurs were asked to rate both the favorability and importance of each condition with respect to their venture. Ten-point ratings of favorability were rescaled to range from −4.5 (highly unfavorable) to 4.5 (highly favorable), with 0 indicating average conditions along some dimension. An overall measure of munificence was obtained from the mean of the favorability ratings, with each one weighted by its relative importance to the entrepreneur.

A separate variable controlled for the amount of first-stage financing available to the venture, independently of external funding and resource mobilization efforts. This resource base includes endowments deriving from the entrepreneurs' personal savings, family savings, asset-based (e.g. real estate) or quasi-equity financing. All finance amounts are adjusted by the consumer price index (CPI) for inflation to 1999 dollars and subjected to a natural log transformation for purposes of analysis.

A statistical control was also included to address the fact that organizational founding processes may proceed at different rates in industries with lower fixed capital costs (e.g. service industries) than those with high capital costs (manufacturing). A dummy variable distinguishes service industry ventures from those devoted exclusively to manufacturing.

Missing Values

For the first-stage financing variable, a conditional mean imputation procedure was employed to replace missing values and ensure that a maximum number of cases could be retained for analysis (see Little 1992). Cases with missing values on any of the remaining independent and control variables were removed by listwise deletion. This reduced the total number of organizations in the analysis to 532.

Methodology

Event history analysis was employed to model the rate with which founding activities were pursued in the sample of emerging organizations. To allow for the concurrence of startup processes, the seven activities identified in

Table 1 were represented as separate event streams. The time clock for each stream began with the first month in which a nascent entrepreneur reported a founding activity for his or her venture. Nonparametric exploratory analyses revealed a monotonic decrease in founding activity rates over the period of organizational emergence. For instance, a firm that had not hired an employee by time point t was more likely to do so at that point than at any later time point $t + \Delta t$. The following Gompertz model captures this effect of organizational aging:

$$r(t) = \exp(B'X)\exp(Ct) \tag{1}$$

where $r(t)$ is the hazard rate for a founding activity, t indexes organizational age, X is the matrix of independent variables, B is the vector of coefficients indicating the effects of the variables in X, and C is a constant term indicating the rate at which startup activities decrease with organizational age. Right-truncation of organizational histories occurs when organizations are dissolved, merged, acquired or when the end of the study period (October 1999) is reached. Maximum likelihood techniques were applied to obtain the model estimates.

RESULTS

I estimated the effects of contextual factors on rates of founding processes using Rohwer's (1999) Transition Data Analysis (TDA) program. Table 2 reports the results for resource mobilization and operational startup, while Table 3 reports estimates for initiation, legal establishment, and social organization.

Rates of resource mobilization tend to be higher among organizations claiming innovative practices and products than those who implement established routines (see Table 2, Models 1 and 2). Potential stakeholders are attracted to the novelty offered by innovators, while entrepreneurs relying on such novelty must be quick to mobilize lest competing organizations gain first mover advantages. A similar, though statistically less significant, effect can be noted for specialist organizations. Ventures having a narrow niche width are better able to focus the presentation of strategic blueprints (e.g. business plans) to potential stakeholders than generalist organizations. This mobilization advantage, however, does not translate into significantly higher rates of external funding events among specialists.

The expected difference in resource mobilization between autonomous (*de novo*) startups and structurally dependent foundings is reflected modestly in

Table 2. Factors Affecting Rates of Resource Mobilization and Operational Startup among Sampled Organizations ($N = 532$)[a].

	Resource Mobilization		Operational Startup	
Variable	Business plan (Model 1)	External funding (Model 2)	Product/service announced (Model 3)	Product/service sale (Model 4)
B vector constant	1.296 (0.196)***	−0.030 (0.207)	−0.793 (0.225)***	−0.674 (0.204)***
C vector constant	−0.559 (0.054)***	−0.415 (0.037)***	−0.613 (0.049)***	−0.511 (0.043)***
Structure				
Independent startup	0.056 (0.112)	−0.181 (0.121)ξ	0.111 (0.123)	0.140 (0.112)
Strategy				
Generalist	−0.102 (0.055)*	−0.055 (0.059)	0.066 (0.055)	0.009 (0.052)
Innovator	0.132 (0.042)***	0.149 (0.044)***	0.042 (0.046)	−0.040 (0.042)
Environment				
Competition	0.014 (0.056)	0.026 (0.062)	−0.148 (0.058)**	−0.084 (0.049)*
Regulation	0.010 (0.050)	0.019 (0.055)	−0.075 (0.057)	−0.035 (0.051)
Legitimation (cognitive)	0.052 (0.049)	−0.019 (0.057)	0.101 (0.056)*	0.092 (0.048)*
Process				
Resource mobilization	—	—	0.406 (0.116)***	0.309 (0.106)**
Legal establishment	−1.261 (0.134)***	0.014 (0.127)	−0.097 (0.125)	0.091 (0.115)
Social organization	−0.593 (0.167)***	0.044 (0.132)	0.084 (0.125)	0.320 (0.111)**
Operational startup	−1.135 (0.210)***	−0.609 (0.141)***	—	—
Control Variables				
Resource base	−0.001 (0.010)	−0.021 (0.011)*	−0.005 (0.010)	0.012 (0.009)
Munificence	0.049 (0.038)	0.100 (0.041)*	0.036 (0.039)	−0.063 (0.036)ξ
Service industry	−0.262 (0.121)*	−0.338 (0.131)**	0.184 (0.138)	0.445 (0.128)***
Number of events	429	356	366	449
Number of spells	2515	2515	2515	2515
−2 Log likelihood (d.f.)	424.39 (14)	1410.80 (14)	1289.22 (14)	1182.12 (14)

One-tailed tests for hypothesized effects, two-tailed otherwise.
[a] Standard errors are in parentheses.
ξ $p \leq 0.10$.
* $p \leq 0.05$.
** $p \leq 0.01$.
*** $p \leq 0.001$.

Table 3. Factors Affecting Rates of Initiation, Legal Establishment, and Social Organization among Sampled Organizations ($N = 532$)[a].

Variable	Initiation (Model 1)	Legal Establishment (Model 2)	Social Organization (Model 3)
B Vector constant	1.188 (0.198)***	1.026 (0.182)***	−0.117 (0.203)
C Vector constant	−0.446 (0.068)*	−0.683 (0.064)***	−0.563 (0.046)***
Structure			
Independent startup	0.335 (0.119)**	0.234 (0.104)*	−0.196 (0.110)*
Strategy			
Generalist	−0.000 (0.057)	−0.007 (0.048)	−0.066 (0.050)
Innovator	0.039 (0.045)	−0.027 (0.040)	0.039 (0.041)
Environment			
Competition	−0.091 (0.059)	−0.038 (0.050)	−0.007 (0.054)
Regulation	0.000 (0.056)	−0.045 (0.047)	−0.067 (0.050)
Legitimation (Cognitive)	0.086 (0.052)⁺	0.072 (0.047)	0.074 (0.051)
Process			
Resource mobilization	−0.440 (0.121)***	0.010 (0.093)	0.331 (0.100)***
Legal establishment	−0.876 (0.162)***	—	0.220 (0.105)*
Social organization	−0.588 (0.216)**	−0.475 (0.162)**	—
Operational startup	−0.060 (0.279)	−0.575 (0.189)**	−0.136 (0.127)
Control variables			
Resource base	−0.003 (0.009)	0.005 (0.009)	−0.010 (0.009)
Munificence	0.078 (0.042)⁺	0.008 (0.034)	0.036 (0.035)
Service industry	0.326 (0.127)**	−0.154 (0.114)	0.077 (0.124)
Number of events	395	501	446
Number of spells	1,981[b]	2,515	2,515
−2 Log likelihood (d.f.)	262.66 (15)	341.60 (14)	1,148.19 (14)

⁺$p \leq 0.10$.
*$p \leq 0.05$.
**$p \leq 0.01$.
***$p \leq 0.001$; one-tailed tests for hypothesized effects, two-tailed otherwise.
[a]Standard errors are in parentheses.
[b]Analysis is limited to those organizations with more than one founding team member ($N = 395$).

the timing of external financial support. A prior infrastructure conveys slight positional advantages to spin-offs and franchises seeking external funding ($p < 0.10$). The analysis identifies a more significant influence on external funding rates based on the resource base enjoyed by an emerging venture. The negative effect suggests that entrepreneurs with a sizable endowment of assets from a sponsoring organization can bootstrap their new venture and put off resource mobilization during the founding process. Entrepreneurs in industries with lower fixed capital costs (the service sector) are also likely to delay resource mobilization.

In general, environmental influences on resource mobilization are limited. Competitive pressures do not encourage entrepreneurs to pursue mobilization efforts more aggressively than those positioned in less competitive environments. The main environmental influence on rates of external funding is munificence. Resource-rich environments for these ventures encourage substantially higher rates of funding (up to a rate multiplier of 1.57) than environments perceived as having an average level of munificence.

Process variables in the founding sequence suggest that resource mobilization is typically initiated early among other startup stages. Entrepreneurs who delay developing an organizational blueprint (business plan) are significantly less likely to do so once other startup events – such as legal establishment, social organization, and operational startup – have been accomplished. To a large extent, this reflects a fundamental difference between those entrepreneurs who opt to code the blueprint of their venture into documented form before engaging in organizing activity and those who forego the exercise in abstraction entirely in favor of practice. External funding events are not as sensitive to startup sequence as business plan development, although entrepreneurs are less likely to pursue external resources once they have achieved operational startup.

Consistent with predictions, the operational startup of new organizations is affected by their cognitive legitimacy and technical environment (Table 2, Models 3 and 4). Operational startup is accelerated for emergent ventures adopting widely recognized (legitimate) organizational forms. Those ventures enjoying the greatest cognitive legitimacy announce products or services at a rate that is 1.38 times that of forms having limited legitimacy. Meanwhile, technical pressures dampen rates of operational startup, with the most competitive environments yielding product-to-market cycles that are half as fast as environments with low levels of competition.

The analyses do not support the hypothesis that a prior stock of organizational routines and competencies among franchises and spin-offs speeds up operational startup. Examining the process variables, it appears that the influence of funding is largely reserved for resource mobilization efforts (which encourage operational startup) rather than initial assets provided by entrepreneurs or sponsoring organizations. There is also no clear impact from the pursuit of an innovator strategy on operational startup. As suggested previously, this ambiguous result is likely when the opportunity costs of creating new products or services are not separated analytically from the opportunity costs of conforming to an existing organizational architecture.

Influences on founding activities that target aspects other than material-resource factors are summarized in Table 3. Rates of initiation – i.e. the organization of an entrepreneurial founding team – subsume only those ventures that have more than one founder and therefore eliminate trivial initiation events. The formation of a founding team is often slowed among ventures built on a prior infrastructure, given the structural inertia inherited from pre-existing organizations. Michels' "law of oligarchy" (1968[1915]) suggests that the conservative and staid leadership of established organizations may politicize the selection of new leadership, especially when the development of spin-off organizations is considered. Process variables also reveal the difficulty of bringing together a viable founding team when other key aspects of the organizing process – resource mobilization, legal establishment, and hiring – have already been accomplished.

The results for legal establishment (Table 3, Model 2) stand out among the other founding processes insofar as there are few factors of theoretical interest that appear to influence these activities substantially. The estimate for the effect of complex regulative environments does not suggest a positive impact on rates of legal establishment and fails to reach statistical significance. The decoupling between legal emergence and organizational context may, of course, be due to a number of aspects of the research design: i.e. attention limited to business organizations, insufficient variance in regulatory structures, or an overly general characterization of institutional detail across a variety of industries and organizational fields. In Model 2, one intriguing finding is that independent startups tend to be quick to establish themselves legally. The lack of backing from extant juristic actors, especially via sponsorship or franchise arrangements, encourages *de novo* startups to seek legal approval to an extent that seems unnecessary for startups with other corporate support.

Rates of social organization – the initial hiring of employees – are also affected by the structure of an emerging venture (Model 3). Sponsored foundings allow templates for authority structures, incentive systems, and roles to be transferred from an extant formal organization to a new venture, increasing rates of social organization in the process (1.22 times that of comparable de novo foundings). Initial resource endowments do not accelerate social organization, but subsequent resource mobilization events have a highly significant impact (increasing hiring rates by a factor of 1.39). As in the case of initiation and legal establishment, environmental context has no clear effect on the timing of social organization among new ventures.

DISCUSSION

In contrast to previous studies of founding processes, which have characterized them as chaotic and disorderly, the results noted here suggest several relationships between founding activities and the social context confronted by entrepreneurs. Structural features of an emerging venture have a marked influence on rates of founding team formation, social organization, and, to a lesser extent, resource mobilization. The strategies embraced by nascent entrepreneurs are reflected in the prevalence and speed of resource mobilization. Features of an organization's technical and institutional environment primarily influence operational startup. Indeed, the one aspect of founding that is only modestly affected by social context is the emergence of an organization as a juristic actor (legal establishment).[7] The analyses do suggest that independent startups pursue legal establishment more aggressively than sponsored startups. Additional research is required to determine whether legal establishment is decoupled from the institutional environment of an emerging venture or whether this decoupling is an artifact of the present research design, reflecting somewhat limited variation in the institutional environment of the organizations studied.

Like contextual variables, process variables also have a substantial impact on the occurrence of startup events. In some cases, aspects of the entrepreneurial process appear to drown out independent or control variables. For instance, the initial resource base of entrepreneurs has no significant effect on the operational startup or social organization of a new venture, but subsequent resource mobilization events accelerate these startup activities considerably. More generally, the process effects point to an underlying founding pattern that begins with initiation activities, proceeds to resource mobilization, legal establishment, and social organization, and concludes with operational startup.

Given the impact of contextual factors, observed sequences of organizational founding behaviors are not likely to reveal fixed patterns. Instead, sequences display predictable departures from each other based on organizational structure, strategy, and environment. These empirical results suggest the relevance of contingency views of formal organizations (see Lawrence 1993 for a review) to the definition and analysis of organizational vital rates. Contingency theorists have long claimed that the routines and structures of established formal organizations should depend on key aspects of organizational form and environment. Translated into an evolutionary-ecological framework, this claim implies that the emergence of formal organizations should likewise be analyzed with some attention to the socially embedded character of organizing processes (see also Ruef 2002b).

CONCLUSION

Organizational founding can be characterized by two underlying micro-dynamics. One micro-dynamic considers a risk set of *potential* entrepreneurs (individual or collective) that are exposed to social, technological, and economic opportunities and constraints over their life course. A small number of these potential entrepreneurs make a serious commitment to starting one or more formal organizations, thus becoming *nascent* entrepreneurs (Reynolds and White 1997). In the second micro-dynamic, the nascent entrepreneurs embark on a series of startup activities that construct a new collective entity. Discrete-event accounts of this founding process pick up on a narrow subset of the startup activities and conceptualize organizational emergence in those terms.

By virtue of the level of analysis employed (that of the emerging organization), the emphasis in this paper has necessarily been limited to the second micro-dynamic in the founding process. An account of both aspects of organizational founding cannot rely on the organizational unit of analysis, since "'non-events' (the absence of foundings in some period) are as important as are observed foundings for testing theories about founding rates" (Hannan and Carroll 1992: 197). A complete micro-analytic of organizational founding begins with potential entrepreneurs as the units of analysis (Zucker 1989), while corresponding macro-analytic accounts consider founding rates at the level of the organizational population or industry. Despite the fact that the results presented here are conditional on a committed founding effort by the nascent entrepreneur, several preliminary insights can be drawn with respect to these more general models of organizational founding.

At the organizational (micro-) level, the effect of context and unobserved heterogeneity on relative rates of founding activities may serve to accentuate or diminish observed dynamics at the population (macro-) level, depending on what operationalization of founding events is employed. As Carroll and Hannan emphasize, an ecological perspective relates "events occurring to individuals... back to the population level by the use of counting procedures... [I]n the simplest case, population size gets incremented and decremented as a result of the simple aggregation of birth and death events"

(2000: 25). If empirical studies emphasize a particular stage of organizational founding (e.g. legal establishment) and many organizations dissolve before achieving that stage, then these studies may undercount foundings. Moreover, if the undercount is not uniform across the history of a population (if, for instance, legal establishment is more difficult early on), then empirical findings involving population dynamics can be affected.

Additional research and simulation studies are required to determine how founding event timing impacts the evolution of organizational populations (see Ruef 2004 for some initial steps in this direction). Such research can relate the present study to a more general sociological issue: how can the actions of ordinary entrepreneurs, assessed on a time scale of months or years, possibly make any difference in the evolution of industries, assessed on a time scale of decades or centuries? Further research is also required to clarify the relationship between founding processes and the micro-dynamics of entrepreneurship: the decision of potential entrepreneurs to become committed founders. In contrast to the present study, this line of research requires attention to individual life histories; in particular the human and cultural capital that entrepreneurs are able to develop, as well as the social contexts that they are embedded in. Representative samples of potential entrepreneurs from the general population, such as the PSED, are central in developing this broader micro-level account of the dynamics of organizational founding.

NOTES

1. One survey, conducted in 1992, considered a representative sample of 1,200 adults in Wisconsin, while the other, conducted in 1993, considered a representative sample of 1,016 adults across the United States. Reynolds, White, and colleagues used the concept of a *nascent entrepreneur* – an individual who is thinking about starting a business and has taken at least two major steps toward realizing this goal – to define "organizations in the making." Applying this criterion, 80 and 40 nascent entrepreneurs were ultimately identified for the Wisconsin and national surveys, respectively. Such small-scale surveys of entrepreneurs have now largely been superseded by more ambitious efforts, such as the Panel Study of Entrepreneurial Dynamics (PSED) (Reynolds 2000).

2. Given the variability with which accreditation and certification processes apply to different organizational forms, they have not been included as a feature of the five generic founding stages.

3. Arguably, similar processes of imitation could apply to other founding stages – initiation, legal establishment, social organization – among cognitively legitimate organizational forms. In those cases, however, the demand-side aspect of the argument (focusing on the recognition of organizational output in some market or non-market arena) is not as pronounced.

4. Selected information was also collected on the role of these individuals in creating nonprofit organizations and other nonbusiness entities. To limit the heterogeneity of organizational forms being analyzed, the present empirical study is concerned exclusively with the founding of business enterprises.

5. At the same time, it must be acknowledged that rates of entrepreneurial activity for this group are likely to be far greater than those found in the general population and that their distinctive human capital may lead to more successful startup activities than those of other entrepreneurs.

6. Note that the initiation process (creation of a founding team) is effectively a "trivial" startup activity in 167 of the cases that involve only a single entrepreneur.

7. Stated more formally, there is no significant improvement in model fit between the model of legal establishment and a baseline Gompertz specification that only includes process variables (likelihood ratio $\chi^2 = 11.6$, $\Delta df = 9$, ns).

ACKNOWLEDGMENTS

This research was supported by the Center for Entrepreneurial Studies at the Stanford Graduate School of Business. I am grateful for the comments of Howard Aldrich, Glenn Carroll, and Lisa Keister on earlier versions. Correspondence may be addressed to Martin Ruef, Department of Sociology, Princeton, NJ 08544.

REFERENCES

Aldrich, Howard. 1979. *Organizations and Environments.* Englewood Cliffs, NJ: Prentice-Hall.
------. 1999. *Organizations Evolving.* Thousand Oaks, CA: Sage.
Aldrich, Howard and Udo Staber. 1988. "Organizing Business Interests: Patterns of Trade Association Foundings, Transformations, and Deaths." Pp. 111–126 in *Ecological Models of Organization,* edited by G. Carroll. Cambridge, MA: Ballinger.
Aldrich, Howard, Catherine Zimmer, Udo Staber, and John Beggs. 1994. "Minimalism, Mutualism, and Maturity: The Evolution of the American Trade Association Population in the 20th Century." Pp. 223–239 in *Evolutionary Dynamics of Organizations,* edited by J. Baum and J. Singh. Oxford: Oxford University Press.
Amburgey, Terry and Hayagreeva Rao. 1996. "Organizational Ecology: Past, Present, and Future Directions." *Academy of Management Journal* 39:1265–1286.
Baron, James, Diane Burton, and Michael Hannan. 1996. "The Road Taken: The Origins and Evolution of Employment Systems in Emerging High-Technology Companies." *Industrial and Corporate Change* 5:239–276.
Baron, James, Michael Hannan, and Diane Burton. 1999. "Building the Iron Cage: Determinants of Managerial Intensity in the Early Years of Organizations." *American Sociological Review* 64:527–547.

Barron, David, Elizabeth West, and Michael Hannan. 1994. "A Time to Grow and a Time to Die: Growth and Mortality of Credit Unions in New York, 1914–1990." *American Journal of Sociology* 100:381–421.

Baum, Joel and Christine Oliver. 1992. "The Institutional Embeddedness and Dynamics of Organizational Populations." *American Sociological Review* 57:540–559.

Baum, Joel, Helaine Korn, and Suresh Kotha. 1995. "Dominant Designs and Population Dynamics in Telecommunications Services: Founding and Failure of Facsimile Service Organizations, 1965–1992." *Social Science Research* 24:97–135.

Bollen, Kenneth. 1989. *Structural Equations with Latent Variables.* New York: Wiley.

Brittain, Jack. 1994. "Density-Independent Selection and Community Evolution." Pp. 355–378 in *Evolutionary Dynamics of Organizations*, edited by J. Baum and J. Singh. Oxford: Oxford Press.

Budros, Art. 1993. "An Analysis of Organizational Birth Types: Organizational Start-Up and Entry in the Nineteenth-Century Life Insurance Industry." *Social Forces* 72:199–221.

Carroll, Glenn, Lyda Bigelow, Marc-David Seidel, and Lucia Tsai. 1996. "The Fates of De Novo and De Alio Producers in the American Automobile Industry, 1885–1982." *Strategic Management Journal* 17:117–137.

Carroll, Glenn and Michael Hannan. 2000. *The Demography of Corporations and Industries.* Princeton, NJ: Princeton University Press.

Carroll, Glenn and Anand Swaminathan. 1992. "The Organizational Ecology of Strategic Groups in the American Brewing Industry from 1975 to 1990." *Industrial and Corporate Change* 1:65–97.

Carter, Nancy, William Gartner, and Paul Reynolds. 1996. "Exploring Start-up Sequences." *Journal of Business Venturing* 11:151–166.

Coleman, James. 1974. *Power and the Structure of Society.* New York: Norton.

Delacroix, Jacques and Glenn Carroll. 1983. "Organizational Foundings: An Ecological Study of the Newspaper Industries of Argentina and Ireland." *Administrative Science Quarterly* 28:274–291.

Delacroix, Jacques and Michael Solt. 1988. "Niche Formation and Foundings in the California Wine Industry, 1941–84." Pp. 53–70 in *Ecological Models of Organizations*, edited by G. Carroll. Cambridge, MA: Ballinger.

Dobbin, Frank. 1995. "Railroads." Pp. 59–86 in *Organizations in Industry: Strategy, Structure, and Selection*, edited by G. Carroll and M. Hannan. Oxford: Oxford University Press.

Gartner, William. 1988. "Who is an Entrepreneur? Is the Wrong Question." *American Journal of Small Business* 12:11–32.

Halliday, Terence, Michael Powell, and Mark Granfors. 1987. "Minimalist Organizations: Vital Events in State Bar Associations." *American Sociological Review* 52:456–471.

Hannan, Michael T. 1998. "Rethinking Age Dependence in Organizational Mortality: Logical Formalizations." *American Journal of Sociology* 104:126–164.

Hannan, Michael T. and Glenn R. Carroll. 1992. *Dynamics of Organizational Populations: Density, Competition, and Legitimation.* Oxford: Oxford University Press.

Hannan, Michael., Carroll. Glenn, Dundon. Elizabeth, and Torres. John. 1995. "Organizational Evolution in a Multinational Context: Entries of Automobile Manufacturers in Belgium, Britain, France, Germany, and Italy." *American Sociological Review* 60:509–528.

Hannan, Michael T. and John Freeman. 1977. "The Population Ecology of Organizations." *American Journal of Sociology* 82:929–964.

------. 1984. "Structural Inertia and Organizational Change." *American Sociological Review* 49:149–164.

------. 1987. "The Ecology of Organizational Founding: American Labor Unions, 1836–1985." *American Journal of Sociology* 92:910–943.

------. 1989. *Organizational Ecology.* Cambridge: Harvard University Press.

Homans, George. 1950. *The Human Group.* New York: Harcourt, Brace & World.

Ingram, Paul and Crist Inman. 1996. "Institutions, Intergroup Competition, and the Evolution of Hotel Populations Around Niagara Falls." *Administrative Science Quarterly* 41:629–658.

Katz, Jerome and William Gartner. 1988. "Properties of Emerging Organizations." *Academy of Management Review* 13:429–441.

Kaufman, Herbert. 1976. *Are Government Organizations Immortal?.* Washington, DC: Brookings.

Khandekar, Rajendra and John Young. 1985. "Selecting a Legal Structure: A Strategic Decision." *Journal of Small Business Management* 23:47–55.

Kimberly, John. 1979. "Issues in the Creation of Organizations: Initiation, Innovation and Institutionalization." *Academy of Management Journal* 22:437–457.

Lawrence, Paul. 1993. "The Contingency Approach to Organizational Design." Pp. 9–18 in *Handbook of Organizational Behavior,* edited by R. Golembiewski. New York: Dekker.

Little, Roderick. 1992. "Regression with Missing X's: A Review." *Journal of the American Statistical Association* 87:1227–1237.

McCarthy, John, Mark Wolfson, David Baker, and Elaine Mosakowski. 1988. "The Founding of Social Movement Organizations: Local Citizens' Groups Opposing Drunken Driving." Pp. 71–84 in *Ecological Models of Organization,* edited by G. Carroll. Cambridge, MA: Ballinger.

Meyer, John and Richard W. Scott. 1983. *Organizational Environments: Ritual and Rationality.* Beverly Hills, CA: Sage.

Michels, Robert. 1968. *Political Parties: A Sociological Study of the Oligarchical Tendencies of Modern Democracy.* New York: Free Press (first published in 1915).

Miles, Robert and W.A. Randolph. 1980. "Influence of Organizational Learning Styles on Early Development." Pp. 44–82 in *The Organizational Life Cycle,* edited by J. Kimberly and R. Miles. San Francisco: Jossey-Bass.

Oberschall, Anthony. 1973. *Social Conflict and Social Movements.* Englewood Cliffs, NJ: Prentice-Hall.

Olson, Mancur. 1968. *The Logic of Collective Action.* New York: Schocken Books.

Ranger-Moore, James, Jane Banaszak-Holl, and Michael Hannan. 1991. "Density Dependent Dynamics in Regulated Industries: Founding Rates of Banks and Life Insurance Companies." *Administrative Science Quarterly* 36:36–65.

Reynolds, Paul. 2000. "National Panel Study of US Business Start-Ups: Background and Methodology." Pp. 153–227 in *Advances in Entrepreneurship, Firm Emergence, and Growth* vol. 4, edited by J. Katz. Stamford, CT: JAI Press.

Reynolds, Paul and Sammis White. 1997. *The Entrepreneurial Process: Economic Growth, Men, Women, and Minorities.* Westport, CN: Quorum Books.

Rohwer, Götz. 1999. *Transition Data Analysis* (TDA) 6.2. Working Papers. Institut für Empirische und Angewandte Soziologie, University of Bremen, Germany.

Ruef, Martin. 2002a. "Strong Ties, Weak Ties and Islands: Structural and Cultural Predictors of Organizational Innovation." *Industrial and Corporate Change* 11:427–449.

------. 2002. "Unpacking the Liability of Aging: Towards a Socially-Embedded Account of Organizational Disbanding." Pp. 195–228 in *Research in the Sociology of Organizations* vol. 19, edited by M. Lounsbury and M. Ventresca. Stamford, CT: JAI Press.

------. 2004. "Boom and Bust: The Effect of Entrepreneurial Inertia on Organizational Populations." Working Paper, Department of Sociology, Princeton University.

Ruef, Martin, Howard Aldrich, and Nancy Carter. 2003. "The Structure of Founding Teams: Homophily, Strong Ties, and Isolation among U.S. Entrepreneurs." *American Sociological Review* 68:195–222.

Ruef, Martin and W. Richard Scott. 1998. "A Multidimensional Model of Organizational Legitimacy: Hospital Survival in Changing Institutional Environments." *Administrative Science Quarterly* 43:877–904.

Schumpeter, Joseph. 1947. *Capitalism, Socialism, and Democracy* 2nd ed. New York: Harper & Row.

Scott, W. Richard. 2001. *Institutions and Organizations* 2nd ed. Thousand Oaks, CA: Sage.

------. 2002. *Organizations: Rational, Natural, and Open Systems* 5th ed. Upper Saddle, NJ: Prentice-Hall.

Schoonhoven, Claudia B., Kathleen M. Eisenhardt, and Katherine Lyman. 1990. "Speeding Products to Market: Waiting Time to First Product Introduction in New Firms." *Administrative Science Quarterly* 35:177–207.

Singh, Jitendra, David Tucker, and Agnes Meinhard. 1991. "Institutional Change and Ecological Dynamics." Pp. 390–422 in *The New Institutionalism in Organizational Analysis*, edited by W. Powell and P. DiMaggio. Chicago, IL: University of Chicago Press.

Stinchcombe, Arthur. 1965. "Social Structure and Organizations." Pp. 142–193 in *Handbook of Organizations*, edited by J. March. Chicago: Rand McNally.

Tolbert, Pamela and Lynne Zucker. 1996. "The Institutionalization of Institutional Theory." Pp. 175–190 in *Handbook of Organization Studies*, edited by S. Clegg, C. Hardy and W. Nord. Thousand Oaks, CA: Sage.

Van de Ven, Andrew, Douglas Polley, Raghu Garud, and Sankaran Venkataraman. 1999. *The Innovation Journey*. New York: Oxford University Press.

Weber, Max. 1889. *Zur Geschichte der Handelsgesellshaften im Mittelalter (Nach Südeuropaischen Quellen)*. Stuttgart, Germany: F. Enke.

Zucker, Lynne. 1989. "No Legitimacy, No History (Comment on Carroll and Hannan)." *American Sociological Review* 54:542–545.

Zuckerman, Ezra. 1999. "The Categorical Imperative: Securities Analysts and the Illegitimacy Discount." *American Journal of Sociology* 104:1398–1438.

APPENDIX. : SELECTED COMPONENTS OF SURVEY INSTRUMENT

I. General Information

1. Many new ventures are built on a pre-existing organizational infrastructure. Which of the following statements most accurately describes your venture? (**check one only**)

Independent Start-Up	Purchase/ Takeover of Existing Business	Franchise	Start-Up Sponsored by Existing Business	Other (SPECIFY)
❑	❑	❑	❑	_____

2. Using the identifiers below, please enter the code(s) that most accurately reflect the industry (or industries) your venture competes within.

Service

1 Accounting
2 Advertising
3 Architecture
4 Arts
5 Commercial Banking
6 Construction/Real Estate Development
7 Diversified Financial Services
8 Education
9 Electronic Commerce-Retail
10 Electronic Commerce-Other Services
11 Entertainment/Leisure/Sports
12 Environmental/Waste Management/Recycling
13 Food/Lodging
14 Foundation
15 Government
16 Hardware/Software/Systems Services

17 Health Care Services
18 Import/Export/International Trade
19 Insurance
20 Investment Banking/Brokerage
21 Investment Management
22 Legal Services
23 Management Consulting
24 Marketing Services
25 Multimedia Services
26 Public Relations
27 Radio/TV/Cable/Film
28 Real Estate Finance
29 Religious Service
30 Retail/Wholesale
31 Social Services
32 Telecommunications Services
33 Transportation Services/Shipping
34 Utilities
35 Venture Capital
36 Diversified Service

Manufacturing

37 Aerospace
38 Agriculture
39 Apparel/Textiles
40 Automotive/Transportation Equipment
41 Biotechnology
42 Chemical
43 Consumer Products

44 Energy
45 Extractive Mineral/Natural Resources
46 High Tech-Computers/Hardware
47 High Tech-Computers/Software
48 High Tech-Consumer/Electronics
49 High Tech-Multimedia Products
50 High Tech-Networking
51 High Tech-Optics

52 High Tech-Semiconductors
53 High Tech-Telecommunications Products
54 High Tech-Other
55 Industrial Equipment

56 Medical Instruments & Devices
57 Pharmaceuticals
58 Printing/Publishing
59 Rubber/Plastics
60 Diversified Manufacturing

II. Creating the Organization

3. When did you first accomplish the following activities?

	Never	Month/Year
a. Bring together a founding team	❑	_____
b. Legally establish the company	❑	_____
c. Prepare a business plan	❑	_____
d. Obtain first external financing	❑	_____
e. Hire an employee	❑	_____
f. Hire an outside CEO	❑	_____
g. File a patent/trademark application	❑	_____
h. Announce a product/service	❑	_____
i. Sell first product/service	❑	_____

4. What innovations did you hope to deliver when your organization was founded? (**check all that apply**)

		Comments
a. Introduce a new type of product/service	❑	_____
b. Introduce a new method of production	❑	_____
c. Introduce a new method of distribution	❑	_____
d. Introduce a new method of marketing	❑	_____
e. Develop new supplier linkages	❑	_____
f. Enter an unexploited market niche	❑	_____
g. Reorganize the industry	❑	_____
h. Other type(s) of innovation	❑	_____

III. Environment of the Organization

5. *Please rate each of the following items on a scale of 1 to 10, with '1' being the lowest and '10' being the highest. Use 'n/a' to indicate that a question does not apply to your organization.*

	At Time of founding	Factor Loadings
How significant was the competition faced by the organization...	—	
(a) In terms of the product or service overlap with existing organizations?		1.00
(b) In terms of attracting a qualified labor pool to the organization?		1.06
(c) In terms of attracting venture/investment capital?		0.91
(d) In terms of acquiring production inputs (materials or technologies)?		0.78
(e) In terms of protection of patents/intellectual property?		0.45
How recognizable were the organization's product(s)/service(s)...	—	
(f) Among actual or potential customers?		1.00
(g) Among actual or potential competitors?		1.26
How relevant are the following kinds of regulation to the organization...	—	
(h) Employment/labor law?		3.11
(i) Trade regulation/tariffs?		2.28
(j) Environmental law?		2.49
(k) Securities law?		1.29
(l) Product liability/consumer protection law?		3.13
(m) Other regulations?		1.00

TECHNOLOGICAL RESOURCES AND NEW FIRM GROWTH: A COMPARISON OF START-UP AND ADOLESCENT VENTURES ✩

Shaker A. Zahra and Bruce A. Kirchhoff

ABSTRACT

New ventures contribute to the competitiveness of the United States in global markets, creating jobs and wealth. Understandably, public policy makers and researchers alike have shown an interest in understanding the factors that spur these ventures' growth, which is also an important research issue in the field of entrepreneurship. Researchers have highlighted the role of owners' needs and aspirations and industry conditions as determinants of new ventures' growth. This study proposes that new ventures' resource endowments influence their growth in domestic and international markets. Using the resource-based view (RBV) of the firm, the study examines the effect of select technological resources on the domestic and international sales growth of 419 new ventures. Start-ups (5 years or

✩ An earlier version of this chapter was presented at the Babson-Kauffman Entrepreneurship Research Conference (BKERC). Major parts of this chapter were completed while the first author was a visiting research professor of entrepreneurship at Jönköping International Business School, Sweden.

Entrepreneurship
Research in the Sociology of Work, Volume 15, 101–122
ISSN: 0277-2833/doi:10.1016/S0277-2833(05)15005-5

younger) benefit from using a different set of technological resources in
achieving growth than those of adolescent firms (6–8 years old). These
differences persist in low vs. high technology industries, reflecting the
maturation of these ventures.

New ventures firms 5 years or younger play an important role in developing
and commercializing new technologies that create new industries, improve
productivity, create wealth, and enhance the growth of national economies.
Yet, the odds of new ventures' survival are low and many of those ventures
that survive may not achieve their growth goals. Given the social, economic
and political consequences of new firm growth, researchers have shown
considerable attention to the factors that influence this growth.

Earlier research has discussed the processes by which new ventures evolve
(Aldrich 2000) and achieve growth (Cooper 1986; Davidsson and Wiklund
2000; Davidsson, Delmar and Wiklund 2002) as well as the effect of founders' aspirations and environmental factors on a firm's growth (Cooper and
Bruno 1977). Researchers have also tracked the various stages of the firm's
evolution and related them to the challenges associated with maintaining
and nurturing growth. While disagreements continue to persist regarding
the definition and measures of growth (Delmar, Davidsson and Gartner
2003; Wiklund, Davidsson and Delmar 2003; Weinzimmer, Nystrom and
Freeman 1998), recent studies have begun to recognize the importance of a
firm's resource endowments for its ability to achieve and sustain growth in
domestic and international markets.

Several researchers have proposed that resources significantly influence
the direction and pace of NVG (Davidsson and Wiklund 2000; Penrose
1959; Wiklund 1998). These researchers noted that resources of different
types could be bundled creatively to give competitive advantages to new
ventures that allow them to capture viable market positions and achieve
superior rates of growth. Technological resources, in particular, can be an
important source of such a competitive advantage and growth (Cooper and
Folta 2000). Technological resources are usually embedded in the firm's
knowledge base and therefore it might be difficult for competitors and other
outsiders to observe or imitate, giving the new venture an opportunity to
develop unique and innovative products that create value for the founders
and owners. It also takes time for competitors to build or acquire these
technological resources and combine them in ways that create value, further
protecting the competitive advantage of those ventures that already have

these resources. These factors have led some (Penrose 1959; Roberts 1968, 1991) to highlight the contributions of technological resources to the creation and subsequent growth of new firms. Studies of knowledge-based industries have also shown that technological resources spur NVG (e.g. Deeds, DeCarolis and Coombs 1998).

Prior research on the effect of technological resources on new venture growth had three shortcomings. Firstly, with the exception of Singh (1992), past research has failed to recognize that companies over time learn to deploy their technological resources differently. Companies learn by doing and by interacting with customers and the market, in general. This learning could be multifaceted, covering the way the resources could be bundled together; how they are integrated into innovative products as well as when and how the products are taken to the market (Zahra, Ireland and Hitt 2000). This learning can change the way new ventures build and commercialize their technologies and, as a result, influence the associations between technological resources and NVG. Start-ups, those firms five years or younger, usually do not have the same expertise as adolescent firms (6 to 8 years) (Bantel, 1998). The evolutionary theory of the firm suggests that experience matters in deploying technological resources (Nelson and Winter 1982). Therefore, we need to empirically document the major differences between new ventures' various technological resources and growth among start-ups and adolescent firms.

Secondly, new ventures compete in environments that vary in their technological sophistication, defined as the skills and capabilities firms have, and how they are employed in exploiting their technological resources. These differences reflect new ventures' unique organizational histories, track records and innovativeness. Differences in these skills can influence the potential gains achieved by new ventures from their various technological resources (Zahra 1996b). Some ventures are better skilled and equipped to exploit these resources than others and as a result are apt to gain differential competitive advantages. However, past researchers appear to have ignored the effect of technological resources on NVG in low vs. high technology industries. This gap in the literature is surprising because technological resources may not generate growth within particular environments but the same resources fuel sales and employment growth in other environments (Porter 1980; Zahra and Covin 1993). Demand and supply conditions as well as competitive rivalry might augment, neutralize or even decrease the payoff from these technological resources. Appreciating the differences that might exist between technological resources and new firm growth in low vs. high technology industries could be informative. Public policy makers have encouraged the creation of technology-based new ventures in different industries to improve employment and quality of life. Public policy makers have also encouraged new ventures to apply new technologies in their operations, hoping to improve their competitiveness and the odds of their survival. If significant technological resources influence the success (e.g., growth) of new ventures differently in different environments, we need to document the sources of these differences and then use this information in shaping and crafting public policy choices.

Thirdly, researchers often ignore geographic sources of new firm growth. In particular, we do not know if technological resources would influence growth in domestic vs. international markets differently. Evidence suggests that new firms are important players in global markets (Autio, Sapienza and Almeida 2000; OECD 2002). Indeed, many new firms are born international and, from inception, target markets in several countries (Bloodgood, Sapienza and Almeida 1996; Zahra, Ireland and Hitt 2000). Given that different variables (e.g., technological resources) might influence domestic and international markets differently, it is important to separate domestic from international sales growth.

This study examines the association between various technological resources and sales growth in start-up vs. adolescent firms. It also explores these associations in low vs. high technology industries, seeking to clarify the financial effects of technological resources on NVG in different competitive settings. High technology industries are usually important arenas for growth; technological change creates opportunities for product differentiation and innovation. Radical innovation, both in products and processes, also thrive in these industries. Thus, identifying those technological resources that enhance sales growth can be useful in developing effective managerial strategies that exploit new firms' technological resources. Understanding these differences can also improve our knowledge of how new firms gain a competitive advantage at different stages of their life cycles, which is a research gap in technological entrepreneurship (Deeds, DeCarolis and Combs 1998; Zahra and Hayton 2004).

THEORY AND HYPOTHESES

Understanding the determinants of NVG has been a subject of much interest in the literature (Hoy, McDougall and D'Souza 1992). Growth creates opportunities for employment and profitability (Davidsson and Wiklund 2000), generating wealth for founders and other members of the top management team (TMT). Yet, NVG can increase conflicts and tensions among members of the TMT. Poorly planned growth might cause the loss of organizational focus, leading to an inability to meet the challenges associated with the increasing complexity of a firm's operations. Growth can also strain a firm's resources and magnify the mismatch between the skills of the TMT and those of the growing organization. Given these concerns, some venture owners and managers may not support or pursue growth (Davidsson, Delmar and Wiklund 2002; Delmar, Davidson and Gartner 2003).

Past researchers have sought to link a firm's resources to its growth. They agree that a new venture's stock of financial resources can determine the magnitude of its growth. Researchers have used multiple theoretical perspectives in examining the factors that determine this growth, including the population ecology, resource dependency, evolutionary economics (Aldrich 2000), and resource-based (Penrose 1959) perspectives. Despite differences on the exact nature of the link between resources and firm growth, there is agreement that a new venture's stock of financial, technological, marketing and administrative resources influence its competitive success, if not survival. However, new ventures often experience serious shortcomings in these various resources and therefore have to work hard to overcome such weaknesses. Some ventures have shown a remarkable ability in overcoming resource limitations by leveraging their limited resources in pursuit of superior market positions. This resourcefulness is consistent with the resource-based view (RBV) (Penrose 1959), which recognizes the importance of valuable, rare and inimitable resources for achieving a competitive advantage that leads to the growth of the firm (Barney 1991; Conner and Prahalad 1996). Tangible (e.g., machinery) and intangible resources can give a venture a sustainable competitive advantage (Alvarez and Busenitz 2001).

One of the major resources of a new venture is its technology. These resources influence the founding of these firms (Aldrich 2000; Cooper 1986). Also, these resources include the machinery, tools, equipment, knowledge and skills that a firm has or controls. They are also usually embedded in a firm's patents, capturing the knowledge and skills the firm has attained from deploying other technological resources such as the talents of its scientists and engineers.

To date, limited research has sought to identify which technological resources specifically influence NVG (Zahra and Hayton 2004). This study fills this gap in the literature. Technological resources define a company's product base; influence the scale and scope of its operations; offer a foundation for product differentiation; are the foundation of knowledge-based competition; and influence the accumulation of other resources such as capital (Autio 2000). Hence, a focus on technological resources is consistent with past research that has linked these resources to company growth (Roberts 1968, 1991).

Most past research on the effect of technological resources on NVG has been prescriptive, failing to distinguish between start-ups and established firms. Past research has followed the industry economics tradition, exploring major variations in deployment of technological resources across the various stages of an industry's life cycle. Typical of this research is Porter's (1980, 1985) proposition that different phases of an industry's cycle require different technological skills. Another example is Zahra and Covin's (1993) study that fit between technology strategy and a firm's environmental conditions is important for successful company performance. Similarly, Zahra and Bogner (2000) have found that certain technological resources influence new software companies' performance (including growth) and that this relationship is contingent upon the characteristics of a firm's competitive environment. Covin, Slevin, and Covin (1990) also concluded that technological resources influence new firm growth differently across industry settings, especially low vs. high technology industries.

The above-cited studies appear to hold a deterministic view of the role of industry variables, where an industry's key factors of success are believed to determine the optimal choices firms make about their technological resources. This view ignores the ability of companies, even very young ones, to employ technological resources in innovative ways that alter the dynamics of competition in an industry. Indeed, one of the distinguishing qualities of new firms' is their ability to do new things that established companies do not do; they also do these things quite differently from industry incumbents. Findings from earlier studies may not apply well to newer competitive arenas where, new ventures shape industry boundaries, evolution, and rules of competitive rivalry. In addition, most past studies were conducted in established, traditional (rather than high technology) industries. Young, high technology industries have unique characteristics that can influence the payoff from the technological resources used by the companies to attain growth (Oakey, Rothwell and Cooper 1988). These industries, for example, are dynamic in that demand and supply conditions that change rapidly and frequently. In turn, this makes it difficult for companies to hold their market positions and, therefore, need to change the mix of technological resources that they use in their operations. Failing to adapt can lower a new venture's competitive advantage.

Still, prior studies support the RBV's proposition on the importance of having and deploying unique and inimitable technological resources as a way of achieving growth (Barney 1991; Miller 2003). For example, a study of new ventures is biotechnology found that R&D spending, new product development and introductions, and the use of patents were significantly associated with sales and market share growth among corporate-sponsored new ventures (Zahra 1996a). The same study concluded that a focus on applied R&D was positively associated with sales and market share growth among both independent and corporate new ventures.

Start-Up vs. Adolescent Ventures

Using the RBV, we examine how different technological resources influence a company's growth over time and in different industry settings. We do this by looking at start-ups vs. adolescent companies that compete in low vs. high technology industries. Bantel (1998) suggests that these companies differ significantly in their experiences, skill bases and competitive approaches. These differences arise because of the learnings these companies achieve as they address the various challenges when positioning themselves in their chosen markets. Further, as new firms become relatively established in their markets, they gain credibility with suppliers and other key stakeholders. This allows these firms to acquire different types of resources, possibly from different sources. Following this line of reasoning, we expect start-ups and adolescent companies to use different sets of technological resources to achieve future growth. This proposition is consistent with Miller and Camp (1985) who found that successful adolescent businesses were aggressive in their deployment of various resources, including technology, to achieve their goals. Lambkin (1988) has also observed that start-up and adolescent firms differed significantly in their competitive strategies, particularly in their use of technological resources such as patents. McCann (1991) has also noted that start-up businesses were more likely to focus on enhancing existing products and services as their core technology strategy. Later in the organizational life cycle, upgrading existing products and introducing radically new products were viable technological choices for these ventures that could influence the growth of the firm (McCann, 1991).

There is an extensive body of research on the firm's life cycle (Kazanjian 1988; Kazanjian and Drazin 1990). This research proffers that companies change over time, facing different challenges. Firms use different resources to address these challenges. Start-ups usually experiment with alternative strategies to make the effective use of their limited resources. These firms usually do not have an extensive repertoire of competitive skills and organizational recipes to make effective technological resource allocations. Therefore, start-ups have to test and probe the market and learn from the feedback they receive from suppliers, customers and competitors' reactions. These activities are consistent with Bahrami and Evans' (1989) organizational life cycle model that labels the first phase of a firm's evolution as "experimentation". In this phase, high R&D spending and the aggressive recruitment of scientists and engineers are expected to be the key organizational priorities (Hanks et al. 1993). These investments enable the new ventures to transform their inventions into products and goods that they can quickly commercialize, create a defensible market position and make a profit (Roberts 1992). Without such skills, start-ups cannot gain a competitive advantage. In turn, start-ups could use their profits (along with other financial resources) to broaden their market reach by expanding their sales activities in domestic and international markets (Zahra et al. 2000). Technological resources could serve as an important signal to key stakeholders in the new markets where the firm aspires to expand its operations, making it possible for it to overcome the liabilities of newness and foreignness. As profits materialize, the firm could undertake aggressive marketing and distribution that will make domestic and international growth possible and profitable.

By the time a firm reaches its adolescence, it would have gained some experience in assembling, managing, deploying, and integrating its resources. This learning through experience positions the firm to use its technological resources in ways that can achieve sales growth (Zahra et al. 2000). Learning also enables the firm to develop routines that will allow it to harvest its investments in technological resources, possibly increasing its gains from these investments. The efficient use of technological resources also permits the adolescent firm to attain profitability while achieving growth. Learning further enables the firm to change the mix of the technological resources it will use in pursuit of growth. Clearly, adolescent firms have to transform the initial investments they have made during the experimentation phase into concrete successes and attain growth. Consequently, prior R&D investments, recruitment of scientists and engineers, use of applied R&D, frequent product development, and the use of patents are expected to be positively and significantly associated with adolescent firms' sales growth, both domestic and international. This discussion leads to the following hypothesis:

Hypothesis 1. Compared to start-up ventures, adolescent companies will exhibit significantly stronger positive associations between sales growth and: (a) R&D spending, (b) applied R&D, (c) the proportion of engineers and scientists, (d) new product development, and (e) patents.

Low vs. High Technology Industries

Industrial organizational economics suggests that different industries have unique structures that determine the efficacy of different technological resources (Porter 1980). These structures evolve overtime, reflecting the key requirements for successful organizational performance. Participating in a given industry requires new ventures to have particular technological resources. However, growth demands deftness in selecting, managing and deploying these resources in order to create a competitive advantage (McGrath, MacMillan and Tushman 1992; McGrath, MacMillan and Venkataraman 1995). Thus, new ventures face a dual challenge of matching the industry's technological requirements *and* then leveraging these resources in ways that give them an advantage that leads to higher sales growth.

High and low technology industries differ significantly in the intensity of the knowledge embedded in their structures, the types of knowledge needed to participate in them, and the infrastructure necessary to create goods and services (Oakey et al. 1988). These industries represent different competitive settings, with very different competitive rules of engagement (Covin et al. 1990). New ventures that compete in high technology industries, therefore, often benefit from using different technological resources than those used in low technology industries. The dynamism of high technology industries also necessitates constant innovation through frequent product introductions and upgrades (Covin et al. 1990).

In the high technology industry, there is a need for a strong focus on applied R&D and upgrading the firm's products in order to capitalize on the opportunities created by continuous change. In turn, this requires heavy R&D spending and the effective recruitment of scientists and the maintenance of a strong knowledge base. Companies in high technology industries also have to carefully protect their intellectual property because diffusion of innovation is commonplace. While it is not always possible (or even desirable) to protect intellectual property entirely in a high technology industry (Zahra and Bogner 2000), patenting can give the firm a competitive advantage. Patents often protect the firm against unwanted leakage of information about important discoveries and serve as a signal of the firm's strong technological capabilities, enabling companies to obtain the capital necessary to achieve sales growth. Patents also allow the firm to enter those alliances that give it access to marketing, manufacturing and distribution resources, fostering sales growth. Therefore, the use of patents in high technology industries is expected to enhance the probability of firm success (Roberts 1992) and growth (Covin et al. 1990).

In low technology industries, change is not as fast or persistent as it is common in high technology industries. Companies do not experience the same pressure as their high technology counterparts. In low technology industries, therefore, companies may not benefit from aggressive spending on R&D or frequent product introductions. Studies has found that, in such industries, firms that spent heavily on R&D had lower company perform- ance (Zahra and Covin 1993). This finding signaled the possibility that in low technology industries companies had to be careful in deploying scarce technological resources, otherwise they might experience low performance including sales growth. Finally, while the value of patenting cannot be dis- puted, it is less likely that companies in low technology industries will gain as much advantage from patents in their growth as their counterparts in high technology industries. Major discoveries in low technology industries that could lead to important patents are infrequent, raising a question about the potential contributions of patents to sales growth.

The foregoing discussion indicates that the type of industry in which a new venture competes (high vs. low technology) can significantly moderate the relationships proposed in H1. Experienced, adolescent firms that com- pete in high technology industries are more likely to exhibit stronger, pos- itive and significant associations between their technological resources and sales growth than their counterparts that compete in low technology new ventures or start-ups in high technology industries. These observations sug- gest the following hypothesis:

Hypothesis 2. Industry type will moderate the relationships reported in H1 such that adolescent high technology firms will report stronger pos- itive correlations between technological resources and sales growth more than (a) start-up ventures in low or high technology industries and (b) adolescent firms in low technology industries.

METHOD

Sample

To test the study's hypotheses, we completed a series of interviews with 13 new venture managers to understand the role of technological resources.

Information gathered from interviews was then used to construct a mail questionnaire that was sent to 1700 new ventures in 11 industries, six of which were high technology and five were low technology companies. Companies competed in 10 industries (and number of firms): electronic components, chemicals, surgical appliances, machine tools, fabricated metals, and measuring and testing devices. Low technology industries included frozen food processing, fabricated metal products, leather products, furniture, and rubber and plastics products.

The names and addresses of companies and the two highest-ranking executives have been purchased through commercial on-line services (Hoover's online). We also used the online directory of membership of the American Electronics Association (AeA) as well as published state business directories. We focused on five states that differed in their technological bases and infrastructure but invested heavily in promoting science and technology-based industries. They were California, Georgia, Massachusetts, New York and Texas. The 1700 names were chosen randomly, representing 10% of the companies fewer than 8 years in the 11 industries in these five states.

Two mailings, combined with the use of faxes and e-mail yielded 419 completed responses, a response rate of 24.6%. We sent a second questionnaire to another senior executive in each of the responding ventures, yielding responses from 103 companies. We used responses from the two managers to establish inter-rater reliability on the study's variables ($r = 0.69$, $p < 0.001$). Finally, we compared data from secondary (AeA Online Membership Directory, company websites and online publications) and survey sources to ensure that the survey data were valid, as reported later in the "measures" section. These results supported the validity of the survey data.

Response rates for new venture-related survey are notoriously low. Owners are busy building their businesses and do not have the support system needed to respond to surveys. Some owners may not respond simply because they are afraid to share sensitive information with outsiders, including academic researchers. Thus, though the response rate achieved in this research is as good as achieved in other recent studies (for a comparison, Zahra and Bogner 2000), it could have been higher had we secured the support of well-known trade associations or state agencies.

Still, we tested for sample representation using the χ^2 and *t*-tests, using company age, size, location, industry type (low vs. high technology) and, where possible, sales growth. There was no evidence of systematic response bias. Next, an orthogonal factor analysis (with a varimax rotation) yielded in three significant factors, each of which had eigenvalues exceeding 2.0 and explained 10% or more of the variance. These results indicated that the source bias was not a serious concern in the study.

Responding companies ranged between 3 to 9 years (avg = 4.2, sd = 2.8), had 29 employees (sd = 44.67), and reported an overall average sales growth of 14.35% (sd = 16.27). We used the *t*-test to determine if significant differences existed in these attributes between responding and non-responding ventures. All tests were statistically insignificant ($p > 0.05$).

Measures

Using survey and secondary data, we constructed the following measures for the study's variables.

Dependent Variable: Sales Growth
We measured sales growth using the average year-to-year change in new ventures' sales for 3 years. Information was collected through surveys and where possible validated through secondary sources (company websites, newspaper articles and interviews with executives and company publications). We separated domestic from international sales growth because many new ventures have gone international in pursuit of growth opportunities. International sales growth was achieved from a company's international operations over the proceeding three years. Domestic sales were achieved in the US during the same 3-year period. This distinction between domestic and international sales growth made it possible to identify a prominent source of the differences in new ventures' performance: their market definition.

Independent Variables
Included R&D spending, employment of scientists and engineers, R&D portfolio, the number of products, and the use of patents. These variables were measured as follows:

R&D spending. Managers provided data on annual spending as a percent of their company's sales over the preceding 3 years. This measure has been used widely in past research (e.g. Oakey et al. 1988; Zahra 1996a, 1996b). We validated this measure by collecting data from the secondary sources listed earlier for 170 new ventures. Correlations between the data provided by managers and secondary data sources was high and significant ($r = 0.87$, $p < 0.001$).

Scientists and engineers. Managers reported the percentage of their labor force that were dedicated full time to science and engineering activities in their companies, as a percentage of the total labor force (Oakey et al. 1988). We were able to find information from secondary sources for 113 new ventures, using online websites, newspaper articles, and company publications. We correlated these figures with those that were received through the survey and the correlations were significant ($r = 0.66$, $p < 0.001$).

Research portfolio. Managers distributed 100 points between two options that showed the extent to which their companies have used each over the past 3 years. The first was basic R&D, focusing on original research with a goal to advance science but may not have immediate commercial objectives. The second was applied R&D that focused on developing specific products or technologies for market commercialization. This procedure followed Zahra (1996a).

Number of new products. Managers also provided the number of new products, including modification in existing brands and lines, their companies have introduced to the market over the past three-year period (Zahra 1996a, 1996b). We collected data from company websites and *Lexis.Nexis* on new product introductions by 139 new ventures. The simple correlation between data from the survey and secondary data resources was high and significant ($r = 0.82$, $p < 0.001$).

Patents. Managers reported the number of patents their company has secured over the past 3-year period, as done in prior studies (Teece 1986). We collected data (US Patent Office and company websites) on the number of patents held by 201 firms. Correlations between these data and the figures provided by managers were significant ($r = 0.84$, $p < 0.001$).

Control Variables
Analyses controlled for the following two variables:

Company ownership. We controlled this variable by coding independent ventures as 1 and publicly owned ventures as 0. Control for venture ownership was essential because it could influence the types of resources the firm would have, especially its capital, which would influence sales growth. In-formation for this variable came primarily from company websites.

Liquidity. We controlled this variable using the current ratio as a control variable because liquidity could influence investments in technological re-sources. Liquidity was also expected to create the slack resources needed to support experimentation and innovation. Data came from the mail survey as well as company publications, online company newsletters, and websites.

ANALYSIS AND RESULTS

We examined the simple correlations between the study's variables. We also considered variable inflation factors. There was no evidence of multicolin-earity among the study's variables. Next, to test the hypotheses, we ran eight separate regressions based on a combination of three sets of variables (a) source of sales growth (domestic vs. international), (b) venture life cycle status (start-up vs. adolescent), and (c) industry type (low vs. high technol-ogy). The results of these analyses appear in Table 1.

Domestic Sales Growth

As the data in Table 1 show, the results for start-ups competing in low technology industries were marginally significant and only applied research was positively associated with domestic sales growth ($p < 0.05$). The regres-sion equation for adolescent new ventures in low technology industries was significant ($p < 0.01$). Three technological resources were positively and sig-nificantly associated with domestic sales growth: applied R&D ($p < 0.01$), number of new products ($p < 0.01$), and patents ($p < 0.05$). Liquidity was also positively but marginally significant ($p < 0.10$).

The regression equation for high technology start-ups was significant ($p < 0.01$). However, as Table 1 shows, only applied research was positively associated with domestic sales growth ($p < 0.05$). Liquidity was also posi-tively and marginally associated with domestic sales growth ($p < 0.10$). The results for adolescent high technology new ventures were significant ($p < 0.001$). All technological resources were positive and significant: number of engineers and scientists ($p < 0.05$), applied R&D ($p < 0.05$), number of new products ($p < 0.001$), patents ($p < 0.05$), and R&D spending ($p < 0.10$). Li-

Table 1. Regression Results: Effects of Technological Resources on New Ventures Domestic and International Sales Growth.

Industry type	LT	LT	HT	HT	LT	LT	HT	HT
Venture status	S	A	S	A	S	A	S	A
Sales source	D	D	D	D	I	I	I	I
R&D/sales ratio	−0.03	0.07	−0.01	0.14^a	0.02	0.19*	0.27**	0.39**
Engineers/employee ratio	−0.03	0.05	−0.02	0.17*	0.09	−0.00	0.02	0.09
Applied R&D focus	0.11	0.28**	0.09	0.21*	0.17*	0.23*	0.09	0.27*
New product development	0.09	0.31**	0.24*	0.41***	0.19*	0.11	0.12	0.25*
Patents	0.15*	0.23*	−0.04	0.18*	−0.08	0.19*	0.29**	0.18*
Ownership (1 = independent)	0.03	−0.03	0.02	0.07	0.03	0.25*	−0.05	−0.07
Liquidity	0.07	0.11^a	0.13^a	0.19*	−0.10	0.19*	0.18*	0.14^a
Adjusted R^2	0.08	0.15	0.14	0.19	0.09	0.13	0.18	0.22
F-value	1.73^a	4.03***	3.17**	5.31***	1.89	2.98*	2.74*	4.89**

LT = low tech; HT = high tech; S = start up; A = adolescent; D = domestic sales growth; I = international sales growth.
^{a}$p < 0.10$.
*$p < 0.05$.
**$p < 0.01$.
***$p < 0.001$.

quidity was also positively and significantly associated with domestic sales growth ($p < 0.05$).

International Sales Growth

Table 1 indicates that in low technology industries, the regression equation for international sales growth for start-ups was not significant, but the equation was significant for adolescent firms ($p < 0.05$). Focusing on adolescent ventures, R&D spending, applied R&D and patents all had positive and significant coefficients. The remaining independent variables were not significant. Liquidity and a corporate-venture status were both positive and statistically significant.

The regression equation for start-ups in high technology industries was significant ($p < 0.05$). R&D spending and patenting were also significant and positively associated with international sales growth. Liquidity was associated with international sales growth. Finally, the regression equation for adolescent firms competing in high technology companies was also significant ($p < 0.01$). Four technology resources were positive and significant (at $p < 0.05$ or greater): R&D spending, patents, applied R&D, and new product development. Liquidity was marginally significant ($p < 0.10$).

DISCUSSION

Understanding the determinants of NVG is an important research issue in the study of entrepreneurship. While not a goal of every new venture, sales growth has important implications for a company's survival and continued ability to create the resources needed to support its different operations. The availability of slack resources that are created by new ventures' growth often encourage managers to innovate, preserving their companies' leading edge in their markets. Though different tangible and intangible resources might influence sales growth, this study has highlighted the importance of technological resources in this regard. Using the RBV, the study has argued that some technological resources create new opportunities for growth whereas others enable the firm to pursue those opportunities that exist in their domestic and international markets.

Applying the RBV, the study has examined the effects of several technological resources on new ventures' domestic and international growth. The study's results support the key propositions of the RBV by showing that a firm's technological resources can generate a competitive advantage that improves its sales growth. This is particularly true among technology-based ventures in high technology industries. These firms are widely considered as the hotbed of innovation, job creation and strong global competitiveness.

These results add to the growing literature on the RBV where discussions have been mostly theoretical and its limited empirical research has directly tested the key propositions of this perspective. In particular, the results corroborate the importance of technological resources for new ventures' domestic and international sales growth. While not universally consistent with predictions in hypotheses 1 and 2, the results support the study's two hypotheses by showing that the effect of these resources on growth varies between start-ups vs. adolescent firms in low vs. high technology industries.

Comparing the regression across each two consecutive equations in Table 1, we found that adolescent ventures benefit from investing more in R&D as a percent of sales in gaining domestic and international sales. Three out of four of the differences between regression coefficient pairs were statistically significant, consistent with hypothesis 1a. The exception was the comparison between the two groups of ventures in low technology industries and pursuing domestic growth. The results also support hypothesis 1c and 1d on the importance of applied R&D and new product for growth with three out of the four pairs of regression coefficients were in the predicted direction. The results also indicated that two out of four pairs of regression coefficients were statistically different and in the direction predicted in hypothesis 1e about the importance of patents. Finally, the results were not particularly strong in the case of the employment of engineers, raising a question about hypothesis 1b. It would appear that adolescent firms might have developed special routines and skills that allowed them to bundle and deploy their resources differently from their younger and relatively less experienced start-up venture counterparts. These observations reinforced the importance of organizational learning in accumulating and deploying new ventures' technological resources in ways that enhanced growth (Aldrich 2000; Autio, Sapienza and Almeida 2000; Zahra et al. 2000).

The results shown in Table 1 also support hypothesis 2, indicating that the effect of technological resources on the growth of start-ups is different from those observed within adolescent ventures in low vs. high technology industries. We have just summarized these differences in discussing the results for hypothesis 1. It is important to reiterate the need to customize the strategic choice of technological resources with industry conditions in mind. New venture managers who seek to achieve growth at home or abroad, therefore, should understand the strategic imperatives of their industry. This is a challenging task for some new venture managers who do not have the resources and skills to conduct thorough competitive analyses. Moreover, these managers need to learn to compete differently by working around the accepted norms of rivalry in their industry. New ventures often excel by altering the rules of competitive engagement in their industry.

Limitations

Care should be exercised in interpreting the results which might suffer from survivor bias, a common problem in entrepreneurship studies. Also, the analyses do not consider the interrelationships that exist among new ventures' technological resources. The gestalt of these relationships might profoundly influence new ventures' sales growth. The synergy that exists among the various components of a new venture's technological resources might have a significant effect on the way the firm competes and achieves sales growth. The study's short time frame also raises the possibility that the observed patterns of relationships shown in Table 1 might differ across different time periods, reinforcing the need for a longitudinal design in future research. Finally, we have studied a few of the technological resources new ventures have; other tangible and intangible technological and non-technological resources could determine the pace and magnitude of a new venture's sales growth.

Implications for Entrepreneurs and New Venture Managers

The results also emphasize the importance of customizing technological choices at specific stages of new ventures' life cycles. Different stages of the organizational life cycle usually demand different skills and capabilities (Kazanjian and Drazin 1990), the development of which requires the use of different technological resources. The study helps to identify the technological resources that foster growth in two important stages of a firm's evolution. To understand the full range of technological resources that could influence sales growth, entrepreneurs need to conduct environmental and competitive analyses.

Entrepreneurs should be cognizant of the fact that different technological resources drive domestic vs. international growth. Interestingly, the stock of the technological resources new ventures induces these companies' international expansion, allowing them to capitalize on lucrative growth opportunities. With the growing internationalization of high technology new ventures (Zahra et al. 2000), it is important to understand which technological resources improve international sales growth. Deftness in using these various resources could help new ventures map their strategic choices in terms of the pace and scale of international expansion.

Implications for Future Research

The results also suggest several issues for future research. Notably, the definition of technological resources should be expanded to include intangibles, such as reputation and networks. These intangibles might play a significant role in determining the speed of internationalization among high technology new ventures. Firms might leverage their technological resources by bundling them effectively with non-technical resources such as unique administrative processes and systems.

Future studies should also differentiate between biological vs. mechanical types of high technology industries. These two types of industries differ in their structures and systems of innovation, possibly influencing the results reported in this chapter. Innovation in engineering and mechanical industries builds on each other, in a cumulative fashion. This process usually allows new ventures to recoup their R&D investments quickly, make a profit and achieve higher sales growth. Innovation in biology-based industries, however, is often discrete. In these industries, one innovation may not build on others. As a result, companies need to have longer investment horizons, leading to longer lags between the accumulation of technological resources and sales growth.

Researchers need to use and explore other indicators of domestic and international sales growth. The use of the measures of growth in employment, revenue and profits might provide additional insights to the findings reported in Table 1. Future analyses should also consider the appropriate lag effect between the accumulation of technological resources and measures of growth; an issue we did not address in this study. It is likely that the accumulation of certain technological resources will take time to influence the firm's performance. Finally, these analyses should seek to uncover any tradeoffs that might exist between profitability and growth and how new managers venture address these tradeoffs, if they exist.

Our results highlight the importance of the experience in leveraging technological resources in pursuit of sales growth. Therefore, researchers should explore the ways in which new ventures learn, especially about assembling and deploying their resources and how they apply their learning in pursuit of growth. Also, future studies using organizational life cycle models would benefit explicitly from examining the implications of a firm's transition from one stage to the next on learning and the approaches the firm can use to learn about the effective configuration of their technological resources. Since competitive advantage does not result simply from having or owning resources, future analyses should also examine how new managers venture to integrate these resources to create and commercialize innovative products that ensure growth.

CONCLUSION

New ventures play a prominent role in today's economy. Consequently, understanding the factors that spur NVG is an important research issue. Using the RBV of the firm, our results clarify the role of technological resources in promoting domestic and foreign sales growth within start-ups vs. adolescent ventures in low vs. high technology industries. With the growing internationalization and expansion of high technology new ventures, the results invite future research on the accumulation and effective deployment of technological resources for enhancing NVG.

REFERENCES

Aldrich, Howard. 2000. *Organizations Evolving.* New York: Sage.
Alvarez, Sharon A. and Lowell Busenitz. 2001. "The Entrepreneurship of Resource-based Theory." *Journal of Management* 27:755–775.
Autio, Erkko. 2000. "Growth of Technology-Based New Firms." Pp. 329–347 in *The Blackwell Handbook of Entrepreneurship*, edited by D.L. Sexton and H. Landstrom. Oxford, UK: Blackwell Publishers Ltd.
Autio, Erkko, Harry J. Sapienza, and James G. Almeida. 2000. "Effects of Age at Entry, Knowledge Intensity, and Imitability on International Growth." *Academy of Management Journal* 43:909–1014.
Bahrami, Homa and Stuart Evans. 1989. "Strategy Making in High-Technology Firms: The Empiricist Mode." *California Management Review* 31:107–128.
Bantel, Karen. 1998. "Technology-Based, "Adolescent" Firm Configuration: Identification, Context, and Performance." *Journal of Business Venturing* 13:205–230.
Barney, Jay. 1991. "Firm Resources and Sustained Competitive Advantage." *Journal of Management* 17:99–120.
Bloodgood, James, Harry Sapienza, and James G. Almeida. 1996. "The Internationalization of New High-Potential US Ventures: Antecedents and Outcomes." *Entrepreneurship Theory and Practice* 204:61–76.
Conner, Kathleen R. and C.K. Prahalad. 1996. "A Resource-based Theory of the Firm: Knowledge Versus Opportunism." *Organization Science* 7:477–501.
Cooper, Arnold C. 1986. "Entrepreneurship and High Technology." Pp. 153–168 in *The Art and Science of Entrepreneurship*, edited by D.L. Sexton and R.W. Smilor. Cambridge, MA: Ballinger.
Cooper, Arnold C. and Albert V. Bruno. 1977. "Success among High-Technology Firms." *Business Horizons* April: 16–23.
Cooper, Arnold and Timothy Folta. 2000. "Entrepreneurship and High-Technology Clusters." Pp. 349–367 in *The Blackwell Handbook of Entrepreneurship*, edited by D.L. Sexton and H. Landstrom. Oxford, UK: Blackwell Publishers Ltd.
Covin, Jeffrey G., Dennis P. Slevin, and Teresa J. Covin. 1990. "Content and Performance of Growth-Seeking Strategies: A Comparison of Small Firms in High- and Low-Technology Industries." *Journal of Business Venturing* 5:391–412.
Davidsson, Per. and Johan. Wiklund. 2000. "Conceptual and Empirical Challenges in the Study of Firm Growth." Pp. 26–44 in *The Blackwell Handbook of Entrepreneurship*, edited by D.L. Sexton and H. Landstrom. Oxford, UK: Blackwell Publishers Ltd.
Davidsson, Per, Fredrick Delmar, and Johan Wiklund. 2002. "Entrepreneurship as Growth: Growth as Entrepreneurship." Pp. 328–342 in *Strategic Entrepreneurship: Creating a*

New Mindset, edited by M.A. Hitt, R.D. Ireland, S.M. Camp and D.L. Sexton. Oxford, UK: Blackwell.

Davidsson, Per and Johan Wiklund. 2000. "Conceptual and Empirical Challenges in the Study of Firm Growth." in *The Blackwell Handbook of Entrepreneurship*, edited by D. Sexton and H. Landström. Oxford, MA: Blackwell Business.

Deeds, David L., Donna DeCarolis, and James Coombs. 1998. "Firm-specific Resources and Wealth Creation in High-technology Ventures: Evidence from Newly Public Biotechnology Firms." *Entrepreneurship Theory and Practice* 22:55–73.

Delmar, Fredrick, Per Davidsson, and William Gartner. 2003. "Arriving at the High-growth Firm." *Journal of Business Venturing* 18:189–216.

Hanks, Steven H., C.J. Watson, E. Jansen, and Gaylen N. Chandler. 1993. "Tightening the Life-Cycle Construct: A Taxonomic Study of Growth Stage Configurations in High-Technology Organizations." *Entrepreneurship Theory and Practice* 18:5–29.

Hoy, Frank, Patricia P. McDougall, and Derrik E. D'Souza. 1992. "Strategies and Environments of High-Growth Firms." in *The State of the Art of Entrepreneurship*, edited by D.L. Sexton and J.D. Kasarda. Boston, MA: PWS-Kent Publishing Company.

Kazanjian, Robert K. 1988. "Relation of Dominant Problems to Stages of Growth in Technology-Based New Ventures." *Academy of Management Journal* 31:257–279.

Kazanjian, Robert K. and Robert Drazin. 1990. "A Stage-Contingent Model of Design and Growth for Technology Based New Ventures." *Journal of Business Venturing* 5:137–150.

Lambkin, Mary. 1988. "Order of Entry and Performance in New Markets." *Strategic Management Journal* 9:127–140.

McCann, Joseph E. 1991. "Patterns of Growth, Competitive Technology, and Financial Strategies in Young Ventures." *Journal of Business Venturing* 6:189–208.

McGrath, Rita G., Ian C. MacMillan, and S. Venkataraman. 1995. "Defining and Developing Competence: A Strategic Process Paradigm." *Strategic Management Journal* 16:251–275.

McGrath, Rita G., Ian A. MacMillan, and Michael L. Tushman. 1992. "The Role of Executive Team Actions in Shaping Dominant Designs: Towards the Strategic Shaping of Technological Progress." *Strategic Management Journal* 13:137–161.

Miller, Danny. 2003. "An Asymmetry-based View of Advantage: Towards an Attainable Sustainability." *Strategic Management Journal* 24:961–976.

Miller, Alex and Bill Camp. 1985. "Exploring Determinants of Success in Corporate Ventures." *Journal of Business Venturing* 1:87–105.

Nelson, Richard. and Sidney Winter. 1982. *An Evolutionary Theory of Economic Change*. Cambridge, MA: Harvard University Press.

Oakey, Roy, Ray Rothwell, and S. Cooper. 1988. "Defining High-Technology Industries: Some Conceptual and Methodological Observations." in *The Management of Innovation in High Technology Small Firms: Innovation and Regional Development in Britain and the United States*. New York, NY: Quorum Books.

OECD 2002. *Small and Medium Enterprise Outlook*. Paris: OECD.

Penrose, Edith. 1959. *The Theory of Growth of the Firm*. New York: Wiley.

Porter, Michael E. 1980. *Competitive Strategy*. New York: The Free Press.

------. 1985. *Competitive Advantage*. New York: The Free Press.

Roberts, Edward. 1992. "The Success of High-Technology Firms: Early Technological and Marketing Influences." *Interfaces* 22:3–12.

Roberts, Edward B. 1968. "Entrepreneurship and Technology: A Basic Study of Innovators." *Research Management* 11:249–266.

------. 1991. *Entrepreneurs in High Technology*. Cambridge, MA: Oxford University Press.

Singh, Harbir. 1992. "The Evolution of Corporate Capabilities in Emerging Technologies." *Interfaces* 22:13–23.

Teece, David J. 1986. "Profiting from Technological Innovation." *Research Policy* 15:185–305.

Wiklund, Johan. 1998. *Small Firm Growth and Performance: Entrepreneurship and Beyond*. Jönköping: Jönköping International Business School.

Wiklund, Johan, Per Davidsson, and F. Delmar. 2003. "Expected Consequences of Growth and their Effect on Growth Willingness in Different Samples of Small Firms." *Entrepreneurship Theory and Practice* 27:247–269.

Weinzimmer, Laurance G., Paul C. Nystrom, and Sarah J. Freeman. 1998. "Measuring Organizational Growth: Issues, Consequences and Guidelines." *Journal of Management* 24:235–262.

Zahra, Shaker A. 1996a. "Technology Strategy and New Venture Performance: A Study of Corporate-sponsored and Independent Biotechnology Ventures." *Journal of Business Venturing* 11:289–321.

------. 1996b. "Technology Strategy and Financial Performance: Examining the Moderating Role of the Firm's Competitive Environment." *Journal of Business Venturing* 11:189–219.

Zahra, Shaker A. and William Bogner. 2000. "Technology Strategy and Software New Venture Performance: The Moderating Effect of the Competitive Environment." *Journal of Business Venturing* 15:135–173.

Zahra, Shaker A. and Jeffrey G. Covin. 1993. "Business Strategy, Technology Policy and Company Performance." *Strategic Management Journal* 14:451–478.

Zahra, Shaker A. and James Hayton. 2004. "Technological Entrepreneurship: Current Debates and Emerging Research Issues." Pp. 185–207 in *Emerging Research Issues in Entrepreneurship*, edited by G. Corbatta, D. Ravsie and M. Huse. Amsterdam: Kluwer Publishers in press.

Zahra, Shaker A., Duane R. Ireland, and Michael Hitt. 2000. "International Expansion, Technological Learning and New Venture Performance." *Academy of Management Journal* 43:925–950.

MANAGEMENT PARADIGM CHANGE IN THE UNITED STATES: A PROFESSIONAL AUTONOMY PERSPECTIVE

Bruce C. Skaggs and Kevin T. Leicht

ABSTRACT

The social organization of work has become more entrepreneurial and less bureaucratic over the past 20 years. How is this development consistent with managerial control over the labor process? This paper develops a professional autonomy perspective to explain the acceptance of new management ideas in the United States, including the recent turn away from bureaucratic organizational forms. The focus on professional autonomy helps to create a theoretical link between past and current managerial practices, including the latest anti-bureaucratic phase that we label neo-entrepreneurialism. We conclude by exploring future research implications of studying managerial practice from a professional autonomy perspective.

INTRODUCTION

Any way you look at it, the organization of work has changed in fundamental ways over the past 25 years. The stable job in the midst of a

Entrepreneurship
Research in the Sociology of Work, Volume 15, 123–149
Copyright © 2005 by Elsevier Ltd.
All rights of reproduction in any form reserved
ISSN: 0277-2833/doi:10.1016/S0277-2833(05)15006-7

corporate bureaucracy, complete with steady and rising earnings, generous fringe benefits, regular promotions, and lifetime work commitment is giving way to a just-in-time, contingent, outsourced, globalized, telecommuted, and subcontracted job populated by contingent workers. In place of simple sets of long-term rules that virtually guaranteed success there are "career consultants," "investment consultants," and "life consultants" to tell us how to read the tea leaves of our complex and globalized labor market.

Regardless of where you work in the United States or the rest of the developed world, entrepreneurship in – bureaucracy is out. Self-employment and small business ownership have reached unprecedented highs (U.S. Census Bureau 2003). Business magazines and newspapers repeatedly tout the different roads to independence where you dictate your own terms and conditions of work, market yourself as an entrepreneur who provides sub-contracted services, and control your own destiny (see, for example Pennington 2004).

There is no place where this shift is more apparent than in the development of management thought and practice. Management thought provides a cultural rhetoric for interpreting workplace change and provides templates and courses of action for reacting to new organizational environments. Though the advent of new technology can influence aspects of work, the application of new technology causes change in work organization (see, for example Barley 1986). Instead of seeing the embrace of entrepreneurial organizational forms as a radical break with the past, we think that much of 20th century management history can be viewed through the lens of professional autonomy.

The present paper examines the historical development of management paradigms in the United States by combining insights from principal-agent models, transaction-cost theories, resource dependence theories, and research on the development of professions into an autonomy-based perspective of managerial acceptance of new ideas and practices. This perspective provides for continuity with past accounts of managerial actions and motives by refocusing the description around the professional project of managers as an occupational group. Changes in management paradigms result from managers' desire to maintain professional autonomy in light of changing relationships with employees and owners. Managerial autonomy is altered by environmental shocks that (in part) result from attempts by significant stakeholders to change firm-specific uncertainties in response to prior managerial actions.

We begin by outlining the basic elements of our professional autonomy perspective. We apply this perspective to successive historical shifts in management paradigms. Using managerial autonomy as a sensitizing concept, we then advance tentative ideas of what the next management paradigm will look like. We label this new paradigm *neoentrepreneurialism.* Finally, we discuss the organizational and research implications of this new managerial paradigm.

We should say a few words about the scope of our paper. First, our intention is not to explore every event that could affect managerial paradigm change over the past 150 years. Instead, we want to focus on the sensitizing concept of professional autonomy to enlarge our understanding of managerial paradigm change and to provide continuity with prior explanations of managerial behavior (see Chandler 1977; Burawoy 1985; Barley and Kunda 1992). Instead of offering a theory that is ready for validation, we offer an alternate *perspective* on historical events affecting management paradigm change. By viewing managerial history through the lens of professional autonomy, we hope to aid management scholars and social scientists in generating more elaborate and testable theory concerning the phenomenon of paradigm change and provide insights into the current appeal of debureaucratized, neoentrepreneurial organizational forms.

PROFESSIONAL AUTONOMY AND PROFESSIONAL PROJECTS

Our perspective draws from several organizational theories to explain changes in management paradigms. We suggest that all of these insights combine to produce a relatively coherent, professional autonomy-based view of management paradigm change. Our perspective deals with three interest groups in work organizations: investors and employees (whom we label "significant stakeholders"), and managers. A central dynamic involved in explaining shifts in managerial paradigms is the professional project of managers as an occupational group. A *professional project* is a set of activities that attempt to define and defend an occupation's task domain from competing occupational groups and the actions of immediate workplace stakeholders (see Abbott 1988). A *profession* (for our purposes) is an occupational group whose knowledge base is linked to theories and complex intellectual ideas and whose status and prestige is based on the relationship between occupational tasks and key societal values (see Wilensky 1964; Leicht and Fennell 2001). The profession defines the occupational group whose incumbents are deemed worthy of societal rewards for performing important and complex tasks. Professional projects describe how professional incumbents (and their professional associations) defend the profession's task domain from encroachment by the would-be competitors.

Management as a Professional Project

According to Freidson (1986) and Abbott (1988) most professional projects attempt to (1) enhance the autonomy and freedom of action for occupational members under a set of well-defined professional prerogatives (Freidson, 1986); and, (2) defend a specific task domain from encroachment by competing occupational groups and stakeholders (Abbott, 1988). Drawing on this literature, we suggest that the professional project of managers would involve (1) attempts to increase their freedom of action within the firm and (2) a defense of their task domain against encroachment by competing occupational groups and organizational stakeholders (i.e. employees and owners).

Using professional autonomy as the lens for viewing paradigm change, there are two major factors that affect freedom of action in the managerial task domain. One of these factors is environmental shocks (Barley and Kunda 1992). Events in the external environment such as industrialization, government action, and the globalization of markets affect the autonomy of managers within firms. The second factor is the action of significant stakeholders (i.e. investors and employees). Borrowing from resource dependence theory, employees and investors are motivated to reduce their dependence/uncertainty surrounding future employment and returns from specific firms (Pfeffer and Salancik 1978). The avoidance of firm-specific uncertainty is a specific type of dependency avoidance behavior. Firm-specific dependence refers to the exposure of an organizational stakeholder to the performance variation of a single firm.

For employees, firm-specific dependence increases with investments in firm-specific human capital. For investors, firm-specific dependence means investment exposure to a single firm. Investors expose themselves to firm-specific dependencies by investing heavily in firm-specific assets that are not easily convertible to other uses without incurring significant transaction costs. As these stakeholders move to reduce firm-specific dependence, their actions may affect managers' professional autonomy. In response, managers adopt rationales to protect their task domain.

In summary, historical changes in management paradigms can be viewed as the product of professional projects by managers attempting to increase their freedom of action in response to environmental shocks and stake-holder actions. In the section that follows, we begin by discussing the organizational landscape as it existed in the United States during much of the 1800s. From there, we examine the increase of successive managerial paradigms (scientific management, human relations management, and human resource management) through the sensitizing lens of professional autonomy. (The dates of the various paradigms are approximations, though they are derived in large part from Wren 1994.) We then discuss the next management paradigm, *neoentrepreneurialism* and discuss the organizational implications of this emerging management ideology. A brief outline of our historical argument and a graphic representation of our model are provided in Table 1 and Fig. 1, respectively.

ENTREPRENEURIALISM, 1860–1910

Around the mid-19th century, sole proprietorships were the predominant form of firm ownership in the United States. Corporate organizational forms existed but their use was limited to public works ventures (Hurst 1970). Most businesses were owned and managed by the same person who supplied much if not all of the investment capital (Berle and Means 1932). The owner possessed a completely undiversified portfolio; return on capital was dependent on the success of their entrepreneurial venture.

The dominant form of employee organization was the inside contract (see Stone 1974; Littler 1982). Entrepreneurs would contract with individual craft workers to perform different operations associated with the production process. The craft worker would then hire assistants to actually perform the operations outlined in the contract. In sharp contrast to the entrepreneur, who was invested heavily in a single firm where ownership and management were lodged in the same individual, craft workers possessed vital human capital skills that were portable. While craft workers were never the dominant occupational group in terms of employment (Form 1987), their skills were critical to the production process (see Marglin 1974; Stone 1974). Craft workers bore few transaction costs in transferring their skills to different employers (see Montgomery 1979). Entrepreneurs were invested heavily in specific firms. Craft workers were not.

Towards the end of the century, the capital demands of rapid industrialization required larger investments than the individual entrepreneurs could manage. As a result, the corporate form was beginning to emerge as the preferred arrangement in for-profit enterprises (Berle and Means 1932).

Table 1. Factors Contributing to Paradigm Change.

	Scientific Management	Human Relations Management	Human Resource Management	Neoentrepreneurialism
External shocks which lead to paradigm	Growing capital requirements with rising industrialization	Great Depression Labor legislation Immigration and urbanization	Change in capital markets to promote stability and efficiency Declining unionization Portfolio investment theory Rise of top managers from finance backgrounds	Rising global competition Skilled labor diversification Steep declines in unionization among employees Further investment diversification Management compensation ties to short-term stock fluctuation
Change in managerial autonomy	Dependence on skilled workers and/or subcontractors	Legislation-sponsored increases in union bargaining power Constraints on employment-at-will Growth in collective bargaining	Human relations approach is not isomorphic with portfolio investment theory Placated employee no longer necessary	Rapid capital movement Reduced environmental beneficence Competition for skilled workers
Management action	Time and motion studies Job redesign Replacement of skilled workers and/or subcontractors with unskilled workers	Greater focus on human behavior and interaction within the firm Employee-centered supervision Concern for employee needs Internal labor markets	Treating employees as human capital (similar to physical capital) Conglomerate is managed as a portfolio of investments Performance goals are thrust on enterprise managers Parts of conglomerates are acquired and discarded	Hiring temporary workers Contingent workforce Subcontracting Network organizations Outsourcing

			Bureaucratic employment practices		
Change in stakeholders' level of dependence	Loss of knowledge monopoly by skilled workers	Expanded pool of potential employees Greater labor market discipline	An initial decrease in employee firm-specific uncertainty, though this becomes reversed with the onset of ILMs	Firm-specific risk rises for SBU employees	Greater firm-specific dependency for unskilled employees
			Increase in investor risk due to uncertainties surrounding production	Employees with marketable skills begin "opting-out" of traditional employment contracts	Skilled workers continue to reduce firm-specific dependencies by diversifying contractual ties
Change in stakeholder action	Rising support for unionization		Employees begin unionising at first, though union support declines as ILMs become more prevalent		
		Investor incorporation Lower employee investment in human capital	Investor diversification		

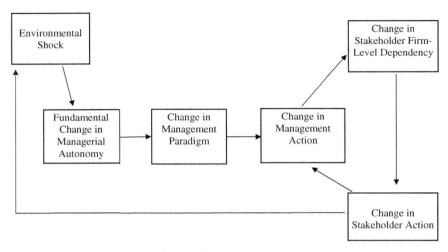

Fig. 1. A Model of Paradigmatic Change.

The corporate form of capital structure divided property rights, separating the suppliers of capital from those who acted on their behalf. This split produced the professional domain that came to be occupied by managers (Abbott 1988; Berle and Means 1932). The other effect of this particular shift in capital structure was a decrease in investors' dependence on the performance of a single firm. The owners of the firm were able to reduce some of their dependence on the firm while continuing to maintain some control over the firm's decisions (Fligstein 1990).

However, financial markets were in a rather embryonic stage of development. The free flow of financial capital that we take for granted was relatively nonexistent. The number of stocks available on stock exchanges were few (Berle and Means 1932; Hurst 1970). These environmental factors made the purchase of stock in a company rather risky. Though the corporate form did serve to reduce some investor uncertainty, individual investors were still exposed to high levels of firm-specific dependence as they were affected by the market fortunes of particular firms.

On the shop floor, entrepreneurs possessed little or no knowledge of how jobs were performed. The skills required to perform necessary tasks were largely controlled by craft guilds or learned through apprenticeship from other craft workers (Wren 1994). Due to the almost proprietary nature of craft knowledge, employees possessed a great deal of freedom and mobility (Stone 1974; Littler 1982). Craft workers were independent entrepreneurial contractors. Owners' reliance on skilled workers served to increase their firm-specific dependence.

FROM ENTREPRENEURIALISM TO SCIENTIFIC MANAGEMENT, 1910–1940

Ownership in a firm has always carried a certain degree of risk. Much of that risk result from the owners' dependence on employees. As the demands of industrialization began to affect owners in the late 19th century, the relationship between investors and workers began to change as well. As firms grew and investors were less involved in the day-to-day operations of specific firms, managers became a vital intermediary representing the interests of owners in the production process. Managers began looking for ideologies and paradigms that would allow them to stake out and defend a professional domain. At the same time investors sought to tie compensation schemes for managers to returns on their investments so that the interests of managers and investors would coincide (see Edwards 1979). But both groups were dependent on mobile and skilled human capital. In order to obviate this dependence and gain professional autonomy, managers turned to scientific management.

Frederick Taylor, the father of scientific management, believed production inefficiencies were due to variations in work methods. Taylor (1903, 1911) felt that these inefficiencies could be reduced by studying the work process itself. Systematic study would yield insights into the most efficient production methods. Managers would record these procedures for the purposes of training their present and future employees. With all of the workers following standardized procedures based on the conservation of time and motion, worker productivity would increase.

Although the rapid growth of Taylor's ideas can be attributed to the productivity concerns of investors, another reason for the quick acceptance of this method was that scientific management reduced managers' reliance on skilled employees and increased their professional autonomy. Scientific management broke the knowledge monopoly of skilled contractors. Though scientific management did increase managerial dependence on unskilled employees, this dependence was less onerous because unskilled workers were more easily replaceable. The new written and formalized procedures gave managers the ability to train workers themselves. This allowed managers to make greater productivity, hours, and wage demands which served to stabilize the production process. Managers could now lessen their dependence on skilled employees while reducing the uncertainty of returns to investors. Both changes increased their would-be professional autonomy.

FROM SCIENTIFIC MANAGEMENT TO HUMAN RELATIONS, 1940–1970

Beginning around 1910 and continuing throughout the 1930s, scientific management became a major guide to managerial thought and practice in the United States (Wren 1994). But by the mid-1920s, the social structure of work in the United States was changing. Millions of Americans were leaving firms and moving to cities (see Bogue 1959). This, combined with the continued immigration of foreigners into metropolitan areas (Bogue 1959), had a dramatic affect on the dependency relationship of workers. As the available labor force for factory work increased, the bargaining power of employees declined. With less ability to make wage or job security demands, and with heightened competition for jobs, employees found themselves increasingly dependent on specific firms.

While scientific management and changes in the social structure of work were altering employees' dependence on the firm, the Great Depression would have monumental affects on all three constituents. In the early 1930s, the unemployment rate in the U.S. rose to approximately 25%. Congress expressed concern for the plight of workers by passing the Norris-La Guardia Act in 1932. This Act strictly limited the use of injunctions against unions and outlawed the use of "yellow-dog" contracts (contracts stating that the worker could not join a labor union as a condition for employment). Though managers now enjoined judicial protection from strikes and boycotts, the loopholes in the Act and the economic climate of the depression meant that they could merely dismiss striking workers and replace them with others at a lower wage (Cihon and Castagnera 1988).

In 1933, the National Industrial Recovery Act (NRA) contained sections specifically intended to address these issues. When the Supreme Court found the NRA unconstitutional in 1935, Congress moved that same year to pass the Wagner Act, otherwise known as the National Labor Relations Act (NLRA). The concern of Congress was again with the power of employees relative to employers. This is exemplified by Senator Wagner's opening remarks before debate on amendments to the bill, where he stated:

> It [the NLRA] is the next step in the logical unfolding of man's eternal quest for freedom.... [W]ith economic problems occupying the center of the stage, we strive to liberate

man from destitution, from insecurity, and from human exploitation.... In this modern aspect of a time-worn problem the isolated worker is a plaything of fate. Caught in the labyrinth of modern industrialism and dwarfed by the size of corporate enterprise, he can attain freedom and dignity only by cooperation with others of his group (Congressional Record, 1935: 7565).

Meanwhile investors continued to reduce their dependence on specific firms by pursuing the corporate organizational form. Although far from perfect, corporate formation did allow investors to continue to decrease their financial liability in the firm. Congress' recognition of this dependency differential between employees and investors can be found in the pre-amendment wording of Section 1 of the NLRA:

> The inequality of bargaining power between employer and individual employees...arises out of the organization of employers in corporate forms of ownership and out of numerous other modern industrial conditions... (Congressional Record 1935: 9717).

The corporate organizational form changed the relative dependence of employees and investors on specific firms, increasing employee dependence and drastically decreasing investor's dependence. And in 1937, when the Supreme Court upheld the constitutionality of the NLRA, it signified the first time that both the judicial and legislative branches were in agreement regarding employees' increased dependence on large corporations.

The timing of this convergence of views in no small way reflects the economic environment of the early 20th century (1920–1944). The growth of the corporate form was reducing the number of potential employers in the labor market. In 1909 there was one small manufacturing firm for every 250 people in the United States; by 1929 there was only one for every 900 people. The increase in the ratio of people-to-firms (partially) was the result of the growth in the corporate form (from the speech of Senator Wagner, Congressional Record 1935) as well as immigration and the movement of labor from farms to the cities (see Bogue 1959). These developments served to increase the firm-specific dependence of employees.

The Liabilities of Scientific Management in a New Institutional Environment

With the Supreme Court's 1937 decision to uphold the constitutionality of the Wagner Act, the employment relationship changed dramatically. This was an external shock that affected the professional autonomy of managers. Employment-at-will was no longer the only doctrine that governed the association between the employer and the employee. Instead, unionization and collective bargaining became options available to workers. With the advent of forced bargaining, union contracts, and strike funds, employees decreased their level of exposure to firm-specific uncertainties. Further, government restrictions on managers' ability to bargain and terminate employees had the effect of increasing the degree of uncertainty associated with investment in a firm, as volatility in earnings were now more likely. As this uncertainty increased, so did the possibility of heightened investor scrutiny of managerial decisions, another potential infringement on managerial autonomy.

The external shock of these legal changes led managers to realize that their current management practices would be unable to nullify these new intrusions on their professional autonomy. Scientific management was an excellent method for managers to establish and defend their professional domain when it was threatened by a lack of knowledge of job skills and work processes. But it offered very little help against legislated union bargaining power. As the 1930s came to a close, managers were searching for a new rationale to regain their professional autonomy. One of the fruits of that search was the human relations approach.

Enter the Human Relations Paradigm

Although it is often identified with the Hawthorne studies in 1929, the human relations approach would not find its way into the management mainstream until the mid-1940s (Sherman and Bohlander 1992; Wren 1994). Unlike scientific management's focus on production efficiency, the human relations approach focused on aspects of human behavior as these affected the firm. One area of attention focused on manager's ability to be sensitive to the needs and feelings of their employees and to recognize the individual differences among them. This approach also emphasized the need for increased worker participation and employee-centered supervision (Sherman and Bohlander 1992; Wren 1994).

The human relations approach was radically different from its pre-decessor that stressed the use of time–motion studies to achieve uniformity and maximum efficiency. This extreme shift in emphasis was an attempt on the part of managers to regain professional autonomy. Given the prevailing legal environment of the late 1930s, the use of scientific management would only exacerbate existing tensions between managers and employees. It would increase the uncertainty of continued, stable profits and heighten investor scrutiny of managerial decision making. What managers needed, given labor's increased power in organizational matters, was a method that would appease workers in order to prevent them from exercising their newly created rights.

This attempt at appeasement was embodied in the human relations approach to management. By focusing on such areas as the needs and feelings of workers, managers could hopefully avoid any costly confrontations (Bendix 1956; Braverman 1974) and stabilize firm output (Gillespie 1991). This would have the effect of reducing labors' power, decreasing investors' scrutiny of managerial actions, and restoring managerial autonomy.

FROM HUMAN RELATIONS TO HUMAN RESOURCE MANAGEMENT, 1970–2000

From the passage of the Wagner Act to the late 1950s, unionization in the United States increased rapidly. In 1935, 13.2% of the nonagricultural work force was unionized; by 1960 this figure had grown to over 30% (Hamermesh and Rees 1988). After 1960 these percentages began falling (Freeman and Medoff 1984; Hamermesh and Rees 1988). Researchers have provided numerous explanations for this decline from continued government intervention and the institutionalization of union efforts to successful "union-busting" on behalf of corporations (Cihon and Castagnera 1988; Hamermesh and Rees 1988). As union membership began decreasing after 1960, the bargaining power of employees started to decline as well. We contend that this loss in power gave managers greater freedom of action in organizational matters. Union decline combined with three other developments to foster the development of human resource management.

The Development of Internal Labor Markets

The internal labor market (ILM) consists of well-defined job ladders, with movement up these ladders dependent upon the acquisition of firm-specific skills (cf. Pfeffer and Cohen 1984). The development of ILMs was the result of complex institutional and environmental interactions between government intervention in manpower activities, industrial unions, and growing personnel departments (Baron, Dobbin and Jennings 1986). Industrial unions were ambivalent about some aspects of ILMs – many of the provisions that increased management's control over the work process protected workers from layoffs and arbitrary treatment (see Baron et al. 1986; Gordon, Edwards, and Reich 1982).

ILMs altered the firm-specific dependence of employees in a dramatic fashion. An employee joins the organization at a particular point-of-entry and moves up the organization by way of a highly defined job ladder. As workers progress through the organization, they acquire skills that tend to be highly firm-specific (Pfeffer and Cohen 1984). Workers are tied to their current organization because movement to new organizations would result in decreased wages because the skills accrued at the old firm would not be transferable to the new one. The development of ILMs throughout the 1960s caused the welfare of many employees to become highly dependent on the success of their current workplace.

One could also argue that ILMs increase the dependence of managers and investors on firm-specific human capital. It is true that ILMs do increase the reliability and predictability of relationships between investors, managers and employees. But ILMs do not keep investors from moving their financial capital to other locations and ILMs give managers a stable labor pool to draw from.

The Rise of Portfolio Investment Strategies

Concurrent with the growth of ILMs, other events were unfolding that would dramatically affect investors' exposure to firm-specific uncertainties. Post-depression regulations made the stock market much more efficient in terms of access to information, reducing the risk associated with stock ownership. The expansion in the number of stocks traded and the number of companies available for purchase further reduced the firm-specific dependence of investors by increasing capital mobility.

An important event in decreasing the dependence of investors came in 1952, when Harry Markowitz published his work on portfolio selection. Markowitz (1952) hypothesized that by focusing on the standard deviations of stocks, as well as the covariance between them and the market, investors could diversify away nearly all the firm-specific risk inherent in any one stock, exposing themselves only to the risk of the overall market. With portfolio investment tools, investors could now exercise control over a number of firms without being exposed to the risk of any one.

Shifts in the Backgrounds of Top Corporate Executives

By the 1970s, managerial autonomy was increasing as workers became immersed in firm-specific ILMs and investors were shedding firm-specific uncertainties by diversifying their portfolios. These changes were accompanied by a shift in the backgrounds of top executives. Prior to the 1970s, the ranks of top management were filled with individuals whose training and corporate background involved marketing, sales, and engineering. Beginning in the 1970s, a growing number of top executives with finance backgrounds were being selected for key positions in organizations (Fligstein 1990). As this cadre of managers grew, portfolio investment theory began to emerge as the organizing mechanism for large firms (see Fligstein 1990).

This change in organizing principles and backgrounds of top executives produced a major split within the managerial ranks. The human relations paradigm was built from a different set of principles that were not isomorphic with the new financial tools of top management. The human relations paradigm was designed to pacify employees in response to newly created union power. But decreasing union ranks and ILMs were making this pacification unnecessary. These occurrences, along with the conflict in ideology between top executives and mid-level personnel managers, led to the rise of human resource management.

Enter the Human Resource Management Paradigm

Human resource management reflects the underlying tenets of portfolio theory as practiced by top managers. The decision by top managers to diversify was based on the notion that the whole was more important than the individual parts of the organization. Top managers would add and discard firms based on their financial contribution to the overall corporation, while the welfare of the individual firms under the corporate umbrella was of secondary importance. Human resource management viewed employees in a similar fashion. Workers were no longer seen as important in and of themselves (as in the human relations approach). Rather, the employees were viewed in the context of their contribution to the specific firm with decisions to add or discard employees reflecting this heuristic (Sherman and Bohlander 1992; Wren 1994).

Though this is a far cry from the previous perspective where worker satisfaction was of paramount concern, this shift from human relations to human resource management was a reaction to environmental changes affecting the professional autonomy of managers. Managers, whose future was increasingly tied to the performance of the individual firms they managed (see Donaldson 1963), sought to reduce their dependence on specific employees and make the employment relationship more predictable

(Monsen and Downs 1965). They further sought to align their managerial paradigm with the dominant paradigm of portfolio investment theory as articulated by the new cadre of top managers. The increase in the use of ILMs and the decrease in the strength of unions made this possible. Most of the changes involved in the shift from human relations to human resource management were invisible to non-supervisory employees on a day-to-day basis. What did change slowly was the implied contract between managers and employees regarding their place within the larger corporation.

When viewed in historical context, the paradigmatic shift from human relations to human resource management was an attempt by firm-level managers to enhance their professional autonomy. As top managers in conglomerate corporations continued to manage using the "corporation-as-portfolio" model, the productivity of the workforce at the firm level became of paramount importance to firm level managers. If the productivity of a particular firm within the conglomerate began to decline, the inclination on the part of top-level managers would be either divestiture or liquidation. In order to remain in the conglomerate, firm-level managers needed a continually productive workforce; this constraint affected the autonomy of firm-level managers. Human resource management supplied the analytical tool necessary for firm-level managers to obviate much of this impact and regain their autonomy. However, this new paradigm would make the employment relationship much more dynamic.

NEOENTREPRENEURIALISM: THE EMERGENCE OF A NEW PARADIGM

At present, the human resource management perspective is the dominant paradigm governing the relationship between organizational constituents. It is practiced in some form virtually in every major firm in the United States and taught nearly in every business school. But the conditions that led to the rise of this paradigm in the 1970s have changed substantially; environmental forces have continued to alter the relationship between the organizational stakeholders. In this section, we will discuss the current state of these relationships. The changes over the past 30 years (since the adoption of human resource management) have affected managerial autonomy to such a degree that a new paradigm is poised to emerge. We call this new paradigm *neoentrepreneurialism*.

The trends that gave rise to the human resource management approach in the 1970s have continued over the past two decades, further altering the relationships among organizational constituents. Unionization now stands at roughly 9.2% of the non-governmental and the non-agricultural labor force (Baird 1990; United States Bureau of Census 2003). Investors have continued to diversify their holdings to the point where they bear almost no firm-specific risk. The existence of the "corporation-as-portfolio" model of managing corporate assets has tied managerial compensation to gains in stock prices at a time when investor control over specific firms has been drastically reduced (Fligstein 1990).

Global competition has altered the dependence exposure of investors, employees, and managers as well. In the 1970s, global markets were in a rather embryonic stage of development. U.S. firms were relatively unaffected by international competition. Today, with the creation of the EC, NAFTA, and GATT, global markets have become much more efficient. Investor returns are no longer tied to firms in specific countries. Further, the conditions of global competition favor factions of management who lessen their dependence on investments in high-wage labor (see Fligstein 1990). This has had the effect of forcing US firms to adapt to global economic changes more quickly.

Financial and physical capital has not had many problems adapting to the demands of global competition. Managers can sell off units, move their products to another market, or transfer funds from one area of the world to another, all in order to achieve higher investment returns. Human capital has not adapted so easily. Employees cannot be effortlessly transferred from one area of the world to another. The response of human resource managers to globalization was to dismantle ILMs and make rapid staffing changes in response to global market competition.

Skilled Knowledge-Intensive Labor is Opting Out

In response to this uncertainty, a split is occurring in the employee ranks. In order to obviate firm-specific dependence, high-skilled employees have begun "opting-out" of traditional employment contracts (see Handy 1989). Instead of remaining beholden to a particular firm, these workers are beginning to resemble independent contractors with renewable contracts, or in some cases multiple contracts with various firms. This action by high-skilled labor is an attempt to reduce their dependence on specific firms in the face of managerial staffing actions (e.g. downsizing, outsourcing). However, the effect this has on managerial autonomy is rather pronounced. In the present economy, managers need high-skilled labor for their firms in order to compete effectively; but global competition favors firms who lessen dependence on high-wage labor (see Fligstein 1990). The human resource management paradigm worked well for managers throughout the 1980s and 1990s as managers could alter staffing levels depending on the demands of the global market. But when high-skilled labor began opting out of traditional employment contracts, a firm's pool of this type of resource became less predictable. This volatility served to reduce managerial freedom of action.

With the dramatic changes in the relationships among managers and significant stakeholders over the past 20 years, we believe that the U.S. is on the verge of entering into a new paradigm of employment relations. The impetus for such a movement is the change in managerial autonomy resulting from reduced environmental slack associated with global competition and the managerial staffing actions that resulted from it. These actions permanently altered employment relationships as employment became more temporary and contingent (see Sherman and Bohlander 1992). Human resource management is ill-equipped to handle these changes because it will only continue to exacerbate tensions between managers and high-skilled labor, causing further reductions in managerial autonomy. What managers need is a new paradigm of employment relations that grants greater autonomy to managers in the face of environmental changes and stakeholder actions.

Enter Neoentrepreneurialism

Neoentrepreneurialism is a change in the mindset of the employment relationship where workers are viewed not as employees but as independent contractors. This new paradigm is the result of managements' desire to attract high skilled, high-wage labor in a manner that allows managers to respond quickly to fluctuations in the global market. By constructing the employment relationship in this manner, managers are able to tap into larger pools of skilled labor, thereby making staffing more predictable. By designing employment contracts to be project and time specific, managers preserve their flexibility of action in firm-level decisions. As a result of this paradigm, growing numbers of firms, skilled workers, and investors are in networks of contractual relationships that resemble a diversified investor's stock portfolio. Workers with different types of skilled human capital will return to their former entrepreneurial status as "inside contractors" with groups of investors and small firms housed under a loosely coupled corporate umbrella (Boyett and Conn 1992; Handy 1989; Leicht and Fennell 2001).

The Implications of Neoentrepreneurialism

Neoentrepreneurialism will have profound effects on two specific actors within the organizations: mid-level managers and unskilled workers. The role of mid-level managers under neoentrepreneurialism will almost completely disappear. These functions either will be outsourced like the remaining skilled human capital or will be eliminated entirely as supervisory requirements are reduced. The key issue for the managers that remain will be their ability to motivate and coordinate a temporary and contingent workforce whose composition may change from job to job (Handy 1989).

Neoentrepreneurialism will profoundly affect organizational culture as well. With temporary arrangements for both high- and low-skilled employees (the former through contracting and the latter through turnover and termination), the existence of a distinctive corporate culture will be difficult to maintain at best. Indeed, this new paradigm leads one to question whether the cultivation of an organizational culture is even desirable. Given the flexibility that organizations require in responding to global competition, notions of loyalty and commitment may only serve to impede a firm's adaptability.

For unskilled workers, the result of this new, evolving management paradigm will be quite different. Unskilled workers may return to their role as "assistants" to skilled workers, a position, a vast majority of factory workers occupied in the 19th century. Here, there will be little but the continued creation of temporary, unskilled work with low pay and few benefits. Under neoentrepreneurialism, only those with human or financial capital are enfranchised players in the system. Actors without human or financial capital may see little in the way of firm investment in their future and (in some cases) work will be subcontracted to offshore facilities (Boyett and Conn 1992).

This perspective also has implications for management as a professional project. The development of neoentrepreneurialism represents a definitive step in the direction of permanently professionalizing management. The rapid development of business consulting and fee-for-service compensation that is the hallmark of the subcontracting process represents the definitive step in the direction of further professionalization for management (see also

Leicht and Lyman forthcoming). Indeed, one can see this development placing professionalized managers on par with physicians and lawyers in their ability to establish and maintain independent, fee-for-service practice delivery to corporate clients. In this sense, personnel management under neoentrepreneurialism may be headed in the same direction as auditing services in accounting.

Our explanation of the development of managerial paradigms also has implications for Williamson's (1975) transaction-cost perspective of the development of hierarchies within firms. In Williamson's perspective, hierarchies and bureaucracy develop because of the high transaction costs involved in monitoring contracts in situations where actors have incentives to act opportunistically or where the ability to negotiate favorable contracts is impaired by small numbers bargaining. From our perspective transaction costs are a form of firm-specific dependence that affects managerial autonomy. Managers act to reduce these transaction costs by altering the makeup of the human capital they use in their firms. Attempts to lessen dependence on skilled human capital may be viewed in this light.

However, the attempt to reduce this dependence occurs at the same time as the ability to monitor transactions is drastically improving (largely through the development of computers and information technology). Given that the ability to measure individual and group performance in a timely fashion has risen drastically, and that flexible manufacturing technologies and relatively short, specialized production runs have reduced asset specificity for firms, markets can now more easily discipline deviant performers. In short, we envision the Williamson process of hierarchy creation "running in reverse" because many of the original conditions that led to the gradual creation of hierarchies are disappearing.

How does our perspective compare with prior perspectives on changes in management ideas and behavior?

PROFESSIONAL AUTONOMY IN CONTRAST TO OTHER EXPLANATIONS OF EMERGING MANAGERIAL THOUGHT AND ACTION

While we consider ours a critical approach to the study of management paradigm change, the professional autonomy approach does differ in important ways from more traditional critical approaches to the evolution of managerial activity (see Edwards 1979; Burawoy 1985). Our approach also differs significantly from functionalist approaches to management change (see Chandler 1977; Barley and Kunda 1992). Though our perspective has much in common with these, it differs on a number of issues. These past approaches to paradigm change either down-play the role of certain stakeholders in favor of others (e.g. Braverman 1974), dismiss the actions of all stakeholders as pre-determined moves in the face of macro-sociological forces (e.g. Barley and Kunda 1992) and/or view process control and efficiency as the only motives governing managers (cf., Chandler 1977). We believe that these assumptions limit the explanative power of their theoretical models. Our approach to management paradigm change relaxes these assumptions by granting greater agency to organizational actors.

Critical Approaches Compared to the Professional Autonomy Perspective

Critical writers from neo-Marxist perspectives focus on the *increase in managerial control* as the central thrust in the evolution of management action (see Burawoy 1985; Edwards 1979; Marglin 1974). Here, managers act as agents of capital to extract profits from the disciplined labor of workers (see Marglin 1974). Edwards' (1979) historical descriptions of the evolution of managerial control correspond to different solutions to the problem of disciplining workers to the rhythms of the factory. Entrepreneurial control produced compliance through personal loyalty and leadership through the entrepreneur. This solution was satisfactory when firms were small, but became impractical as manufacturing interests grew in the early 20th century. Hierarchical control attempted to reproduce the conditions of simple control through the use of foremen and assistants. This solution was organizationally conservative but otherwise quite explosive since there were few constraints on the behavior of foremen and personal identification with foremen and managers (the glue of entrepreneurial control) was lacking. Technical control linked productivity to machine-paced production, combining principles of scientific management with de-personalized leadership. Finally, bureaucratic control linked evaluation and performance to formal rules. Satisfactory work was associated with the internalization of rules and compliance to them. Edwards' explanation leaves off at approximately the time that human resource management becomes the dominant rationale for managerial activity.

Burawoy (1985) develops the same themes by linking the employment relationship to two core concepts, the *production of consent* and the *factory regime*, that describe managerial behavior and the context where it occurs.

Early capitalism is labeled the "despotic regime" because factory discipline
on the shop floor and labor market discipline in the community are reinforced by negative sanctions and force. More recent capitalist efforts (20th
century capitalism after the Depression) are labeled the "hegemonic regime." This regime is based on consent and effort bargaining. The purpose
of the management system is to get the requisite amount of effort from the
workforce by securing active consent. This consent is secured through a
range of benefits provided to employees and implicit effort bargains that
provide a measure of autonomy on the shop floor without fundamentally
disrupting production. Overall, the major goal of hegemonic system is
smooth production at pre-specified levels in an environment with little economic competition.

Burawoy's arguments regarding the future development of capitalism
point in the direction of our arguments here. As globalization and capital
mobility increase, Burawoy talks about the development of "hegemonic
despotism", a factory regime where discipline is enforced through the ability
of capital to move from place to place looking for the least resistance and
the best investment climate. Central to this "good climate" are compliant
and inexpensive workers and compliant communities that allow firms to
operate with impunity. Recalcitrant workers, and their communities that
fight back, are punished by the logic of the global market as they are replaced by those willing to let managerial capitalists to do as they please.

Our approach differs from past critical approaches not so much in the
emphasis on autonomy and freedom of action, but with regard to the
terms and conditions of their use. The managerial autonomy perspective suggests that managers are (1) a distinctive interest group whose
interests diverge from those of non-supervisory employees and investor/
capitalists, and that (2) solutions that advance the managerial and professional autonomy of managerial incumbents are preferred over solutions
that either wantonly abuse employees as members of the working class
or increase investors' profits. If controlling and de-skilling employees
will lead to these ends, managers will do those things. If controlling and
de-skilling employees will not serve those ends (as the neoentrepreneurial
paradigm suggests) managers will "surrender" direct control over employees in order to garner greater absolute control in other areas. In this
case, the ability to hire and discard specific human capital for specific
purposes, and the ability to claim distinctive expertise in combining what
the labor market will provide to produce a specific product, overrides
whatever advantages can be gained by permanently employing workers
whose working lives can be extensively controlled. In this way managerial

autonomy is increased while managerial responsibility for workforce welfare is displaced permanently.

Functionalist Approaches Compared to the Professional Autonomy Perspective

The functionalist approach has two main variants. The first involves the use of the transaction cost perspective as a lens for viewing change in managerial paradigms. For example, in his analysis of the rise of the managerial class, Chandler (1977) suggests that scientific management was the result of management's desire to decrease coordination costs associated with human capital (i.e. transaction costs). With the industrial revolution under way and with the growth in consumer markets, firms found it more economical to internalize a large number of previously external functions. These large investments in plant and machinery required governance structures that would reduce the costs associated with the coordination of the work process. As a result, foremen, who were once independent contractors, were hired as line workers and their power of coordination and control was relegated to a growing class of managers.

A second functionalist approach that addresses management paradigm change is the business cycle theory articulated by Barley and Kunda (1992). Incorporating theories from sociology and economics, they propose that paradigmatic shifts in managerial ideologies are the result of cultural shifts occurring within economic long waves. The movement of the economy through long waves of growth and decline causes vacillations between rational and normative rhetoric which lead to shifts in managerial paradigms.

There are important similarities and differences between the managerial autonomy perspective and the functionalist perspectives as well. We have already suggested that transaction costs are declining in importance. This not only lessens demand for middle managers who communicate directives up and down a managerial hierarchy, it also eliminates many incentives to internalize employment relationships in hierarchies rather than markets. The market now occupies a distinctive role in advancing managerial control. Managers can be viewed as people with the expertise to bring together distinctive skills and competencies from the external market, figure out ways to employ them and maximally utilize them for the exact length of time necessary to execute specific projects, and then discard them so that firm expenses are minimized and output and profits are maximized.

Our perspective shares with Barley and Kunda the idea that conditions external to specific firms affect managerial ideas and paradigm development. However, the professional autonomy perspective views alternative managerial choices as more activist than Barley and Kunda's response to cultural shifts and economic long waves. Long waves also leave the impression that managerial change returns to old ideas and that economic change produces no permanent change in how firms are organized. It seems unlikely that the current shift toward arms-length, market mediated, and subcontracted network relationships is going to reverse itself any time soon, even if there is a prolonged recession that ends the current economic long wave.

In summary, our perspective differs from functionalist perspectives and critical approaches by attributing distinctive interests to managers as an occupational group (managers represent themselves, not capital), downplaying the role of class domination as an overarching goal of managerial action, and by suggesting that many of the current changes in firm organization that are a product of neoentrepreneurialism are permanent and unlikely to shift backward as the present economic long wave comes to a close.

CONCLUSION

There have been numerous attempts to describe historical changes in management paradigms over the course of the 20th century. Our perspective ties together transaction cost theories, resource dependence theories, principal/agent models, and research on the development of professions to explain changes in management paradigms. Our perspective is distinctive because it discusses changes in paradigms from the perspective of managers themselves. It also acknowledges that managers have distinctive interests that result from their unique locations in firms that mesh with the desired development of management as a professional project.

The professional autonomy perspective suggests that each management paradigm took a different approach to increase or maintain managerial autonomy. Scientific management accomplished this by reducing dependence on skilled workers and substituting unskilled workers in their place. Human relations management attempted to tie the loyalty of employees to firms so that newly found rights to organize and unionize would not lead to excessive disruptions in production. Human resource management sought to regain the professional autonomy of managers by viewing human capital as a portfolio investment, acquiring and discarding such capital as firm's profitability increased and decreased. Finally, neoentrepreneurialism takes advantage of the pressures of global competition and new developments in information technologies to eliminate reliance on specific people for specific tasks. Human capital is outsourced so that reliance on specific employees is nearly eliminated. All of these actions served to increase managerial power and autonomy, two central goals of most professionalization projects (see Abbott 1988).

Our theoretical endeavor has just scratched the surface of the possibilities for examining changes in managerial paradigms and the managerial incentives for instituting these changes. Our analysis is limited in scope. But there are a number of broader social scientific implications that can be pursued by scholars interested in developing a sociology of managerial knowledge;

(1) Where do new management ideas actually come from?

(2) What roles do business schools play in shaping the environment for management paradigm change rather than passively reacting to changes suggested by environmental stakeholders?

(3) Will the current wave of well-publicized business scandals lead to new challenges to the professional autonomy of managers? If so, what are those challenges likely to be and will they work to limit corporate management malfeasance?

(4) What are the career and larger social implications of a new entrepreneurial economy where skilled human capital works in a fee-for-service, subcontracted environment? Can stable communities and social arrangements be sustained in an environment where economic rewards are so variable and short-term?

(5) How can the growth of managerial professional autonomy in the neo-entrepeneurial economy be squared with ever increase in the attempts to limit the professional autonomy of long-standing professionals (lawyers and physicians) through bureaucratic interventions and the end of fee-for-service practice? (see Leicht and Fennell 2001; Leicht and Lyman forthcoming).

(6) More philosophically, if "everyone becomes an entrepreneur" what are the social, ideological and political implications for cultures like the United States that glorify entrepreneurial activity as distinctive, path breaking, and novel? Can politicians and others continue to endow the entrepreneur with distinctive social virtues if (in effect) "everyone" is doing it?

We hope that this preliminary exploration inspires others to develop more elaborate theories of managerial behavior that can be applied to the growth and change in the emerging global managerial class.

ACKNOWLEDGMENTS

The authors wish to thank Dan Wren, Charles Wrege, Martin Kilduff, Dan Brass, Lisa Keister, and the faculty of the Penn State Labor Relations Department and the Sociology Departments at Vanderbilt University and The University of Iowa for comments on an earlier draft of this paper. An earlier version of this paper was presented at the Academy of Management meeting in 1997 in Boston, Massachusetts.

REFERENCES

Abbott, Andrew. 1988. *The System of Professions*. Chicago: University of Chicago Press.
Baird, Charles W. 1990. "Labor Law Reform: Lessons from History." *Cato Journal* 10:175–208.
Barley, Stephen R. 1986. "Technology as an Occasion for Structuring: Evidence from Observations of CT Scanners and the Social Order of Radiology Departments." *Administrative Science Quarterly* 31:78–108.
Barley, Stephen R. and Gideon Kunda. 1992. "Design and Devotion: Surges of Rational and Normative Ideologies of Control in Managerial Discourse." *Administrative Science Quarterly* 37:363–399.
Baron, James N., Frank R. Dobbin, and P. Devereaux Jennings. 1986. "War and Peace: The Evolution of Modern Personnel Administration in U.S. Industry." *American Journal of Sociology* 92:350–383.
Bendix, Reinhard. 1956. *Work and Authority in Industry: Ideologies of Management in the Course of Industrialization*. New York: Harper & Row.
Berle, Adolf A. Jr. and Gardiner C. Means. 1932. *The Modern Corporation and Private Property*. New York: Macmillan.
Bogue, Donald J. 1959. *The Population of the United States*. Glencoe, IL: The Free Press.
Boyett, Joseph H. and Henry P. Conn. 1992. *Workplace 2000: The Revolution Reshaping American Business*. New York: Plume.
Braverman, Hary. 1974. *Labor and Monopoly Capital: The Degradation of Work in the Twentieth Century*. New York: Monthly Review Press.
Burawoy, Michael. 1985. *The Politics of Production: Factory Regimes Under Capitalism and Socialism*. London: Verso Press.
Chandler, Alfred D. 1977. *The Visible Hand: The Managerial Revolution in American Business*. Cambridge: Harvard University Press.
Cihon, Patrick J. and James O. Castagnera. 1988. *Labor and Employment Law*. Boston: PWS-Kent.
Donaldson, Gordon 1963. "Financial Goals: Management Versus Stockholders." *Harvard Business Review*, May–June, 116–129.
Edwards, Richard. 1979. *Contested Terrain*. New York: Basic Books.
Fligstein, Neil. 1990. *The Transformation of Corporate Control*. Cambridge, MA: Harvard University Press.
Form, William. 1987. "On the Degradation of Skills." *Annual Review of Sociology* 13:29–47.

Freeman, Richard B. and James L. Medoff. 1984. *What Do Unions Do?*. New York: Basic Books.

Freidson, Elliot. 1986. *Professional Powers: A Study of the Institutionalization of Formal Knowledge*. Chicago: University of Chicago Press.

Gillespie, Richard. 1991. *Manufacturing Knowledge: A History of the Hawthorne Experiments*. Cambridge: Cambridge University Press.

Gordon, David M., Richard Edwards, and Michael Reich. 1982. *Segmented Work, Divided Workers: The Historical Transformation of Labor in the United States*. Cambridge: Cambridge University Press.

Hamermesh, Daniel S. and Albert Rees. 1988. *The Economics of Work and Pay* 4th ed New York: Harper & Row.

Handy, Charles. 1989. *The Age of Unreason*. Boston: Harvard Business School Press.

Hurst, James W. 1970. *The Legitimacy of the Business Corporation in the Law of the United States, 1780–1970*. Charlottesville: University Press.

Leicht, Kevin T. and Mary L. Fennell. 2001. *Professional Work: A Sociological Approach*. Oxford, UK: Blackwell.

Leicht, Kevin T. and Elizabeth C.W. Lyman. 2005. "Detours on the Road to the Professionalization of Everyone: Contemporary Issues in the Study of the Professions." *Research in the Sociology of Organizations*.

Littler, Craig 1982. *The Development of the Labor Process in Capitalist Societies*. London:Heineman.

Marglin, Stephen A. 1974. "What Do Bosses Do? The Origins and Functions of Hierarchy in Capitalist Production." *Review of Radical Political Economics* 6:33–60.

Markowitz, Harry M. 1952. "Portfolio Selection." *Journal of Finance* 7:77–91.

Monsen, R. Joseph and Anthony Downs. 1965. "A Theory of Large Managerial Firms." *Journal of Political Economy*, June, 221–236.

Montgomery, David. 1979. *Worker's Control in America*. London: Cambridge University Press.

Pennington, April Y. 2004. "You're Hired." *Young Money* 3:2–3.

Pfeffer, Jeffery and Gerald R. Salancik. 1978. *The External Control of Organizations: A Resource Dependency Perspective*. New York: Harper & Row.

Pfeffer, Jeffery and Yinon Cohen. 1984. "Determinants of Internal Labor Markets in Organizations." *Administrative Science Quarterly* 29:550–572.

Sherman, Andrew W.Jr. and George W. Bohlander. 1992. *Managing Human Resources*. Cincinnati: South-Western Publishing Co.

Stone, Katherine. 1974. "The Origins of Job Structures in the Steel Industry." *Review of Radical Political Economics* 6:61–97.

Taylor, Frederick W. 1903. *Shop Management*. New York: Harper & Row.

------. 1911. *The Principles of Scientific Management*. New York: Harper & Row.

United States Bureau of Census 2003. *Statistical Abstract of the United States*. Washington, DC: US Government Printing Office.

United States Congressional Record. (1935).

Wilensky, Harold L. 1964. "The Professionalization of Everyone." *American Journal of Sociology* 70:137–158.

Williamson, Oliver E. 1975. *Markets and Hierarchies*. New York: The Free Press.

Wren, Daniel A. 1994. *The Evolution of Management Thought* 4th ed New York: Wiley.

UPSIDE-DOWN VENTURE CAPITALISTS AND THE TRANSITION TOWARD PYRAMIDAL FIRMS: INEVITABLE PROGRESSION, OR FAILED EXPERIMENT?

Noam Wasserman

ABSTRACT

The early-stage venture capital (VC) industry has long been dominated by small firms comprising senior venture capitalists and few junior staff. However, during the late 1990s, a group of firms changed their internal structures, adopting pyramidal structures and redesigning internal processes to leverage the efforts of junior staff. In doing so, they followed first-movers in other professional services industries that transitioned to pyramidal models in the 20th century. Has the recent industry downturn terminated the transition, or simply delayed it? This chapter analyzes the events that led the VC firms to transition, the barriers to doing so, and related issues affecting the industry's future.

Entrepreneurship
Research in the Sociology of Work, Volume 15, 151–208
ISSN: 0277-2833/doi:10.1016/S0277-2833(05)15007-9

INTRODUCTION

INEVITABLE PROGRESSION. "This is a cottage industry in its infancy – it will mature and move into the organizational form of more-mature industries." {GP in early-stage California firm}

FAILED EXPERIMENT. "This is an artisans' business, full of specialists, that doesn't lend itself to pyramids. It's like a surgeon's business."..."At the end of the day, it's an art. Would you really think that Mozart could've been a lot more productive if, instead of writing his own music, he stayed at the top and reviewed and edited what his people did? Would it work?" {GP and COO of California firms}

Until the 1920s, the Dutch accounting industry was dominated by "P-form" organizations consisting of small firms with only partners (Lee and Pennings 2002). However, in the 1920s, several early-mover firms transitioned to a "PA-form" that included both partners and more-junior "associate" professionals, an organizational form that soon dominated the industry in that country and enabled the development of large accounting firms. During the 1900s, similar large-scale transitions occurred in other professional services industries, such as law (Sherer and Lee 2002), management consulting (McKenna 2001), and investment banking (Eccles and Crane 1988; Hayes III and Hubbard 1990). Small "non-pyramidal" professional services firms (PSFs), which had previously been comprised of senior partners transformed themselves into the large "pyramidal" organizations that dominate these industries today. To do so, they significantly increased their ratio of junior staff to senior staff, created processes with which the senior people could leverage the time and efforts of their junior employees, and developed junior and mid-level specialists who could perform their tasks with increased expertise and efficiency. Moving to pyramidal structures enabled these firms to increase their effectiveness and scope of operations, to economize on coordination and governance costs (Galanter and Palay 1991), and to increase their chances of survival compared to firms that did not change their models. The fact that large number of firms changed their structures, capabilities, and processes helped each industry escape from its "cottage industry" status (e.g. Baumard 1999) and changed the overall competitive landscape within the industry.

Past studies (e.g. McKenna 2001; Lee and Pennings 2002; Sherer and Lee 2002) have assessed these transformations retrospectively, often decades after they occurred. Therefore, they were not able to directly study the process of transformation and the range of issues faced by the people experiencing and participating in the transition. In addition, as analyses of completed transitions, these "ex post" studies were susceptible to the assumption that the change was the inevitable next stage in an evolution (Lamoreaux, Raff et al. 2003). In contrast to these studies, this chapter focuses on current changes in venture capital (VC), an industry in which non-pyramidal firms have predominated for several decades (Wasserman 2002), and does not take it for granted that a transition toward pyramidal structures will be completed and be a positive development for the firms involved. In the late 1990s, several VC firms, such as Crescendo Ventures (Wasserman 2003), Atlas Venture, and Battery Ventures, began attempting to transition toward pyramidal structures by undergoing the same "institutionalization and professionalization" (McKenna 2001:673) that had previously occurred in management consulting firms and other PSFs. However, as described below, many of the firms ran into problems transitioning toward the pyramidal models adopted on a widespread basis in other professional services industries, raising questions about whether VC can evolve in a similar way. The debate over this evolution is captured in the competing quotes at the beginning of this chapter.

Therefore, consistent with past studies, this study explores the reasons why some firms began to change. However, it also focuses on the barriers that might prevent such a change from becoming widespread or permanent. Doing so can help illuminate the challenges faced by "organizational entrepreneurs" who attempt to pioneer new organizational structures, much like Nike did in its industry (Abrahamson and Fairchild 2001), in that success in the "introduction" stage must be followed by success in the "diffusion" stage or else the organizational innovation will not be sustained. The focus on barriers to change can also inform past entrepreneurship research that has examined the persistence of organizational characteristics and strategies. For instance, founding strategies often persist for decades after founding (Stinchcombe 1965; Boeker 1989), and this chapter sheds light on structural and strategic persistence in the context of the VC industry, an industry where research has neglected to study the internal organizational characteristics of firms (Gompers and Lerner 2001; Wasserman 2002).

In this chapter, I draw primarily on extensive field research with first-mover firms who began transitioning, but also use illustrative data from a unique large-scale panel dataset of 327 VC firms.[1] The sections below integrate the analyses into a model of the motivations for and obstacles to achieving structural transformation toward a pyramidal model. The diagram below summarizes the issues addressed in these sections regarding the trigger events, barriers to transitioning, and organizational contexts that facilitated or hindered the adoption of pyramidal structures.

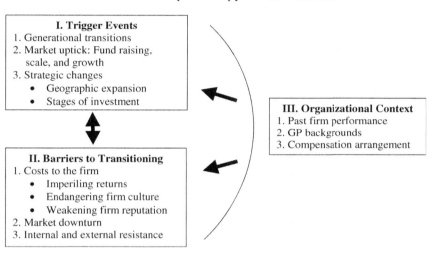

ORGANIZATIONAL STRUCTURE AND PROFESSIONAL SERVICES FIRMS

Within modern organization theory, in-depth exploration of pyramidal organizational structures was sparked by the work of Max Weber. A century ago, Weber created a typology of organizations dominated by the "rational-legal" type of authority system, which he saw as the dominant institution of modern society (Weber 1946 trans.). The organizational form of this rational-legal system is the pyramidal, bureaucratic organization. Technically the most efficient form of organization possible, bureaucratic organizations consist of offices arranged in a hierarchy, with each higher-level office encompassing several offices below it. Work is divided and allocated to each set of lower-level offices, which contain experts who have specific areas of responsibility and the specialized skills necessary to accomplish their tasks. As in "machine" organizations (Mintzberg 1979) and "mechanistic" organizations (Burns and Stalker 1961), the division of labor in these organizations entails the separation of work into standardized routine tasks, which are controlled using formalized rules and regulations.

However, some of the patterns in the pyramidal industrial firms of past research may not hold in PSFs. Compared to capital-intensive firms, PSFs provide clients with services that are largely intangible and difficult to "inventory," their businesses are subject to information economies, and their core assets are the people who work in them – the proverbial "elevator assets" (Maister 1993). These knowledge-intensive firms include such PSFs as investment banks (Eccles and Crane 1988), law firms (Gilson and Mnookin 1989; Sherer 1995), management consultants (Maister 1993), and venture capital firms (Gompers and Lerner 1999). Even compared to other service organizations, which use a large base of fixed assets to deliver relatively standardized and simple products to clients and customers, the products of PSFs are relatively complex and usually feature "entrepreneurial problem solving" and customized solutions (Morris and Empson 1998; Lam, 2000). From an economic perspective, PSFs are formed to share risks by pooling expertise (Gilson and Mnookin 1985). The key input in these firms is the expertise of a firm's employees (Prahalad and Hamel 1990; Drucker 1993), and the emphasis in such firms is on esoteric (or "tacit") expertise over widely shared (or "explicit") knowledge (Polanyi 1966). As a result, these firms "present particular problems of organization and management." (Blackler 1995:1028) For instance, they rely on apprenticeship relationships because tacit knowledge has to be conveyed through strong personal ties between the source and recipient (Hansen 1999), and the junior staff must acquire necessary tacit knowledge via mentoring and socialization (Nonaka 1994; Lam 2000).

Early in their lives, the most striking structural characteristic of these PSFs is the fact that many are *not* structured as pyramids (Wasserman 2002). Instead, they are often structured as "upside-down" pyramids, with multiple people at the top of the organization and fewer people at each successive level down. In short, the people at the top of these organizations decide *not* to gain the presumed benefits of hierarchies, such as the increased efficiencies of delegation, the development of specialized expertise at different levels of the organization, and the use of promotion as an incentive. However, in industries such as law, investment banking, accounting, and management consulting, firms transitioned away from these structures and toward large pyramidal structures. This chapter examines an emerging transformation in the VC industry, both to gain a better understanding of the transformation itself and to begin to assess whether the VC industry will follow in the footsteps of these other industries.

Gaining a better understanding of these organizations is particularly important today, given the significant increase in similar knowledge-based

organizations within the economy (Starbuck 1992) and the important economic role played by venture capitalists (Gompers and Lerner 2001). It can
also provide insights into the broader issue of transformational change (e.g.
Miller and Friesen 1980; Tushman and Romanelli 1985; Romanelli and
Tushman 1994) helping us understand the factors that can either trigger or
hinder the "revolutionary" changes that punctuate longer periods of "convergence" within organizations. Below, I describe the work performed by
VCs and the structures historically adopted in their firms, my approach to
studying the structural transformations within the industry, and the findings
from my field-based research with almost two dozen VC firms from 1998 to
2002, including three months spent working as an associate inside a VC firm.

Venture Capital Firms

Venture capitalists are professional private-equity managers who invest
capital in young companies. Before investing, VCs expend a lot of time and
effort collecting information on each candidate investment, examining the
company's management team, its ability to develop products or services, its
business model, and the market it is targeting. Much of this information is
subjective, instinctive, and holistic. In collecting this information and making decisions about whether to invest in a company, VCs must rely heavily
on their intuition, years of experience in working with young companies,
and tacit knowledge about business and technology. Once this information
has been assessed, they decide whether to invest in the company and, for
those in which they invest, help the company grow and develop.

   There are two major ways in which VCs try to manage the risks of investing in such companies. The first is by building a portfolio of investments,
in an effort to diversify risks across many companies in ways that an investor in a single company cannot. The second is by performing extensive
pre-investment due diligence in order to assess the quality of each potential
deal. They assess the entrepreneur's abilities (and those of her team), the
chances of developing an operational product, the market need for such a
product, how competitors might respond, and the potential responsiveness
of the stock markets to an IPO of the company's equity. Once they have
decided to pursue an investment, the VCs negotiate the terms of that investment with the entrepreneur. During negotiation over the terms of their
investments, VCs seek to craft terms that both will provide entrepreneurs
with incentives to build their company's value and will protect the VCs from
losing their entire investment.

Within these firms, general partners (GPs) are the senior leaders of the firm who raise capital from and sign funding agreements with the limited partners (LPs) who invest in venture firms. The GPs are responsible for crafting firm strategy, attracting and investigating business plans from high-potential start ups, and making the final investment decisions that implement their chosen strategies. After investing in a company, they play an active role in helping shape and build the company, sometimes also serving on the company's board of directors. Internally, GPs are incharge of VC-firm governance, and decide whether and when to hire additional (junior) staff to assist them with performing their jobs. These junior staff include both mid-level Principals and junior Associates. Principals are "GPs in training": younger, less experienced VCs who draw upon several years of experience to perform many of the tasks that otherwise would be performed by the GPs, but which can be performed by the Principals with only a small loss in effectiveness. Associates are recent graduates with little or no work experience, who work alongside one or more of the GPs or Principals, perform tasks delegated to them, and facilitate communication within the firm. They often bring with them technical or business/financial skills gained in school, and spend years working under more senior VCs to learn the business.[2]

Almost as a rule, VC firms are very small organizations, in contrast to the industrial firms of past research, which often needed to grow to a substantial size in order to have a significant economic impact. This is because PSFs can have a large impact even while consisting of only a few people (Baker and Smith 1998).[3] Therefore, the effects of size and growth may be particularly important to examine for these firms. As we will see below, the firm's stage of development, capital availability, and the nature of the work performed within the firm all played key roles in the transition toward pyramids.

Structures within VC Firms
Consistent with the finding that the dominant type of knowledge in an organization affects organizational form (Lam 2000), a VC firm's strategy and the associated predominant mode of knowledge have a powerful effect on the structure adopted within the firm (Wasserman 2002). Most importantly, the stage of company on which the firm focuses its investments plays a pivotal role in its structuring. For "later-stage" VCs, who assess mature companies that have been in existence for several years and have a lot of historical performance data that can be analyzed, their tasks are more separable and codifiable, which enables the GPs in these firms to delegate discrete subsets of their job to junior staff. For this reason, later-stage firms

are able to build structures that are more pyramidal and leverage the efforts of junior staff. In contrast, "early stage" investors assess young companies that have little or no history and must base their decisions on intuition and the pattern recognition that comes from years of working with young companies. In these firms, VCs' jobs are holistic and based on tacit knowledge that either cannot be codified or would suffer from being codified, so the GPs are not as able to separate their job into discrete tasks that can be delegated. Because junior staff are of little use to these GPs, early-stage firms rely predominantly on GPs and cannot use many junior people.

To illustrate the difference in structure between early- and late-stage VC firms, the chart below shows how, for 2000, these different types of structures were distributed in my large-scale dataset.[4] Firms whose structures were GP-only made up 38% of the dataset, with the other firms split between majority-GP (39%) and majority-non-GP (24%) firms. Non-pyramidal structures were particularly dominant in early-stage VC firms, but less prevalent in late-stage firms.

	GP-only	Majority GP	Majority non-GP	Total firms	% of firms	*Shading Key*
Early stage	44%	37%	19%	78	24%	41-50%
	41%	40%	19%	132	40%	31-40%
	32%	39%	28%	82	25%	21-30%
Late stage	29%	34%	37%	35	11%	11-20%
Total firms	123	126	78			
% of firms	38%	39%	24%			

In quantitative terms, we can use the metric of structural leverage to refer to the degree to which firms are GP-only versus pyramidal. Structural leverage is the ratio of the number of lower-level staff to the number of higher-level staff, and indicates the extent to which organizational leaders try to use the efforts of lower-level employees to achieve the organization's objectives (Sherer 1995). The higher the structural leverage, the more pyramidal the organization; GP-only firms have structural leverage of 0 (a ratio of 0 non-GPs to the number of GPs), while pyramidal firms have structural leverage of greater than 1 (more non-GPs than GPs). The chart below shows the distribution of structural leverage across the firms in my dataset during 2000. While there are some pyramidal firms (i.e. structural leverage of 1.0 or above), non-pyramidal firms are much more common in the VC industry, whether we compute structural leverage using all personnel in the firm (i.e. including full-time support personnel and others who are not investment professionals) or using just investment professionals (i.e. GPs, principals, and associates).

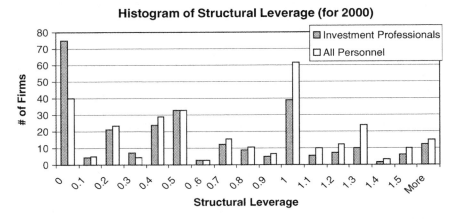

Histogram of Structural Leverage (for 2000)

While performing field research in the late 1990s to understand the difference in structures between early- and late-stage firms, I found a small number of firms that were in the process of trying to transition from their long-standing upside-down structures toward pyramidal structures, consistent with the past transitions in other PSFs. As an emerging transition, studying the transformations within these firms promised to fill in many of the details that could not be examined in past PSF-transformation studies. However, as I followed the evolution of these firms over time, it also became apparent that most of the firms were encountering strong barriers to transitioning that imperiled such a major change. These barriers to change could prevent the firms in this industry from following in the footsteps of the "formerly cottage" firms in other PSF industries. Therefore, I spent the next couple of years trying to understand the events that were leading these firms to try to transition and the process by which they were trying to do so, but also delved into the barriers that might prevent such a change and the organizational contexts that might facilitate or hinder such a change.

An Overview of the Structural Changes

The first institutional VC firm, American Research and Development, was founded in 1946 by Harvard Business School professor General Georges Doriot and MIT president Karl Compton. Since then the non-pyramidal organizational structure has predominated in the industry. Indeed, many VCs in firms I studied said that they still felt little pressure to change their long-standing structures. Their current approaches had been performing very well, their GPs were relatively young and planned to be active VCs for many more years, and they had not recently made any strategic changes. The following comment was representative of the thinking in such firms:

> With the Sequoia guys, the inner sanctum of managing partners are all in their early 40s, with no interest in going anywhere. … Bringing in Associates isn't good if you do it too quickly, when you don't need to make a generational transition. You have to do it only when you want, in 4 or 5 years, to have developed a full-fledged GP. {Principal in large California firm}

However, other firms were undergoing fundamental changes. Rather than making small, incremental changes on a person-by-person basis, firms were changing their approaches and structural models in ways that signaled a fundamental shift in how they performed their work as VCs. The people in these firms insisted that this new model had become necessary as the industry matured.

> This is a cottage industry in its infancy – it will mature and move into the organizational form of more-mature industries. {GP in early-stage California firm}

In the "traditional" VC arrangement, each GP typically performs all tasks for each of the potential and actual investments for which the GP serves as sponsor. The same person performs due diligence, negotiates terms of the deal, and works with the company after investing in it. However, several firms I studied decided to make a dramatic shift in the GP's job. They split the job into multiple, discrete tasks, and hired specialists to perform some of them. For instance, some firms hired junior staff to whom a GP could delegate analysis tasks, while other firms brought in "venture partners" to sit on boards of directors instead of the GPs. Other firms hired functional specialists, such as executive recruiters or turnaround specialists, to work with portfolio companies on specific tasks that used to be performed by the GPs. As a result, these firms added a relatively large number of non-GPs, thereby making a fundamental shift in both their structures (toward pyramidal organizations with functional specialists) and their work processes (toward discrete tasks).

> At firms like Crescendo and Battery, they aren't just supplementing the orthodox model with a couple of discrete tasks that can be handled by support staff. They are entirely

revamping the way that VC firms operate by relegating [to them] some of the vital GP functions – domain expertise and assisting companies. {Industry analyst}

For instance, one Boston firm, which was comprised almost solely of GPs 5 years ago, hired eight Associates in 2000–2001 and made plans to transition to a classic pyramid over the next two years.

> We're now talking about building our "power pyramid." … We've had a lot of discussion about "how steep should the sides be?" We're thinking that 1:2 would be too much for us, just given the senior partners we have and the limits on their abilities to take the time to mentor junior people, but we're looking to go to 1:1.5 in the near term. Our plan is to go to 8 investing GPs plus the MP and COO, 12 Principals, and 20 Associates. {COO of Boston firm}

Instead of being a "one-man show," GPs in these firms now played more of a coordination role in which they performed tasks that only GPs could perform, but spent the rest of their time facilitating the efforts of the junior or specialized personnel working for them.

The tasks that these VCs separate and delegate to junior staff seem to share four main characteristics (Wasserman 2002). First, the inputs into the tasks and outputs out of the tasks are well defined, which facilitates the interactions between the people performing the tasks and those performing related tasks. Second, the processes required to perform the tasks that can often be codified and formalized, enabling the firm to provide detailed guidance to the junior staff and to check the quality of their work. Third, the people performing the tasks can become more productive by developing specialized expertise in them. Fourth, having an Associate or Principal perform the tasks would not harm the relationship that a GP has with the entrepreneurs or LPs with whom the GP interacts.

In addition to splitting up the job, many of these VCs also broadened the scope of their work by bringing some tasks in-house, hiring their own people to perform them instead of outsourcing. In some firms, these were pre-investment analytical tasks that they used to "farm out" to investment bankers, while in other firms they included such post-investment tasks as executive search, which had been outsourced to external executive search firms. Some of these post-investment tasks included those which GPs used to perform themselves, but which specialists – even those with fewer years of experience than the typical GP – could perform with higher quality. For instance, one Boston firm hired mid-level people who specialized in helping turn around portfolio companies that encountered major problems as the market turned down. The firm's MP stated, "We now push our problem children to our specialists and let them handle them." Similarly, a New York firm hired a team of mid-level specialists:

> We have an in-house consulting firm now. For example, if company has an issue, we have a couple of Director-level people who've been CFOs in troubled situations who come in to help. {Principal in large New York firm}

Other firms tried to broaden the range of services they provided to their portfolio companies, in an effort to become "full-service providers." Firms that used to focus on delivering a particular type of value to their portfolio companies, such as technical guidance, added specialists, marketing consultants, and in other areas.

> This is meant to be a selling point at a time when cash is a commodity, and firms are driven to differentiate themselves to get the best deals. {Industry analyst}

Once again, these shifts resulted in the hiring of more junior level or specialized staff, broadening the pyramidal structure of the firm.

It is important to note that the transition from being GP-only or "upside down" to a pyramid could take different paths. For instance, in the Salta case (Wasserman 2002), the firm moved from being GP-only to being upside down (hiring a couple of non-GPs), to have an hourglass shape (many GPs, many Associates, almost no mid-level Principals), to pyramidal (as some people from the initial wave of Associates have moved into mid-level positions), before regressing toward a less-pyramidal structure (and parting with the COO who had been hired to lead the transformation toward a pyramidal structure). Other firms skipped the "hourglass" stage by hiring mid-level people from the outside at the same time as they were hiring Associates. At the same time, another firm first built a hierarchy within its GP team, by creating a Managing Partner position and a small management committee at the top of the GP team, before beginning to build a pyramid at the bottom of the organization. Therefore, while the initial starting point and the target ending point for these firms is similar, their interim transitional structures may differ.

We can use my quantitative dataset of VC firms to explore the structural changes on a larger scale. To examine structural changes between 1997 and 2000, I selected the firms that were in the dataset throughout those 4 years, and then calculated summary statistics of how they changed their structural leverage between 1997 and 2000. As shown in the histogram below, with regards to the structural leverage within each firm, there was a wide range of changes across the industry. Overall, the firms increased their structural leverage by an average of 0.031 between 1997 and 2000. However, 110 of the firms did not change structural leverage during this period, 34 decreased their structural leverage at least by 0.25, and 55 increased their structural leverage at least by 0.25 (of which 14 increased by a very substantial 1.00 or more).

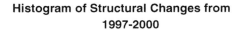

Histogram of Structural Changes from 1997-2000

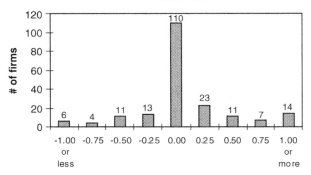

4-year change in Structural Leverage

RESEARCH APPROACH

One of the major approaches used to develop organizational theory is field-based research in which the researcher delves into a real world phenomenon in order to understand it in all its richness (Glaser and Strauss 1999). To uncover the critical elements shaping the phenomenon, whether they are pervasive or not, case-based research uses "theoretical sampling" (Glaser and Strauss 1999), which is sampling driven by the development of the emerging theory. As a category emerges and the researcher has to sample more data in order to elaborate the category, the researcher selects cases that might be able to illuminate the category. New cases are selected not to assess the representativeness of the new category, but for their theoretical relevance (Eisenhardt 1989:537).

Inductive techniques have an overriding requirement to seek negative cases (Eisenhardt 1989). By seeking negative cases, we can both modify or correct the emerging explanation, and enrich the explanation in new ways. For instance, my initial explanation for the difference between pyramidal and upside-down firms was that "it is a size issue." However, in seeking to disprove this, I sought – and found – some small firms that were relatively pyramidal and some relatively large firms that were still upside down. These negative cases forced me to modify my explanation and led me to explore whether it was a combination of size and firm age. For instance, the prototypical GP-only firm is Benchmark Capital, a relatively young firm that was founded in 1995, while Atlas Venture was founded in 1980 and is relatively pyramidal. However, in seeking to disprove this possibility, I found Greylock, which was founded in 1965 and is almost GP-only, and Crescendo Ventures, which was founded in 1998 and is an extremely pyramidal organization while being a similar size (in terms of active capital and number of people) to Greylock. I continued to revise and iterate through these memos as I conducted more interviews and added new cases until I reached "theoretical saturation" (Charmaz 1983; Eisenhardt 1989; Glaser and Strauss 1999), the point at which the researcher feels that his incremental learning is minimal because the patterns have already been seen.

In this study, for each case study, I reviewed documents and archival records, interviewed key participants, performed direct observation of several cases, and was a participant-observer while working as an Associate in a VC firm for 3 months. When I thought that it would add more insights – e.g. in firms that were undergoing fundamental changes, were dealing with sensitive issues, or were grappling with problems that might affect multiple hierarchical levels in different ways – I made sure to conduct interviews with more than one member of the organization. Overall, in about one-third of the organizations I studied, I spoke with multiple participants in the firm. For firms that were undergoing important changes, I followed these firms for up to a year and a half, conducting a series of interviews spread out over the time period, to trace how they were changing.

In addition to interviewing 40 people from 22 VC firms, I also interviewed six limited partners, four industrial analysts, five venture-backed entrepreneurs, one executive search firm that performs searches for start-ups, and one law firm that works with venture-backed companies. In crafting my theoretical-sampling strategy, I included small firms (e.g. tiny Catamount Ventures, with a single GP) and large firms (e.g. behemoth Chase Capital) those that had recently been started and those that were very established. Most of the firms were based in California and Boston, the two largest markets for VC, but my interviewees also included VCs working in other parts of the Northeast and in the Midwest. I interviewed both senior GPs and more junior Principals and Associates, from firms that invested in every stage of company development. Some of the VC firms had a single office, while others had multiple offices. Finally, the firms included some that focused their investments in a single business sector, and many that invested across a wide range of sectors.

TRIGGERS, BARRIERS, AND ORGANIZATIONAL CONTEXTS

In this section, I describe the "trigger events" that led firms to make changes,[5] the barriers they encountered in doing so, and some of the organizational characteristics that seemed to increase or decrease the chances that they would make such changes.

I also use my large-scale dataset to present summary statistics to complement the qualitative findings and model that are the focus of this chapter. More specifically, with regards to the triggers described below, I created data tables to explore whether the firms that experienced each trigger increased structural leverage more than firms that did not experience each trigger.[6] In those data tables, I split the firms into three major buckets, based on the histogram above: (1) those firms that decreased structural leverage by 0.25 or more (the 34 firms at the left half of the histogram above), (2) those that did not change (the 110 in the middle of the histogram), and (3) those that increased structural leverage by 0.25 or more (the 55 in the histogram). I present each data table in the section that describes the field findings about that trigger.

Trigger Events

Among the firms I studied, I found three major types of events that precipitate a fundamental shift in VC blueprints. On their own, none of these events was enough to effect a fundamental change in the firms I studied. However, the firms that experienced more than one event were more likely to transition than the firms that did not experience them, since these events increased the benefits of pyramidalization. The three events are generational transitions, the raising of a second fund or of a fund much larger than previous funds, and a shift in strategy.

Generational Transitions
The first major event is when firms are approaching a generational transition in which a central GP or a group of GPs are nearing retirement and beginning to reduce their involvement in investing.

In the early years of the industry, according to several GPs, firms were formed with the intention of raising a fund to invest, without worrying about building a firm that would last multiple funds.

> Before, people thought firms were single-fund firms. One-offs, where "let's do something together." You couldn't see that, "My career will be in VC." Now, it's built-in that firms are here to stay, that longevity is here to stay. {MP of Boston firm}

Even for new firms that plan to be around for many years, the founding GPs are often young enough that they do not worry about how their far-off retirement would affect the firm. However, as founding GPs near their retirement, their firms' continued existence comes into question. As an increasing number of founding GPs have neared retirement in recent years, the issue of whether their firms would survive through a new generation has become more pervasive, as stated by a Principal in a Boston firm: "The generational problem is now a big problem in the industry." This is particularly true for GP-only firms that never hired and developed junior people. The retirement of their GPs is much more likely to imperil the future of these firms. According to the COO of a Boston firm, "Historically, GPs would leave and it would be a train wreck." Their firms either neglected to proactively prepare for such a transition, or had powerful GPs who resisted any such preparations.

> It's like watching a thunderstorm in Texas – you see clouds forming, and then they're used up all their energy and can't sustain it, and then there are others that develop into a full-blown storm. {Industry consultant}

This problem is particularly salient for LPs, who commit their money to each VC fund for a decade. (The influential role played by LPs in this phenomenon resembles the power held by central resource providers in other contexts (e.g. Emerson 1962; Pfeffer and Salancik 1978).) According to the LPs I interviewed, such "generational problems" catch their attention and can make them think twice about investing in a new fund. One large California LP stated that "the reason we exist is primarily to monitor internal dynamics, chief among which is generational transitions."

> You're giving them a lot of money. Once you sign on the bottom line, you're stuck, so you want to make sure that they're going to be around. ... I don't want to be age discriminating, but if you're 65 years old and starting a new 10-year partnership fund or you're the only GP, that's a problem. ... To be a great VC firm you have to be able to make the transition. {LP in large university endowment}

> When we're looking at a fund that's going to last 10 years, when we're evaluating a team and their business strategy, we're listening to and watching their current interactions but also wondering, "Is this an organization that's going to be able to perpetuate itself?

Who's the leader and if something happens to him, who would fill his shoes?" {LP in large Boston institution}

Furthermore, many LPs said that they like to invest in firms with the intention of continuing to invest in multiple funds the firm will raise over a long period of time.

We want to invest in the same firms throughout. We want a long-term relationship. In a ten-year period, we'll have at least 3–4 funds from a firm on average, so it turns into a twenty-year relationship at that point. It's not worth the time, effort, and risk of investing in a one-time fund. {LP in large university endowment}

Therefore, LPs assess what each firm will look like throughout the next couple of decades or more.

To see this, we look at turnover, at the career development of the important people, and we meet separately with the younger partners to get their perceptions of where the firm is going and what role they'll play in getting it there. {LP in large institutional investor}

Similarly, a COO I interviewed stated that, "LPs used to want to invest in a fund. Now, they want to invest in a firm, an institution." This COO's LPs were looking for longer-term relationships that would endure through multiple funds. Other LPs made similar arguments for doing so.

Investing in a venture capital fund is very labor intensive for an institutional investor. ... To put a billion to work in VC requires scores of separate negotiations and due diligence on dozens of private equity teams. When an institutional investor has gone through the effort to establish a relationship with a private equity team, they want to be able to reuse all of the research and relationships for future funds. It makes sense than an institutional investor would be looking to forge a relationship with an institution. {California LP}

Other VCs report, and the LPs I interviewed confirm that their LPs have begun asking such questions as, "Do you have a long-term infrastructure in place?" in an effort to assess whether the firm is susceptible to the loss of a single GP, or if it would be able to survive the retirement of the current generation of LPs. They are particularly concerned by firms that depend on a single GP – or on a group of GPs who are close to retirement – for much of their success.

When you look at the GPs in the industry, there's a select group that's rich now and moving on. There is a real need to grow people with real experience, to have people who can step into their shoes. Otherwise, there's knowledge that hasn't been passed on, board seats that haven't been transitioned. ... Individual portfolio companies can be hurt by the abrupt retirement of a key board member before another member of that VC's firm has been able to take over the reins. {COO of Boston firm}

One COO, who had just returned from his firm's annual meeting with its LPs, said that the LPs had been very supportive of the firm's efforts to transition toward a pyramidal structure.[7]

> Our LPs were very supportive of our current transitioning efforts. They like that we're making our GPs leveragable and that we're developing an infrastructure. They were very supportive of the fact that we're developing a scalable organization – with a larger fund, we need to create more capacity for our people, and all the things we're doing are helping that. They also feel good that when a senior partner leaves, we won't have to go outside to hire someone to replace him. {COO of Boston firm}

Sometimes, the impetus for the older generation to hand over the reins comes from the senior GPs themselves, who realize that they will soon need to reduce their involvement in the firm.

> How does a GP know when to move down? It becomes readily apparent. Especially on the tech side, you have to be younger. The sweet spot is when you know enough to know what you're doing, but you're fresh enough that you're still current. It's usually about a 15-year period of time. {GP in established Boston firm}

> There will be a Greylock 37, and Henry McCance [Greylock's MP] knows he will have nothing to do with it. {MP of Boston firm}

However, as described later in this chapter, the senior GPs can also resist changes for several reasons.

When it comes to making a smooth transition, one solution might be to hire GPs from outside when the need arises, rather than having to take the time to develop people into GPs over a number of years. However, many VCs I interviewed saw such a solution as sub optimal. The main reason is that firms emphasize maintaining their tight-knit cultures, and avoid imperiling these cultures by hiring senior outsiders who might not fit.

> Especially when you have a number of partners who will be retiring within the next five years, you need to have people who can step into their shoes, and it is better to grow them from within than to bring them in from outside. Just having a certain number of years of direct experience in the firm is important. {COO of Boston firm}

In addition, some firms see the hire-a-GP approach as a riskier solution because, "We can't rely on getting lucky and hiring a future star," as one Principal stated.

Therefore, firms that want to proactively develop a new GP often hire an Associate and develop him or her into a GP over a series of years. Such firms try to develop the next generation of firm leadership in advance and plan for a smooth transfer of leadership to the new generation. An Associate in a life-sciences firm said that such approaches were relatively common in past years, and may still predominate among firms that want to remain small.

> The historical model for generational shifts is based on a one-to-one mentor model: after some number of years, some number of funds, the person is brought up to GP. This is the "slow-growth model." You're just looking to replace yourself. {Associate in health-sciences firm}

To LPs, such an approach shows that the firm is concerned about how it will be able to continue investing the capital committed to it.

> The better firms, you can see them planning it. There's a partner who's 50, another 48, another 41, and a partner-to-be who's 35. It's very hard if there are four guys who are 55–65 and one guy who's 40. {LP in large university endowment}

> You have to have a commitment to bring people in and developing them. It can be one per decade or three per decade, but you have to be bringing them in. {COO of California firm}

For instance, one prominent Boston firm recently hired its first new Associate since the current MP was hired as an Associate in the mid-1980s. According to the Associate, a big reason he was hired was a generational transition that would occur in a few years.

> The forcing event was the need to get in some young people and take care of some long-term succession worries. The GPs realized, "We're not going to be around forever." {Associate in prominent Boston firm}

However, many other firms believe that they do not have the luxury of hiring a single Associate who will become a GP. Doing so leaves them vulnerable to the Associate's leaving the firm and setting back their transition-preparation efforts by several years. Therefore, when they get within a few years of needing to transition to a new generation, these firms begin hiring multiple Associates for each future GP slot, and then "weed out" the best candidates.

> To the extent you hire more than one or two junior people for each future-GP position, you have to be looking at culling some of the junior people. {COO of Boston firm}

> We will have 4 more Associates over the next four years. For every two, one will make it to Senior Associate, and then maybe makes it to Principal. So we'll have 2–3 more Principals. Our steady state is to have 6 partners. {Principal in small California firm}

One large California firm has spent a considerable amount of time planning its next generational transition. Most of the current GPs experienced rocky transitions in their previous positions, both within the firm and at other firms, and seem to be determined to avoid a repeat.

> Many of the second-generation guys left their previous firms because the senior guys there didn't focus attention on generational issues. The foundation of the firm are people who had been at other firms. They hated the cultures there and how the firms were being built, and decided to do it differently. {Principal at large California firm}

The transition plan crafted by the firm's current GPs calls for the development of two new levels of leadership within the firm, in an effort to ensure that the firm will be able to continue its success for atleast two more generations.

> The second-generation guys are running the admin side of the firm, setting compensation and titles, managing the infrastructure. They're now bringing along the third-generation guys on the administrative side, and bringing along the fourth-generation so in 3–4 years, when the second generation slows down, they'll have two generations incredibly active at the GP level. It's also very well thought out at the sector levels. {Principal at large California firm}

One approach, used by three of the firms I studied, was to hire COOs from industries that had learned how to make smooth transitions. For instance, one COO had been a partner in a law firm. He pointed to the predominance in that industry of large law firms that was able to transit from their founding partners to later generations of partners, and to one prominent venture firm that had been able to do likewise.

> Thinking about large institutional law firms, if you name the fifty most prominent law firms in America, the people with their names on the door have been dead for decades, so the current head guys – the "law firm GPs" – inherited it. They didn't start it. ... At KP [Kleiner Perkins], Byers is the only one still there. The rest have moved on, and the most prominent people don't have their name on the door. {COO of California firm}

In helping his firm make a similar transition, this COO hoped to draw on lessons from his legal career.

Among the firms I studied, the best transitions were those where the senior partners proactively reduced their involvement and share of the carry (profits). They hired promising junior staff on a regular basis while they could still mentor them and develop them into GPs, and delegated work to them. Easing out the senior partners while developing a new generation of GPs enabled these firms to live for another generation, and enabled them to gain the confidence of LPs.

> In the clubby, congenial atmosphere of a VC partnership, it's a way for [senior GPs] to exit without an abrupt transition. It's good for both the individual and for the firm, because it's hard to abruptly change who is sitting on boards and LPs don't like abrupt changes. {COO of Boston firm}

Market Uptick: Fund Raising, Scale, and Growth

The second major trigger event is the raising of a new fund. For both legal and practical reasons, VC funds are almost always limited to a life of 10–12 years, forcing VC firms to raise a new fund every few years (Gompers and Lerner 1999). In the late 1990s, the funds invested by LPs in VC increased dramatically. In such an environment, it becomes much easier for firms to raise large funds to invest. At the same time, it also became more necessary for firms to have large funds. For instance, in "boom" markets, the valuations of start-ups increase dramatically. With an increase in valuations, VCs have to invest more money in a start-up if they want to maintain the same percentage ownership as before, so it becomes more necessary for VCs to raise larger funds.

I found that fund raising affects firms' structural choices along several dimensions. Sometimes, the *number of funds* the firm has raised is the important factor. In some of the firms I studied, when they raised their first funds, the GPs could not be sure if their firms would survive to raise a second fund. Therefore, they delayed hiring other people to work with them. However, once the firm had raised its second or third fund, the GPs became more willing to build a full organization. More generally, once GPs have gained confidence that their firm will continue beyond the first fund, they often look to "scale up" quickly.

> [Our GPs] couldn't make long-term plans with the first fund because they weren't sure how it would go. Now, we can start to see about hiring Associates. {Principal in young Boston firm}

However, beyond the number of funds that have been raised, the *amount of capital raised* is also critical. Many of the GPs I interviewed stated that having a lot of capital was important in the industry for several reasons. These reasons include the desire of entrepreneurs to have VCs with "deep pockets" who will be able to fund all of their needs while they are still a private company,[8] the desire of the VCs to have a large stream of management fees,[9] and the desire of large LPs not to spread small amounts of capital across a huge number of VC funds.[10] In addition, firms began using the increased management fees to broaden the range of services they provided to portfolio companies, both to increase their attractiveness as investors and to increase their portfolio companies' chances of success. These services – such as helping set up systems and policies, performing market research, and assisting with executive recruiting – could often be performed by non-GPs, leading firms to hire junior people and become more pyramidal.

Pyramids come from groups scaling up massively in funds, and looking to create new advantages. {Venture partner in Boston firm}

A prominent school of thought in the industry right now is that you have to differentiate yourself and build your services {Principal in Boston firm}

It's a function of how we want to be perceived. ... It's about marketing, all about where the sources of parity are and where the sources of differentiation are. ... In VC, you can be high quality as a 3–4 person firm, but you will have a harder time in the marketplace. {GP in established Boston firm}

Once they had raised large funds, several GPs I interviewed said that they then "had to figure out how we'd invest it." A common concern was that the GPs would become "overloaded," either having to manage a much larger number of portfolio companies or having to investigate and make many more investments than in the past. This was particularly true if the firm's growth in capital was much faster than growth in the number of GPs investing the capital, resulting in dramatically higher *capital per GP*.

The firms who raised $1B funds – the number of deals they're going to have to do is insane. They're not going to be able to do the due diligence. {Principal in young Boston firm}

Firms that are looking for high growth find it more chaotic. It's an issue how they load up their partners. {Venture partner in Boston firm}

Sometimes, the firms anticipated this problem and began to address it in advance, while other firms did not begin to address it until it became an actual problem. However, for both types of firms, the most common solution was to enlarge the firm by hiring people who could help them invest the large amount of capital.

Typically, the VCs who raise large funds don't view capital as a limited resource. Instead, their limited resource shifts to being their people. {Principal in young Boston firm}

One firm that had experienced a huge increase in the volume of investment between 1995 and 2000 went from having almost all GPs in 1995 to having a "rectangular" organization (in 2000) in which the number of Associates and Principals was nearly equal to the number of GPs. The main reason for doing so was "to provide more leverage for the senior guys." In the Boston firm that had hired its first Associate in 15 years due to generational-transition issues, the second reason given for hiring the Associate was because "our funds are getting bigger now and we'll need some new people to invest it."

If you're swamped, bring in [junior people]. They're smart guys, you can teach them to do due-diligence and to help on the front end – give you scale. It's a great experience for them, and you get lots of leverage. {Principal in large California firm}

> Having a pyramidal organization is a great way to source deals. {Principal in Boston firm}

In addition, as these firms grew, they often changed their processes in ways that facilitated a move toward pyramidal organizations. In almost all of the firms I studied that had grown substantially, the face-to-face meetings and informal processes that had worked when their firms were small (and when they were comprised of GPs who had worked together for a long time) began to deteriorate, and they began to adopt formal processes and a "hierarchical" structure of meetings that did not include all members of the firm.

> There are communication issues. The weekly meeting thing gets too big, and you start talking about different things. It's not worth spending everyone's time talking about those things. You change to another model or you get chaos. {Associate in health-sciences firm}

In order to get an industry wide view, I split my quantitative sample into those firms that increased their capital-per-GP markedly during 1997–2000 (defined here as an increase of 33%)[11] versus those that did not. As a whole, the firms that increased capital-per-GP by 33% raised their structural leverage by 0.080 over the 4 years, while the remaining firms raised it by 0.027 over the 4 years. With regards to the "buckets" that came out of the histogram shown earlier, Table 1 shows the distribution of buckets according to whether the firm raised capital-per-GP markedly. As shown, the firms that did *not* increase capital-per-GP markedly were as likely to raise structural leverage as they were to decrease it (16.5% versus 16.5%). In contrast, the firms that did increase capital-per-GP markedly were more likely to raise structural leverage than to reduce it (by a gap of 5.5%).

Table 1. Impact of Changes in $/GP.

	Did not Increase $/GP Markedly	Increased $/GP by 33% or More
(1) Reduced structural leverage	16.5%	14.3%
(2) Maintained structural leverage	66.9%	66.0%
(3) Increased structural leverage	16.5%	19.7%
(4) Difference between (3) and (1)	0.0%	5.5%
Obs.	118	60

Strategic Changes: Geographic Expansion, and Change in Stages of Investment

A final trigger, which was often linked to fund raising but could also occur on its own, was a strategic change that caused a shift in structure. In the VC industry, firms are usually very careful about the initial strategies they choose to pursue. One reason is the need to "sell" LPs on the strategy, by pointing to why their backgrounds and skills will enable them to execute the strategy well. Another reason is the fact that VCs publicize their strategies – for example, the stage of companies in which they want to invest and the sectors they target – in order to attract potential investment candidates that meet their criteria and in order to begin building a clear identity and reputation in those areas of focus.

However, as the investing markets shift and make a new stage of investment or a new sector more attractive for investments, firms may decide to shift their strategies in a search for better returns. Doing so can trigger a change in their fundamental models, as stated by a venture partner in a prominent Boston firm: "Firms can bring in some new business models that force them into a pyramid." In particular, I found two major strategic changes that could lead firms to transition to new structures: geographic expansion and a change in the stage of companies in which they invest. As a COO observed:

> You throw the geographic issue in and any changes in your focus, and it all changes for the firm. {COO of Boston firm}

Regarding the fund raising trigger described above, these strategic changes can happen whether or not the firm has raised a large fund. At the same time, firms that raise larger funds might be more likely to change their strategies, in order to be able to invest all of their newly raised capital either in additional locations or in later stage start-ups that require more capital.

> How do they say they'll invest [the new capital]? Is the size-per-deal going up, or the number of deals going up? In either case, they can't follow the strategy that got them to this point. {LP in large university endowment}
>
> The risk with a billion-dollar fund is that you've got a big fund and over time you start modifying your behavior and two years later your business has changed. {GP in established Boston firm}

The sections below describe these two types of strategic changes and how they may affect transitions toward pyramids.

Geographic Expansion

In general, VCs like to invest in companies that are near their offices, so that they can perform due-diligence tasks and work with their portfolio companies in person.

> There's something better about having investments nearby – when time is a scarce resource, you don't want to fly across the country. You want to be able to pick up the phone, let the guy know you're coming, and just drop in on them. {Principal in Boston firm}

Many of the firms I studied had been founded in a single office and had remained single-location firms. However, more than half of the firms I studied had opened one or more other offices, most of them within the last few years.[12] I found two major reasons why these VCs expanded geographically. First, and most basic, was the decision to increase the number of deals they make. As one GP stated, "We don't want to overdo it in any particular market, because then we would be reaching down into the lower-quality deals."

For those firms that had recently raised large funds and had to find investments for all of that capital, this issue took on added importance. In order to increase their volume of deals without sacrificing the quality of the deal pool, they branched out into new geographic markets by opening offices in those regions. As one VC stated, "We now get to look for good deals all over."

> When you have more than a billion dollars to invest, multiple locations make sense, because you can't put that much money to work in one location. You have to reach farther to get good deals and not just be an index fund. {Associate at life-sciences VC firm}

Increasing the number of deals was not enough to trigger a change within these firms on its own. Firms that only wanted to increase their volume of deals could do so by opening new offices that were independent of the main office. These new offices would find, investigate, and manage their own investments without having to coordinate with the main office, thereby enabling the main office to maintain its existing structure and processes. In perhaps the most extreme example, Benchmark has opened two "clones" of itself that have a similar GP-only structure and even raise their own "regional funds" from which they invest. Therefore, in these firms, opening a new office usually did not trigger a transition to pyramids.

However, in firms where a second factor was at work, opening a new office did tend to help trigger a transition. This second factor was where the VCs opened new "synergistic" offices that would work closely with the main office and whose presence was meant to strengthen the work of the main office, rather than being independent of it. For instance, some firms opened offices in new regions to gain local information that they could disseminate across the firm. They believed that having a comprehensive grasp of the competitive outlook in multiple geographic markets would be important both for their decision making about what investments to make and for their ability to help portfolio companies craft strategies once they have joined their boards. In short, they would know more and have a broader perspective than if they remained single-office firms.

> Our firm had been Boston-based since its founding, but now we have about 40 percent of our staff in Silicon Valley, and the goal is to have 50 percent there. A big reason for our expanding to there was to increase our deal flow, but it was also to keep tabs on the companies in Silicon Valley, and to transmit the knowledge we gain there throughout the rest of the firm. {GP in Boston office of large firm}

Opening new offices forced many of these firms to change their *modus operandi*. GPs said that, while they were single-office firms, they could exchange information in person and could engage in extensive dialogues about which investments to make. However, when they opened up new offices and therefore spread themselves across multiple locales, the GPs had to change their decision-making processes. As one GP stated, when his firm opened up its second office, "That's where our consensus model really broke down and we had to find a new way of doing things." The firms could no longer gather in a single room to make decisions and were forced to find other approaches. The VCs in these firms often moved to hierarchical decision making processes, in which subsets of the firm participated in various stages of decision making. For instance, the GPs designated a small group of GPs who would be responsible for final decisions about firm direction and policies. This resulted in the adoption of processes that led them toward pyramidal organizations.

Furthermore, in order to spread local information across the firm, these VCs adopted several communication practices that helped them move toward pyramids. Because some of the most valuable "local" information was of high richness, they placed a premium on practices that transferred this information through rich media, such as face-to-face meetings. However, almost all of these multi-office firms found it too hard to conduct face-to-face meetings on a regular basis, and had to find alternatives to these meetings. These alternatives often included the development of a central firm infrastructure for sharing information. To facilitate cross-office sharing of information, many of the multi-office firms codified and formalized some of their communication processes, which further accelerated their ability to change the ways they worked. In addition, rather than taking on all of the

Table 2.   Impact of Opening and Closing Satellite Offices.

	Closed Office	No Change	Opened New Office
(1) Reduced structural leverage	18.2%	17.5%	4.5%
(2) Maintained structural leverage	63.6%	68.1%	63.6%
(3) Increased structural leverage	18.2%	14.5%	31.8%
(4) Difference between (3) and (1)	0.0%	−3.0%	27.3%
Obs.	11	166	20

responsibility for developing the infrastructure and for facilitating information flows within the firm themselves, the GPs often hired junior staff to help facilitate the spreading of local information throughout the firm, especially when that information would not lose critical richness by being transferred this way. Therefore, an increase in the need to spread local information across the firm resulted in the hiring of additional junior staff.

> When you're internally trying to harness synergies, you need more organizational resources to tie it together. As a Principal, I bear a lot of the load of communicating things across the firm. I spend a lot of my time documenting stuff, making sure the GPs know various things from elsewhere in the firm. You need more people to keep it a unified firm. {Principal in California office of early-stage firm}

In short, as these firms broadened their geographic strategies by opening new offices in other regions, they tended to transition toward pyramidal models that included more junior staff and were based on processes that were more formalized and were more hierarchical in nature.

With regards to my quantitative data, I split the sample into those firms that closed an office during 1997–2000, those that kept the same number of offices during the period, and those that opened a new office during the period. As shown in Table 2, as a whole, the firms that kept the same number of offices were a little more likely to reduce structural leverage, by a gap of −3.0%. Those firms that closed an office were equally likely to increase as to decrease structural leverage. The firms that opened an office were far more likely to increase structural leverage, by a sizable gap of 27.3%.

Change in Stage

VC firms can focus their investing on young early-stage companies, mid-stage companies, or mature late-stage companies. A strategic change that can occur on its own is a change in the stage of company in which the VC firm invests. Firms may make such a strategic change when they anticipate that as a result of a shift in the market, later-stage firms will have relatively attractive returns.

At the same time, in several firms, I found changes in stage focus to be closely tied to the raising of large funds. According to the VCs I interviewed, when an early-stage firm has a large amount of capital to invest, one of the most tempting changes the firm can make is to change its focus to later-stage companies. These companies are more mature and usually have capital requirements that are far higher than early-stage companies. Therefore, the firm can put a lot more capital to use with a few later-stage investments than it can with a similar number of early-stage investments. Tempted to do this, some early stage firms that have raised large funds have migrated toward a later-stage focus.

> The hardest challenge is when you go down the path of growth, and it makes you migrate into another business. Eighty percent of Sand Hill Road VCs are in a different business from when they started – they're now [later-stage] "money managers," not early-stage investors. {GP in early-stage California firm}

The tasks performed by later-stage VCs are much more amenable to pyramidal structures (Wasserman 2002). Later-stage VCs can separate their jobs into discrete tasks that can be delegated to junior staff, while GPs' jobs in early-stage firms tend to be more holistic and dependent on the intuition and experience of senior VCs. Therefore, as these firms have migrated from early-stage investments to later-stage investments, many have also transitioned toward pyramidal organizations.

To assess this event using my quantitative dataset, I split the sample into those firms that moved to a later-stage focus during 1997–2000 versus those that did not. As a whole, the firms that moved to a later stage raised their structural leverage by 0.093 over the 4 years, while the remaining firms raised it by 0.029 over the 4 years. With regards to the "buckets" that came out of the histogram at the beginning of this chapter, Table 3 shows the distribution of buckets according to whether the firm moved to a later-stage focus or not. As shown, the firms that did not move to a later stage were slightly more likely to raise structural leverage than to decrease it (a gap of 0.9%). The firms that did move to a later-stage focus were more likely to raise structural leverage than to reduce it, by a gap of 3.2%.

Summary of Trigger Events
The causal diagram below shows each of the events described in this section and how they are linked to a transition toward pyramidal structures. From my field research, in firms where multiple events existed, the chances that the

Table 3. Impact of Changing Investment Focus.

	Did not Change Stage	Changed Stage
(1) Reduced structural leverage	15.8%	16.1%
(2) Maintained structural leverage	67.4%	64.5%
(3) Increased structural leverage	16.7%	19.4%
(4) Difference between (3) and (1)	0.9%	3.2%
Obs.	147	31

firm would choose to attempt a transition seemed to be much higher than in firms where no events were evident.

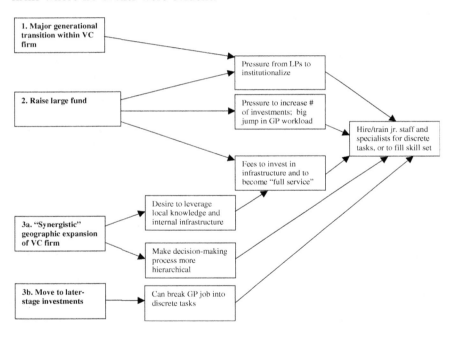

It is important to note that each of these three events may differ in its effects over time. At its core, generational transitions can come in waves, where a firm "transitions out" sets of GPs within a relatively short period of time, replacing them with new GPs who were hired and developed for a few years before the transition. While the new generation is running the firm for a decade or two, there is little pressure to prepare for an upcoming transition, and the firm reduces its junior hiring and pyramidal structure. When the next generation is ready to move on, the cycle would start again.[13] With regards to growing fund sizes, firms have historically, steadily grown their fund sizes as they raised each new fund. For firms for which this pattern holds, the pressure to transition may increase steadily over time as the capital-per-GP in these firms rises.[14] Finally, strategic changes (e.g. opening the second office, making a concerted effort to move to later-stage investing) can be one-time shifts that increase the pressure to transition at the time of the change.[15]

In addition, as mentioned above, the relative strength of each event within a firm can also affect the path that it takes toward becoming pyramidal (e.g. whether the transition starts by hiring a lot of junior personnel or by building a hierarchy within the GP team), and may have fundamental implications for the performance or survival of the firms that are changing.

Barriers to Transitioning

As described at the beginning of this chapter, a critical way in which the transition within VC seems to have differed from the transitions in other professional service industries is that many transitioning firms have run into major problems changing their models. In some firms, the issues involved became salient before any change was attempted, preventing the firms from even initiating a transition. In other firms that had begun to change during the late 1990s, the emergence of these issues caused them to rethink their changes and to reverse the transition toward pyramids. In both types of firms, the barriers they encountered raise the question of whether VC will follow the footsteps of the other professional service industries that succeeded in transitioning toward pyramidal structures on a widespread basis. The sections below describe the major firm-level costs of transitioning, the problems introduced by the downturn in the early 2000s, and the internal and external sources of resistance to change.

Costs to the Firm

Transitioning toward a pyramidal organization is a fundamental change that firms do not take lightly. This is because there are costs introduced by a transition toward a pyramidal blueprint that counterbalance the benefits of the "events" described above. In some firms, the costs are not high enough to prevent a transition, while in others, they prevent any attempt to transition. This section describes the major costs of transitioning.

Degrading Investment Performance

One early-stage VC questioned whether it was possible for his firm to shift tasks to junior staff, given the "esoteric knowledge" required to perform his job. He feared that if his firm were to transition to a pyramidal organization, its investing performance "would substantially deteriorate." In addition, VCs believe that the best investments are those where the same person, usually a GP, performs all tasks necessary to investigate and then build a company, rather than delegating tasks to others or having multiple people perform different parts of the job. These VCs focused on the cost incurred when an early-stage GP's job is separated into discrete tasks and delegated to junior staff. In this case, the GP lacks a "gut feel" for candidate investments and may make poor investment decisions. As one such GP stated, "We believe that, 'He who hunts also has to kill.'"

> A lot of the judgments that partners make are hard to translate, and require a lot of intuition and subtle understanding. At the seed stages, you are often dealing with a company that doesn't have a product and is dealing with a rapidly shifting market. There is a lack of traditional metrics, and you are making subjective judgments about crucial factors, such as the caliber of a management team. {Industry analyst}

> This is an artisans' business, full of specialists, that doesn't lend itself to pyramids. It's like a surgeon's business. ... VCs are actively involved with building businesses, making value-added contributions to their formation and growth. It's a big step function, going from apprentice to master. {GP in early-stage California firm}

The costs also include the "distraction" of having to manage younger people and the risks that adding such people to the firm would change its processes and modes of communication in detrimental ways.

> The other "school" in our firm said that you can't leverage GPs by throwing poor people around them. It dilutes their ability to invest. ... Managed appropriately, it enables GP to leverage their time, but otherwise, it creates more work for you than before. You risk having a breakdown in communications, with things going on within the firm that someone doesn't know about who should. {Principal in Boston firm}

> GPs are so busy with "revenue generating responsibilities," they can't mentor Associates. {COO of Boston firm}

> The reason VC is different is it's an art, best practiced by people doing their own work. You don't get better performance out of someone by putting a lot of staff around them. {COO of California firm}

> The theory is to extend the guys you've got, but does it take your best guys off the road? Does it keep them from making the investments they have to make? {MP of Boston firm}

Some of the VCs I interviewed went even further saying that many GPs are simply not capable of managing other staff, and forcing them to do so would degrade their performance as investors.

> Do you want to know why VCs don't hire junior staff? It's our dirty secret: VCs are bad people-managers. ... They realize that what they say they do and what they actually do are very different things. They say they do the numbers, but don't have Excel open more than 10 minutes a day. A lot say ... "I don't have time to management someone – I'm too busy," or "I can't boil it down or teach it to someone." These really mean, "I don't want anyone working with me to see the emperor doesn't have any clothes." {Principal in small California firm}

> My boss [at another firm] told me, "I don't want to manage people and be a personnel guy – I want to do deals and work with companies! I want to be a great venture-capital investor, not build an asset-management firm here." He wanted to focus on external issues, not internal ones. {Principal in Boston firm}

In a similar vein, one COO admitted, "Ever since we hired some Associates, I've had to spend a lot of my time giving some of our GPs remedial management training."[16]

Many VCs believe that they must improve their networks of contacts and their ability to provide board-level guidance to portfolio companies – i.e. skills and resources that only GPs can add.

> Our key asset is our credibility and the networks of our partners. {Associate in health-sciences firm}

> Our constraint is Board capacity, not analytical capacity. {GP in established Boston firm}

> Analysts don't help increase returns, just the # of deals ... they just help you manage day to day. If I'm alone, without someone below me, I can sit on 12 boards; if I have someone below me, I can still only sit on 12 boards. {MP of Boston firm}

Therefore, bringing in junior staff would not strengthen a firm in any of these areas, while introducing costs and risks.

> You could bring in a large number of low-paid, no-carry Associates to maximize deal flow and conserve carry for the partners, but you could say that that model only makes the easy calculations. ... The best deals aren't the ones that walk in the door. You need to have as wide a web as possible, to have a Jeff Hawkins from Palm walk in and tell you he wants to do Handspring. You don't get that with adding an Associate. If you're generous and hire another GP, you have a better chance of getting a homerun investment, and you'll return far more than you gave up. {Industry analyst}

A COO who was hired to help his firm transition to a new structure acknowledged that there had been fierce debates within the firm before he had been hired, and that vestiges of the debates still remained. In his two years in the industry, he had seen that there was much validity to the arguments against making fundamental changes.

> In the last few years, people thought that VC was easier than it is. They thought you could do it like they do in investment banking: be national, go international, build and scale the business. On the one hand, you really do need to scale. This is a business that *needs* to scale, and if you don't take up the challenge, you lose. But on the other hand, it's really hard to do it. You can leave big, smoking craters, because it's a thing that's really hard to do well. {COO of California firm}

In a later conversation, he acknowledged:

> At the end of the day, it's an art. Would you really think that Mozart could've been a lot more productive if, instead of writing his own music, he stayed at the top and reviewed and edited what his people did? Would it work? {COO of California firm}

Therefore, some of the firms I studied restricted their fund raising to keep the amount of capital per partner relatively constant, enabling them to maintain their existing size and blueprint.

> [An established Boston firm] has decided at this point to stay a certain size. They believe they are at an optimal number of partners, each with a comfortable number of deals, and that from an organizational standpoint they have a good model. When they want to scale up or grow, they will use the same type of model. They'll grow stepwise, maintaining the same load on their GPs. {Venture partner in Boston firm}

Firms such as ComVentures have become known within the industry as resisting the lure of raising large funds.

> They're a top-tier firm, have returned 10-12X on their funds. In their last fund, raising a billion dollars was possible, but they still took only $500 M. They make sure they're not getting ahead of themselves in terms of cash flow, like the rest do. {Boston LP}

One COO suggested that these firms emphasize getting a high return on their small funds, rather than risking a lesser return on a much bigger amount of capital.

> The biggest returns come not from investing a lot of money, but from investing in a company early on and getting big returns on the money you do invest. Matrix knows that if they have more money per partner, it's harder to get the great returns. They want to stay local, and say, "To get high returns, we need to stay small, have good communication, spread ourselves across no more than 2 offices." {COO of Boston firm}

Endangering Firm Culture

In a related vein, many VCs I studied were unwilling to change their work processes and styles. They liked to work as "lone guns" or "solitary cowboys," and feared that moving to a new structure would imperil that style of working. Even more important, they believed that their previous success as investors had been due to the tight-knit cultures they had developed within their firms. Moving to a different structure would change the culture of the firm and endanger their investment performance. For instance, firms that have developed a deep GP-only culture fear that building pyramidal organizations will imperil that culture.

> You risk losing the culture that made you successful, made you unique. {Principal in Boston firm}

> Blow it on process and learning, that can be fixed; blow it on culture, you've blown it. {COO of Boston firm}

> An alternative model uses the assumption that it's better to hire another GP and slice the pie a little smaller than hiring four Associates and changing the culture. {Industry consultant}

One cultural aspect was the emphasis on "investing above all else." As mentioned above, having to mentor and train Associates would distract from investing tasks. In one firm, an analyst observed, "[The GPs] don't have a training orientation. It would be a major cultural change for them." Hand in hand with this "cowboy" style is an attitude that shuns hierarchy and "the feel of large organizations."

> Most VC firms don't want to expand. ... They don't want to be part of a large organization. Twice as many guys investing doesn't mean you get twice the returns. The cost of adding additional people can be more than the incremental value-added. {Principal in large California firm}

> There are some fundamental challenges. An entrepreneurial demeanor has been part of the reason that VC firms are successful, and I wonder whether they can scale in this fashion. {Industry analyst}

Much of this hesitancy regarding pyramidal structures is grounded in the VCs' past experiences in large or hierarchical organizations.

> A lot of VCs came from operating backgrounds, came to VC to work in a collegial environment without a lot of bureaucracy. {COO of Boston firm}

One GP stated that "Bureaucracies kill the fun," and worried that "the move to hierarchy encourages politics." Another GP said he wanted to avoid "the frustration of working through a lower-level stratum." An observer of a GP-only firm echoed this statement.

> If they would add an Associate, they would have 2 strata – a shadow of a hierarchy forming – where they had just one. Ipso facto, they would have a small hierarchy. {Industry observer/analyst}

Weakening Firm Reputation

With an eye on the entrepreneurs who approach them for investments and on the LPs who invest capital in their firms, many VCs I interviewed stated that moving to a pyramidal structure would hurt their firms' reputations and their ability to differentiate themselves from competitors. This is particularly true for firms that emphasize the value they add through direct interaction between their GPs and their portfolio companies.

> Bringing people in can dilute the perception of the firm. Kleiner Perkins is known as a firm of ex-CEOs. If you have a lot of junior people, you do not have as strong an image or reputation. ... When stay upside-down, the message you're sending to entrepreneurs is, "You're going to deal with me directly; there will be no layer of support staff between us." {Principal in Boston firm}

> There are limits to how much you can delegate, when you try to leverage too far. When there are a lot of board seats going to Associates, it starts to hit the reputation issue. {Associate in health-sciences firm}

> We liked to brag that we had more experience-per-partner than anywhere else. {MP of Boston firm}

Some of the transitioning firms I studied had hired junior staff and delegated to them such pre-investment tasks as performing reference checks and conducting the initial "filtering" meetings with entrepreneurs. However, other GPs argued that, "Even if you *can* delegate those things, you shouldn't." Even if a junior person could conduct an initial meeting it might be harmful to have them do so.

> Our experience and the ability to be a great contributor on the Board is best communicated by the person who is going to be that Board member – the GP – himself, from the very first meeting on. ... We could hire an Associate for the Boston office, but part of how we differentiate ourselves, part of the philosophy we articulate to entrepreneurs is that if you come to Greylock, you're dealing with a decision maker. {GP in established Boston firm}

> Part of our pitch, what we're offering, is that every first meeting is attended by a GP, to give you immediate, direct feedback. With us, they don't waste 4–5 weeks just getting to the GP. {GP in early-stage firm}

Some firms, such as Benchmark Capital, have built their reputations based on a GP-only structure that "differentiates us from our competitors," and the partners believe that giving up that differentiator would be detrimental.

> Benchmark would revisit the question of hiring an Associate from time to time [but] they liked saying to entrepreneurs, "You're always talking to a decision maker with us." They

were very concerned about an entrepreneur walking in and being able to say, "You're talking to a decision maker." {Industry analyst}

An Associate in a Boston firm admitted that his doing key parts of the work could harm his firm's reputation.

> When it's clear the Associate is doing all of the due-diligence work, it becomes known as "Todd's deal." Then, the entrepreneur has to ask himself, "Would you prefer to do it with Todd or with a full GP elsewhere?" {Associate in health-sciences firm}

After making an investment, a VC firm can also get a bad reputation if it delegates key tasks to junior staff, especially when the entrepreneurial firm expects the GP who invested in the company to be its main or sole point of contact.

> There's a limit to how wide you can make the pyramid and make it work. ... It's not good if you get a bad reputation among entrepreneurs – "What we got is not what we bought" – and it gets passed when entrepreneur A speaks to entrepreneur B. {Associate in health-sciences firm}

Increasing Risks by Making Irreversible Moves

Heightening the perceived risk of moving to a pyramidal structure is the fear among some VCs that the change is irreversible. An Associate in a firm that had aggressively transitioned voiced doubts about his firm's recent moves.

> Locking yourself into sustaining that infrastructure means you have to raise successively bigger funds, which changes your strategy. {Associate at Boston firm}

Other VCs echoed the opinion that many of the changes would be hard to reverse, increasing the risk of making them. These changes included hiring new people, raising large funds, and bringing specialist in-house.

> Once you become a "money raising machine" it's hard to go back. Junior people are attracted by the expectation that they'll have the opportunity to be in the next fund. And bringing in all those young people – what happens if, in your next fund, you don't raise $1B but $200M? They're not going to have a role! {Principal in Boston firm}

> You create incredible management overhead as soon as you transition. When you have $100M and 4 guys, so each has $25M to invest, why go to $200M and 8 guys? Why complicate things, having to worry about people development, management issues, and compensation hassles??

> Even if you bring recruiting in-house, who's the best recruiter changes every couple of years, and you're bringing them in house for 10 years at a time? {Associate in prominent Boston firm}

Why are we raising a big fund, raising even more money? I think because we can, but it drags you down a path you won't want to be on. {Associate in international Boston firm}

Summary of Costs and Benefits

Table 4 summarizes the costs and benefits of transitioning toward a pyramid that have been described so far in this chapter.

Market Downturn

A section above described the central role played by the state of the venture market. All of the firms I studied that began to transition toward pyramids began to do so during the pre-2000 boom market. Many of them had raised large funds during that period, helping to trigger their explorations of pyramidal models. Anticipating a continued plethora of capital from their LPs, they began adopting pyramidal organizations as a way to be able to investigate and invest in a much larger number of young companies. After 2000, the state of the venture market played a powerful role in stunting or reversing the efforts of many firms to transition toward pyramids, at least partly by increasing the costs and risks described above. As the market turned down, as firms realized that LPs might not continue to fund them at the same rate, and as their portfolio companies ran into problems that only

Table 4.   Costs and Benefits of Transitioning Toward a Pyramid Structure.

Benefits of Transitioning	Costs/risks of Transitioning
• Generational transitions: Support the development of future GPs who will be able to take over leadership of the firm. • Growth in funds: Enable GPs to leverage their time over more investments to increase capital invested per GP. • Synergistic geographic expansion: Facilitate communication across offices (e.g. via mid-level liaisons). • Shift to later stage investing: Enable GPs to separate job into discrete tasks and delegate to junior staff.	• Degrades investment performance: GPs lose holistic feel for potential investments, firms lose tight-knit culture. • Changes firm culture: Endangers "cowboy" style, introduces bureaucratic feel. • Weakens firm reputation: Perception that junior staff add less value results in weakening of firm image and a decrease in firm's ability to differentiate itself from competition. • Risks of irreversible moves: Moves to increase firm's scale and scope by investing and hiring may be hard to reverse.

a GP could help solve, they began to rethink such a move and began to stretch their existing funds for a longer period of time.

> A lot of firms have been caught "mid-scaling" now. Hiring is flat this year. They've frozen in their tracks. {MP of Boston firm}

Another GP, from a firm that had been largely GP-only for two decades before it began hiring Associates and Principals in 1999 and 2000 (when it also raised its first billion-dollar fund), said that his firm did not plan to hire any more junior staff for the foreseeable future.

> Our constraint in 1999 was that we needed to get more capacity for our GPs. [One GP] was on 13 or 14 boards, and the same with [another]. ... Now, that constraint has been lessened as the market has settled down. {GP in established Boston firm}

In short, the late-1990s boom market was characterized by rising LP funding, a high level of deal flow and attractive exit possibilities, which led to increased pyramidalization in first-mover firms. The subsequent "bust" market was characterized by stagnant or declining LP investments, depressed deal flow and IPO/acquisition markets, and a rethinking of pyramidalization in these firms. As described in detail in the final section of this chapter, a central question is whether the post-2000 downturn has ended the transition-to-pyramids experiment or has only temporarily delayed it.

Resistance to Change from Senior GPs and External Parties
Sources of resistance include the costs to the senior GPs, and pressures from external parties, such as LPs, entrepreneurs, and syndication partners.

Personal Costs to Senior GPs

Many firms I studied had not proactively built pyramids in preparation for a generational transition because the senior GPs in such firms viewed the personal costs of such a move to be too high. For instance, some GPs feared losing control of the firm. Much like an entrepreneur who has founded a company and resists giving up leadership of it (Wasserman 2003), these GPs resist changing their involvement in running and building their firms.

> It's their baby, you can't punt them. ... If they foster a culture within the firm, they can make the generational transition seamlessly. But it's rare. VCs are entrepreneurs, and they don't know when it's time to give up their baby. Some of the great VCs are egomaniacs, some are great team players. You can get some hints about it from the partnership chemistry. If there's one guy who's an egomaniac, no, he won't be able to transition out smoothly. The real thing you can see is, does he give it up along the way?

That's the best way to know if he'll give it up in the end. {LP in large university endowment}

Several VCs agreed with this assessment. One venture partner stated:

The typical entrepreneur suffers from the founder's syndrome. VC firms are just like any other start-up: a strong founder wants to hold on to power until the firm outgrows him. {Venture partner in Boston firm}

Some of these founding GPs try to hold on for a financial reason: once they retire their ability to share in the firm's carry disappears.

If the old guy is really greedy and wants to keep the carry, it's very tough to pry it out of his hands. However, if the old guy wants to do charity when he gets older or wants to develop the junior people, it's different. It's very much the individual's personality, his philosophy and time horizon – build a firm that's around for 100 years, or grab all the money? {Associate in health-sciences firm}

One LP suggested that such GPs might also resist hiring or developing people who would be able to take over in order to delay such a transition. A GP admitted that had his firm not proactively prepared for the retirement of its MP and one of its senior GPs by developing a generation to replace them, the MP would probably have pushed off his retirement: "If we hadn't hired a few new guys, there would have been less impetus for him to move off."

Indeed, organizational inertia is one of the most powerful impediments to internal change (Hannan and Freeman 1989). Inertia is the greatest when powerful parties want to maintain the same practices and arrangements that have been around for a long time. Within the VC firms I studied, the barriers to change were usually the highest when the main resistance came from the top partner in the firm.[17]

We have decided not to continue moving to a pyramid. Our senior partner said, "You're trying to make me into someone I'm not. I don't want to make the management decisions." He doesn't even want to have to attend partner meetings. He realized that changing the organization would mean that he would have to change his own way of working, his own processes. ... The rest of the organization wants to go the pyramidal route, but the top guy is an unwilling participant. He says, "I made it as a gun-slinger, you should be able to also." {Principal in small California firm}

Two of the COOs I interviewed also stressed how the top partner can also be the key facilitator or roadblock to their being to do their jobs.

For a COO to be effective, he has to not be completely emasculated by the top guy. The top partner has to give his authority to the COO, has to lend processes and credibility to them. {Principal in small California firm}

One of the COOs, who had recently left his firm after 2 years, said:

> I was brought in because the partners knew intellectually that we had to change things at Atlas. But emotionally, they weren't ready for it. They weren't willing to delegate any of the key decisions to me. ... They weren't willing to give up any of the strategic decision making, so the job became very tactical. {COO of Boston firm}

When all GPs are equal, the GP team may collectively resist any changes. In order to maintain the same style of work, when it wants to expand by opening offices, Benchmark takes several steps to assure that the core Silicon Valley office will not be affected by the expansion.

> When they've expanded by opening new offices, they always set up separate funds with separate structures that don't affect how they work within the main office. When they were hiring for London or for Tel Aviv, it could happen without their feeling that they were changing anything for themselves. {Industry analyst}

Interestingly, one of the COOs hired to effect a transition said that his hiring increased the opposition to pyramidalization within the GP team.

> To them, I represented that bureaucracy, what they were trying to avoid when they came to the industry. {COO of Boston firm}

Resistance from External Parties

External parties that provide critical resources to an organization can have a material impact on the decisions and internal changes made within that organization (Pfeffer and Salancik 1978). To a VC firm, there are three major external parties on whom it may be dependent: the LPs who invest money in the firm's funds, the entrepreneurs in whom the firm invests, and other VCs with whom the firm might want to syndicate investments. When a VC firm's transition toward a pyramidal structure introduces costs for these external parties, they may withhold resources from the VC, further increasing the costs of transitioning.

First, in contrast to the LPs quoted earlier who were in favor of a transition within the VC firms in which they invested, some of the LPs I interviewed want to invest in GP-heavy firms. They believe that VC can only be performed by GPs, and resist putting money into firms that are hiring junior staff, which they believe will be mediocre investors.

> This is a "GP business." It is very hard to do this as an "Associate business." GPs have to make the investments themselves. When I look at a group that's hired a bunch of Associates or Analysts so they can have cheap labor, I don't like what I'm seeing. They [the junior staff] source the deals and do all the running around, then a GP comes in at

> 10:10 in the morning, takes a long lunch break, and isn't attached to the deal flow
> and what's going on in the world. He's relying on his Associates and Analysts to do
> everything. ... The GP doesn't know it, doesn't see it, can't touch it, or feel it. Seeing and
> touching are different things. {LP in large university endowment}

Second, some entrepreneurs said that they would resist a move by their VCs to make a junior staff person into their main point of contact, because they want to deal with GP-level VCs.[18] They said that they would resist taking money from firms that did not convince them that they would receive GP-level attention whenever they wanted it. In particular, they want to deal with the individual who first invested the money, for it was that person's skills and contacts that sold them on having that firm as an investor.

> Entrepreneurs see it as an individual putting money into their firms, not the VC firm
> investing it. They say, "We want the guy who invested in us to be along for the whole
> ride." {COO of Boston firm}

For instance, within their existing portfolios, some firms have begun transitioning board responsibilities to junior staff. However, many entrepreneurs resist such a move. One entrepreneur referred in disgust to his VC's attempts to "downgrade" the level of attention the entrepreneur received from the GP who had been on his board. A Principal admitted that such transitions are "a hard sell" to entrepreneurs.

> It's hard to transition a portfolio company to a junior person who has little credibility
> {Principal in small California firm}

VC firms that try to "strong-arm" such a move onto a portfolio company risk sullying their reputations among entrepreneurs.

Finally, resistance can also come from syndication partners. Other VC firms that might want to syndicate with a VC firm may think twice if they know that the firm might assign a junior person to it.

> Among peer VCs, the question is, "We're doing a new round – who should we show it
> to?" If you ... get a reputation for being passive, then people only set aside a tiny piece
> of each round for you, and it becomes a self-fulfilling prophecy that you're passive.
> {Associate in health-sciences firm}

The Organizational Context

In comparing the transitioning firms to those that were not changing their blueprints, I found three contextual characteristics that could either increase or decrease the chances of making a transition (and possibly the chances of long-term success after the transition). These characteristics are the firm's past performance, the backgrounds and orientations of the GPs, and the firm's compensation arrangement.

Past Firm Performance
In the VC firms I studied, the second-tier firms seemed to move toward pyramids sooner than did the most successful firms. (This is consistent with the argument that "organizations at the margin" are more likely to make organizational innovations first (DiMaggio and Powell 1983).) After all, a GP in one of the top VC firms said, "This has worked well for us in the past – why should we risk changing it?"

> Matrix has been such a phenomenal success, they figure that if the organization ain't broke, they shouldn't try to fix it. {COO of Boston firm}

Therefore, the top firms I studied tended to make only incremental changes to their structures while steadfastly avoiding fundamental changes. Rather than transitioning to a radically different blueprint that might imperil that success, these firms tended to make smaller changes, such as hiring venture partners, that enabled them to add skills and resources while maintaining the core of their existing structures.

> We're definitely pushing hard in this direction, with EIRs, etc., but without our affecting deeper structural issues. It's just a reaction to the immediate symptoms and the needs for more deal flow and more board help. {Associate in prominent Boston firm}

In another example, according to an industry analyst who considers Benchmark a top-tier VC firm, in the late 1990s, Benchmark's partners debated hiring junior staff and building a more pyramidal organization, but decided not to because of their initial success using a GP-only structure.

On the other hand, second-tier firms were usually much more open to pyramidal transitions, seeing it as a potential way to "leapfrog" into the top tier. Almost all of the transitioning firms I studied were second-tier firms that had seen some success but wanted to find ways to break into the top tier of firms within the next decade. Likewise, one VC compared the stances of two communication-focused firms. One of the firms, Crescendo Ventures, has transitioned to a pyramidal organization with the goal of breaking into the top tier of firms (Wasserman 2003). In contrast, ComVentures has resisted instituting such a structure.

> ComVentures, the old, extremely successful firm, has made it a point to keep the structure the same. ... [Their] returns are significantly higher, hence a lower motivation to change. ... It might present insight into the motivations and therefore the nature of the firms. Are these top performing funds looking to extend their leads through innovative

models? Or are these under-performers looking for a way to evolve from losing models? In many cases, it's the latter. {VC at communications firm}

GP Backgrounds

Past research has found that differences in the backgrounds of the people who run entrepreneurial firms can play a big role in how they decide to structure and run their firms (Burton 2001). Among the VC firms I studied, I likewise found that the backgrounds of GPs played an important role in their receptivity to transition toward pyramidal organizations. For instance, some GPs with operating experience told me that they feel very comfortable working in pyramidal organizations. When they were founding their VC firms, many of these GPs formed GP-only firms. However, as they began raising follow-on funds, they were faced with a choice of whether to maintain their old model or whether to transition toward pyramidal organizations. Among the VCs I interviewed, the GPs who had enjoyed working in pyramidal organizations in the past seemed to be among the most forceful proponents of moving toward pyramids in their own VC firms. They welcomed the chance to delegate tasks to junior personnel and to leverage their time by doing so.

> People here are comfortable in an environment where there are a lot of people reporting to them. They are used to being leveraged. They say, "A lot of stuff here takes time to do, and sure doesn't take 20 years of experience to do it!" {COO of large California firm}

> It also depends on whether they've managed big teams before. There are a lot of nuances to managing people, and if you haven't done it before, you're worried you'll make mistakes that won't be obvious until much later. ... The guys who have managed before tend to be more focused on developing the firm and on being involved in growing the organization. {Principal at California firm}

However, for GPs with other backgrounds, their past experiences often lead them to make the opposite decision: they resist hiring junior staff and avoid building pyramidal organizations. For instance, GPs with financial backgrounds often said that they preferred to maintain a top-heavy structure within their own VC firms. Their past work experience was based on a sharing of analytical tasks among peers, and they preferred a similar arrangement within their own firms.

More interesting, though, were the GPs who had operating experience in pyramidal organizations, but who refused to adopt a pyramidal organization within their own VC firms. Some of these GPs said that they had grown weary of working within bureaucracies and therefore, steadfastly avoided creating one within their own firm.

> The guys here don't want to be part of a large organization. That's what they're running *from*, not to. {Principal at California firm}

Others who had worked in hierarchical organizations had been disappointed with how those organizations had performed.

> Where did our GP-only model come from? The model came from the partners' experience at previous firms which did have leveraged structures and didn't seem to work too well. {COO of prominent California firm}

A final group of operating-experience GPs had crafted strategies which they believed left little room for junior staff.

> Our whole theme is "We're the entrepreneur's VC" with significant operating experience. ... So going forward, our GPs might not need to have anyone under them, because they don't need junior people to follow that strategy. {Principal at young Boston firm}

> Enterprise Partners in San Diego is one of the best. They have four GPs, and don't believe in Associates. ... They only want to hire GPs with operational experience, not anyone from business school or McKinsey. They pride themselves as wanting to be only ex-operators, and believe those are the best people to do VC. {Boston LP}

Compensation Arrangement

Across almost all firms in the industry, VC compensation comes in two forms: "carry" (a share of the profits earned by the VC firm) and salary. However, the ways in which firms split the carry among their members vary markedly, in ways that can affect a firm's willingness to transition toward a pyramid.

> There's always some element played by the compensation factor, with regards to how many people you bring in and how you split the carry. {Venture partner in Boston firm}

Among the firms I studied, some are very "hierarchical" in how they split the carry, with some members earning far less carry than others. Other firms are very egalitarian in how they split the carry, with every carry-earning member of the firm earning exactly the same amount. In the latter type of firm, each person's ability to receive carry is "all or nothing": either a person gets a full share of carry or gets none at all. Egalitarian carry systems can have cultural advantages. For instance, they may foster a higher level of teamwork (which tends to make GPs in egalitarian-carry firms adverse to compromising the egalitarian nature of the compensation system). According to the VCs I studied, egalitarian-carry systems can also have important implications for whether firms can transition toward pyramidal structures. The all-or-nothing arrangement can prevent egalitarian firms from luring high-potential junior staff by offering them small shares of carry. In contrast, in hierarchical carry systems, the GPs can offer small slices of carry to junior staff. In fact, in recent years, some of the hierarchical-carry firms I studied have indeed begun giving a small slice of carry to promising junior members of the firm, both to attract them to the firm and to motivate them. These firms hope that, by doing so, they can attract better junior staff than can the egalitarian firms. VCs in these firms believe that their firms benefit from having higher-quality junior staff, both regarding the work they perform now and regarding the probability that they will mature into quality GPs.

> If that's what it takes to get someone who'll be good enough to be one of our GPs years from now, sure – I'd do it. It's nice to have the flexibility to use in that way. {GP at small California firm}

In addition, hierarchical-carry firms may have an easier time retaining their promising junior staff even before they receive any carry. This is because junior staff in these firms can begin earning some carry several years before they would be able to earn carry in an all-or-nothing egalitarian firm, and look forward to doing so. One Associate admitted:

> If I can get a piece of the action here now, why should I go somewhere else where I won't see anything for years? {Associate at Boston firm}

> The pie is so doggone big that even a small piece is worth a huge amount. {GP in early-stage California firm}

One LP acknowledged that hierarchical-carry systems may lead a firm to build toward the future more than an egalitarian system might.

> It's not always true that an even split is the best thing. An even split today won't ensure a smooth generation transfer later. {LP in large university endowment}

In short, hierarchical-carry firms have more flexibility regarding the compensation of junior staff.

A second compensation-related factor to which two VCs pointed is a firm's incentives to grow. In hierarchical carry systems, firms may have added incentive to grow, as one GP described.

> There was a long time in the industry where growth wasn't important. [But] when there's a chieftain with the lion's share of the profits and the supporting cast gets little, it necessitates that the firm pursue growth so small pieces of the pie grow. The people with a small piece of the pie need it to grow rapidly. {GP in early stage California firm}

Summary of Contextual Issues
Table 5 summarizes how each of the elements described in this section can either support or hinder a transition toward pyramids.

Table 5.   Impact of Organizational Context on Structural Transitions.

	Supporting Transition	Hindering Transition
Past performance	2nd-tier performance (or worse); desire to break into top tier	Top performance; do not want to imperil "what's made us successful"
GP backgrounds	Positive experiences in pyramids	Antipathy toward bureaucracies
Compensation	Desire to "grow the pie" without hiring only GPs	Belief that junior staff cannot help "grow the pie"
	Ability to lure promising junior staff with small slices of carry (hierarchical carry systems)	Egalitarian carry systems that prevent giving small slices of carry to junior staff (egalitarian carry systems)

DISCUSSION

The concept of a pyramidal organization is, literally, Biblical. Exodus, the second book of the Bible, describes life for the Hebrews immediately after they left Egypt. One aspect on which it focuses is Moses' daily schedule: from sunrise to sunset, people with legal questions or disputes would line up outside his tent and he would personally arbitrate or pass judgment on each dispute (Exodus 18:14). One day, Moses' father-in-law, Yisro, came to join the Jews from his home in nearby Midyan, and watched Moses maintain this grueling schedule. At the end of the day, Yisro told Moses, "The thing that you do is not good. You will surely become worn out, you as well as this people that is with you, for this matter is too hard for you, you will not be able to do it alone." (Exodus 18:17–18, Artscroll translation) For one thing, many of the cases did not require Moses' expertise. For another, the nation could benefit from a system that developed judicial skills among a broader segment of the population. Therefore, instead of handling all cases himself, Yisro suggested that Moses set up a five-layered court system, in which a large group of low-level judges would be in charge of handling routine and simple cases for each group of ten people ("leaders of tens"). Above them would be a smaller number of judges who would each handle harder cases for a larger unit of the population ("leaders of fifties"), followed by two more levels of progressively more qualified judges ("leaders of hundreds" and "leaders of thousands"). At the top of this pyramid would stand Moses himself, judging only the most important and complex of cases. Yisro pointed out that, in addition to giving Moses more time to do the things that only he could do, such a system would also be a healthier one for the nation as a whole. Moses transformed the judicial organization into a pyramidal structure, and for the remainder of their 40-year stay in the desert the Jews used such a pyramidal court system to efficiently adjudicate disputes.

In a sense, the VC industry is still in what might be termed the "pre-Yisro" stage of development. According to one industry analyst I interviewed, "VC is still more craft and apprenticeship than a business – more Old World cabinet-makers circa 1820 than modern company," akin to Baumard's Indigo case, which is situated in a "cottage industry [where] we work on an individual scale." (Baumard 1999:148) The firms that are trying transition to pyramidal structures are trying to transform VC from a cottage industry into one that looks like other more-professionalized PSF industries, such as accounting, consulting, and investment banking. As described in this chapter, some big events, such as an upcoming generational transition, the raising of a large fund, or a strategic shift, prompted firms to attempt this transition. In addition, some of the VCs I interviewed believe that the entire VC industry will soon become dominated by the large, pyramidal organizations found across other professional services industries. These VCs are therefore trying to be first-movers in this transition.

At the same time, other experienced GPs deride such attempts at pyramidalization as the "regional sales manager model," "splitting into a lot of little firms," and a "failed experiment." Adding ammunition to the arguments of these anti-transition GPs is the fact that many of the transitioning firms have run into barriers preventing them from increasing their structural leverage. These barriers include institutional momentum, a lack of trained mid-level VCs who can help mentor new junior staff, and decision-making processes that emphasize face-to-face interaction.

Many of the firms I studied have stepped back from their plans to adapt a pyramidal organization because of such barriers and intense resistance. For example, one large Boston firm has cut back its Associate-hiring target, and has backed away from some of the process changes it had made. It has also reversed moves it had taken to integrate its dispersed international offices as part of its attempt to build an integrated pyramidal structure.

> The synergies of having an international firm didn't pan out, so they made a decision to decentralize. Each of the office heads will play more of a role. Things within the firm will be more local than global. There will be a lot more duplication, but they view it much more as a local business, especially with the foreign offices. {COO at large Boston firm}

Similarly, a Founding GP from another firm I studied had initially decided to begin hiring Associates for his 4-GP firm in order to help him increase the number of companies he could investigate and manage. However, as our discussions continued and after I probed his thinking, he informed me that they had rethought their plans to increase their leverage. Given the high-value image they had fostered, and given the premium they placed on investing in the earliest-stage companies, he feared that moving toward a more pyramidal organization would cause more problems than it would solve. Instead, he informed me, they were going to remain a GP-only firm. These cases are consistent with the fact that a firm's founding strategy gets locked into place by the investments the firm makes to pursue that strategy, and by the internal organizational consistencies that are developed to support it (Miles and Snow 1978).

The resistance to pyramidalization also extends to some of the process changes that have accompanied the transition toward pyramids in some firms. On the one hand, some firms have formalized their processes, enabling them to separate their processes into discrete tasks, some of which can be performed by junior staff. Such processes include online tools or paper documents that facilitate and act as inputs into the decision making, in addition to face-to-face meetings. On the other hand, in firms where the investment decision making process is based on heavy, face-to-face inter-action between partners, the VCs believe that such formalization would be counterproductive. As an MP of a Boston firm stated, "How much can we put process in, to substitute for personal interaction?" Furthermore, past research has speculated that performance can begin to degrade in firms that try to use less-rich information media than are required by the complex work they do (Daft and Lengel 1984). Early-stage VC firms that go too far in breaking holistic tasks into discrete subtasks, and building pyramidal and functionally-specialized organizations to perform them may be endangering the quality of the work that GPs have been performing themselves until now. Whether firms like Crescendo Ventures (Wasserman 2003) can address such challenges will provide deeper insights into which tasks truly can be separated and delegated effectively, and which tasks must be kept whole.

Industry Downturn: Experiment Over, or Just Delayed?

There is little doubt that even beyond the challenges described above, the current extended downturn in the venture industry has had a powerful impact on the internal characteristics of VC firms. During the exploding market of the late 1990s, many firms in the industry raised large funds and began preparing organizationally for a continuing "boom market." However, with the sustained market downturn that began in 2000 and continued for several years, many of these firms have rethought their plans and reversed many of these changes. Firms that had planned to invest their latest funds within 2 years have decided to stretch that investment horizon to 4 or more years, and some have even refunded to their LPs significant amounts of the capital that had been committed to their funds. Firms that hired COOs to lead their transitions have let those COOs go, and have scaled back their plans to hire and develop large numbers of junior staff. Firms that had loosened their investment processes and requirements during the market upswing have had to tighten those requirements dramatically, and have moved toward more restrictive processes for investigating potential investments. And firms, like Salta Partners (Wasserman 2002) that moved to new structural models have reexamined those moves and have altered those approaches to be more like their pre-boom models.

Therefore, the VC industry is in the midst of a significant upheaval. The recovery from the slump will have a major organizational impact on VC firms. Does the downturn represent a temporary detour from the growth trajectory of the late 1990s, or does it represent a return to the historical level of investing? Will firms return to making the changes they began in 1999, or were those changes – and such experiments as functional-pyramidal structures – fleeting trials that do not have a place in the industry? In the words of a VC I interviewed, "Are VC firms adolescents or are they dwarfs?" In other words, are they young, small firms that will mature and grow into large, more developed firms, or are they destined to remain small, cohesive firms? Will the industry see another long "convergent" period (Tushman and Romanelli 1985) of little change before firms try again to transform themselves into large pyramidal organizations during a "revolutionary" period of fundamental change?

Given the evidence presented above and the sustained market downturn, it is tempting to conclude that the move toward pyramids will recede within these firms. However, many GPs still argue that such a move is necessary and a natural progression. For one thing, when I asked them to compare today's GP job with the challenges they faced when they first became GPs, several GPs stated that today's job is much more complex. They said that the companies in which they invest are more complex, require expertise that is more specialized, and often require global contacts and assistance that were not required in past years. As a result, these GPs felt added pressure to leverage their time effectively and to be able to draw upon

specialized expertise within their organizations leading them to build pyramidal organizations.[19]

For another, one of the major "triggers," an imminent generational
transition within the firm will only be increasing in frequency in the coming
years. These changes are continuing to lead GPs to take actions that build
their firms into "institutions" in ways that go beyond just the development
of new GPs. They are also beginning to build their firms' brands, rather than
relying on the coattails of a single prominent GP. As one COO commented,
"In the past, we never thought about the firm-level image. We relied on [one
GP's] high profile. Now, with him retiring, we're trying to build our organizational brand."

One COO believed that the delay in his firm's efforts to transition was
only temporary, and that its efforts would continue anew shortly.

> The reversal at [my firm] is not just due to market conditions. I still fundamentally
> believe that our upside-down organization has to go to a pyramid. {COO at large Boston
> firm}

Debates over the efficacy of transition toward pyramids have not just been
occurring between firms, but also within firms, as some GPs push their firms
to make a transition while other GPs fight such a change. When faced with
ambiguous signals, people derive subjective interpretations of those signals,
and "try to cram events into familiar frames of reference rather than try out
totally new frames" (McCall 1977:117). Other people interpret ambiguous
signals as conflicting with their familiar frames of reference. When members
of an organization differ in their interpretations of signals that may affect
the organization in important ways, they try to resolve the contradictory
perceptions. In many of the firms I studied, the debate over the future
evolution of the VC industry resembled such a process. GPs who perceived
the future of the industry as being pyramidal engaged in a dialogue with
GPs who saw the current structure of VC firms as necessary. The latter set of
VCs interpreted signals about changes in the industry as "deviations that fit
[their] current frames of reference" (McCall 1977:113), while the former set
of VCs interpreted them as suggesting or confirming a frame of reference
that contradicted the old frame.

In the process of resolving these competing interpretations, the GPs
within these firms were collectively trying to make sense of the evolution of
the VC industry. Two ways of doing so are the questioning of implicit
assumptions, such as the assumption that GPs in early-stage VC firms cannot leverage their time by delegating to junior staff, and "the discovery of
hidden analogies." (McCall 1977:117) One such analogy is the precedent set

in other professional services industries, like investment banking, accounting, and law. Along these lines, a comment from a GP at a prominent midsize firm that has remained very upside-down is illuminating:

> VC doesn't scale very well. It's very different from the more transaction-oriented, commoditized firms. We have a long relationship cycle, on a one-to-one basis for each GP. ... But maybe investment banks felt the same 50 years ago! ... I can't say with 100% conviction that the industry won't institutionalize. Maybe I'm just being myopic. A few years ago, even the idea of having a $1B fund in early-stage VC was unheard of, and now even we have one!

Although it is possibly the most radical of the current experiments in the VC industry, the transition toward pyramids is but one of many current experiments. In recent years, firms have also experimented with being early-stage incubators and with developing joint ventures with non-VC firms (e.g. the Accel-KKR joint venture). Some firms, such as Draper Fisher Jurvetson (DFJ), have tried to expand using a "franchising" approach. They open branches of DFJ in new regions, hire people to staff each new office, and let them operate independently. This allows them to keep the same structure and processes in place in their main office, while being able to invest in new regions. Other firms, led by Accel Partners and others, have hired venture partners and entrepreneurs-in-residence (EIRs) in order to strengthen their deal-finding and company-building capabilities while maintaining the core structure of the firm – in Scott's (1992) terms, "augmenting the hierarchy." Within the core structure, they created hierarchical distinctions within the GP team, by forming Managing Partner positions and management committees. To augment the core investment-professional structure, they have added COO positions (in addition to longstanding CFO positions) and specialized support groups. These additions help expand the volume and range of deals the firm can reach, and increase the services to portfolio companies. However, there is an interesting contrast between those firms that have chosen to transition to a new blueprint and those that have chosen to make small changes to their existing models without radically changing those models. By adding EIRs and venture partners while maintaining their upside-down structures, are the latter type of firms solving the issues facing them, without taking the huge risks associated with changing blueprints? Or, are they just "putting band aids on the problem," as one GP stated?[20]

Underlying these divergent perspectives are strikingly different philosophies about the value created by GPs. VCs who create GP-only firms often believe that they will maximize the performance of their investments if they perform all tasks themselves. Other VCs believe that GPs can delegate substantial parts of their job to junior staff in order to free themselves to focus on the tasks that only GPs can perform, thereby maximizing their performance in a very different way.

> One of the current debates within the industry is whether VC firms are dwarfs who will always be this shape, or adolescents, who will eventually grow up. {VC industry analyst}

> The heart of the question is, "What is the nature of VC?" {GP at early-stage California firm}

My fieldwork indicates that these very different views of VC can have substantial implications for the ways GPs structure their firms. Furthermore, organizational transformations that require a reorientation in the philosophies and values that underpin an organization are the hardest transformations to effect (Tushman and Romanelli 1985), leading these very different perspectives to play a central role in a firm's ability to change its organizational model. Is it possible for VC firms to become large, pyramidal organizations, or must they remain small and GP-heavy in order to succeed? Do VC firms inherently have to remain small and structured as they have been for decades, or are they going to have to "grow up" in ways that mirror the growth of firms in other professional services industries?

A Disruptive Organizational Form?

The downturn in the industry seems to have frozen or reversed efforts to change the standard VC blueprint. At the same time, it may be worthwhile to explore another possibility. In the technology-development realm, dominant technologies often begin life as inferior technologies that are derided and dismissed by the existing leaders of an industry (Christensen 1997). Initially, these technologies under-perform the market standard and only appeal to the lowest end of the industry. However, as firms improve their knowledge of the new technology and develop and improve it over time, these technologies begin to outperform the old dominant technologies and come to dominate.

In the organizational realm, an analogy may be drawn to these "disruptive technologies." New organizational forms may emerge in an industry that initially are inferior to the dominant model, but that are improved over time. In early-stage VC, such an organizational form might be the pyramidal organization, compared with the dominant non-pyramidal model. It is entirely possible that pyramidal models like Crescendo's simply cannot meet or beat the performance of the predominant model in early-stage VC firms, and will never be reach equality with that model. However, at the same time, over time, this new organizational form might improve as the early-mover pyramidal firms learn which tasks can be codified and/or delegated without imperiling their quality, learn how to integrate them with tasks that can only be done by GPs, and develop systems and processes that support the application of pyramidal structures to early-stage VC.

Should such an organizational form continue to improve, it may become what might be called a "disruptive organizational form" that comes to dominate the older organizational form in its effectiveness, efficiency, and scale. Much like Crescendo has continued to learn and refine its organizational model as it has seen its results in different investing environments, the early movers toward pyramidalization – currently derided by the existing heavyweights within the industry – may in the end develop a powerful organizational model that can outperform the GP-heavy model in many respects. If such a scenario comes to pass, the VC industry may, indeed, begin to look like the current-day legal, investment banking, consulting, and accounting industries. As Schumpeter observed, the development of similar "new types of organization" can "strike not at the margins of the profits and the output of the existing firms, but at their foundations and their very lives" (Schumpeter 1942:84), resulting in fundamental changes to industries experiencing such gales of creative destruction.

NOTES

1. Because the structural transformations that I was studying only occurred in a small set of first-movers, I could not perform significant quantitative analyses of these changes across the industry. However, should the transition be sustained across more firms, it may become feasible to perform such analyses to complement the field findings described in this chapter.

2. Another important difference between GPs and non-GPs is how they are compensated. Associates and Principals are paid salaries and, sometimes, annual bonuses based on their performance. While GPs are also paid salaries, the vast majority of their compensation comes from the share of profits, or "carry" that they receive from their investments. The GPs then split the carry among themselves. Therefore, whenever a firm hires a new GP, the share received by each of the existing VCs usually declines. This causes many firms to resist hiring senior staff unless they can make a compelling case to do so, and can increase their preference for hiring "non-carry" junior staff over carry-earning GPs. This makes it even more remarkable that upside-down pyramids predominate over pyramidal structures in the VC industry.

3. For instance, the VC firms that played a crucial role in funding and helping build such multi-billion-dollar companies as Apple, Microsoft, Intel, and Lotus were almost all smaller than 10 people.

4. This unique large-scale dataset was compiled from three major sources: the internal database maintained by the National Venture Capital Association, a database of VC firms compiled by Asset Alternatives, and original data collection by the author. The panel dataset was comprised of 327 VC firms, covered 1997–2000, and included data on firm strategies (stage of investment targeted, industries targeted, number of non-headquarters offices), firm structures (number of investment professionals at each level of the hierarchy), capital managed (number and size of funds raised), and other firm-level factors.

5. In order to specify, which firms seem most inclined to make such changes, I also briefly highlight the types of firms that seem not to be affected by each type of trigger.

6. I was able to compute summary statistics for the fund-raising, stage-change, and geographic-change triggers, but could not do so for the generational-transition trigger for which systematic data was not available.

7. His firm's LPs are mostly large institutions that have been involved in VC investing for a moderate amount of time, prefer to invest in diversified VC firms instead of picking a heterogeneous set of specialist VC firms themselves, and are not very active with regards to monitoring the internal dynamics within the firm.

8. A GP in a prominent Boston firm echoed what many other VCs had told me:

> The key thing with a lot of entrepreneurs is the size of the fund – the amount of money you'll be able to use to back them. You want to have parity with the other top VCs. {GP in prominent Boston firm}

9. Management fees are based on the amount of capital the VCs manage, and are used to pay salaries, invest in firm infrastructure, and pay other expenses.

10. According to the COO of a large international firm, "Some LPs want to put a lot of their own money to work, so they like the bigger funds."

11. A similar analysis of an increase of 50% showed a more extreme pattern, but had much fewer firms that had experienced such an increase, so I use the "33% increase" data here.

12. The firms were predominantly non-California firms that were opening offices in California in order to increase their presence in Silicon Valley.

13. At the same time, in firms where individual GPs retire at different intervals (e.g. 8–10 years apart), the firm may not experience such "waves" and instead face a regular, but reduced, impetus to bring in junior staff.

14. During the subsequent downturn in the industry, many firms that had previously raised large funds had trouble raising larger (or even similarly sized) funds. Even more extreme, firms, such as Crosspoint Venture Partners that raised overly large funds (and then could not productively invest the capital from those funds) returned to their LPs a large percentage of the unused capital. Therefore, this "trigger event" may also come in waves for some firms.

15. Once again, however, the pattern may swing back and forth if the firm reverses the strategic change – e.g. closing its new office or moving back into early-stage investing.

16. The COO also stated that some of these problems could be alleviated if the firm had mid-level people who could help manage and mentor the new Associates. However, given the long period over which the firm had not hired and developed

non-GP staff, it currently lacked mid-level personnel, and was loathe to hire any directly for fear of their not fitting in with the firm's culture.

17. At the same time, resistance could also come from lower down in the organization. For instance, at the bottom of the organization, firms that break the job into discrete tasks and delegate only a subset of the job to junior staff may have trouble retaining top junior staff.

> If someone said, "You're going to do X and not Y," they'd leave and would lose interest. Good athletes want to play a lot of sports. {Principal in New York firm}

> I wouldn't want the typical Associate's job – look through pile after pile of sh***y business plans, doing due diligence up the a**. It's a fairly narrow task then. ... None of my friends would want to work for Battery, being one of a hundred Associates. ... You're engineering the job into bits and pieces and divvying it up? You're hiring the best people to be what – staff people? {Associate in prominent Boston firm}

18. Interestingly, two of the entrepreneurs I interviewed stated that they did not know what went on within their VCs' firms, and did not care. They suspected that they would not even notice a pyramidal transition with the VCs' firms, and one stated, "Even if I did, what business is it of mine?" The other said:

> I have very little visibility into my VCs' firms. I have no idea what their processes are. I only know the things that directly affect us. I have no idea when their partner meetings are, when they do status checks, how Steve [the GP who sits on the company's board] is evaluated, etc. I read about them raising a new fund in Venture Wire, and don't know anything about their business' functioning otherwise. To some degree I don't even know what a VC does when he's not at a board meeting! {Founder-CEO of business-services company}

19. Some VCs who initially oppose a change later come to think that there is some value in adopting some elements of the pyramidal model. During my initial chat with him, a managing partner at one of the oldest VC firms stated that "If I'm alone, without someone below me, I can sit on 12 boards; if I have someone below me, I can still only sit on 12 boards." After discussing the gains that he might have from being able to delegate tasks to an Associate, thereby freeing up his time to focus on higher-level tasks, this same MP grudgingly admitted, "Okay, maybe they let you extend yourself to cover more: if I can manage to do 14 boards instead of 12 and keep the quality up, then we could theoretically increase our returns." Similarly, another GP stated when we first talked that "VC firms have to be upside down. We need to do all our own stuff without having Associates or Principals get in the way." Our discussion then proceeded to explore what the differences were between VC firms and consulting firms in which senior partners often make extensive use of junior staff to increase their leverage. When we spoke 2 months later, he began the conversation with, "I'm starting to question our model. When we first talked, I thought we had to be this way."

20. More graphically, during a recent presentation, Rosabeth Moss Kanter referred to such changes in another industry as "putting lipstick on a bulldog. ... Even after that, it's still beastly and ugly!"

ACKNOWLEDGMENTS

I would like to thank Nitin Nohria, Paul Gompers, George Baker, Peter Marsden, Vishesh Kumar, Dan Wadhwani, and participants in Harvard's Work, Organizations, and Markets seminar for their comments on an earlier draft of this chapter.

REFERENCES

Abrahamson, Eric and Gregory Fairchild. 2001. "Knowledge Industries and Idea Entrepreneurs: New Dimensions of Innovative Products, Services, and Organizations." Pp. 147–177 in *The Entrepreneurship Dynamic: The Origins of Entrepreneurship and the Evolution of Industries*, edited by Claudia Bird Schoonhoven and Elaine Romanelli. Palo Alto, CA: Stanford University Press.

Baker, G.P. and G.D. Smith. 1998. *The New Financial Capitalists: Kohlberg Kravis Roberts and the Creation of Corporate Value*. Cambridge: Cambridge University Press.

Baumard, P. 1999. *Tacit Knowledge in Organizations*. London: Sage Publications.

Blackler, F. 1995. "Knowledge, Knowledge Work and Organizations: An Overview and Interpretation." *Organization Studies* 16(6):1021–1046.

Boeker, W. 1989. "Strategic Change: The Effects of Founding and History." *Academy of Management Journal* 32:489–515.

Burns, T. and G.M. Stalker. 1961. *The Management of Innovation*. London: Tavistock.

Burton, M. Diane. 2001. "The Company they Keep: Founders' Models for Organizing New Firms." Pp. 13–39 in *The Entrepreneurship Dynamic*, edited by Claudia Bird Schoonhoven and Elaine Romanelli. Stanford, CA: Stanford University Press 2001.

Charmaz, Kathy. 1983. "The Grounded Theory Method: An Explication and Interpretation." Pp. 109–126 in *Contemporary Field Research*, edited by R.M. Emerson. Boston: Little, Brown.

Christensen, C.M. 1997. *The Innovator's Dilemma: When New Technologies Cause Great Firms to Fail*. Boston, MA: Harvard Business School Press.

Daft, R.L. and R.H. Lengel. 1984. "Information Richness: A New Approach to Managerial Behavior and Organization Design." Pp. 191–233 in *Research in Organizational Behavior* vol. 6, edited by B.M. Staw and L.L. Cummings. Greenwich, CT: JAI Press.

DiMaggio, P.J. and W.W. Powell. 1983. "The Iron Cage Revisited: Institutional Isomorphism and Collective Rationality in Organizational Fields." *American Sociological Review* 48:147–160.

Drucker, P.F. 1993. *Post-Capitalist Society*. Oxford: Butterworth-Heinemann.

Eccles, R.G. and D.B. Crane. 1988. *Doing Deals: Investment Banks at Work*. Boston, MA: Harvard Business School Press.

Eisenhardt, K.M. 1989. "Building Theories from Case Study Research." *Academy of Management Review* 14(4):532–550.

Emerson, R.M. 1962. "Power-dependence Relations." *American Sociological Review* 27:31–40.

Galanter, M. and T. Palay. 1991. *Tournament of Lawyers: The Transformation of the Big Law Firms*. Chicago, IL: University of Chicago Press.

Gilson, R.J. and R.H. Mnookin. 1985. "Sharing Among the Human Capitalists: An Economic Enquiry into the Corporate Law Firm and How Partners Split Profits." *Stanford Law Review* 37:313–392.

------. 1989. "Coming of Age in a Corporate Law Firm: The Economics of Associate Career Patterns." *Stanford Law Review* 41:567–595.

Glaser, B.G. and A.L. Strauss. 1999. *The Discovery of Grounded Theory: Strategies for Qualitative Research.* New York: Aldine de Gruyter.

Gompers, P. and J. Lerner. 1999. *The Venture Capital Cycle.* Boston: MIT Press.

------. 2001. *The Money of Invention.* Boston: Harvard Business School Press.

Hannan, M.T. and J. Freeman. 1989. *Organizational Ecology.* Boston, MA: Harvard University Press.

Hansen, M.T. 1999. "The Search-transfer Problem: The Role of Weak Ties in Sharing Knowledge Across Organization Subunits." *Administrative Science Quarterly* 44:82–111.

Hayes, S.L.III. and P.M. Hubbard. 1990. *Investment Banking: A Tale of Three Cities.* Boston, MA: Harvard Business School Press.

Lam, Alice. (2000). "Tacit Knowledge, Organizational Learning, and Societal Institutions: An Integrated framework." in *Organization Studies.* Berlin: 2000 vol. 21, Iss. 3; Pp. 487–513.

Lamoreaux, N.R., D.M.G. Raff, and P. Temin. 2003. "Beyond Markets and Hierarchies: Toward a New Synthesis of American Business History." *American Historical Review* 108(2):404–433.

Lee, K. and J.M. Pennings. 2002. "Mimicry and the Market: Adoption of a New Organizational Form." *Academy of Management Journal* 45(1):144–162.

Maister, D.H. 1993. *Managing the Professional Service Firm.* New York, NY: Free Press.

McCall, Morgan W. 1977. "Making Sense with Nonsense: Helping Frames of Reference Clash." Pp. 111–123 in *Prescriptive Models of Organizations*, edited by P.C. Nystrom and W.H. Starbuck. New York, NY: North-Holland Publishing.

McKenna, C. 2001. "The World's Newest Profession: Management Consulting in the Twentieth Century." *Enterprise & Society* 2:673–679.

Miles, R.E. and C.C. Snow. 1978. *Organizational Strategy, Structure, and Process.* New York, NY: McGraw-Hill.

Miller, D. and P.H. Friesen. 1980. "Momentum and Revolution in Organizational Adaptation." *Academy of Management Journal* 23(4):591–614.

Mintzberg, Henry. 1979. *The Structuring of Organizations.* Englewood Cliffs, NJ: Prentice-Hall.

Morris, T. and L. Empson. 1998. "Organisation and Expertise: An Exploration of Knowledge Bases and the Management of Accounting and Consulting Firms." *Accounting Organizations and Society* 23(5–6):609–624.

Nonaka, I. 1994. "A Dynamic Theory of Organizational Knowledge Creation." *Organization Science* 5:14–37.

Pfeffer, J. and G.R. Salancik. 1978. *The External Control of Organizations: A Resource Dependency Perspective.* New York, NY: Harper & Row.

Polanyi, M. 1966. *The Tacit Dimension.* Garden City, NY: Doubleday.

Prahalad, C. K., and G. Hamel. 1990. "The Core Competence of the Corporation". *Harvard Business Review* (May–June): 79–91.

Romanelli, E. and M.L. Tushman. 1994. "Organizational Transformation as Punctuated Equilibrium: An Empirical Test." *Academy of Management Journal* 37(5):1141–1166.

Schumpeter, J. 1942. *Capitalist, Socialism, and Democracy.* New York, NY: Harper & Brothers.

Scott, W.R. 1992. *Organizations: Rational, Natural, and Open Systems.* Englewood Cliffs, NJ: Prentice-Hall.

Sherer, P.D. 1995. "Leveraging Human Assets in Law Firms: Human Capital Structures and Organizational Capabilities." *Industrial and Labor Relations Review* 48:671–691.

Sherer, P.D. and K. Lee. 2002. "Institutional Change in Large Law Firms: A Resource Dependency and Institutional Perspective." *Academy of Management Journal* 45(1):102–119.

Starbuck, W.H. 1992. "Learning by Knowledge-intensive Firms." *Journal of Management Studies* 29(6):713–740.

Stinchcombe, A.L. 1965. "Organizations and Social Structure." Pp. 153–193 in *Handbook of Organizations*, edited by J.G. March. Chicago: Rand McNally.

Tushman, M.L. and E. Romanelli. 1985. "Organization Evolution: A Metamorphosis Model of Convergence and Reorientation." Pp. 171–222 in *Research in Organizational Behavior* Vol. 7, edited by L.L. Cummings and B.M. Staw. Greenwich, CT: JAI Press.

Wasserman, N. 2002. "Knowledge, Structure, and the Upside-down Venture Capitalist." *Academy of Management Annual Meeting* (Business Policy and Strategy Division).

Wasserman, N. 2002. *The Venture Capitalist as Entrepreneur: Characteristics and Dynamics Within VC Firms.* Ph. D. thesis, Harvard University, Boston, MA.

Wasserman, N. 2003. "Building to a Crescendo." *Harvard Business School case #804–009.*

Wasserman, N. 2003. "Founder-CEO Succession and the Paradox of Entrepreneurial Success." *Organization Science* 14(2):149–172.

Weber, M. 1946 tran. *From Max Weber: Essays in Sociology.* New York: Oxford University Press.

ENTREPRENEURSHIP, INDUSTRIAL POLICY AND CLUSTERS: THE GROWTH OF THE NORTH CAROLINA WINE INDUSTRY

R. Saylor Breckenridge and Ian M. Taplin

ABSTRACT

This paper examines the late 20th Century emergence of wineries in North Carolina, using the concepts of clusters and industrial policy to explain the dynamics of entrepreneurship in an embryonic industry. Specific attention is paid to how changing resource conditions (available agricultural land and financial capital) interact with an entrepreneurial climate that has fostered individual interest in winemaking to precipitate institutional changes that consolidate cluster formation. Using a model of small business growth in which firms gain credibility through identification with a cluster we trace the success of key wineries in this geographic region.

INTRODUCTION

This study examines the growth of retail wineries and commercial wine production in North Carolina. Commercial winemaking first presented itself

Entrepreneurship
Research in the Sociology of Work, Volume 15, 209–230
Copyright © 2005 by Elsevier Ltd.
ISSN: 0277-2833/doi:10.1016/S0277-2833(05)15008-0

in the state in 1835, but the industry closed at the onset of Prohibition.[1] Its rejuvenation began in the 1980s following the development of commercial grape and wine production, at the Biltmore Estate – the immense Vanderbilt family home in the western part of the state that was turned into a public museum and tourist destination in 1930. The mass of growth in the industry occurred around the turn of the 21st Century with the formation of many small, boutique wineries – these are primarily located in the central portion of the state, where weather and agricultural conditions are favorable to grape production. Specifically, between 1996 and 2003 the number of wineries in North Carolina increased from 9 to 25, with approximately 21 new wineries scheduled to open by late 2004. Similarly, wine production has increased from 220,136 gallons to 654,296 gallons in this seven year span (North Carolina Grape Council 2003). In conjunction with this growth in wine-production organizations, the number of commercial vineyards increased from 68 in 1991, to 128 in 1998, to 200 in 2001, and to 240 in 2003 – this constitutes an increase of over 250% in the space of a decade (NC Department of Agriculture 2003). From the perspective of raw grape production, aggregate data from Department of Agriculture (2003) reveals that production doubled from 900 tons of grapes utilized in 1996, to 2000 tons utilized in 2001.[2] These developments set the stage for our research. Our essential questions are then: (1) How can this phenomenon of industrial growth be explained? and (2) How does this develop an understanding of the principal forces in the story of entrepreneurship?

It is our assertion that a combination of institutional changes and stable resource conditions (agricultural land and capital for its exploitation) are supportive of an embryonic industry, and have facilitated the growth of this industry since the mid-1990s. Furthermore, this critical mass of linked resources and institutions have come together in such a way as to provide relational attributes and inter-dependencies that further stimulate entrepreneurial activity. By invoking the notions of clusters (Porter 1998) and niches (Hannan and Freeman 1989; Carroll and Hannan 2000; see Delacroix, Swaminathan and Solt (1989) for a related example), we focus on how and in what way organizational start-ups draw sustenance from their environment.

Of particular interest in this study is the way new specialist organizations emerge within a particular geographic area, and in doing so draw upon internal and external resources of that area (Saxenian 1994). We propose that this process is associated with the ecological notion of legitimacy (Hannan and Freeman 1989; Carroll and Hannan 2000): as an organizational population grows, a critical mass is reached, which can confer credibility to existing and new firms in this location, and further encourages corollary institutional changes that sustain a growth infrastructure. Further, we consider that networks and associations among firms work to further promote the legitimacy and stability of the new industry (see Brown and Butler (1995) for an example within the wine industry). By enhancing the ability of firms to extract resources and improve their chance of success, this, then further contributes to the stabilization of niche boundaries and taken-for-grantedness of the industry.

We begin with a brief review of the relevant entrepreneurship and organization literature, then examine recent institutional changes and resource conditions in NC. This is followed by a description of the typology we developed to classify the firms in our sample and subsequently an analysis of their organizational genesis. We conclude with a discussion on how the growth of firms in an emerging sector confers legitimacy upon that sector, creates opportunities for dialog and information sharing that facilitate organizational learning and enhance individual efficiency then stimulate further organizational founding.

ENTREPRENEURSHIP AND ORGANIZATIONAL FOUNDING

Traditionally, studies of entrepreneurship have focused upon individual traits that are seen as requisites for a successful new business venture (Gartner 1988). Succinctly stated these refer to an individual who perceives opportunity, defines the circumstances as being suitable for the pursuit of such an opportunity, and when acted upon presumes the possibility of success (Stevenson and Jarillo-Mossi 1986). In some instances, individuals possess unique product knowledge that sets them apart from others. In other cases, individuals have the resources (typically financial but also time) that permit them to experiment in an area, where information is imperfect but knowledge acquisition is possible in a market that encourages information sharing and a degree of co-operation. Research with this focus tends to examine the supply of individuals and their enthusiasm for entrepreneurial roles, with the more explicit sociological dimension looking at how social class and ethnicity shape such action; in other words how group characteristics might be imputed to describe the attributes of entrepreneurial initiative (Aldrich and Waldinger 1990; Light and Rosenstein 1995). In the management literature, the approach has focused more on how to sustain small business growth, with the focus more explicitly on internal development processes and personality characteristics of owners (Vinnell and Hamilton 1999).

Despite an almost intuitive assumption that explanations for entrepreneurial initiative should be adduced to individual traits, recent criticism has pointed to methodological flaws in such an approach as well as a disregard for context factors and events (see Thornton (1999) for a summary). Here, context focuses upon problems in identifying causal forces within the sphere of entrepreneurial activity; and events refers to what Glade (1967:251) described as "opportunity structure" or the conditions that encourage and facilitate entrepreneurial activity. From such critiques has emerged a greater emphasis upon entrepreneurship as being context-dependent (Reynolds 1988). This demand-side perspective not only allows the examination of broader social settings and the availability of resources (Romanelli 1989) and social networks (Aldrich 1999) that encourage start-ups, but also how individual agency interacts with such forces and vice-versa (Martinelli 1994). In other words, organizational founding is a product of the interaction between some distinctive individual attributes of entrepreneurs and broader social and economic processes, with each conferring legitimacy on the other as the growth process unfolds.

In this study of an emerging industry, we argue that institutional and political changes reorient the use of material resources and produce a new market niche that stimulates growth of new enterprises. They do so at a time when institutional forces and material resources provide incentives for individuals who otherwise might not have seized the opportunity for innovation. Furthermore, entrepreneurial activity increases as organizations flourish but this occurs within a context of cooperation and information sharing within the cluster of firms: when a critical mass emerges, it can be said that a "shared business culture" acts as catalyst for further entrepreneurial activity by attracting requisite human capital to continue developing the organizational population (Mulholland 1997). This builds upon the concept of industrial districts developed by Piore and Sabel (1984) and more recently by Schmitz (1995, 1997) who focuses upon collective efficiency. The latter, he argues, is the result of an emerging division of labor and specialization among small producers, which is followed by the emergence of suppliers of raw materials, then agents who are linked with regional distribution networks, as well as pools of workers with sector-specific skills (Schmitz 1995, 1997). In other words, clusters of similar firms themselves do not confer advantages; it is when their joint actions trigger new initiatives by supplemental industries that the competitiveness of the entire sector may be upgraded.

It is our contention that continued organizational founding in this particular sector is predicated on information sharing as a means of collectivizing organizational learning, which increases the critical mass, net of actual organizational density, that eventually confers legitimacy on the local industry. Practically, this can then lead to greater brand recognition and presumably more interest from incipient entrepreneurs; and it provides the stimulus for further small firm growth in related supply and technical services industries.

RESOURCES AND INSTITUTIONAL CHANGES

Given our emphasis upon external rather than individual factors that shape entrepreneurial behavior, which specific events help us to understand the rapid rise of a new industry such as winemaking in NC? The availability of land and capital are crucial resources for wine production among both the vineyard and winery-forms of organizations. Although barriers to entry are not high and the majority of these organizations remain small in terms of volume of grapes grown or wine produced, access to land in regions that are conducive to grape production is essential to the formation of a geographically integrated industry (Swaminathan 2001). Since most vineyards and wineries start out and remain small in size, the actual acreage does not have to be large; but the availability of agricultural land suitable for cultivation and individuals with the skill sets necessary for these endeavors is crucial.

We consider two categories of grape growers. First are those whose interest is in an integrated organization including a commercial winery. Typically, they seek out available land, initially as a site for grape growing and then locate a winery to process the harvested grapes on that land. These are people who fit the traditional entrepreneurial archetype. The second group is those who grow grapes for delivery to local wineries and who engage themselves in non commercial wine production. This group can be further subdivided. For one subset, grapes represent an embryonic interest in the industry and a first stage toward possible commercial production. Information on this group remains imprecise mainly because anecdotal evidence suggest many people have started growing grapes but have not registered their land as agricultural production for tax purposes; and even those whose land is registered for agricultural purposes often consider this activity as a hobby that is subsidized by full time employment elsewhere. Aside from data received from wineries about such purchase of grapes there is not much way of accurately determining how much grape production of this nature exists. The second sub-set refers to farmers who have systematically diversified from an existing crop. Data on this group are just emerging, largely because of the infancy of this transition and its association with the secular decline of tobacco growing in the late 1990s. Such individuals do not easily fit the entrepreneurial stereotype but their commitment to this nascent industry through risk taking behavior (and agricultural experience) is vital to its growth.

In NC, land suitable for grape production has been available in recent years as farmers have moved out of tobacco growing. Tobacco acreage is small (sometimes merely several acre plots) and is often farmed by individuals on a part-time basis outside the context of a larger agricultural enterprise; but following a recent decline in demand for tobacco crops and the creation of a fund to help farmers switch to alternate crops, grape production has been stimulated among some farmers and others have been encouraged to acquire farmland to start wineries.

The dollar value of tobacco yields has been high (approximately $4,000 per acre from an annual $1,500 per acre investment in seed and fertilizer) and consequently this crop historically has proved lucrative for small farmers. Tobacco was still the principal crop by value in NC in the mid-1990s, providing earnings of $1 billion per year for growers and sustaining 30,000 jobs within the state (Tursi, White and McQuilkin 2000:363). Tobacco growing has been based upon a quota system, in which individual farmers acquired rights to grow and harvest tobacco. This system has been rigidly enforced, effectively restricting the supply of the product but in doing so ensures a high crop value. In addition, farmers were protected with a price support system that provided further certainty in earnings. Many individuals with growing rights used tobacco as a supplemental income source, with their other employment activities often non-agricultural related.

Tobacco growing, however, has been dramatically transformed since the late 1990s following extensive litigation against tobacco companies over product liability. Facing spiraling legal costs and potentially bankrupting settlements for class action lawsuits, plus increasing public revulsion of the use of cartoons in cigarette advertising and a decline in the number of people smoking, cigarette companies have been forced to retrench and cut production or switch to export markets.[3] This has led to a decline both in the quotas for tobacco leaf and the price paid for it at auction, following a drop in demand for the crop.

By switching to grape production, such individuals can continue to extract high value from small acreage and also remain part-time if necessary. Their agricultural experience with a cash crop is transferable and they are also eligible for financial support to diversify. Following a spate of unsuccessful lawsuits against tobacco companies, a more coordinated effort on behalf of states' Medicaid systems resulted in a settlement between the big four tobacco companies (Philip Morris, RJ Reynolds, Brown and Williamson, and Lorillard) and 46 states in November 1998 (Tursi et al. 2000). According to this agreement, tobacco companies would pay the states $206 billion over 25 years and thereby insulate the industry from FDA regulation.[4] Another significant part of the agreement was the creation, in early 1999, of the Golden Leaf – a foundational fund used, in part, for farmers to offset the projected decline in tobacco use – as part of the North Carolina tobacco litigation settlement. The cigarette companies agreed to pay $5.15 billion over 12 years to this trust fund for farmers, of which almost $2 billion was assigned to NC farmers and allotment holders (Tursi et al. 2000:387). When combined with a reduction in quota allotments, the provision of such cash grants for diversification has encouraged tobacco farmers to switch crops. As of late 2003, approximately 2% of such farmers have used this money to purchase vines and the equipment necessary for cultivation and made the switch (NC Grape Council 2003).[5]

Aside from the fiscal incentives that have provided tobacco farmers with the resources to switch to grape growing, two institutional changes have provided a broad framework for sustained industry growth. In the state's only federally approved official wine region (Yadkin Valley Appellation), Surry County Community College's Viticulture and Enology program provides training and short courses for individuals interested in grape growing and wine making. Started in the late 1990s, the program has seen enrollment grow and has provided a useful source of local instruction for former tobacco farmers making the switch to grapes as well as others with not much or no agricultural experience. Regular short courses on commercial grape growing and wine-making are geared explicitly for those in the community who wish to learn new skill sets or complement their existing agricultural knowledge. Together with the agricultural extension service of North Carolina State University that has developed experimental vineyards to determine the grapes most appropriate to North Carolina's soil and climate, these educational facilities offer an institutional framework that is supportive of and helps to nurture growth in this industry. Many of the farmers who have switched to grape growing, report having taken courses at Surry Community College and been in contact with the agricultural extension agents.

Second, North Carolina uses its tax dollars from wine sales to fund the Grape Council, an umbrella organization whose aim is to promote and facilitate the growth of wineries and winemaking in the state. In addition to working with NC State University to develop experimental vineyards, it has also become a de facto marketing arm for the industry, disseminating information on grape growing, location of wineries, plus information on auxiliary production equipment in the state. In doing this, it has also conferred incipient cluster legitimacy to the local wine industry.

To summarize, consistency in land conditions, but decreasing tobacco profits for farmers combined with additional fiscal incentives to diversify and an institutional framework supportive of wine making, have come together to provide a crucial resource dynamic in sustaining the new organizational forms of wineries and the transformation of agricultural operations toward grape production.

FARMERS AND ENTREPRENEURS: GROWTH OF WINE-MAKING

Two forms of agricultural transformation are occurring in NC. As noted earlier, one is the increase in grape growing, the other of wineries. The former grow grapes for their own personal wine-making or sell to wineries; while the latter are bonded firms that can sell wine to the general public – and may, or may not, grow their own grapes. The remainder of this chapter focuses upon commercial wineries since this represents the more significant type of entrepreneurial activity in terms of risk and interdependency with market forces. It includes farmers who have diversified not just into grape growing but actual winemaking as well as others with non-agricultural backgrounds who have acquired land specifically for a vineyard and commercial wine sales. Fig. 1 presents a list of current operational wineries in NC as of 2003, with details on production and type of grape used.

In terms of capital, there are minimal barriers for entry into the small commercial vineyard or winery: they can be located in as little as a backyard or basement in some cases, and many firms rely heavily upon a pattern of familial self-exploitation to sustain the initial venture. Our research shows that owners of commercial wineries generally fit into one of two categories. They are middle aged (45 plus) and of a professional background and have made the investment decision as part of a lifestyle change; where this investment is predicated on the acquisition of relevant knowledge and skill sets and access to (either directly or indirectly) available capital sources. Furthermore, such individuals are more likely to be successful in identifying

	North Carolina Winery Production Statistics - Gallons			**(sorted by 2001 production)**		
	Winery	**Type**	**1996**	**Est. 1997**	**2000**	**2001**	**Est. 2002**
1	Biltmore Estate Winery	V	134,715	150,000	240,000	263,000	290,000
2	Duplin Winery	M	60,000	50,000	190,000	148,000	200,000
3	Shelton Vineyards	V	n/a	n/a	30,000	39,000	45,000
4	Dennis Vineyards	M	0	500	7,500	14,000	16,000
5	Westbend Vineyards	v,h	15,385	19,000	36,000	12,000	15,000
6	RayLen Vineyards	V	n/a	n/a	n/a	11,000	18,000
7	Chatham Hill Winery	v,h	n/a	n/a	11,000	8,025	11,000
8	Moonrise Bay Vineyard	v,h,f	n/a	n/a	2,500	6,000	9,000
9	Waldensian Heritage Wines	A	1,476	1,771	3,000	4,751	5,706
10	Chateau Laurinda	v,h,f	n/a	n/a	14,000	3,600	3,600
11	Windy Gap Vineyards	v,h	n/a	n/a	840	2,865	4,200
12	Rockhouse Vineyards	v,h	n/a	n/a	2,100	2,500	3,600
13	Hanover Park Vineyard	v,h	n/a	n/a	2,500	1,800	2,200
14	Martin Vineyards	v,m	2,100	2,500	2,500	1,800	2,000
15	Germanton Vineyard and Winery	h,v	1,000	1,000	1,000	1,000	2,000
16	Cerminaro Vineyard	v,h	n/a	n/a	300	900	1,100
17	Bennett Vineyards	M	5,160	10,000	8,000	800	2,400
18	SilkHope Winery	H	n/a	n/a	300	580	190
19	Ritler Ridge Vineyards	V	n/a	n/a	300	328	500
20	The Teensy Winery	V	300	300	300	300	300
21	Silver Coast Winery	V	n/a	n/a	n/a	17,100	20,000
22	Thistle Meadow Winery	V	n/a	n/a	n/a	n/a	2,500
23	RagApple Lassie	V	n/a	n/a	n/a	n/a	?
24	Hinnant Farms	M	n/a	n/a	n/a	n/a	?
25	Stony Mountain Vineyards	M	n/a				
	Total Gallons		**220,136**	**235,071**	**552,140**	**539,349**	**654,296**

n/a = not in production   v = vinifera
                                 h = Irbid
                                 a = american
                                 m = muscadine
                                 f = fruit
                                 (listed in order of predominance)

Fig. 1. North Carolina Winery Production Statistics – Gallons (sorted by 2001 production).

and networking with existing organizations and acquiring resources – most specifically grapes from other vineyards – within the emerging niche. Alternately, winery owners are farmers, whose crop holdings are diversified and whose background has made them less risk averse and willing to embrace new business opportunities. Identification of this group is consistent with the studies on self-employed farmers that show them to be more educated and better able to adjust to economic disequilibrium and hence are more likely to innovate, and to do so successfully (Schultz 1975). In either case, any onsite land that is used for grapes is quite likely to have been formerly devoted to tobacco production; and its availability (either on the market or through crop diversification) is a direct consequence of the secular decline in the tobacco crop in recent years.

Within vineyard operations, once vines are planted, it is 3–5 years before they bear significant grape harvests of the quality and quantity necessary for winemaking. Consequently, the up-front costs are highly relative to realized potential, and this requires a longer term orientation or expenditure indifference to business than is normal among entrepreneurial foundings. Furthermore, once a particular type of grape is planted, this investment is relatively fixed and invariable. This imposes restrictions on switching to meet variable demand for products and pre-disposes winemakers to a medium term production outlook. However, wineries with sufficient fiscal resources can purchase different grape types from external producers to make a variety of wines and exploit new consumer niches. In doing this, firms typically leverage their competencies derived from the winemaking process, moving laterally and further contributing to product diversification within the cluster. This form of product differentiation can be as important as economies of scale in realizing cost advantages (Bain 1956), although excessive brand proliferation can inhibit specialist growth in areas where mass producers have established identities (Swaminathan 2001). Yet, if a cluster is to establish a robust identity without recourse to individual marketing, then it must initially rely upon brand replication and locational identification with that brand to confer operational legitimacy.

DATA AND METHODS

In addition to descriptive statistics we have relied heavily upon organizational ethnographies. As key players in the growth of this industry, owners of wineries, and in some cases the wine makers who are employed by the owners, are crucial sources of information. The rich contextual details derived from interviews with these informants enabled us to chronicle individual narratives, the aggregate of which depict the genesis of the recent growth as well as the current status of the industry.

Starting in late 2002, we interviewed owners or wine makers in 14 wineries in North Carolina (56% of the total population of wineries in the state as of late 2003). In determining our sample, we wanted to focus primarily but not exclusively upon the Yadkin Valley Appellation, a geographical area in the central portion of the state, where the majority of new wineries are located and actual vinifera grape cultivation occurs.[6] Our sample therefore includes 100% of the wineries in this geographic area (the cluster), plus those who purchase grapes from farmers in this cluster region. Other wineries outside of this area were selected on the basis of convenience and to determine how much variation existed outside of the central area.

Interviews typically lasted an hour or more, and were followed by a tour of the winery. We used an interview questionnaire designed to elicit information on organizational founding, capital sources, ownership structure, size, and basic production figures together with sales data. We also asked open-ended questions about the current state of the wine industry in NC as well as reasons for its possible growth. We used these questions to probe for additional explanatory factors not necessarily included in our analytical framework. See Appendix A for a copy of the survey questionnaire and Appendix B for a list of the wineries where interviews were conducted.

We also interviewed individuals from the key institutional agencies (NC Grape Council, Surry County Community College, Yadkin County Agricultural Extension Agency) to elicit further information on policy measures and growth initiatives that have shaped the industry's evolution.

We developed a simple typology that allowed us to classify NC wineries into three types based upon size and resources.

- First are the large, capital intensive, wineries; of which there are two in the current sample. Typically, this type of enterprise has been found by one or more individuals using existing wealth to cross-subsidize start-up and current/future operating costs. Profitability is an eventual goal but not necessary in the years immediately following inception. Such wineries seek to produce over 100,000 gallons of wine per year and may have 30 acres or more of vines. Here, start-up capital costs can exceed $500,000 and the firms employ at least one full-time professional winemaker.
- Second are the small to medium sized wineries producing between 10,000 and 50,000 gallons of wine per year of which there are four in the current sample. These were started by farmers who owned agricultural land, then switched from tobacco (and other crops such as corn and soy beans) to grapes in search of greater profitability. Land under vines is anywhere between 10 and 40 acres, and start-up capital costs are generally in the

$250,000–500,000 range. In these case, some have learned winemaking whereas others have brought in professional full-time or part-time winemakers.

- Finally, there are small, boutique wineries, producing less than 10,000 gallons of wine per year, with generally less than 10 acres under vines. There are eight such operations in our sample. These are low volume operations, with minimal capital start-up costs (probably less than $100,000), but a greater imperative for more immediate profit-making since they are self-financed and with limited financial resources. Individuals running these wineries typically started growing grapes and making wine for their own consumption, then moved to commercial operations (albeit small scale) to cover their increased production costs. Their goal is typically to stay small (<2000 cases per year) and focus upon higher value-added production and/or serving low cost niche markets. In all cases, one of the owners is the winemaker.

The crucial feature of large wineries is that their founders have been able to massively subsidize the cost of start-up by recourse to private capital sources. However, it is precisely such individuals who have been in the forefront in both creating an institutional environment supportive of the wine industry and then capitalizing upon such subsequent support. For example, the owners of one of the largest wineries in the state were instrumental in setting up a formal Viticulture and Enology Program at the community college within the Yadkin Valley Appellation area in an attempt to provide training for farmers interested in growing grapes and making wine. Although they might not necessarily have used such a program themselves, it was seen as part of the legitimacy building process necessary for the NC wine industry to be established. As one of the owners said, "we are building a wine making culture in this area and we really hope, and expect, more and more folks to start wineries around here."

This winery, located on a 383 acre estate, some of which originally was devoted to tobacco, saw vines planted in 1999. The growth of their professional and administrative staff has enabled them to specialize in different facets of production. This has included hiring both a full-time experienced wine maker, who previously worked in another state's well-established wine industry, and an experienced vineyard manager. It has also enabled them to spearhead the often cumbersome and lengthy (2 year) process of securing appellation status for the Yadkin Valley where they are located (On the Vine 2003:3). This viticultural designation draws attention to NC wines and allows the area to be distinguished from others by virtue of the character of wine. The existence of at least one large winery and several medium-sized ones within the Yadkin Valley American Viticultural Area (AVA) helps to further consolidate the awareness and credibility of winemaking in the region.

Among small to medium sized wineries, many have been found by individuals who owned agricultural land, some of which was devoted to tobacco, but who have sought an alternative crop that is more profitable. With the decline in tobacco quotas – contracted volumes of tobacco to be grown for buyers – and the price paid for tobacco leaf, such farmers were looking for a substitute, more viable crop. A growing awareness of the possibilities of winemaking and profitability of vinifera has encouraged the switch, money from the state-based Golden Leaf foundation helps cover start-up costs for transformation away from tobacco based agriculture (in this case, vine purchase), and the availability of winemaking classes at local colleges provides valuable skill acquisition. For example, one farmer in Yadkin Valley saw his tobacco allotment drop by 53% over the past few years. Coupled with insufficient returns from alternative crops he had planted, he has decided to try grapes where he hopes to earn four times as much as he was doing with tobacco. After planting the vines and establishing a winery, he has seen considerable interest from neighboring farmers who are also making the switch for the same reasons.

Another former tobacco and soybean farmer in the central part of NC started growing grapes 30 years ago to supplement his income. For years, he sold them to a local winery but recently started his own winery following a further reduction in his tobacco allotment. Golden Leaf money has been helpful ("manna from heaven" he indicated) in that it helps subsidize some of his operating costs. He also welcomes the addition of more wineries since it brings further exposure to the industry. When asked about competitive pressures, his response was

> The more wineries, the better as far as I am concerned. I'd like someone to start one next to me, or down the road since it would make people realize that there's something going on here. We'd all make slightly different wines and it would get the word out. I talk to friends and other farmers around here and try and convince them that this would be a good thing to do. You can make money out of it and it's just the same as other farm work.

Another winery owner said that Golden Leaf money has been good to help the transformation from tobacco to grapes because in earlier years there was not much support for the industry. This particular winery was one of the first to be established and has slowly built a reputation. However, the owner felt that it is only recently that the state has started paying attention to the viability and commercial potential (tourism related) of wineries unlike neighboring Virginia where the state has played a more active role. According to this owner, the establishment of enology programs has clearly helped by increasing the local pool of skilled workers in this area, as the NC grape council, which provides assistance with start-up information. It has been the tobacco settlements that provide the impetus for much of this change, since it has forced many farmers to look for alternative crops.

There are difficulties that farmers acknowledge in growing grapes let alone starting a winery. Compared to existing crops with established markets grapes are a niche crop. Furthermore, it is a long term investment, with new skill sets and a greater need for marketing the end product. Compared to tobacco it will probably never be as profitable.[7] This probably explains the reluctance of many farmers in the area to make the switch. These farmers have sometimes concentrated merely on grape growing for sale to established wineries. Those who have started wineries are nonetheless quite sanguine about their move. A fourth generation farmer commented on the stark reality of switching to winemaking stating that the alternative would probably be to lose his family farm. "It is a risk and a big investment, but agriculture is all about risk. I think wine is the future for this area so I might as well get into it now. The opportunity is good and there is enough people around here to help me learn."

Small, boutique wineries are the fastest growing categorization of wineries and also the one where profits (albeit small) are most likely to be made at the present time. Largely self-financed, often by individuals who have taken early retirement, these wineries are in many respects classical entrepreneurial enterprises. Stimulated by an abiding interest in wine, individuals in this category have found themselves with an opportunity to pursue their interest. Taking advantage of a growing market segment and interest in local wines, they have used modest resources and patterns of familial self-exploitation to start the enterprise. Skill in winemaking has been initially self-taught ("a process of trial and error to figure out what would grow and then what is the best way to make the wine" – comments of a four and a half acre winery owner), but local agricultural resources have been used as the winery production grew.

As these wineries have grown, and their winemaking skills improved, some have bought grapes to supplement their own production. One owner commented

I figured out two years ago that I was better at making wine than growing grapes so I've cut back on my own vineyard expansion plans and started buying more locally. There's more and more grapes being grown by local folks and the quality has improved. The prices are still good so it's viable for me to do it this way and then I can concentrate on making different types of wines. I've also been able to blend similar grapes from different growers and that's been good.

This same winery owner said that some of his grapes that are bought come from former tobacco farmers who have switched to grapes and he foresees that increasing in the future. As he went on to say, "the more local grapes there are the better the choice for me. Quality is bound to improve, especially since buyers are becoming more picky about what they buy." On this same point, another small winery owner said that in the past few years more and more people have been calling him and offering to sell him grapes. He did not know if these were former tobacco farmers, but did comment that the quality was varied when he looked at the grapes suggesting that many growers are still developing the skills necessary to grow optimal grapes.

Another owner of a small winery adjacent to his residence commented on the initial difficulty he had in gaining the relevant information and resources to start his winery. He bought the house when he took early retirement because it had sufficient land that was appropriate for vines. In early years, he had to go out of state to learn winemaking and gain specialist help. Now, he said much of this is available locally. Even though his location is outside of the primary wine growing region in NC he nonetheless is able to secure the necessary resources for production at a lower cost than in his early growing years. He also said his sales have increased as more people come to the area specifically to visit wineries and buy wines.

Yet another owner sought capital from several friends who thought "it would be fun to open a winery," but soon found that the work was hard, but that modest profits could be made. This particular individual chose to locate his winery adjacent to a large metropolitan area in the state, but sourced his grapes from a vineyard 100 miles away where the climatic and soil conditions where most suitable for the type of wine he wanted to make. He entered into a partnership with the vineyard owner whose land was formerly tobacco land but had been acquired from a local farmer who wanted to retire from farming.

Similarly, another recently opened winery close to the coast, where conditions do not permit the growth of vinifera grapes, was located there precisely because of market factors. The owner (a recent executive who took "very" early retirement) reasoned that the sales potential in this area, where close to 250,000 people live and with a high tourist market, would enable the business to grow faster than if the winery was located in the area where the grapes are grown. The owner commented

> "When it rains they can't go to the beach or play golf so they have to do something else. I'm trying to fill that gap and give tourists something to do when the weather's bad. I think of myself as being in the tourism industry as much as wine making. That's why I have built this banquet facility, and have the small art gallery and shop as part of the winery."

Initially, this winery's grapes were bought from another state but now are under contract from growers in the Yadkin Valley where the owner noted that the quality of crop has improved in the last few years.

In both these cases, owners of wineries made strategic decisions regarding location to maximize their sales potential. They also chose to focus exclusively upon local grapes in their production, capitalizing upon what they see as increasing credibility of NC wines.

CLUSTERS AND COOPERATION

Every informant, no matter what the size or category of firm, reported a high degree of information sharing between wineries, especially in the inception period. New owners went in search of information from existing owners who were willing to share it with them. Nobody indicated that such cooperation might be inimical to competitive behavior – instead it was seen as normative in this geographic concentration of firms. This practice appears to have become institutionalized and has minimized the costs associated with start-up. When asked about grape purchases, several owners said they relied upon an informal network of contacts that provided accurate information about quality and reliability of products. Contracts for purchases were similarly either on the spot market or involved little formalism in specifying amounts, etc.

The more wineries that exist, the more this informational cluster grows. Not only does this help legitimize the industry, but also creates an opportunity for dialog and organizational learning for firms whose access to information can be difficult. Instead of distorting competition, such co-operation enhances individual efficiency by providing informational co-ordination and minimizing the impact of negative externalities. As more wineries are established, the provision of traded and non-traded inputs increases in variety and at a lower cost. This growth also complements and enhances the institutional provisions that support industry establishment.

CONCLUSIONS AND CONTINUING RESEARCH

The data presented here intertwine the histories of three organizational populations – tobacco farms, vineyards, and wineries – arguing that these paths are linked via the unique conjuncture of key contextual processes. Precisely, we find evidence that it is the legislation against the tobacco industry that reduces the ability of small land-holding farmers to acquire the contracts necessary to farm tobacco; and reduce the profits of large land-holders who incorporate tobacco into their crops. The similar agricultural demands of viticulture, combined with state encouragements then produces increased orientation to grapes; and combined with tax incentives toward wine production and state and industry-based initiatives enable the growth of the wine industry in North Carolina. Parallel to such processes has been the existence of a set of individuals, with resources and desire for a change in life style, who have individually pioneered the winery concept. They have been in the forefront of articulating its importance in the local economy, either pro-actively through lobbying or implicitly by their persistence in marketing the finished product (wine). Their modest success, demonstrated by production levels and sales, has been achieved through cooperation and an explicit willingness to further the legitimacy of the industry by encouraging new winery start-ups. By externalizing organizational learning and making it a community property, they have eliminated many of the imperfect information risks entrepreneurs typically face.

This research then confirms the notion that externalities are a significant locus of entrepreneurial endeavors. Following the general recommendations of Thornton (1999), while focusing on relationships between inter-dependent industries and the institutional environment, forces driving entrepreneurial efforts can be isolated alongwith individual desire and capital. As such, a synergistic formula is presented that encourages a sociological approach on entrepreneurship: examining market and political forces as the context within which individual action can take place. From an applied perspective, recognizing changes in organizational clustering is a valuable tool to understand social environments, structures, and cultures in general and specifically how they shape entrepreneurial behavior. Geographically oriented clusters of organizations manifest as key features of the social environment, in part, by locally affecting types of jobs and careers, employment rates, general economic conditions (Schmitz 1995), and broadly affecting the nature of social life (Enright 1998). For example, the structure of social relationships has been shown to be associated with the clustering of the cattle and meat-packing industries in the U.S. plains states; the clustering of the textile industry; and different regions of California are alternately identified via clustering in the computer industry (Porter 1998) or – key to the focus of this research – the wine industry (Swaminathan 2001). Although future research is necessary on the cultural and psychological attributes of individual entrepreneurs, the conditions that shape their initial success and the way external forces sustain organizational growth will continue to yield rich explanatory data on such foundings.

In addition to the pursuit of more direct ecological analyses of founding and failure of organizations (Hannan and Freeman 1989; Carroll and Hannan 2000; see Baum (1999) for a review), of particular note for future research on this topic are contrasting stories about power at the intersection of vineyards and wineries. Is it that – as Gohdes (1982) indicates – the state encouraged the transformation of tobacco agriculture to viticulture and a marginal market in adjacent states led to vineyard expansion into winery operations? Or, have winery owners encouraged the tobacco-to-grape transformation in order to acquire the resources necessary to expand from hobbyist operations into profit-oriented business? Or, perhaps more reasonably, does this power systematically vary over time in response to external conditions (e.g. legitimation and competition)?

NOTES

1. North Carolina's first commercial vineyard, Medoc vineyard, was founded in 1835 in Halifax County and the state's Scuppernog vine can be traced even further back in history: to Walter Raleigh's Colony on Roanoake Island in the 16th century (Gohdes 1982).

2. It is, however, difficult to determine exactly what acreage is currently devoted to grape production, as well as what percentage of the production is used for commercial wine making. There is significant anecdotal evidence of grape growing on small (less than 10 acres) plots, but that the land is often not registered as agricultural property for tax purposes. This is quite remarkable since much of this land is in areas where non-agricultural property is taxed at a higher rate than agricultural property, thereby providing owners with fiscal incentives to record their property accurately.

3. Smoking rates (defined as those people 18 years of age or older who currently smoke every day or some days and have smoked at least 100 cigarettes in their life time) have gradually declined from 31.9% in 1983, to 25.3% in 1990, to 24.6% in 1995 and to 22.7% in 2001 (U.S. Department of Health and Human Services 2003).

4. There continues to be questions raised in the general press about whether new legislation might eventually modify this agreement. For example, current discussions in Congress over the tobacco quota buy-out might conceivably place further restrictions on the industry in terms of advertising and FDA regulation.

5. This number might seem small in percentage terms, but given the large number of tobacco farmers the absolute numbers are nonetheless significant. Strawberry plants are another crop that tobacco farmers have diversified into through grants from the Tobacco Communities Reinvestment Project. Like vines, the initial investment can be quite high ($8,000 per acre compared with $10,000–11,000 per acre for vines) hence the attraction of the grants as a fiscal incentive ("Growers hesitant to turn a new leaf," *Winston-Salem Journal*, August 31, 2003).

6. Vinifera refers to grapes specifically oriented to wine making (e.g. cabernet or pinot noir).

7. Tobacco accounted for 22% of the $3.1 billion in cash receipts from crops grown in NC in 2001; fruit accounted for 2% and vegetables 9.5%. "Growers hesitant to turn a new leaf" *Winston-Salem Journal*, August 31, 2003.

ACKNOWLEDGMENTS

Earlier versions of this chapter were presented at the American Sociological Association annual meeting, Atlanta, 2003 and at the Department of Sociology, UNC-Charlotte. We appreciate the many useful comments received at these presentations and also would like to acknowledge the research help of Arwen Hunter in the early phases of this project.

REFERENCES

Aldrich, H. 1999. *Organizations Evolving*. Thousand Oaks, CA: Sage Publications.

Aldrich, H. and R. Waldinger. 1990. "Ethnicity and Entrepreneurship." *Annual Review of Sociology* 16:111–135.

Bain, J.S. 1956. *Barriers to New Competition*. Cambridge, MA: Harvard University Press.

Baum, Joel A.C. 1999. "Organizational Ecology." in *Studying Organization: Theory and Method*, edited by S.R. Clegg and C. Hardy. Thousand Oaks, CA: Sage Publications.

Brown, B. and J. Butler. 1995. "Competitors as Allies: A Study of Entrpreneurial Networks in the U.S. Wine Industry." *Journal of Small Business Management* 33(3):57–66.

Carroll, G. and M.T. Hannan. 2000. *The Demography of Corporations and Industries*. Princeton: Princeton University Press.

Delacroix, J., A. Swaminathan, and M.E. Solt. 1989. "Density Dependency versus Population Dynamics: An Ecological Study of Failings in the California Wine Industry." *American Sociological Review* 54:245–262.

Enright, M.J. 1998. "Regional Clusters and Firm Strategy." in *The Dynamic Firm*, edited by A. Chandler, P. Hegstrom and V. Solvell. Oxford: Oxford University Press.

Gartner, W.B. 1988. "Who is an Entrepreneur? is the Wrong Question." *American Journal of Small Business* 12/4:11–32.

Glade, W.P. 1967. "Approaches to a theory of entrepreneurial formation." *Explorations in Entrepreneurial History*, 2nd Ser., 4(3):245–259.

Gohdes, C. 1982. *Scuppernong: North Carolina's Grape and Its Wines*. Durham, NC: Duke University Press.

Hannan, M.T. and J. Freeman. 1989. *Organizational Ecology*. Cambridge, MA: Harvard University Press.

Light, I. and C. Rosenstein. 1995. *Race, Ethnicity and Entrepreneurship in Urban America*. New York: Aldine De Gruyter.

Martinelli, A. 1994. "Entrepreneurship and Management." Pp. 476–503 in *Handbook of Economic Sociology*, edited by N.J. Smelser and R. Swedburg. Princeton: Princeton University Press.

Mulholland, K. 1997. "The Family Enterprise and Business Strategies." *Work, Employment and Society* 11(4):685–711.

North Carolina Department of Agriculture. (2003). www.agr.state.nc.us/.

North Carolina Grape Council. (2003). www.ncwine.org/gchist.htm.

On the Vine. (2003). www.onthevine.net.

Piore, M.J. and C.F. Sabel. 1984. *The Second Industrial Divide*. New York: Basic Books.

Porter, M. 1998. "Clusters and the New Economics of Competition." *Harvard Business Review* 76/6:77–90.

Romanelli, E. 1989. "Organization Birth and Population Variety: A Community Perspective on Origins." Pp. 211–246 in *Research in Organizational Behavior* vol. 11, edited by L.L. Cummins and B.M. Staw. Greenwich, CT: JAI.

Saxenian, A. 1994. *Regional Advantage: Culture and Competition in Silicon Valley and Route 128*. Cambridge: Harvard University Press.

Schmitz, H. 1995. "Collective Efficiency: Growth Path for Small-Scale Industry." *Journal of Development Studies* 31/4:9–128.

------ 1997. "Collective Efficiency and Increasing Returns." Working Paper No.50. Brighton: Institute of Development Studies, University of Sussex.

Schultz, T.W. 1975. "The Value of the Ability to Deal with Disequilibria." *Journal of Economic Literature* 13(3):827–846.

Stevenson, H.H. and J.C. Jarillo-Mossi. 1986. "Preserving Entrepreneurship as Companies Grow." *Journal of Business Strategy* 7(1):10–23.

Swaminathan, A. 2001. "Resource Partitioning and the Evolution of Specialist Organizations: The Role of Location and Identity in the U.S. Wine Industry." *Academy of Management Journal* 44/6:1169–1185.

Thornton, P. 1999. "The Sociology of Entrepreneurship." *Annual Review of Sociology* 24:19–46.

Tursi, F.V., S.E. White, and S. McQuilkin. 2000. *Lost Empire: The Fall of R.J. Reynolds Tobacco Company*. Winston-Salem, NC: Winston-Salem Journal.

Vinnell, R. and T. Hamilton. 1999. "A Historical Perspective on Small Firm Development." *Entrepreneurship, Theory and Practice* 23/4:5–18.

APPENDIX A

Interview Questions

Name of winery_____

Location of winery_____

Owner (s) _____

Age (s) _____

1. Date of founding
2. What made you interested in making wine commercially?
3. Capital source?
4. Capital expenditures (type of equipment)?
5. What determined your choice of grapes?
6. From whom did you buy your vines? How was your knowledge of this product determined? How was additional knowledge about production acquired?
7. What did you know about winemaking and general viticulture prior to embarking upon this venture?
8. When were wines first sold?
9. Size – acreage
10. Yield – lbs per acre
11. Volume – # of bottles/cases produced
12. Profits; costs/sales ratio
13. Ratio of grapes bought to wine produced? How has this changed?
14. From whom are grapes bought and how were contacts established?
15. Number of employees
16. Skill level of employees
17. Sales volume (1) direct sales from winery (2) retail outlets (wine shops, supermarkets (3) restaurants
18. Sales: in state v out-of-state

APPENDIX B

List of Wineries Included in the Sample Plus the Key Informant

Shelton Winery	General manager
Dennis Vineyards	Owner
Westbend Vineyards	Owner
RayLen Vineyards	Winemaker
Windy Gap Vineyards	Owner
Chateau Laurinda	Owner
Hanover Park Vineyards	Owner
Germanton Vineyard	Owner
Cerminaro Vineyard	Owner
Silver Coast Winery	Owner
Rag Apple Lassie	Winemaker
Hinnant Farms	Owner
Stony Mountain Vineyards	Owner
Chatham Hill Winery	Manager

PART III:
CONTEXT AND OPPORTUNITIES

SOCIALIZING THE ETHNIC MARKET: A FRAME ANALYSIS

Louis Corsino and Maricela Soto

ABSTRACT

The Mexican-American population has experienced a dramatic increase in ethnic entrepreneurship over the last several decades. In an attempt to explain this development, 25 Mexican-American entrepreneurs were interviewed in the Chicago area. These interviews focused upon the specific ethnic strategies used by these entrepreneurs to bridge the gap between the opportunity structures for entrepreneurship in the United States economy and the unique group characteristics or capacities for entrepreneurship characterizing the Mexican-American population. Based upon these interviews, we found that the favored ethnic strategy used by Mexican-American entrepreneurs involved attempts at socializing the economic encounter between co-ethnic customers and entrepreneurs. These socializing activities were examined using Goffman's frame analysis, with particular attention devoted to the collective organization of customer and entrepreneur experience in terms of an ethnic frame.

INTRODUCTION

Ethnic entrepreneurship has long offered one of the more alluring, though one of the most difficult routes to success in American society.

Entrepreneurship
Research in the Sociology of Work, Volume 15, 233–256
ISSN: 0277-2833/doi:10.1016/S0277-2833(05)15009-2

Immigrant Jews, Chinese, Italians, and Greeks are just several ethnic groups who have historically included ethnic entrepreneurship as an avenue for mobility. In more recent years, Koreans, Arabs, Cubans, and Pakistanis are among new wave immigrants who have turned heavily to self-employment as a way of overcoming economically marginal positions. Along with the increasing presence of African-American entrepreneurs, this more recent wave of immigrants to America has contributed greatly to a resurgence in ethnic entrepreneurship. Thus, at any given time in the United States, over 10 million people are attempting to create a new business. New business development is as prevalent today as getting married or having a baby and racial and ethnic groups, as a whole, have higher rates of entrepreneurship than do whites (Reynolds et al. 2002). Quite understandably, these trends have also created a renewed interest among scholars attempting to explain the array of personal attributes, cultural resources, and structural opportunities (or disadvantages) that account for successful entrepreneurship (for reviews, see Bates 1997; Light and Karageorgis 1994; Light and Rosenstein 1995; Waldinger et al. 1990).

This general growth in ethnic entrepreneurship, however, obscures important variations within particular ethnic groups. There is, perhaps, no more intriguing example than with the entrepreneurship of Mexican-Americans. Though constituting the largest immigrant population in the United States, Mexican-Americans historically have had one of the lowest rates of business ownership (U.S. Bureau of the Census 1986), have ranked near the bottom in terms of self-employed persons per size of ethnic group (Waldinger and Aldrich 1990:54), and, generally, have not been counted among the more successful ethnic entrepreneurs (see Hoffman and Marger 1991; Light and Rosenstein 1995; Valdivieso 1981; Villar 1994).

As one might expect, there has been no shortage of explanations for this lack of entrepreneurial success. The sojourner status of many Mexican immigrants, the low levels of work skills among the Mexican-American population, the abiding discrimination and prejudice against Mexicans, the political-economic cleavages within the Mexican-American community, and the absorption of Mexican workers into non-entrepreneurial sectors of the economy have all been thought to contribute to an economic, cultural, and social structure that confronts and poses obstacles to the development of Mexican-American ethnic enterprises (Aponte 1990; Chavez 1988; Goodis 1986; Hansen and Cardenas 1988; Portes and Bach 1985; Torres 1988; Waldinger and Bozorgmehr 1996).

While these obstacles continue to limit entrepreneurial opportunities, there is growing evidence that Mexican-Americans, as part of a larger pan-Hispanic movement, have reversed these historical trends and are experiencing substantial growth in self-employment. Thus, a number of case studies point to the development of these ethnic economies in selected urban environments (for example, Alvarez 1990; Spener 1995; Villar 1994). And in more quantitative terms there is ample evidence that Mexican-American firms are increasing in absolute numbers. Thus, the number of Hispanic owned small businesses in the United States increased 80% from 1982 to 1987 and then increased another 76% from 1987 to 1992. This compares favorably with all U.S. business where the increases over these two time spans were 28% and 26%, respectively (U.S. Bureau of the Census 1992, 1996b; U.S. Small Business Administration 1993). With respect to Mexican owned firms in particular, over the 10 year period from 1982 to 1992, the number of these Mexican firms in the United States increased from approximately 143,000 to over 378,000 – a 160% gain. Over this same time, total sales for Mexican-owned business increased more than four-fold from $7 billion to close to $29 billion. And the number of people employed in Mexican owned firms jumped from 106,000 to nearly 324,000 – an increase of over 200% (U.S. Bureau of the Census 1986, 1996b). Although the self-employment *rates* of Mexican-Americans still rank below the average rates for other ethnic/racial groups in the United States (Fairlie and Meyer 1996; Light and Gold 2000), the sheer size of the Mexican-American population offers a compelling argument for our attention to Mexican-American entrepreneurship.

Given these developments, it is important to understand the social and cultural factors that have affected this entrepreneurship. As the Mexican-American population increases in size and economic power, Mexican-American entrepreneurship is likely to play an even more significant role within the Mexican-American population and the larger United States economy. With this in mind, this study will examine what might arguably be the most critical, the most central element in the success of ethnic entrepreneurs (e.g. see Light and Karageorgis 1994; Waldinger, Aldrich and Ward 1990). We will examine the ethnic strategies used by Mexican-American entrepreneurs to create and maintain a successful ethnic enterprise. In doing so, we hope to contribute to a greater understanding of the conditions and possibilities for ethnic entrepreneurship among Mexican-American entrepreneurs and, more generally, for entrepreneurs from a variety of ethnic group contexts.

ETHNIC STRATEGIES, INTERACTION THEORY, AND FRAME ANALYSIS

By ethnic strategies we mean the unique adaptations or manipulations ethnic businesses develop as responses to any number of problems that impede the founding or the maintenance of a business venture. For example, in dealing with problems of recruiting and maintaining reliable workers, many ethnic groups look to family and kinship ties for support; or in dealing with problems of competition from other ethnic groups, entrepreneurs may form mutually supportive trade associations. These types of emergent reactions to the demand and supply side of entrepreneurial ventures stand at the center of successful entrepreneurial activities. They provide the fit between what ethnic groups can supply and what consumers demand.

This focus upon these emergent, ethnic strategies derives from the interaction theory of ethnic entrepreneurship as proposed by Aldrich and Waldinger (1990) and Waldinger, Aldrich and Ward (1990). In this view, the development of ethnic enterprises is explained as a conjuncture of two related processes. First, the business success of any particular ethnic group may be examined in terms of the group's access to opportunity structures in the larger society – i.e., favorable concentrations of co-ethnic customers, a minimum of interethnic competition, or the presence of state policies or resources that favor small business development. Second, entrepreneurial success may be explained by the predisposing sociocultural orientations and capacities for resource mobilization characterizing particular ethnic groups – i.e. cultural aspirations for achievement, networks of kinship and friendship, or access to capital. Taken together, opportunity structures and group characteristics set the stage for the emergence of ethnic strategies. Ethnic entrepreneurs are able to position themselves favorably within a structure of opportunities because their particular mix of ethnic and class resources provide market advantages for which mainstream entrepreneurs are ill-equipped.

In this respect, successful ethnic strategies constitute an amalgam of micro and macro level processes. These strategies can not help but be embedded in and, most importantly, serve as a link between the more personal, the more proximate attributes that entrepreneurs bring to various economic encounters, on the one hand, and the more distal, the more encompassing political and economic structures that constrain or promote these encounters, on the other. In this sense, ethnic strategies are most appropriately viewed as a subset of what Maines (1982) and Hall (1987, 1995) term the mesodomain of social organizations. These strategies serve as the linkages through which ethnic entrepreneurs activate, strengthen, and order the available opportunity structures in the direction of entrepreneurial success and, at the same time, activate, strengthen, and order the predisposing, ethnic group characteristics that are relevant (or irrelevant) to successful ethnic entrepreneurship. By applying Hall's terminology, ethnic strategies are the links through which the consequences of both the opportunity structures and the predisposing group characteristics are turned into the on-going conditions impacting ethnic entrepreneurial success.

There has been considerable research undertaken on identifying these, emergent ethnic strategies (see e.g. Boissevain and Grotenberg 1986; Light and Bonacich 1988; Waldinger et al. 1990). Yet, there has been little detailed analysis of the precise mechanisms that link these micro and macro processes together. We are presented with insightful evidence on the use of protected markets, kinship ties, the provision of special services, and the like, but the social, psychological and structural bridges that produce these ethnic strategies have not been revealed. We are left without a clear understanding of the active agency entrepreneurs, typically employ to create successful business ventures. At the same time, previous studies have been *a*-theoretic. They have largely presented information on ethnic strategies in an ad hoc and idiosyncratic manner, offering descriptions of these ethnic strategies that are especially context specific (for an exception, see Boissevain et al. 1990). Though valuable in their own right, such descriptions make comparisons between different groups of ethnic entrepreneurs most difficult. There is little basis to build a more systematic understanding of the similarities and differences in ethnic strategies across various types of businesses, different stages in the development of ethnic enterprises, different ethnic group ventures, and so forth.

With these questions in mind, one avenue for exploring these ethnic strategies in greater depth is provided by Goffman's *Frame Analysis* (1974). By social frames Goffman means the complex of meanings, rules, rituals, mannerisms, physical settings, and the like that give collective definition to activities and experiences. Frames are socially organized schemata that allow individuals and collectivities to recognize and make intelligible these activities and experiences. Social frames are a product of individual and structural forces. On an individual level, they are dependent upon the cognitive and subjective typifications that individuals call upon to make clear what is going on in a situation. Yet, these frames must be anchored to structural and organizational factors least they lapse into a complete relativism. In this sense, Goffman argues that frames are not simply micro-level, subjective definitions of the situation, but definitions that must find

coherence within the larger social organization. Frames are meaning structures that one "somehow arrives at, not something cognition creates or
generates. Given their understanding of what it is that is going on, individuals fit their actions to this understanding and ordinarily find that the
ongoing world supports this fitting" (1974:247).

Yet, Goffman argues that this framing is far from a mechanical process of
matching individual frames with socially accepted frames. Indeed, the process of framing is incredibly complex because there are innumerable frames
available in the world to organize experiences. On a practical level, however,
the extant *physical, cultural, and structural* resources bind or limit framing
possibilities. For example, the probability of framing a talk as a classroom
lecture is enhanced if the physical surroundings focus attention upon the
lecturer, if lecturing is given cultural legitimacy, if both students and professors act in terms of their respective social roles.

In this sense, this process of building frames in light of the constraints and
opportunities of the more fundamental physical, cultural, and social realities
is a critical part of successful ethnic entrepreneurship. At the situational
level, what ethnic entrepreneurs do when they devise ethnic strategies is to
organize the experience and involvement of customers and clients in an
economic market so as to bring them into a presumably favorable social
exchange. In the process, they create a social organization of experience
embedded within the larger market context where the sale and purchase of
goods and services take place. This social organization of experience, if
anchored to the relevant frames of customers, becomes an essential component of successful ethnic entrepreneurs. Understanding the frame building
process of Mexican-American entrepreneurs will, therefore, provide a more
systematic understanding of the mechanisms involved in ethnic entrepreneurship and the increasing success of Mexican-American entrepreneurial
ventures.

METHODOLOGY AND PROCEDURES

The data for this study consisted of 25 open-ended interviews with successful
Mexican-descent business entrepreneurs. For our purposes, we defined entrepreneurs as people who both owned and operated business enterprises or
those people who not only assumed the financial risk of an enterprise but
also functioned as the manager (Martinez and Dorfman 1998). We defined
as successful those entrepreneurs who had been in business for at least 5
years. In this manner, we sought to eliminate those entrepreneurs who never

emerge from the more formative and unsuccessful forays into entrepreneurship. We defined Mexican-descent as someone who identified himself or herself as Mexican, regardless of whether he or she was born in Mexico or the United States. For our examination of the ethnic economy, the place of birth was not as significant as the more general identification with a set of values or themes that characterize a Mexican, ethnic culture. As Light and Karageorgis have argued, "ethnic economies depend upon ethnicity, not national origins, for their boundaries" (1994:648).

The interviews were conducted between January 1994 and September 1998. These interviews lasted from 45 min to 3 h and were conducted in the business establishments during business hours. We preferred this approach for it allowed us to see the business operations in practice and, thereby, gain an ethnographic context for interpreting the comments in the interviews. The majority of interviews were conducted in Spanish because most entrepreneurs expressed a desire to do so. Tapes of the interview were then translated and transcribed in English.

The interview questions themselves were open-ended. They focused upon common problems confronting most entrepreneurs. Thus, we were intent upon gaining insight into the business background of the entrepreneur, the decisions involved in starting one's own business, and the way various entrepreneurial skills were acquired. We also asked about the businesses themselves such as the relationships with customers and suppliers, the ways workers were recruited and managed, the role of ethnicity in providing opportunities, and constraints upon success. Finally, we asked each entrepreneur to discuss what he or she believed to be the reasons for success, with a special focus upon the strategies deemed important in creating a successful business venture.

Our sample of entrepreneurs came as a result of our initial contact with a key informant. This person was herself a successful Mexican-descent entrepreneur and had extensive ties with Mexican-American business organizations throughout the Chicago area. As a result of her contacts, we were introduced to several other Mexican-descent entrepreneurs, who introduced us to several more, who gave us the name of several others. Thus, our data collection method best approximates what has been termed a snowball sample. This method not only provided us with a variety of people willing to be interviewed, but also gave us insight into the high degree of sociability and cohesiveness among the Mexican-American business community in Chicago. Most significantly, this selection of entrepreneurs was guided by our overall theoretical goal of understanding the more subtle, framing strategies of entrepreneurs. We were most interested in talking to entrepreneurs who would allow us to explore and bring to light a set of strategies that are difficult to articulate and codify.

However, this non-statistical strategy for selecting individuals has a number of drawbacks, most significantly representativeness. Thus, we have no definite way of assessing whether our sample of Mexican-American businesses has characteristics and patterns reflective of Mexican-American businesses more generally (e.g. with respect to locational clustering, number of years in operation, and the like). While a probability sample would have been desirable, the costs of identifying a larger sampling frame were prohibitive, requiring in all likelihood a block by block canvassing and identification of Mexican-American businesses throughout Chicago and the surrounding suburbs.[1]

Despite these limitations, we are able to make several comparisons between our sample and other studies carried out on Mexican-American or Hispanic businesses. For example, while the average starting capital for entrepreneurs in our study was $25,000, Huck et al. (1999) found that the average start-up funds for *Hispanics* in Chicago's predominantly Mexican Little Village was $13,164 and national data compiled by the U.S. Census Bureau estimates that 79% of Hispanic business owners needed $24,000 or less to start or acquire a business (U.S. Bureau of the Census 1998). With respect to numbers of years in operation, the average in our study was 14 years. Raijman and Tienda's (2000) stratified random sample of Mexican businesses in Little Village found that these businesses had been, on average, in operation for 8 years; the study by Huck et al. (1999) put the average at close to 7 years. And finally with respect to number of employees, our sample averaged approximately 11 employees per business. Huck et al. (1999) found a somewhat lower average of four employees for each firm and Soyeon and Eastlick's (1998) random sample of Hispanic-owned businesses (primarily Mexican) in 16 major Metropolitan Statistical Areas found that 59% of the businesses had 10 or fewer employees. Overall, it appears that our sample was comparable to other studies carried out on Mexican-American or Hispanic businesses, but that our sample produced a slightly more well-funded, more established, and larger set of businesses. This bias was perhaps predictable, and even warranted, given our sample selection criteria and our attempt to focus upon entrepreneurs who were particularly successful in marrying opportunity structures with relevant group characteristics.

Table 1 presents more detailed information on the characteristics of the businesses included in this study and reveals three essential characteristics of the businesses in our sample. First, the majority of enterprises were located

Table 1. Characteristics of Businesses in the Sample.

Type	Original Capital	Years in Operation	Number of Employees	Percent Mexican Employees	Est. Percent Mexican Customers
Video store	$20,000	10	6	100	40
Restaurant	NA	14	10	70	30
Book store	$10,000	9	17	100	70
Jewelry store	$80,000	12	5	50	5
Grocery store	$14,000	7	7	100	80
Construction	$1,400	8	70	70	NA
Restaurant	$8,000	5	8	100	90
Craft store	NA	9	7	80	30
Restaurant	NA	15	9	NA	60
Auto parts	$6,000	20	10	90	50
Wedding shop	$1,500	7	2	100	70
Grocery store	$58,000	13	5	100	75
Restaurant	$160,000	10	12	100	50
Grocery store	$55,000	10	4	100	60
Distributor	NA	10	NA	NA	5
Restaurant	$5,000	28	8	60	60
Clothing store	NA	15	6	100	90
Bakery	$7,000	13	NA	NA	90
Grocery	$5,000	11	13	100	90
Beauty salon	$3,000	22	NA	NA	70
Distributor	NA	51	20	90	75
Auto repair	$4,000	19	13	60	75
Clothing store	$6,000	5	5	100	60
Restaurant	NA	7	6	90	40
Jewelry store	$15,000	10	2	100	80

Note: NA = not available.
The values in the table above are based upon information gathered in interviews with the entrepreneurs in this study. The values in the last column should be taken as general "estimations" since they derive from the entrepreneurs' informal assessments of the percentage of Mexican customers.

in the small retail and personal service sectors of the economy (often labeled the "traditional" lines of business). Thus, there were a number of restaurants, clothing stores, groceries, and the like. In this manner, our sample coincides with the general trends for self-employed proprietors in the United States economy as a whole and for ethnic entrepreneurs more specifically

(Hodson and Sullivan 1995:318; Sevron and Bates 1998:426). Second, our sample reflected the major industry distribution of Mexican-owned firms in the United States, where on the national level over 45% of Mexican-owned businesses are located in either the retail trade, food store, apparel and accessory, eating or drinking, personal services, or miscellaneous retail industry groupings (U.S. Bureau of the Census 1996a). Third, the businesses in our sample proved to be an example of an ethnic economy (Bonacich and Modell 1980:110–111) as the Mexican-descent employers created a substantial co-ethnic labor market by hiring, on average, an estimated 85% co-ethnic Mexican-descent employees.

With respect to location, our sample included businesses from both the city of Chicago (including the Little Village and Pilsen areas) and the surrounding suburbs (including Melrose Park, West Chicago, Franklin Park, Cicero, Blue Island, Des Plaines, Addison, and Evergreen Park). The majority of these businesses are situated in Hispanic enclaves with relatively substantial clustering of Hispanic enterprises and institutions and with relatively substantial Hispanic populations. Thus, the Pilsen and Little Village areas have the greatest concentration of Hispanic owned businesses in the Chicago area and a Hispanic population upwards of 95%, predominantly Mexican-descent (Villar 1994). For the most part, the suburban locations also have a substantial number of Hispanic-owned business. For example, while 3.1% of all firms in the United States were Hispanic owned, 19% of all the firms in Cicero, 12% in Blue Island, 9% in Melrose Park, and 6% in Addison were owned by Hispanics (U.S. Bureau of Census 1996a). Most of these communities also have relatively significant Hispanic populations. Thus, while Hispanics comprise 8.8% of the U.S. population, Cicero has an Hispanic population of over 37%, Melrose Park 30%, West Chicago 30%, Blue Island 25%, Franklin Park 21%, Addison 13%, Des Plaines 7%, and Evergreen Park 2% (U.S. Bureau of the Census 1991).

SOCIALIZING THE ETHNIC MARKET

Ethnic markets can not be counted on to produce profits for ethnic businesses in a purely instrumental fashion whereby ethnic consumer needs are automatically matched with ethnic entrepreneurial supply. Instead, these economic relationships have to be socialized. That is, these relationships have to be contoured or made to fit the special social needs of the customers – be these needs of companionship, trust, respect, friendship, knowledge, a friendly atmosphere, and the like (see Levitt 1995). Put in another way, the success of these economic relationships are dependent upon their transformation into social relationships whereby customers and entrepreneurs enter into a structure of obligations and social solidarity. The social character of these economic relationships came out in the comments of one storeowner who said.

> The Mexican customer is very easy to please. If you are pleasant with them, if you are a friend to them, that's it, that's what you need. The treatment you give the customer is probably more important than the product itself. I mean, like if they go to a grocery store and the bread is not fresh, they will forgive you. But if you don't give them good treatment, they might not be able to forgive that,

To use another example, the appeal of the "good taco" was not inherent in a traditional combination of spices or unique preparation of ingredients. The authentic and economically compelling character of this ethnic good was not solely determined by the content of the product per se but by the common rituals, actions, and feelings that surround and infuse the product (see, Lu and Fine 1995). In this sense, the customer not only ate the taco – or in other contexts purchased the wedding dress, had one's car repaired, or bought bread – but ritually consumed ties of solidarity. For example, Eucario, suggested as much when he said that Mexican customers did not come to his restaurant because they wanted to consume Mexican food. More so, they came because his years of experience taught him that Mexican customers "want to know that they are welcome. They want to feel as if you are waiting for them."

This market for ethnic goods, therefore, is best seen in both economic and social terms, for this market is at one and the same time an economic exchange and a social relationship. Co-ethnic customers no doubt evaluate purchasing decisions along rational lines of quality, valuations, and cost. But these decisions are tempered with social concerns of being treated with respect, of not being made to feel out of place, in believing that the co-ethnic entrepreneurs will give them special treatment. These market transactions are embedded in social ties that have a history and a reach beyond the immediate transaction costs. Entrepreneurs who were able to expropriate these markets and weave them into the social needs of their customers were able to establish advantages for themselves such as increasing customer loyalty, reducing costs, and creating a more efficient and predictable operation. A grocery storeowner put it this way,

> Let's talk about cheese. In my twenty years of experience I haven't found a way to slice the ends of a cheese bar. I usually give them away. I tell the person "here is a thick piece of cheese, I'll give it to you free." When I do this, they feel like I am doing something extra for them.

And a video storeowner spoke of his methods for dealing with customers in the following way.

> Well, I tell my employees when I train them, that I want them to always know the customers – to be real friendly with them and ask them how they're doing. If they rent a movie, they should say 'Oh, how was the movie? Did you enjoy it? Did you like the part about this or that?'
>
> Sometimes the staff girls and myself will be talking and laughing and joking and including the customer in our conversations and stuff. And the customers feel good about this, you know. And they come and stay for a half an hour or so. Sometimes they complain about our movies being too expensive. But I tell them, 'But you just had a fun time. I should charge you for the fun time you had while you were here this afternoon.' So you try to be this way with them.

Socializing economic transactions, therefore, proved to be a key element in the success of the ethnic entrepreneurs. The mechanisms by which this was accomplished varied. Still, Goffman's use of the concept framing provides a most useful analytic devise for describing the similarities in the ethnic strategies used by entrepreneurs to link economic exchanges to social markets. As one might expect, the *ethnic frame* was a most powerful way of organizing and socializing the economic encounter. The rituals of ethnicity – be they encased in language, food, dress, mannerisms, and so forth – played a critical role in extending market transactions deep into the social structure and extracting values of trust, mutual understanding, and involvement. Specifically, as entrepreneurs were able to frame, or more properly reframe, the experiences of customers within the bounds of these ethnic solidarities, they were able to activate a series of group or network ties that promised a competitive advantage over other businesses and brought a measure of stability to this small-scale sector of the economy, a sector noted for its unpredictable and fluctuating demand (Piore and Sabel 1984).

As Goffman argues, this movement from one frame to another is typically activated by a set of conventions. These conventions Goffman terms "keys" (1977:44), by which he means those collectively recognized customs that signal that something already understood in terms of some frame is to be transformed into a set of understandings within another frame. The entrepreneurs we studied keyed the ethnic frame in a number of ways.

Physical Keys

In the most fundamental sense we found that the physical setting served as an outer layer or rim for keying the more universalistic, market transactions into an emergent, bounded ethnic solidarity. That is, the organization of the *physical world* played a critical role in transforming and anchoring the experience of customers into a common ethnic focus. Thus, the strategic display of patriotic colors, the placement of authentic bakery goods on counter tops, even the conscious hiring of "Mexican looking" waitresses were frame-building mechanisms tied to the physical world. They were keyings of a Mexican ethnic experience that allowed co-ethnic customers to project feelings of competence, mutual understanding, and ease of interaction into the encounter.

To be sure, this physical organization of the environment took subtle forms. Eva, the owner of an arts and craft store, told us that she sought to evoke feelings of homeland in the way she organized her craft activities.

> When you walk into an arts and craft store in Mexico, you see long tables with sales girls showing displays of how to use certain materials. The stores in the United States don' t have that. So when people come into my store they say they feel different, like they did at home.

And the owner of a Mexican restaurant, attributed his success to the physical keying of a "true Mexican" eating experience.

> The people who come to the United States from Mexico are simple people – rustic people use to typical food, prepared and served fast. That is why you don't see a table clothe, a flower or a candle on this table. This is not an elegant place, but it is clean. I don't want the customers to feel out of place.

Broadly speaking, the physical world is often managed in some fashion to generate ethnic sensibilities. Thus, any number of franchise restaurants with ethnic themes (e.g. *Pepe's, Olive Garden, Taco Bell,* and *Panda Express*) seek to create some caricature of an ethnic experience through architecture, the strategic display of photographs, traditional music, recognizable cuisines, and the like. Because this manipulation of the physical world is so pervasive, ethnic entrepreneurs have to be particularly adept at creating authentic ethnic frames to distinguish them from these corporate fabrications. An owner of a Mexican restaurant in our study spoke specifically to this dilemma in comparing his restaurant to a Mexican chain restaurant, *Pepe's.* "They have a different style. They serve chips and salsa...but when more Mexicans came into the neighborhood, they knew *Pepe's* food wasn't the real thing. The true Mexican restaurant is different."

Cultural Keys

The "different style" of the more authentic Mexican business can be attributed to another set of keyings or frame-building devices. Specifically, the entrepreneurs in our study also relied to a considerable extent upon keyings embedded within a *cultural framework*. Such keyings ranged from knowing how to cut meats to satisfy the distinctive cultural preferences of Mexican customers, to displaying knowledge of Latino/a music tastes, to styling hair in a manner that evokes traditional Mexican fashions, to emphasizing freshness in the preparation of bakery goods and restaurant meals, and so forth. By engaging in such activities, the entrepreneurs were keying a larger, more encompassing set of ethnic, cultural solidarities. Thus, cutting meats according to the traditional preferences of Mexicans was, at one and the same time, a strategy of concluding a successful economic transaction and a framing device that ritually signaled a co-ethnic set of expectations and experiences. To understand these examples of business acumen as simply an economic calculus devoted to matching economic supply with demand is to miss the transforming dimensions of these activities.

Perhaps the most adaptable cultural keying strategy involved the strategic management of ethnic language. By talking to customers in their native language, using ethnic slang, or varying the rhythms of speech the entrepreneurs framed the experiences of customers in ethnic terms and, in so many words, sought to bracket or set these economic exchanges apart from pure transactions. Thus, an auto parts' owner in response to our question regarding successful encounters with customers spoke of the importance of language.

> I can think of at least six customers whom I call *compares* even though they are not related to me. When they come in I'll say 'Hey, how are you *compare*?. How is everything, come let's talk'.

And an owner of a carniceria (butcher shop) said,

> If you speak their language, you are able to communicate with them much more efficiently. I have been in this country for twenty years, yet I do not speak English fluently, nor can I express the same passion in English that I do in Spanish. Being able to communicate with customers in their language is essential.

Eucario, a restaurant owner, suggested that speaking to his customers in the native language had both a practical and symbolic motive.

> If you're Mexican and your English is limited, you would much rather go to someone who understands exactly what you want. But I speak Mexican to many of my customers because we understand each other better in terms of our lives. We have lifetime

experiences together, something that someone who is not from Mexico is not able to compete with.

Structural Keys

Language, thus, provides a common cultural basis for framing an encounter in ethnic terms. Still, the power of language to frame this encounter, as with the manipulation of the physical world, is dramatically enhanced if it is linked to relevant *social structural* frames. Goffman did not systematically examine the social structural relevancies that constrain or promote the possibilities of certain frames, focusing instead upon the anchoring of frames within the physical and cultural realms (Crook and Taylor 1980). Still, Goffman left open the possibilities that frames may be embedded within relevant social organizations and structures. Specifically, if individuals are sociologically cast in situations with structured and recognizable rules, relationships, and relevancies, it is more likely that they will activate, strengthen, and order their experience according to a more predictable range of framing possibilities.

Once again, the entrepreneurs we interviewed demonstrated considerable skill in invoking social structural relations as an ethnic strategy. And in this vein, the most serviceable and effective framing device revolved around the keying of economic encounters in terms of the informal, particularistic norms of the family. Thus, in several different situations customers were cast into familial roles by being addressed on a first name basis, by being given household privileges of serving themselves if the restaurant was especially busy, by being presented with gifts on their birthdays, by being allowed to borrow items from the store, by even serving as babysitters on occasion. As one entrepreneur said, "We're all family. I tell my staff you have to make the customers feel like they are at home." Another entrepreneur offered, "Well all of them, a lot of them anyway, always say that it is like a home atmosphere here. All my children work here and the people like this. They say it creates a family atmosphere."

This recognizable "family atmosphere" in turn evokes ethnic ties. While family frames and Mexican, ethnic frames are not one and the same, they are both a part of a traditional, institutional structure, and are in a great many instances linked in the experiences of many Mexican-American individuals. As such, transforming an economic encounter by keying the normative structure of the traditional, Mexican family creates at least the possibility that customers may view this encounter according to recognizable ethnic ties and solidarities.

The manipulation of physical, cultural, and structural keys created, therefore, an ethnic frame for the entrepreneurs in our study. More than simply cognitive matching schemes between businesses and customers, these frames produced a biding sense of loyalty on the part of co-ethnics by manifesting or making public the ritual ties of ethnicity. In a Durkheimian sense, these frames symbolically affirmed, celebrated a shared collective identity. But as Durkheim suggested and as Goffman explored in scrupulous detail, rituals as frames must inevitably be embedded in the "immediately surrounding workaday world" (Goffman 1974:248), for these rituals draw their sustenance and power as representations of these worlds. In this sense, the perceived *sureness* or *genuineness* of frames are themselves dependent upon another set of keys which anchor them or legitimate them to an ongoing, persistent social order, least these frames be seen as temporary expediencies, as mere deception, calculation, or mimicking. Without these anchoring activities, frames become vulnerable, in Goffman's terms, to fabrications or "the intentional effort of one or more individuals to manage activity so that a party of one or more others will be deduced to have a false belief about what it is that is going on" (1974:83).

This issue of genuineness or authenticity is especially poignant for ethnicity. As presentations of ethnicity have taken on largely symbolic elements in American culture, the social construction and manipulation of ethnicity have become more transparent. And so far as many businesses make claims to an ethnic identity or frame, "ethnicity often becomes a marketing tool, part of an entrepreneurial market" (Lu and Fine 1995:535). Under such conditions, the entrepreneurs in our study could not rely upon physical, cultural, and structural keys, in and of themselves, to produce an authentic ethnic experience for their customers – co-ethnics, especially recent immigrants, are too ethnically savvy for this. So, embedded within these frames were yet other conventions that sought to ground the ritual ties between customers and entrepreneurs in a more convincing, authentic manner.

The most significant of these legitimating conventions involved the strategic manipulation of what Goffman called the "person-role formula" (1974:269). More generally, situations vary in terms of the continuity expected between the performance of certain roles and the person we expect lies behind these roles. For example, theatrical actors performing a role on stage are not assumed to have the self-same attitudes, dispositions, and personalities when they are off-stage. And for the most part, we do not think such actors are less genuine or authentic if the roles they play are far removed from who they "really" are. Ethnicity, as a social status, however, is very different. Co-ethnics, in particular, expect a continuity between public displays or roles of ethnicity and the sort of person that lies behind these displays (Alba 1990:75). Genuine ethnicity requires a cultural competence, a set of experiences, a heritage that grounds and goes beyond the strategic use of key ethnic terms, the arrangement of merchandise, the display of patriotic colors, and the like. The entrepreneurs in our study made repeated reference to this sense of genuineness or authenticity as they talked about "a life-time of experiences together," "express(ing) the same passion," "feeling different," "being with" the customers in a special way. In other words, it was not enough to simply frame an ethnic experience by means of physical, cultural, and structural keys – these frames are, at least theoretically, within the reach of most anyone or any corporation. More so, such experiences had to be seen as genuine, as emanating most directly from the life-experiences of the entrepreneur or "the sense he provides them through his dealings...what sort of person he is behind the role he is in" (Goffman 1974:298).

With this in mind, the entrepreneurs we interviewed sought to organize their experiences with co-ethnics in ways that allowed a tight connection between their role as restaurant owner, butcher, grocery store manager, wedding planner, on the one hand, and fellow Mexican, on the other. This involved a variety of keying or anchoring conventions aimed at authenticity. Some involved overplaying Mexican identity, others underplaying non-Mexican identities. With respect to the former, Goffman's notion of "type-casting" is particularly relevant (1974:285–286). Specifically, a number of entrepreneurs overly embraced facets of a Mexican identity so as to elicit the cultural competency expected of genuine, Mexican entrepreneurs. For example, dress or clothing was cited as a way to enhance authenticity. Thus, one owner of a Mexican restaurant said, "We are simple people. We come from small towns or farm communities. So, when I'm in the store I don't dress up because our atmosphere is very modest. I want my customers to feel comfortable in here wearing a T-shirt." Conversely, Benny, a clothing store owner, carried an entire line of western wear including boots, leather belts, buckles, and hats. In order to enhance his reputation with his co-ethnic customers, Benny would often don this apparel because in Benny's eyes, "Mexicans like to dress up, they love to dance and they love to party." On the other hand Isidra, a restaurant owner, keyed her authenticity more directly. "I let all my customers know that my recipes come from my mother. I don't cook Tex-Mex or Mexican-American food but simply au-thentic Mexican food, the type you can find in the remote farms and ranches of Mexico."

At the same time, there were instances when the entrepreneurs, in the pursuit of an authentic frame, sought to conceal the more entrepreneurial aspects of their relations with customers or create "role-distance" (Goffman 1974:297) between this role and their Mexican identity. For example, in the example cited previously, the grocery store owner who accorded special treatment to co-ethnics by giving away "free cheese" didn't let his customers know that this cheese became available because he couldn't find a way to cut or profit from these end pieces. What passed as sociability, may have also been economic calculations. Similarly, the owner of the wedding store suggested that if customers don't have enough money to pay for the wedding dress, she may "just let them have it for a dollar or two less." While this may be viewed as an act of ethnic solidarity on the part of customers, the entrepreneurial goal of increasing customer loyalty was not emphasized. "I'm not going to get any richer with one or two more dollars," said the store owner, "but the customer might come back. And pretty soon they bring their friends and family. It's like a chain."

Overall, this quest to socialize economic encounters in terms of an authentic, ethnic frame proved a valuable resource for the entrepreneurs in our study. It provided these entrepreneurs with a useful fit, a connection between ethnic demands and entrepreneurial supply. However, as a number of entrepreneurs in our study were aware, appeals to specific ethnic loyalties are also limiting. The other side of ethnic framing is the potential exclusion of non co-ethnics as customers and the limitations that particularistic strategies place upon the growth and size of entrepreneurial ventures. This was especially problematic for the entrepreneurs in our study, for even though the majority of businesses had a predominantly Mexican clientele, few of them could survive on the appeal to Mexican customers exclusively. Instead, entrepreneurial strategies had to be adaptive to the sizeable numbers of non-Mexican, ethnic customers located in most areas. Thus, the presence of Puerto Rican, Guatemalan, African-descent, Italian, Polish, and other Latino/a ethnic groups posed challenges to these ethnic entrepreneurs in terms of finding avenues for socializing these economic encounters. These challenges were dealt with through the use of a higher order, *pan-ethnic frame.* Specifically, several Mexican entrepreneurs attempted to socialize with customers on the basis of a common set of experiences that presumably most ethnic, immigrants encounter – that is, strong familial ties, an unfamiliarity with the dominate culture, a heightened sense of uncertainty and apprehension regarding modern, market transactions. In doing so, these Mexican entrepreneurs found a way to extend the notion of an ethnic market beyond the bounds of the narrow, Mexican ethnicity per se.

Benny, a clothing store owner, provides the best example of the entrepreneurial skill in moving from the Mexican ethnic frame to this pan-ethnic
frame as a way of establishing this sense of trust. In Benny's own words,

> One day I had this particular Italian gentleman come into the store. He needed a suit and
> tie but told me 'I don't want to come out looking like a Mexican.' I didn't take offense to
> this because different ethnic groups have different tastes. However, I know fashion and I
> know what he was feeling. So, I helped him choose a suit. The man seemed happy but
> was concerned that his wife would not approve. I said, 'Your wife will be satisfied, trust
> me. But just in case, you can come back to the store anytime for a full refund.' A couple
> of weeks later this man and his wife come back and the wife says to the husband, 'I
> finally found the store where I don't have to come shopping with you anymore.'

In this way, Benny, as well as a number of other entrepreneurs, found a way
to extend the notion of an ethnic market beyond the bounds of ethnicity per
se. They created an intimacy and familiarity not typically found in non-
ethnic firms and, as a result, increased their chances for more long-term
economic success.

CONCLUSIONS

Mexican-American entrepreneurship has grown substantially over the last
several decades. According to the interaction theory of ethnic entrepreneurship, this growth may be explained in large measure by changes in the
opportunity structures and changes in the capacities for resource mobilization in the Mexican-American community. Interaction theory goes on to
suggest that opportunity structures and predisposing group capacities for
resource mobilization will not alone account for the development of successful entrepreneurial ventures. Such ventures require the active agency of
entrepreneurs and their ability to meld these opportunity structures and
group characteristics into effective, ethnic strategies for dealing with common business problems. For the Mexican-descent entrepreneurs in this study,
the favored strategy for attracting and maintaining customers revolved
around attempts at socializing the encounters between customers and entrepreneurs (or staff) in order to transform these otherwise external economic
exchanges into internalized social relationships. This was accomplished in
varying degrees through the effective use of frames. That is, through the
strategic management of the physical, cultural, and social structural realms,
Mexican-descent entrepreneurs were able to organize the experience of customers into favorable social relationships and purchase the loyalty of these
customers. The most powerful frame involved the use of ethnic ties and

solidarities – an ethnic frame. Specifically, the rituals of ethnicity were displayed in a manner which symbolically reaffirmed an underlying and enduring sense of solidarity between co-ethnic customers and entrepreneurs. In this manner, the relationship between customers and entrepreneurs was extended beyond the pure economic transaction itself and in the process the economic relationship was institutionalized and routinized.

Our discussion of ethnic strategies in terms of Goffman's frame analysis has intended to advance the understanding of ethnic entrepreneurship along theoretic and empirical lines. On theoretic grounds, we have found the interaction theory of ethnic entrepreneurship to be quite compelling, especially in terms of its ability to bring together in systematic fashion the array of structural opportunities and group characteristics that influence such entrepreneurship. Yet, we have found the discussion of ethnic strategies to be largely ad hoc, taxonomic, and underdeveloped. In this respect, we offered Goffman's frame analysis as a useful analytic tool for systematically understanding how successful ethnic entrepreneurs tact between structural opportunities and abiding group characteristics. Specifically, the deft management of the physical world, the cultural realm, and the social structure provide entrepreneurs a measure of control over the way their customers organize their economic involvement and experience. Viewed in this light, we gain insight into how ethnic entrepreneurs systematically incorporate an extant, opportunity structure and a unique collection of group characteristics into an effective business strategy and bring them to bear upon the market place at the interactional level.

Yet, theoretic and empirical challenges remain. Most importantly, the relative significance of the physical, cultural, and social worlds in the creation of frames is still an unsettled issue. In a general sense, Goffman argues for the primacy or foundational character of the physical world of objects. Frames are built in a fundamental manner upon the physical copresence of others in the situation, the material artifacts that attract our attention, the size of a room, the clustering of buildings on a street, and the like. While not focusing upon entrepreneur–customer interaction specifically, there is at least tacit recognition in the literature on ethnic enclaves that the concentration of ethnic firms in a "physical place" or the degree of "entrepreneurial clusters," (Portes and Jensen 1989) has a decided influence on entrepreneurial success. In light of the present study, one can argue that the physical concentration of co-ethnic firms in an enclave, especially those firms in "traditional" lines of business, creates a more immediate, ethnic environment (for example, in terms of the presence of co-ethnic pedestrians, signage, smells, and sounds) and enhances the ability of entrepreneurs to frame economic interactions as instances of ethnic solidarity. In this respect, one can suggest that an ethnic entrepreneur in a less physically ethnic setting would need to resort to different, perhaps more cultural and symbolic, strategies to create a sense of ethnic solidarity. This, of course, is an empirical issue and requires an investigation of ethnic framing, its presence and its variants, in different ethnic economies and ethnic enclaves.

Yet, to focus upon how frames are tied to the physical realm at the cost of examining the impact of cultural and structural arrangements would be a mistake. For example, Goffman did not explicitly examine how experiences are organized within the cultural and structural constraints of social class. Nevertheless, the ability to frame an encounter along ethnic lines, or most any other line, is tied in most intricate ways to social class structures and sensibilities. Here, the work of Bourdieu (1984, 1990) may be particularly useful. Specifically, Bourdieu's notion of "habitus" as a subjectively embodied, structured set of dispositions that generate practices and perceptions is analogous to Goffman's notion of frames both in its attempt to mediate between subjective possibility and objective structure and as a schema that is used by individuals to creatively classify the world(s) and organize experiences in this world(s). However, Bourdieu's "habitus" explicitly incorporates objective social class preferences and structures, especially as these relates to patterns of consumption. As such, Bourdieu's work may help clarify the way that ethnic entrepreneurs draw upon social class conceptions of taste, sociability, manners, and so forth to transform economic exchanges into social interactions. In doing so, the work of Bourdieu may complement Goffman's seminal work on framing and the organization of experience and lead to a more in-depth understanding of the dynamics of ethnic entrepreneurship.

NOTES

1. For an examination of the resources required to identify a probability frame for local entrepreneurs, see Raijman and Tienda (2000) and Vincent (1996); for an examination of a national study see Reynolds et al. (2002).

ACKNOWLEDGMENTS

We thank Roger Waldinger for comments on an earlier version of this paper as part of a National Endowment for the Humanities summer seminar. And we gratefully acknowledge a grant from North Central College, Naperville to allow for the completion of this study.

REFERENCES

Alba, Richard. 1990. *Ethnic Identity*. New Haven, CT: Yale University Press.

Aldrich, Howard and Roger Waldinger. 1990. "Ethnicity and Entrepreneurship." *Annual Review of Sociology* 16:111–135.

Alvarez, Robert. 1990. "Mexican Entrepreneurs and Markets in the City of Los Angeles: A Case of an Immigrant Enclave." *Urban Anthropology* 19:99–123.

Aponte, Robert 1990. "Urban Hispanic Poverty in the U.S.: Theory and Context." Working Paper #6. Lansing, MI: Julian Samora Research Institute, Michigan State University.

Bates, Timothy. 1997. *Race, Self-employment and Upward Mobility: An Illusive American Dream*. Baltimore: Johns Hopkins University Press.

Boissevain, Jeremy and Hanneke Grotenberg. 1986. "Culture, Structure and Ethnic Enterprise: The Surinamese of Amsterdam." *Ethnic and Racial Studies* 9:1–23.

Boissevain, Jeremy, Jochen Blaschke, Hanneke Grotenberg, Isaac Joseph, Ivan Light, Marlene Sway, Roger Waldinger, and Prina Werbner. 1990. "Ethnic Entrepreneurs and Ethnic Strategies." Pp. 131–156 in *Ethnic Entrepreneurs*, edited by R. Waldinger, H. Aldrich and R. Ward, and Associates. Newbury Park: Sage Publications.

Bonacich, Edna and John Modell. 1980. *The Economic Basis of Ethnic Solidarity*. Berkeley and Los Angeles: University of California Press.

Bourdieu, Pierre 1984. *[1979]. Distinction: A Social Critique of the Judgment of Taste*, translated by Richard Nice. Cambridge, MA: Harvard University Press.

------. 1990. *The Logic of Practice*. Cambridge: Polity.

Chavez, Leo. 1988. "Settlers and Sojourners: The Case of Mexicans in the United States." *Human Organization* 47:95–108.

Crook, Steve and Laurie Taylor. 1980. "Goffman's Version of Reality." Pp. 233–251 in *The View from Goffman*, edited by John Ditton. New York: St. Martin's Press.

Fairlie, Robert and Bruce Meyer. 1996. "Ethnic and Self-employment Differences and Possible Explanations." *Journal of Human Resources* 31:757–793.

Goffman, Erving. 1974. *Frame Analysis: An Essay on the Organization of Experience*. New York: Harper & Row.

Goodis, T.A. 1986. *Adaptation Processes of Recent Immigrants to the United States: A Review of Demographic and Social Aspects*. Washington, DC: The Urban Institute (PDS-86-3).

Hall, Peter. 1987. "Interactionism and the Study of Social Organization." *Sociological Quarterly* 28:1–22.

------. 1995. "The Consequences of Qualitative Analysis for Sociological Theory: Beyond the Microlevel." *Sociological Quarterly* 36:397–423.

Hansen, Niles and Gilberto Cardenas. 1988. "Immigrant and Native Ethnic Enterprises in Mexican-American neighborhoods: Differing Perceptions of Mexican Immigrant Workers." *International Migration Review* 22:226–242.

Hodson, Randy and Teresa Sullivan. 1995. *The Social Organization of Work*. Belmont, CA: Wadsworth Publishing Company.

Hoffman, Constance and Martin Marger. 1991. "Patterns of Immigrant Enterprise in Six Metropolitan Areas." *Sociology and Social Research* 75:144–157.

Huck, Paul, Sherrie Rhine, Philip Bond, and Robert Townsend. 1999. "Small Business Finance in Two Chicago Minority Neighborhoods." *Economic Perspectives* 23:1–24.

Levitt, Peggy. 1995. "A Todos les Llamo Primo (I Call Everyone Cousin): The Social Basis for Latino Small Businesses." Pp. 120–140 in *New Migrants in the Marketplace: Boston's Ethnic Entrepreneurs*, edited by Marilyn Halter. Amherst: University of Massachusetts Press.

Light, Ivan and Edna Bonacich. 1988. *Immigrant Entrepreneurs: Koreans in Los Angeles, 1965–1982*. Berkeley and Los Angeles: University of California Press.

Light, Ivan and Stavros Karageorgis. 1994. "The Ethnic Economy." Pp. 647–671 in *Handbook of Economic Sociology*, edited by Neil Smelser and Richard Swedberg. Princeton: Princeton University Press.

Light, Ivan and Carolyn Rosenstein. 1995. *Race, Ethnicity, and Entrepreneurship in Urban America*. New York: Aldine de Gruyter.

Light, Ivan and Steven Gold. 2000. *Ethnic Economies*. New York: Academic Press.

Lu, Shun and Gary Alan Fine. 1995. "The Presentation of Ethnic Authenticity: Chinese Food as a Social Accomplishment." *Sociological Quarterly* 36:535–553.

Maines, David. 1982. "In Search of Mesostructure: Studies in the Negotiated Order." *Urban Life* 11:267–279.

Martinez, Sandra and Peter Dorfman. 1998. "The Mexican Entrepreneur: An Ethnographic Study of the Mexican 'Empresario'." *International Studies of Management and Organization* 28:97–123.

Piore, Michael and Charles Sabel. 1984. *The New Industrial Divide*. New York: Basic Books.

Portes, Alejandro and Robert Bach. 1985. *Latin Journey*. Berkeley and Los Angeles: University of California Press.

Portes, Alejandro and Leif Jensen. 1989. "What's an Ethnic Enclave? The Case for Conceptual Clarity." *American Sociological Review* 52:768–771.

Raijman, Rebeca and Marta Tienda. 2000. "Training Functions of Ethnic Economies: Mexican Entrepreneurs in Chicago." *Sociological Perspectives* 43:439–456.

Reynolds, Paul, Nancy Carter, William Gartner, Patricia Greene, and Larry Cox. 2002. *The Entrepreneur Next Door: Characteristics of Individuals Starting Companies in America*. Kansas City, Missouri: Ewing Marion Kauffman Foundation.

Sevron, Lisa and Timothy Bates. 1998. "Microenterprise as an Exit Route from Poverty: Recommendations for Programs and Policy Makers." *Journal of Urban Affairs* 20:419–441.

Soyeon, Soyeon and Mary Eastlick. 1998. "Characteristics of Hispanic Female Business Owners: An Exploratory Study." *Journal of Small Business Management* 36:18–34.

Spener, David 1995. "Entrepreneurship and Small-scale Enterprise in the Texas Border Region: A Sociocultural Perspective." Ph.D. dissertation, University of Texas-Austin.

Torres, David. 1988. "Success and the Mexican American Business Person." Pp. 313–334 in *Research in the Sociology of Organizations*, edited by Nancy DiTomaso and Samuel Bacharach. Greenwich: JAI Press.

U.S. Bureau of the Census 1986. *Survey of Minority Owned Business Enterprises, 1982 – Blacks, Hispanics and Asia-Americans*. Washington, DC: U.S. Department of Commerce.

------. 1991. *1980 Census of Population and Housing: Summary Tape File 1*. Washington, DC: U.S. Department of Commerce.

------. 1992. *1987 Characteristics of Business Owners*. Washington, DC: U.S. Department of Commerce.

------. 1996a. *1992 Economic Census*. Washington, DC: U.S. Department of Commerce.
------. 1996b. *Survey of Minority Owned Business Enterprises, 1992 – Blacks, Hispanics and Asia-Americans*. Washington, DC: U.S. Department of Commerce.
------. 1998. *Summary Characteristics of Business Owners and Their Businesses: 1992*. Washington, DC: U.S. Department of Commerce.
U.S. Small Business Administration 1993. *The State of Small Business: A Report to the President*. Washington, DC: U.S. Department of Commerce.
Valdivieso, Miguel. 1981. "An Economic Analysis of Successful Hispanic Businessmen." Pp. 35–52 in *Hispanic Business and Economy in the 1980s: Proceedings of the Third National Symposium on Hispanic Business and Economy*, edited by Armando Triana. Chicago: Depaul University.
Villar, Maria. 1994. "Hindrances to the Development of an Ethnic Economy among Mexican Migrants." *Human Organization* 53:263–268.
Vincent, Vern. 1996. "Decision-Making Policies among Mexican-American Small Business Entrepreneurs." *Journal of Small Business Management* 34:1–13.
Waldinger, Roger and Howard Aldrich. 1990. "Trends in Ethnic Businesses in the United States." Pp. 49–78 in *Ethnic Entrepreneurs*, edited by Roger Waldinger, Howard Aldrich and Robin Ward and Associates. Newbury Park: Sage Publications.
Waldinger, Roger, Howard Aldrich, and Robin Ward. 1990. "Opportunities Group, Characteristics, and Strategies."Pp. 13–48 in *Ethnic Entrepreneurs*, edited by Roger Waldinger, Howard Aldrich, and Robin Ward and Associates. Newbury Park: Sage Publications.
Waldinger, Roger, Howard Aldrich, and Robin Ward, Associates. 1990. *Ethnic Entrepreneurs: Immigrant Businesses in Industrial Societies*. Newbury Park, CA: Sage Publications.
Waldinger, Roger and Medhi Bozorgmehr. 1996. *Ethnic Los Angeles*. New York: Russell Sage Foundation.

THE HENNA MAKER: A MOROCCAN IMMIGRANT WOMAN ENTREPRENEUR IN AN ETHNIC REVIVAL

Beverly Mizrachi

INTRODUCTION

Much research claims that immigrant women's entrepreneurship in Western capitalist societies is embedded in the structural and cultural attributes of receiving societies. Other studies maintain that the structural and cultural traits of immigrant groups explain women's entrance into this type of business activity. Together, this body of research underestimates those individual attributes embedded in human agency, in the personalities of immigrant women, that encourage them to engage in this type of business enterprise.

The purpose of this chapter is to present a case-study analysis of Rena, the Henna Maker, precisely because it enables one to theorize about the personality of the actor, the autonomous, individual immigrant woman who chooses to engage in entrepreneurship as well as to consider the cultural milieu within which she created her business. Rena immigrated from Morocco to Israel, where she established a business in which she organizes a Henna, the traditional Moroccan engagement ceremony that, by custom, is organized by the mother of the bride for the couple and their relatives. By

Entrepreneurship
Research in the Sociology of Work, Volume 15, 257–277
Copyright © 2005 by Elsevier Ltd.
All rights of reproduction in any form reserved
ISSN: 0277-2833/doi:10.1016/S0277-2833(05)15010-9

turning this ceremony into a business, Rena is an example of an immigrant woman who, motivated by her desire for individual self-fulfillment through financial success, used her ethnic and gender capital to engage in cultural entrepreneurship within the Moroccan community in Israel.[1] With the demise of expectations of achieving a cultural melting pot and the persistence of ethnicity, an ethnic revival has occurred among Moroccan Jews in Israel (Weingrod 1979; Levy 1997; Peled 1998) that has created a market demand for expressions of cultural affiliation. Rena identified this demand and turned it into a thriving enterprise. Thus, her individual ability to recognize an entrepreneurial opportunity and to exploit it interacted with a cultural event occurring in the society at the time. In light of the fact that other culturally pluralistic societies are also experiencing ethnic revivals (Alba 1990; Wicherkiewicz 1996; Gomez 1997; Sexton 1999; Halter 2000), the Henna Maker can serve as a typical case of how immigrant women, who have a penchant for entrepreneurship, may use their ethnic and gender capital within this unique cultural context to create new opportunities for profitable businesses in their societies, as well. Considering the increasing number of women immigrants (Castles and Miller 1993; Kofman 1999), their presence in entrepreneurial activities and the prevalence of ethnic revivals, it seems that the Henna Maker is deserving of analysis.

IMMIGRANT WOMEN AND ENTREPRENEURSHIP

Studies on Western capitalist societies claim that one of the structural attributes of receiving societies that affects women's entrance into entrepreneurship is the existence of a segmented labor market that offers immigrant women higher returns on their human capital in entrepreneurship than they would receive in the traditional employment that offered them low income, low status, dead-end jobs in domestic work or in industrial labor (Aldridge and Waldinger 1990; Anthias and Lazaridis 2000; Pedraza 1991). However, because of the dual nature of the entrepreneurial business sector, immigrant women's entrepreneurial activities usually do not operate in the large-scale capital intensive branch of this sector that offers high profits and upward social mobility, but in the small-scale, labor-intensive branch that is characterized by low profits and limited or blocked mobility (Baxter and Raw 1988; Josephides 1988; Phizacklea 1988). Cultural factors, such as discrimination against immigrant ethnic groups, particularly against immigrant women of color, and even semi-professional and professional women, in receiving societies (Kim and Hurh 1988; Kibria 1994) provide additional motivation for these women to concentrate their economic activities in entrepreneurship.

Among the structural characteristics of immigrant groups that contribute to immigrant women's entrance into entrepreneurship is the existence of geographic concentrations of co-ethnic, or ethnic enclaves, that provide a clientele for particular ethnic commodities or services that only co-ethnic entrepreneurs can provide (Aldrich and Waldinger 1990; Moallen 1991; Portes and Manning 1994; Dallalafar 1994). These enclaves offer ethnic businesses "a protected market" (Light 1972) because they shield them from non-ethnic competition and give them an advantage over non-ethnic businesses. Among the cultural characteristics of immigrant women that influence their entrepreneurship are definitions of normative gender activities for men and women that create a gender division of labor in immigrant businesses (Moallen 1991; Dallalafar 1994). Also, certain collectivist family ideologies assume that wives will supply voluntary labor for family businesses in which the husbands are usually the owners and the wives are considered only helpers, even if they devote considerable time and energy to the enterprise (Perez 1985; Kim and Hurh 1988; Kibria 1994). In this manner, cultural definitions of feminine gender roles combine women's spousal role with an economic role, and legitimize their unpaid labor (Josephides 1988). As a result, women's economic contribution to the family business is not recognized formally, their economic dependence on their husbands is perpetuated, and their individual mobility is blocked (Westwood and Bachu 1988).

It seems to me and others (Morokvasic 1983; Moallen 1991; Dallalafar 1994) that this reliance on structural and cultural factors has created a stereotypical construct of immigrant women's entrepreneurship. This is true even though Westwood and Bhachu (1988:2) maintained that their analysis "... goes beyond an account of patriarchal relations positing instead the articulation between racism, class relations, cultural forms, and gender." By presenting a category of women who are dependent, in low-profit, limited mobility business activities, most of these studies constructed a stereotype of these women as subordinate and vulnerable, and neglected those women entrepreneurs who are independent owners of their businesses. Although it is true that only a minority of immigrant women are business owners (2–5%) (Morokvasic 1991:408), focusing on those who are helpers in entrepreneurial activities and ignoring those who are entrepreneurs themselves, misrepresents women's activities in this business sector.

In the interest of presenting an alternate construction of immigrant women's activities in this occupational sphere, a few studies concentrated on analyzing the business activities of those women who do own their business (Dallalafar 1994). Morokvasic (1991), in her analysis of 82 such women in five European countries, maintained that all these women used their self-employment as a "strategy of resistance" to their disadvantaged, subordinate position as immigrants. She argued that these women rationalized this strategy by claiming that their desire to be entrepreneurs derived from their personal motivation to own a business, rather than admitting that their business activities were a response to their disadvantaged status.

However, from the theoretical perspective, even this alternate social construction gives insufficient consideration to human agency. Although these few studies focused on women who were business owners, they neglected those non-stereotypical women who chose to establish a business not as an alternate route to economic mobility or as a rationalization or strategy in response to blocked mobility, but as a conscious desire to find self-fulfillment by being an entrepreneur, a desire to establish a successful business in order to be wealthy. In doing so, these studies, too, continued to place great emphasis on the macro structural and cultural level factors that affect immigrant women's entrance into entrepreneurship, but overlooked the micro level individual factors, such as personal motivation, that may encourage these women to engage in business, which may exist independently of their status as immigrants. This oversight disregards immigrant women as active agents in choosing their economic activities and distorts empirical evidence that leads to theoretical biases regarding entrepreneurship among immigrant women.

The case study of Rena, the Henna Maker, is informative because it illustrates how individual level factors may explain an immigrant woman's decision to engage in entrepreneurship. While Rena was an immigrant woman, she chose to establish a business because it suited her personal goal for accumulating wealth and not because it was a response to her vulnerable structural position or status as an immigrant woman or to cultural forces that limited her options in other kinds of employment. However, her entrepreneurial traits led her to capitalize (literally) upon her status as a Moroccan immigrant and as a woman to create a business in a propitious cultural milieu that, eventually, brought her financial success.

IMMIGRANT ENTREPRENEURSHIP IN ISRAEL

During the mass immigration that followed the establishment of the State of Israel in 1948, 740,000 immigrants arrived in the country. Of these, 45.4%

were of European-American (mostly European) ethnic origin, and 54.6% were of North African-Asian (mostly Middle Eastern) ethnic origin. The immigrants from Morocco were the largest group (58.5%) among the Middle Easterners (Lissak 1999:3–10).

The Europeans possessed significantly higher levels of education than did the Middle Easterners, had higher occupational–professional skills and became concentrated in the middle and upper income strata, while the Middle Easterners became clustered in the low income strata (Lissak 1999; Ben-Raphael and Sharot 1991; Peled 1998). As a result of these differences in human capital, socio-economic resources and the greater prestige attributed to the culture of the European groups than to that of the Middle Eastern groups, an ethnic stratification evolved in which the Europeans enjoyed superior status to the Middle Easterners. Within the Middle Eastern group, the Moroccans were in the lowest position in this social hierarchy (Horowitz and Lissak 1989). The low social status of the Moroccans was exacerbated by negative stereotypes of the group and feelings of discrimination against them by Europeans that led to riots and protests (Bernstein 1984). Over the years, some upward mobility of those of Middle Eastern origin has occurred (Ayalon, Ben-Rafael and Sharot 1998) and today about 1/3 of this group, Moroccans among them, belong to the middle class (Peled 1998:710).

Researchers have claimed that entrepreneurship has offered immigrants of Middle Eastern origin, an alternate route to economic mobility than that available to European immigrants who, because of their greater human capital resources, have had greater opportunities in the labor market for accomplishing this mobility (Lissak 1999; Yuchtman-Yaar 1989). Within the entrepreneurial sector, these two ethnic groups displayed different entrepreneurial patterns that were influenced by their different human capital, their different family resources and their different geographical concentrations after their arrival in the country. Middle Eastern immigrants entered retailing more than did the Europeans. The children of the former tended toward small, blue-collar and distributive services, whereas the children of the latter were more inclined toward professional occupations in large public and business white collar services. Moroccans tended less toward entrepreneurial activities than did other Middle Eastern groups. Entrepreneurs of European origin received financial aid from their parents and inherited businesses from them more than did entrepreneurs from Middle Eastern origin. The Europeans settled in the major urban areas that offered greater possibilities for entrepreneurial activities, while the Middle Easterners were concentrated in development towns whose small size and limited economic resources of their inhabitants offered only minimum opportunities for successful business activity (Razin 1997, 1992, 1989).[2]

Little data exist about immigrant women entrepreneurs in Israel. Those that are available reveal a similar pattern as in the general data on this type of business activity among immigrant women. Thus, in Israel, too, entrepreneurship has been considered an alternate route to economic mobility for women with low human capital. Women immigrants from Middle Eastern origin entered entrepreneurship more than women of European origin (Nahon 1993; Razin 1997), presumably because the former had much lower levels of education than the latter. This trend continued into the second generation with a higher proportion of women of Middle Eastern origin engaging in entrepreneurship than women of European origin (Nahon 1993; Razin 1997). While the proportion of Moroccans in entrepreneurship was the lowest among the Middle Eastern ethnic group, the percentage of Moroccan women in small retail establishments was 37.5% (Razin 1997:73). Women's patterns of entrepreneurship also varied according to their geographical concentrations. Women comprised between 17–20% of the self-employed in the major urban areas, but only 14.9% in the development towns. The lower percentage of women in entrepreneurship in development towns is probably indicative to both of their low level of education and of the lesser opportunities for successful business enterprises in these areas not only for women, but also for men (Razin 1989:172).

The latest mass immigration to Israel consisted of approximately 500,000 newcomers from the former Soviet Union who came into the country during 1989–1983. These immigrants have been characterized by low levels of entrance into entrepreneurship. While they possessed high human capital in the form of education, they possessed low human capital in other areas related to establishing a business, such as knowledge of Hebrew, an "entrepreneurial orientation," and managerial experience (Lerner and Hendeles 1998:107). Therefore, a very small percentage of women from this group entered entrepreneurship (Menahem and Lerner 2001).

METHODOLOGY

As Thornton (1999) pointed out, three major disciplines and their leading exponents – McClelland (1961) in psychology, Schumpeter (1934) in economics and Weber (1904) in sociology – presented various explanations for the emergence of entrepreneurs. However, in spite of their different theoretical approaches, the common denominator in their writings was the claim that individuals, acting alone or in groups, display entrepreneurial traits, such as innovativeness, motivation toward high achievement and the desire to succeed in business, and become entrepreneurs within certain social–cultural contexts.

Since I wanted to study how Rena's individual entrepreneurial characteristics intermingled with the social and cultural context in which she lived and led her to decide to establish her own business, I used the qualitative life history methodology to interview her. This methodology was particularly appropriate for this research for several reasons. Firstly, since I wanted to examine the individual-level factors that induced Rena to become an entrepreneur, I wanted to use a methodology that concentrated on the individual, as this methodology does. Secondly, the life history methodology, which is a holistic approach, permits one to study lives as a whole and not just periods or episodes in them. Thus, it reveals biographical processes or life patterns. Since I wanted to know what processes in Rena's life had led her to become a business owner, this methodology supplied precisely the type of information I sought. Thirdly, a life history narrative reveals the interviewee's subjective reconstruction of her life events. As DeVries (1996:860) wrote, "What is important in a person's story is how he or she remembers it. Deconstructing some of the key issues of this person's personal myth, finding a number of salient themes…may be of some help in arriving at conjectures about the entrepreneur's personality structures and the vicissitudes of entrepreneurship." Indeed, this methodology enabled me to understand Rena's interpretation of her life events that had led her to become a business owner. Finally, the life history methodology helps us to understand the social aspects of an individual's life because it positions that life in time and place and, thus, it connects the micro with the macro. In fact, Rena's narrative enabled me to understand her path to entrepreneurship within the context of an ethnic revival that was occurring in Israeli society during her lifetime.

In spite of the importance of analyzing life histories in order to understand the factors that influence individual immigrant women to become business owners, very few studies have used this methodology to research this topic. This is surprising, considering the theoretical argument that maintains that a single case can lead to the development of grounded theory about a particular group (Glaser and Strauss 1970; Langness and Frank 1981). Perhaps this chapter will strengthen the argument with regard to studying immigrant women's entrepreneurship.

This chapter is based on an in-depth study on the gender construction, ethnic construction and social mobility of 25 second generation Moroccan immigrant women in Israel. Within this group, three were entrepreneurs, owners of their own businesses. Among these three, I chose to focus on Rena because she demonstrated most clearly the entrepreneurial traits common to these three and those noted in research on this topic, particularly in the way these characteristics can be applied in specific social contexts. I also concentrated on Rena because she was the most articulate among these three women. I conducted four, one and a half-hour, taped interviews with Rena for a total of six hours of interviewing. I observed several Henna celebrations that Rena organized.

RENA, THE HENNA MAKER

When I met Rena, the Henna Maker, she was in her late fifties, a widow for ten years and the mother of four children. In narrating her life story, she told me that she had immigrated from Morocco to Israel during the mass immigration of North African Jews to Israel during the 1950s. At the time, Rena had been a young girl. She, her parents and ten brothers and sisters settled in a development town near Jerusalem that was populated by religious, traditional Moroccan immigrants like her family. Like many Moroccan immigrants who arrived at the time, her parents did not possess the educational and occupational skills to enable them to become integrated into the Israeli labor market. Her father, who had been a merchant in copper wares in Morocco, did not find work in Israel and was unemployed. Her mother, who had come from a well-to-do family in Morocco, worked as a maid for middle class European families in Jerusalem. The family was poor. Rena found the homogeneous, isolated surroundings of the development town stifling. She told me,

> I always knew that there was more in the big city than just what I saw in the town I grew up in. From time to time, I would take a trip into the city – into Jerusalem – and I saw that there were other people out there, that not everyone was Moroccan and not everyone lived as we did.

Rena finished the academic track at her high school at eighteen and has a high school diploma, but she did not want to do the matriculation examinations that would have enabled her to attend a university. After graduation, she left the town she had grown up in and moved to Jerusalem to join the police force. It was an act that revealed a non-conformist aspect of her personality and a motivation towards achievement, traits that have been associated with entrepreneurship (McClelland 1961; Lachman 1980; DeVries 1996). She recalled,

> I wanted to join the police force, but that was unheard of in the town because everyone there was religious and it was improper for girls to serve in the police. They were afraid that I would become secular and that was like going into prostitution. The rabbi objected. My father was furious. I was expected to marry at 19 and have children. But I came to Jerusalem to join the police and stayed in the police for three years. I left because they would not give me the advancement I wanted. I wanted to advance very much – I wanted to be an officer – but they said that I was too rebellious.

In spite of the fact that Rena did not have a matriculation certificate or a university education, she had various employment options, all of which would have enabled her to be financially independent. She chose to be an administrator of school projects in a vocational high school. This position permitted her to express additional aspects of her personality that proved to be constant motifs in her life story as an entrepreneur – her desire for financial reward, independence and expressing initiative. In talking about this job, she remembered,

> I liked the job. I got a good salary and I was independent – I had the power and the authority to do what I thought was best.

Rena remained in this job until she married. After her marriage, she worked in her husband's family restaurant as a waitress on a volunteer basis, as many immigrant women do. After a while, the couple moved to the United States to improve their financial situation. Her husband prospered in his business there. In order to "do something with myself and not be 'just a housewife,'" Rena studied manicuring, specializing in making artificial nails. In spite of her very rudimentary knowledge of English, she earned a diploma. Her children were born there. When they entered their teens, the family returned to Israel. Shortly after their return, her husband became ill and died of cancer.

> After twenty-one years of marriage, I found myself a widow with four children to support. I had no money and no job. I had to put food on the table.
> I didn't know what to do. But I knew that I wanted self-fulfillment in what ever I would do. I considered lots of things. I knew that I didn't want to be a secretary. I'm capable of more. I knew I didn't want to sit for eight hours a day for a few pennies – even if I didn't have anything to eat. If that suits someone that's fine, but it wasn't for me. And I knew that I wanted to make money – I think that that was the most important thing.

Even at this crisis in her life, Rena had a clear sense of what work would satisfy her, and would not compromise. She had options that would have ensured her and her family's financial survival and could have constituted a path to social mobility. She could have gotten a secretarial job in the civil service, as do most immigrant women when they attain a high school diploma (Central Bureau of Statistics 1995), which Rena had. As Caplow (1954) pointed out, civil service jobs offer status, stability, and security through tenure and social benefits, which may be particularly attractive to women who come from precarious socio-economic origins, as do many immigrant women. However, this occupational sector does not provide high financial rewards, which Rena wanted. But, perhaps, just as importantly, the individual traits required for civil service work and for entrepreneurial enterprises are quite different. In explaining the differences between clerical work and the kind of employment she sought, Rena made a distinction between bureaucratic and entrepreneurial personalities that has been noted by Dimock (1959:123–135). He wrote, "The traits of temperament that seem to accompany achievement motivation also seem to be the key to vitality of ideas ... The conditions of bureaucracy are the worst possible ones in which to expect creativity to flourish. ... bureaucracy invites ossification. In contrast, entrepreneurs ... like to take risks and are not discouraged by occasional failures or even social disapproval. ... findings seem to mean that people with a high achievement motive are independent and non-conformist, want to do well anything they undertake, are predisposed toward innovation, and get a subjective satisfaction out of succeeding. Collectively they constitute the group from which one would expect entrepreneurs to be drawn."

Rena rejected the route of the civil service as a means of economic mobility and chose the route of entrepreneurship. She established a business doing artificial nails. In choosing this specific enterprise, she displayed additional traits that characterize an entrepreneur – rationality, the application of a skill or knowledge, creativity in formulating a business idea and a willingness to take economic and psychological risks that involve uncertainty (Aldrich and Waldinger 1990; DeVries 1996; Schumpeter 1934). The notion to establish a business making artificial nails was not a random one, but was a rational choice that was based on a skill she had acquired during her stay in the United States. It was also innovative in that it was a business that did not exist previously in Jerusalem. Though Rena's decision involved taking a risk, it was a calculated risk because it utilized a skill that only she possessed and, therefore, would operate in a protected market free from competition. She further minimized her risk by running the business from home, which enabled her to save rent and to keep the profits to herself. She told me,

> I tried setting up a business to do manicures and to specialize in artificial nails. No one else in Jerusalem was doing that – I was the first one. And I did it in a corner of my living room. I didn't see any reason to do it in a beauty parlor. Why should I pay rent and why should the owner of the beauty parlor profit from my work? But sitting at home filing nails all day was not for me – even if I could have made a million dollars a day doing it.
>
> So I got the idea that I would teach artificial nails in a cosmetics school. I looked around and saw that no one else was doing it. Because I had studied it in America and had a diploma, I thought that that would give me an advantage. I even thought of opening my own school to teach manicures. In the end I decided that it was not a good business idea.

Although Rena left the artificial nail business, she remained an entrepreneur. Again, she was rational in implementing her decision and was motivated by her need for high achievement. She went to a business school to acquire the skills that would help her be a successful businesswoman. She said,

> I knew that I wanted to go into business. So I went to school. I studied management and marketing. I knew that if I wanted to start a business, I didn't want to be amateurish about it. I knew that I needed to start from scratch. I didn't know exactly what kind of business I would start, that came to me while I was studying. I studied for a year. The studying was very hard. I was studying with people who were young enough to be my children – I could have been their mother. I studied economics, accounting, and public relations. It was easy for them, but it was very, very hard for me. Those things are still hard for me today, but today I can afford to hire an accountant to do it for me.

Rena chose to enter a specific niche within the entrepreneurial sector – cultural entrepreneurship. Halter (2000) has shown that major corporations in the United States have entered cultural entrepreneurship as a business strategy. They have taken advantage of the ethnic revival occurring there to target specific ethnic products to specific ethnic groups in order to increase their sales. However, most research on cultural entrepreneurship has focused on ethnic, small-scale local business enterprises. Within this group of studies, Palmer (1984:90) has pointed out that there are "culture-suppressed entrepreneurs" who deny their ethnicity for business purposes and appeal to a universal, non-ethnic clientele while, in contrast, there are "cultural entrepreneurs" who use their ethnicity to create business opportunities. For them, their ethnicity is their "distinctive product," their "stock-in-trade." They use their "...ethnicity in the launching, sustaining and expanding of their business enterprises." According to Palmer (1984:92), a "cultural entrepreneur" may be regarded as someone who is "manipulating" his ethnicity as a "marketing strategy." Rena decided to use her knowledge of her own Moroccan customs and traditions, her ethnic capital, to establish a business organizing a Henna, the traditional Moroccan engagement ceremony. In doing so, she turned her ethnic capital into a commercial product for her co-ethnics that, she hoped, would give her financial success.

Once Rena decided upon the concept for her business, she was not satisfied with her knowledge of her Moroccan culture to initiate her venture. Motivated by her ambition for high achievement, for making her business successful, she delved into all the details involved in organizing a Henna. She remembered,

> Once I made the decision to set up a business organizing Hennas, I began doing research on Hennas. I went to museums and libraries. I read that the Henna plant is ground into a paste and at the engagement ceremony it is smeared on the palms of the hands of the bride in the hope that it will bring her many children and that the couple exchange golden jewelry to show how much they value each other and as a sign of their social status. I knew all that, but doing the research made me more sure of myself. When I finished studying, I went to Morocco. In itself, going to Morocco was an experience, but I went to buy clothes-the elegant, silk embroidered caftans and the turbans the bride and groom and the guests wear at the ceremony. I also wanted to buy Moroccan chairs, Moroccan samovars, Moroccan glasses, Moroccan candlesticks that decorate the hall where the Henna takes place. I learned the traditional Moroccan music the guests dance to at the ceremony. I learned to make the traditional Moroccan cakes and cookies everyone eats at the celebration. I wanted everything to be Moroccan. I decided that if I was going to produce Moroccan Hennas, I wanted them to be authentic, not an imitation of the original. I wanted to be faithful to the original.

Why was it so important to Rena that the Henna ceremony she organizes be authentic? Both commercial and symbolic reasons may offer an explanation of Rena's insistence that the ceremony be "faithful to the original." On the commercial level, a "real" Henna, one that is not fabricated, but is a replica of the ceremony as it had been celebrated in Morocco, adds to the market value of the product Rena is selling. On the symbolic level, reproducing the ceremony as it had been observed in Morocco represents returning to the roots of Moroccan ethnic culture and tradition and creates a feeling among the participants that they are taking part in a "true" ethnic experience.

Upon her return from Morocco, Rena proceeded to implement her idea for her business.

> When I came back to Israel, I started to publicize the business. I went to halls that people rent for engagement parties and got lists of couples who were planning weddings and offered to arrange a Henna for them. I left my calling card everywhere. I took out ads. I made some mistakes there. I spent too much money on advertising – but I learned from my mistakes. Today I don't have to go looking for customers – they come to me. I get publicity by word of mouth. That's the best kind of publicity.
>
> When I am hired to do a Henna, I rent the hall, I bake the cakes. In the beginning I used to bake the cakes myself. Today I hire a professional baker to do the baking – I want everything to be the best. I hire the orchestra, the singers, I supply the clothes. I

organize the whole affair. Of course, not everyone wants everything that is part of the Henna ceremony. Some people want certain parts of the ceremony, but don't want others. It is also a question of budget. But I always include the basics – the smearing of the Henna, the exchange of golden jewelry, some Moroccan music and Moroccan cakes and, the relatives, of course.

Rena not only used her ethnic capital to establish her business, but her gender capital, as well. Research has documented that women have preserved their ethnicity by perpetuating those customs and ceremonies that, in their culture, are specific to women (Bell 1981; Beoku-Betts 1995; Billson 1995). In Moroccan culture, the engagement ceremony, the Henna, is a gender-specific activity traditionally organized by a woman, the mother of the bride. Therefore, for a Henna business to be successful, to be accepted by Moroccans as an authentic ethnic ceremony, a woman should arrange it. Rena explained,

I don't think that a man could run this business. He could probably do some of what is involved – but he couldn't do everything. He couldn't dress and undress the bride. Do fittings for the costumes. That's intimate. It also has to be someone who understands fashions, costumes, who has a sense for beautiful things. I think that women have a special attachment to the ceremony. In the past it was always women who did the ceremony – the mother of the bride. I take the mother's place. I think that that is one of the reasons that I am successful in this business-people see me as a stand-in, as a substitute for the mother.

It should be pointed out that Rena's ethnic and gender capital constituted a doubly protected market and offered her a double advantage. Her monopoly of her ethnic capital shielded her from competition by non-ethnics and her gender capital sheltered her from competition from co-ethnic males.

Rena's ethnic and gender capital would not have been relevant without the ethnic revival among Moroccans in Israel that constructed a market demand for her cultural product. The influx of immigrants, predominantly from European and Middle Eastern cultures, that followed the establishment of the State of Israel in 1948, was accompanied by a melting pot ideology that expected that the cultural differences between the various immigrant groups would disappear and a new Israeli culture would be formed. Immigrants were encouraged to abandon their cultural traditions through a process of "de-socialization" and adopt a new Israeli culture through a process of "re-socialization" (Bar-Yosef 1966). However, the tenacity of ethnicity among the ethnic groups brought about an acceptance of cultural pluralism. Thus, since the 1960s, there have been increasing indications of an ethnic revival. As Deshen (1974:281–284) has suggested, there have been "... manifestations of cultural ethnicity ... through ethnic actions in which a claim to a common provenance, ancestry or culture is potent. This cultural ethnicity [is] expressed through the increasing popularity of particular traditional festivities of various immigrant groups." I suggest that the desire of Moroccans to celebrate an engagement with the traditional custom of a Henna, or to buy Rena's cultural commodity today, is one "manifestation" of their ethnic revival.

In this sense, the timing of Rena's business was probably crucial to its success. It is hard to imagine that her ethnic enterprise would have been successful during the 1950s, when the melting pot ideology, rather than cultural pluralism, dominated Israeli society's attitude towards ethnicity. Rena's entrepreneurial traits directed her to the new "…situational cues of opportunities …" (Shane and Venkataraman 2000:219) that were presented by the Moroccan ethnic revival while others, who lacked these traits, may not have recognized them and exploited them for business purposes.

Rena articulated the change in her own and in her co-ethnics' attitude toward expressing their ethnicity when she commented,

> When I lived in the development town I grew up in, I saw Moroccans. I didn't like them. They didn't make me proud to be Moroccan. For a long time I denied my Moroccan culture – actually throughout my whole childhood. But later on in my life, I met other Moroccans, too. I met Francine who was a doctor and her husband, Maurice, who was a famous photographer. Getting to know them, I learned that there were other kinds of Moroccans than those I had met in my town. When my husband and I lived in the States, I met other Moroccans – people who were intellectuals, doctors, lawyers, business people. They were not ashamed of being Moroccan – they were proud to be Moroccan and even emphasized that they were Moroccans. They cooked Moroccan food, lived the culture. I began asking myself why I had been ashamed of being Moroccan all these years. The European Israelis treated me as though they were better than I was, as though I was inferior. Why are they better than I? I am sure a lot of Moroccans who grew up when I did, felt as I did.
>
> Today it is different. Today people are proud of being Moroccan, like I am. Brides today want to have a Henna. Young couples born in Israel are the ones who want the Henna. They feel that it is part of their tradition – something that is passed on from one generation to the next. Today there is awareness that one should not be ashamed of who he is.
>
> I did some research on my own. I discovered that of all the Asians and Africans in Israel, 60% are Moroccans. Sixty per cent! When I was a girl, sometimes in the 1950s, probably 60% of all the criminals were Moroccans and 60% of all the prostitutes were Moroccans. It's a fact. But, today, 11 members of Parliament are Moroccans – were born in Morocco. So we have something to be proud of. Then I didn't see many Moroccans that I could be proud of. By doing Hennas I wanted to show people that in spite of what people say about Moroccans, we have a beautiful culture.

These comments emphasized both the personal and the social transformation that has occurred within Rena and within the Moroccan ethnic group in

Israel. The arousal of Rena's own ethnic pride paralleled the same process among her co-ethnics. Thus, she is both a product of the Moroccan ethnic revival and, through her business, a contributor to its construction, especially among those older Moroccan immigrants who may have forgotten all the elements of the Henna ceremony and among those second and third generation immigrants who may not know how it was celebrated in Morocco.

The location of Rena's business was instrumental to its success. The concentration of Moroccans in Jerusalem constituted an ethnic enclave that provided a clientele for her enterprise. It was also an important consideration in her decision to expand her Henna business to organizing other traditional ceremonies for the Moroccan ethnic market. She recalled,

> In fact, I have begun branching out. I began to feel that doing Hennas was too small a scope for me. Jerusalem has a big Moroccan population. So I have expanded my business to doing other Moroccan ceremonies – I have entered another niche. I now do Moroccan weddings and Bar Mitzvahs. I also do 1000 + 1 nights parties – with belly dancing, Moroccan decorations, Moroccan food, Moroccan music. That is beginning to be a big part of my business – it is becoming very popular.

Rena not only identified the potential of an ethnic market among her Moroccan co-ethnics, but she recognized a similar market among other ethnic groups that are also experiencing ethnic revivals in Israeli society. Today she is breaking out of her own ethnic market to capitalize on this cultural phenomenon. In order to do this, she is improving her skills and diversifying her product, while remaining a cultural entrepreneur. She said,

> I think that there is also a demand for ethnic ceremonies of other ethnic groups. I am thinking about expanding in that direction, too. I don't want to be stuck in the same place. I want to be active. I plan to study the customs of other ethnic groups and start doing their ceremonies. That demands a great investment. I want it to be good. I want to expand to other ethnic groups because I'll make more money. I like the work, but my motivation is money. Money is convenience.

Today, Rena's business is almost 10 years old, quite beyond the critical five-year mark that signifies sustainable entrepreneurial ventures (Hisrich 1990). Rena has achieved her wish of making money. She has accomplished significant economic mobility in her lifetime and she places herself within the middle class in Israeli society. In evaluating her success in her business at this period in her life, Rena concluded,

> I am very proud of myself and the business I started. I am only at the beginning and I still have a way to go, but I am at the beginning.

DISCUSSION

In this article I argue that much of the existing research on immigrant women's entrepreneurship has neglected those individual-level traits embedded in human agency, in the personalities of immigrant women, that direct them toward owning their own business. Furthermore, I suggest that Rena's life history supports my argument and may be considered typical of such women. The personality traits that Rena exhibited that were conducive to entrepreneurship may be inherent, as they seemed to be in her case, they may be fostered through socialization (in childhood or in adulthood) or they may be fortified through social policy that offers support and inducements to immigrant women who are interested in owning their business in order to achieve economic mobility. Whatever the source of these traits, incorporating an analysis that includes the autonomous actor, with existing structural and cultural analyses, may enable researchers to broaden the theoretical approach to studying immigrant women as business owners. In this case study, one can discern how individual-level characteristics of entrepreneurship in an immigrant woman interacted with the cultural event of an ethnic revival to create a successful business.

I further argue that cultural entrepreneurship is an avenue for the economic mobility of immigrant women, especially during periods of ethnic revivals. This is a sub-type of immigrant entrepreneurship that has not received much attention in research. This is so, in spite of the economic opportunities it presents for such women.

However, cultural entrepreneurship as a business option for immigrant women depends upon several necessary conditions. Firstly, the existence of culturally pluralistic societies that are composed of ethnic groups who possess distinct cultures. Secondly, co-ethnics need to share a sense of a common membership in that distinctive culture: they need to have an ethnic consciousness. Thirdly, there needs to be a normative acceptance of cultural diversity in these societies. A culturally pluralistic society that is dominated by a melting pot ideology does not create a milieu in which cultural entrepreneurship can thrive. Finally, there has to be a desire for active expressions of culturally valued traditions and ceremonies, for example, in the form of an ethnic revival, that creates a market for ethnic commodities.

Rena drew upon her two identities, her ethnicity and her gender, in conceptualizing her business idea. Basically, she converted these two identities into ethnic and gender capital that she used to achieve her business goal. Coleman (1990:304) referred to social capital as "... resources that can be used by actors to realize their interests." I pose that ethnic and gender capital constitute a type of social capital that can be used in the same goal-oriented behavior. Ethnic and gender groups have used these kinds of capital, through protest, for example, to achieve various ends, such as political goals and social status. Rena demonstrated how ethnic and gender capital might be used for financial gain.

Rena's narrative suggested that Moroccans' ethnic revival might be due to both a greater acceptance of cultural pluralism in Israeli society and to the group's socio-economic mobility. Existing research (Weingrod 1979; Ayalon, Ben-Raphael and Sharot 1988; Peled 1998) supports Rena's perception regarding the Moroccan group's mobility. These scholars have shown that this group has moved from being considered backward, discriminated against and being concentrated in the lowest socio-economic strata to joining the middle class. Therefore, it seems plausible that this upward mobility of some Moroccans has legitimized the desire of members of the group to express their ethnic uniqueness and has created ethnic pride. They may no longer be hesitant about acknowledging their affiliation with a segment of Israeli society that, in the past, was considered low status and subordinate. In fact, Moroccans may even want to flaunt it now that some of their co-ethnics have become upwardly mobile.

This interpretation of the Moroccan groups' ethnic revival may have some bearing upon the complex debate (Gans 1979; Ayalon, Ben-Raphael and Sharot 1988; Alba 1990; Halter 2000) regarding the connection between ethnic ties and social mobility, Broadly stated, this discussion has centered on the question whether mobility strengthens ethnic ties or weakens them. I suggest that, on the behavioral level of expressing cultural ethnicity through the celebration of the ethnic custom and tradition of the Henna, mobility appears to strengthen expressions of ethnic affiliation. Thus, this study supports research that maintains that upward mobility does not inhibit expressions of ethnic affiliation.

This analysis of Rena's narrative and the theoretical implications I have raised that evolve from it, are based on a case study of one immigrant woman's life story as she constructed it for me. They need to be tested and refined through an analysis of the life histories of other immigrant women who are business owners.

NOTES

1. In using the terms "ethnic capital" and "gender capital" I am drawing upon Coleman's theory of social capital which maintains that actors use

various resources to implement their interests (Coleman 1990). I maintain that ethnic and gender resources, such as the knowledge of the cultural traditions and ceremonies of a specific ethnic group and knowledge of feminine gender construction within that ethnic group, can be mobilized to attain various goals, in this case, success in business.

2. Development towns are small urban cities in Israel, usually in peripheral areas of the country. They were set up by the government to absorb immigrants in an urban setting and to distribute the population throughout the country.

ACKNOWLEDGMENTS

I would like to thank Professors Victor Azarya, Reuven Kahane and Moshe Lissak, all of the Sociology and Anthropology Department of the Hebrew University for their helpful comments on earlier drafts of this paper. I gratefully acknowledge the research grants awarded to me by the Memorial Foundation for Jewish Culture, Ashkelon Academic College and the Israeli Ministry of Science, Culture and Sports that enabled me to carry out the study on which this paper is based.

REFERENCES

Alba, Richard. 1990. *Ethnic Identity: The Transformation of White America.* New Haven: Yale University Press.
Aldrich, Howard and Roger Waldinger. 1990. "Ethnicity and Entrepreneurship." *Annual Review of Sociology* 16:111–135.
Anthias, Floya and Gabriella Lazaridis, eds. 2000. *Gender and Migration in Southern Europe-Women on the Move.* New York: Berg.
Ayalon, Hanna, Eliezer Ben-Rafael, and Stephen Sharot. 1998. "The Impact of Stratification: Assimilation or Ethnic Solidarity." *Research in Social Stratification* 7:305–326.
Bar-Yosef, Rivka. 1966. "Desocialization and Resocialization: The Process of Adaptation of Immigrants." Pp. 41–59 in *Immigrants in Israel,* edited by M. Lissak, B. Mizrachi and O. Ben- David. Jerusalem: Akadamon (in Hebrew).
Baxter, Sue and Geoff Raw. 1988. "Fast Food, Fettered Work: Chinese Women in the Ethnic Catering Industry." Pp. 58–76 in *Enterprising Women,* edited by S. Westwood and P. Bhachu. New York: Routledge and Kegan Paul.
Bell, Diane. 1981. "Women's Business is Hard Work: Central Australian Aboriginal Women's Love Rituals." *Signs: Journal of Women in Culture and Society* 7:314–337.
Ben-Raphael, Eliezer and Stephen Sharot. 1991. *Ethnicity, Religion and Class in Israeli Society.* Cambridge, England: Cambridge.

Beoku-Betts, Josephine. 1995. "We Got our Way of Cooking Things." *Gender and Society* 9:535–555.

Bernstein, Deborah S. 1984. "The Case of the Black Panthers in Israel." *Youth and Society* 16:120–152.

Billson, Janet Mancini. 1995. *Keepers of the Culture.* New York: Lexington.

Caplow, Theodore. 1954. *The Sociology of Work.* New York: McGraw.

Castles, Stephen and Mark Miller. 1993. *The Age of Migration.* Houndsmills, England: Macmillan.

Coleman, James. 1990. *Foundations of Social Theory.* Cambridge, MA: Belknap.

Dallalafar, Arlene. 1994. "Iranian Women as Immigrant Entrepreneurs." *Gender and Society* 8:541–561.

Deshen, Shlomo. 1974. "Political Ethnicity and Cultural Ethnicity in Israel During the 1960s." Pp. 281–311 in *Urban Ethnicity*, edited by A. Cohen. London: Tavistock.

DeVries, Manfred. 1996. "The Anatomy of the Entrepreneur: Clinical Observations." *Human Relations* 49:853–883.

Dimock, Marshall. 1959. *Administrative Vitality.* New York: Harper.

Gans, Herbert. 1979. "Symbolic Ethnicity: The Future of Ethnic Groups and Cultures in America." *Ethnic and Racial Studies* 2:1–20.

Glaser, Barney and Anselm Strauss. 1970. *The Discovery of Grounded Theory.* Chicago: Aldine.

Gomez, James. 1997. "Consolidating Indian Identities in Post-Independence Singapore: A Case Study of the Malayalee Community." *Southeast-Asian Journal of Social Science* 25:39–58.

Government of Israel 1995. *Population Census.* Jerusalem: Central Bureau of Statistics, Government of Israel Printing Office.

Halter, Marilyn. 2000. *Shopping for Identity.* New York: Schoken Books.

Hisrich, Robert. 1990. "Entrepreneurship/intrapreneurship." *American Psychologist* 45:209–222.

Horowitz, Dan and Moshe Lissak. 1989. *Trouble in Utopia: The Overburdened Polity of Israel.* Albany: SUNY.

Josephides, Sasha. 1988. "Honour, Family and Work: Greek Cypriot Women before and after Migration." Pp. 34–58 in *Enterprising Women*, edited by S. Westwood and P. Bhachu. London: Routledge.

Kibria, Nazli. 1994. "Household Structure and Family Ideologies: The Dynamics of Immigrant Economic Adaptation among Vietnamese Refugees." *Social Problems* 4:81–96.

Kim, Kwang and Won Moo Hurh. 1988. "The Burden of Double Roles: Korean Wives in the USA." *Ethnic and Racial Studies* 11:51–167.

Kofman, Eleonor. 1999. "Female 'birds of passage' a Decade Later: Gender and Immigration in the European Union." *International Migration Review* XXXIII:269–300.

Lachman, Roy. 1980. "Towards Measurement of Entrepreneurial Tendencies." *Management International Review* 20:108–116.

Langness, L.L. and Geyla Frank. 1981. *Lives.* Novato, CA: Chandler and Sharp.

Lerner, Miri and Yeoshua Hendeles. 1998. "New Entrepreneurs and Entrepreneurial Aspirations among Immigrants From the Former U.S.S.R. in Israel." Pp. 95–111 in *Immigrants to Israel*, edited by E. Leshem and J. Shuval. New Brunswick (USA): Transaction.

Levy, Andre. 1997. "To Morocco and Back." Pp. 25–47 in *Grasping Land*, edited by E. Ben-Ari and Y. Bilu. Albany: SUNY.

Light, Ivan. 1972. *Ethnic Enterprise in America.* Berkeley: University of California.

Lissak, Moshe. 1999. *Social Mobility in Israel*. Jerusalem: Israel Universities Press.

McClelland, David. 1961. *The Achieving Society*. Princeton: Van Nostrand.

Menahem, Gila and Miri Lerner. 2001. "An Evaluation of the Effect of Public Support in Enhancing Occupational Incorporation of Former Soviet Union Immigrants to Israel: A Longitudinal Study." *Journal of Social Policy* 30:307–331.

Moallen, Minoo. 1991. "Ethnic Entrepreneurship and Gender Relations among Iranians in Montreal, Quebec, Canada." Pp. 80–205 in *Iranian Refugees and Exiles since Khomenei*, edited by F. Ashgar. Costa Mesa, CA: Mazda.

Morokvasic, Mirjana. 1983. "Women in Migration: Beyond the Reductionist Outlook." Pp. 13–31 in *One Way Ticket*, edited by A. Phizacklea. London: Kegan Paul.

Morokvasic, Mirjana. 1991. "Roads to Independence. Self Employed Immigrants and Minority Women in Five European States." *International Migration* XXIX 3:407–421.

Nahon, Yaakov. 1993. "Women, Education, Employment and Income." Pp. 90–103 in *Ethnic Communities in Israel–Socio-economic Status*, edited by S.N. Eisenstadt, M. Lissak and Y. Nahon. Jerusalem: The Institute for Israel Studies (in Hebrew).

Palmer, Robin. 1984. "The Rise of the Britalian Culture Entrepreneur." Pp. 89–104 in *Ethnic Communities in Business*, edited by R. Ward and R. Jenkins. Cambridge, England: Cambridge.

Pedraza, Silvia. 1991. "Women and Migration: The Social Consequences of Gender." *Annual Review of Sociology* 17:303–325.

Peled, Yoav. 1998. "Towards a Redefinition of Jewish Nationalism? The Inigma of Shas." *Ethnic and Racial Studies* 21:703–727.

Perez, Lisandro. 1985. "Immigrant Economic Adjustment and Family Organization: The Cuban Success Story Reexamined." *International Migration Review* 20:4–20.

Phizacklea, Annie. 1988. "Entrepreneurship, Ethnicity and Gender." Pp. 20–34 in *Enterprising Women*, edited by S. Westwood and P. Bhachu. London: Routledge and Kegan Paul.

Portes, Alejandro and Robert Manning. 1994. "The Immigrant Enclave: Theory and Empirical Examples." Pp. 509–520 in *Social Stratification*, edited by D. Grusky. Boulder: Westview Press.

Razin, Eran. 1989. "Relating Theories of Entrepreneurship among Ethnic Groups and Entrepreneurship in Space – the Case of the Jewish Population in Israel." *Geografiska Annaler* 71:67–182.

Razin, Eran. 1992. "Paths to Ownership of Small Businesses among Immigrants in Israeli Cities and Towns." *The Review of Regional Studies* 22:277–297.

------. 1997. "Social Networks, Local Opportunities and Entrepreneurship among Immigrants in Israel." Pp. 57–82 in *Immigrant Entrepreneurs and Immigrant Absorption in the United States and Israel*, edited by I. Light and R.E. Israelowitz. Hants, England: Ashgate.

Schumpeter, Joseph. 1934. *The Theory of Economic Development*. Cambridge, MA: Harvard University Press.

Sexton, Rocky. 1999. "Cajun Mardi Gras: Cultural Objectification and Symbolic Appropriation in A French Tradition." *Ethnology* 38:297–313.

Shane, Scott and S. Venkataraman. 2000. "The Promise of Entrepreneurship as a Field of Research." *Academy of Management Review* 25:217–226.

Thornton, Patricia. 1999. "The Sociology of Entrepreneurship." *Annual Review of Sociology* 25:19–46.

Weber, Max. 1904. *The Protestant Ethic and the Spirit of Capitalism*. New York: Scribner.

Weingrod, Alex. 1979. "Recent Trends in Israeli Ethnicity." *Ethnic and Racial Studies* 2:55–65.

Westwood, Sallie and Parminder Bachu. 1988. "Introduction." Pp. 1–20 in *Enterprising Women*, edited by P. Westwood and P. Bhachu. London: Routledge and Kegan Paul.

Wicherkiewicz, Tomasz. 1996. "Ethnic Revival of the German Minority in Poland." *International Journal of the Sociology of Language* 120:25–38.

Yuchtman-Yaar, Ephraim. 1989. "Private Entrepreneurship as an Alternate Route to Socioeconomic Mobility: Another Look at Ethnic Stratification in Israel." Pp. 386–428 in *Stratification in Israeli Society: Ethnic National and Class Cleavages*, edited by M. Lissak. Tel Aviv: Open University (in Hebrew).

ENTREPRENEURSHIP AND SELF-EMPLOYMENT IN TRANSITION ECONOMIES

Akos Rona-Tas and Matild Sagi

ABSTRACT

We argue that claims of an entrepreneurial miracle as a description of private sector development in post-communist Europe conflates entrepreneurship with self-employment. The difference between the two hinges on the Weberian distinction between enterprise- and household-centered businesses. We then present two paradigms, the entrepreneurial that emphasizes the first and the post-Fordist that stresses the importance of the second business type, and provide data on businesses and individual motivation of business owners. We find more support for the post-Fordist approach. Then we show that business forms, primarily associated with self-employment have different recruitment patterns and rewards than other, more entrepreneurial forms. We end with a plea to disaggregate the various forms of independent, private sector activity in future research.

INTRODUCTION

A decade and a half after the collapse of communism, all post-communist countries can claim a sizable and often amazingly lively private sector. In

Entrepreneurship
Research in the Sociology of Work, Volume 15, 279–310
Copyright © 2005 by Elsevier Ltd.
All rights of reproduction in any form reserved
ISSN: 0277-2833/doi:10.1016/S0277-2833(05)15011-0

2001, Hungary boasted 110 registered private businesses for every 1000 inhabitants, more than twice the European Union (EU) average, while Poland had 81, Slovakia 74 and Slovenia 71. Yet Hungary is not the most prolific in spawning enterprises. It is outnumbered by the Czech Republic, where there is a private business registered for every five citizens. The United States would rank with Slovakia in this comparison. Moreover, it did not take a decade or more to create this abundance of private establishments. By the middle of the 1990s these countries were already above the EU average.

To some this came as a great surprise. After 40-plus years of communist rule that actively frowned upon private enterprise of any sort, this quick recovery looked nothing short of a miracle. Others were less astonished. They saw this boom as yet another demonstration that the innate ability for entrepreneurship in humankind, once it is unshackled from the chains of state intervention, will do wonders.

In this chapter, we argue that the entrepreneurial miracle is an overly sanguine description of what happened in post-communist Europe. Its error follows from an inflated notion of entrepreneurship that conflates it with self-employment. After reviewing the literature on entrepreneurship, we will present two paradigms: the entrepreneurial and the post-Fordist. Each has its own take on post-communist private sector development. The difference between the two hinges on the Weberian distinction between household- and enterprise-centered businesses. Then we present data on businesses, individual motivation of business owners, and find that the post-Fordist approach receives more support. Then we show that business forms, primarily associated with self-employment, have different recruitment patterns and rewards than other entrepreneurial forms. We end with a plea to disaggregate the various forms of independent, private sector activity in future research.

LITERATURE REVIEW

Entrepreneurship is a theoretically challenging concept as it includes agency at its core. The entrepreneur is thought of as the creative force of capitalism rather than a predictable cog in its machinery (Schumpeter 1936, 1947/1989, 1949/1989; Kirzner 1973; Kirzner 1980; Casson 1982), an actor who wrestles with uncertainty rather than calculates existing solutions to well-defined puzzles (Knight 1921/1957). Capturing the entrepreneur in theory is therefore an almost impossible task because entrepreneurship begins where structural and rational explanations end. This is why entrepreneurship for a long time was a topic mainly for economic historians who explained its workings after the fact, while economic theory with the exception of the Austrian school had little to say about the protagonist of the capitalist drama. This is reflected in the way entrepreneurs have been treated until recently in economics. Kent (1989), in his review of 15 economics textbooks, found that entrepreneurship was presented inconsistently, almost in an ad hoc manner, tacked on other topics as important miscellany.

The exasperation over the difficulties of conceptually capturing entrepreneurship is evident in a review of the literature on ethnic entrepreneurs by Aldrich and Waldinger:

> Many writers have suggested making a distinction between entrepreneurs and owner/managers on the basis of either innovativeness or risk, but few have done a convincing job. Neither economists nor sociologists have been able to operationalize this distinction so that "entrepreneurs" are clearly differentiated from "owners" or even the self-employed. (Aldrich and Waldinger 1990:112)

In the empirical literature in economics, entrepreneurship and self-employment are often used interchangeably. Self-employment is routinely treated as the best operationalization of entrepreneurship (e.g. Blanchflower and Oswald 1998; Hamilton 2000). Keeping with its implicit theoretical biases, economics thus emphasizes independence and individuality in entrepreneurship. In sociology, entrepreneurship is often equated with the founding of organizations (Thornton 1999; see also Martinelli 1994). Here the indicator of entrepreneurship is the starting of a business firm. Unlike economists, sociologists not surprisingly stress the creation of social structures. By this definition, most self-employed people would not qualify as entrepreneurs as the organizations most command are either non-existent or very small and rudimentary.

This theoretical confusion is mirrored by the conceptual muddle in policy circles. In post-communist countries, the multiplication of private businesses, the vast majority of which are small, is seen as the key to the successful transition to a prosperous market economy (Národná... 1997; OECD 1996:7; Scase 2003.).[1] It is often asserted that this small private sector growth is fuelled by entrepreneurial initiative. There is a curious link between size and entrepreneurship. It is widely believed that entrepreneurial creativity is most evident in the early phase of the enterprise when the initial key decisions are made, when risk and uncertainty are largest, when the business cannot rely on the political and market power large corporations tend to enjoy, and when innovation is not weighed down by a large bureaucratic organization. Therefore, to add to the conceptual chaos, entrepreneurs are often conflated not just with the self-employed but also with the operators of small and medium-sized enterprises (SMEs).

Since we cannot fall back on a clean theory of entrepreneurship to evaluate the recent rise of the private sector in transition economies, we will

	Entrepreneurial	Post-Fordist
Main Actor	Entrepreneur	Self-employed
Main Unit	Enterprise with its own account and space	Household
Main Goal	Accumulation	Consumption
Main Motivation	Exploitation of market opportunities	Job creation
Activity	Innovative, proactive, creative	Defensive, reactive, imitative
Main Asset	Smart combination of factors of production	Labor
Market	Anywhere, potentially even outside the country	Local, geographically bounded
Line of business	Diverse or single	Single only
Genesis	Pull	Push
Commitment to enterprise	High, full-time	Low or intermittent, part-time
Calculation	Rational, accounts well-kept	Traditional, poor bookkeeping
Legal Form	Incorporated Limited liability	Sole proprietorship Unlimited liability
Employment	Employs others	Employs only self, family and people with strong ties
Size	Continuum from small to large	Segmented
Growth	Likely to grow when successful	Keeps its small size even when successful
Source of profit	Market opportunities	Self-exploitation
Business cycle	Expansion in up cycle	Expansion in down cycle
Taxes	Major source of tax revenue	Tax evasion (even when legal!)
Solves Unemployment	Business expansion	New business creation
Policy Intervention	Credit	Training

Fig. 1. Contrasting the Two Approaches.

follow a different route. We will develop two contrasting ideal types emerging from two competing paradigms designed to explain the post-communist transition. The first we call the entrepreneurial, the second the post-Fordist paradigm. Once we identified the two main types, we will supply some data from the region to evaluate each.

THE ENTREPRENEURIAL PARADIGM

Much of the market transition literature (e.g. Nee 1989, 1991; Rona-Tas 1994) is built on the assumption that the heart of private sector development in transition countries is entrepreneurship. Entrepreneurialism is essential in private firm creation, and to making these firms innovative, adaptable, flexible, and able to adopt new technologies. The protagonist is the entrepreneur, Schumpeter's creative genius, whose brilliance in linking the factors of production (capital, technology, personnel, etc.) in a novel way is rewarded by profit for him and economic development for all.

The main unit framing entrepreneurial decisions and activity is the enterprise, which is kept apart from the household and follows its own logic (Weber 1921/1978; 161–164, 375–380). The financial separation between household and enterprise rests on separate bookkeeping: the enterprise has its own account, which is separate from the household budget. The enterprise with its own interests guides entrepreneurial action, and only through the success of the enterprise does the entrepreneur improve his household finances and standard of living. The entrepreneur's business is enterprise- and not household-centered. The entrepreneur follows the logic of profit maximization, market expansion, and accumulation. To achieve these goals, the entrepreneur must calculate rationally and try to find the most profitable combination of production factors. Profit is reinvested into the enterprise but credit is also constantly sought as the enterprise grows (Scase 2003). The market for the small enterprise is limited only by the opportunities available and can reach beyond the boundaries of the locality, the region, and even the nation-state when profitable. The entrepreneur is also ready to diversify his activities if that seems lucrative.

The entrepreneurial paradigm sees economic units in the private sector on a continuum from the smallest, single-person business to the largest company. Each size is a station in the process of entrepreneurial expansion. Of course, not all small businesses will grow into large companies, but all have the potential to do so. The very expression "small and medium-size enterprises" suggests that small and medium-size enterprises are similar in principle and there is a smooth progression from one to the other.

In the creation of new enterprises, the entrepreneurial paradigm emphasizes opportunities and pull factors. People start small enterprises because they notice new opportunities opening up in the market. Entrepreneurship is an active choice and not a forced, defensive move. As a result, enterprise growth follows the business cycle. During bad times, the number and size of small entrepreneurs contract, while during good times there is entrepreneurial expansion. During periods of growth, small enterprises employ greater numbers and hire new people from the open labor market.

The causes of the upsurge of the small private sector, the entrepreneurial paradigm argues, are new opportunities, some of which are, at least initially, the legacies of the socialist economy. Small businesses thrive because they fill the holes created by the weakness of the communist service sector, the poor supply of consumer goods, the deficiencies of socialist trade, and the inefficiencies of a concentrated, overcentralized state-run economy. Coupled with the information revolution and the process of globalization, these factors presented new possibilities upon which entrepreneurs seized.

THE POST-FORDIST PARADIGM

The post-Fordist paradigm offers a contrasting explanation for the sudden burst of the small private sector in transition economies (Laki 1998; Gábor 1997; Laky 1994, 1998; Rona-Tas 1997, 2000, 2001). It proffers a very different appraisal of what has happened in Eastern Europe in the past decade and a half and leads to contrasting policy recommendations. The post-Fordist paradigm perceives the growth of self-employment primarily as a labor market phenomenon. In developed countries, the post-Fordist paradigm points to a decentralization of production, as economies of scale supplying mass markets with uniform standardized products is partially replaced by economies of scope, the production for smaller, more specialized markets (Brusco 1982). Shorter product runs and more frequent changes in the product mix force producers to be more flexible in all respects, including the way they employ labor. Thus, there is a move away from employment contracts and a shift toward subcontacting (Piore and Sabel 1984; Hirst and Zeitlin 1991; Kumar 1995). The post-Fordist paradigm describes the rise of small businesses as a new and more flexible way the economy employs labor (Fig. 1).

The point of departure of the post-Fordist approach is not the adventurous entrepreneur, but rather the risk-averse worker who can choose between various options for deploying time, effort, and skills. Other factors of production are either incidental or serve the sole purpose of enhancing the value of labor. The small private sector is first and foremost a form of self-employment. While the self-employed have more autonomy than most employees and must show some initiative compared with those who work for others, this newly gained freedom is not the freedom to create but the freedom to adapt. Far from being innovative, the self-employed are imitative and reactive.

In many instances, small entrepreneurs are simply employees who lost their benefits and security and now as contractors do very much the same as they did before. The employer is better off because he does not have to absorb fluctuations in demand, which are now pushed onto the contractor. Moreover, the employer does not have to pay payroll taxes (Azudová 1998). Some of these savings may be passed onto the contractors, who must now fend for themselves if they fall sick or grow old.

To receive social security benefits, a large segment of the self-employed run their businesses part-time, merely complementing their salaries and benefit packages from regular employment. Unlike the medium-sized enterprises that function continuously until they go bankrupt, the self-employed business often goes through periods of dormancy, existing only on paper, to resume activity whenever new prospects emerge. During the time of suspension of the operation of the enterprise, the 'entrepreneur' lives off the wages from regular employment. To be able to fold and hibernate, the business must stay small, simple, and with the minimum of ongoing commitments.

The genesis of small enterprises is driven by push factors. At the heart of the post-communist transformation is the restructuring of the state socialist, Fordist industry of large state-owned companies. Under the spell of the 19th and early 20th century success of factory production, state socialism in the European region sought to advance economically by concentrating production into ever larger and fewer organizations run on the principle of Taylorist scientific management (Rona-Tas 1997). Convenient for central planners, the size structure of European state socialist economies by the 1980s was the mirror opposite of what one finds today. While today it is the multitude of dwarfs that make up the bulk of the post-communist economies, at the time, economy consisted of a small number of giants. Through these large, state-owned companies, the socialist state sought to integrate every able bodied adult into the work force, creating a system of universal state employment. This rigid organization of production began to run up against its limitations as early as the 1950s, but it did not start disintegrating until the 1980s. The key to the post-communist transformation in the 1990s then was the restructuring of the economy, which involved breaking up those giants, slimming their work force, closing down loss making companies and ending guaranteed state employment. This squeezed people out of jobs.

Indeed, it is not just the ranks of employees that has shrunk but also the economically active segment of the population. Those who cannot retire on a sufficient pension must fend for themselves. Some retreat into domestic labor, some stay on unemployment, some depend on family for survival or take on informal and irregular jobs, and others launch their own business. People start those enterprises because they have few other choices. They are forced into self-employment precisely when other market opportunities are withering. The expansion of the small private sector, therefore, runs counter to the business cycle. During bad times, the number of small entrepreneurs expands; during good times the entrepreneurial sector contracts (Rona-Tas 2000).

The post-Fordist approach sees radical differences between small and medium-sized units. Small, and especially microbusinesses are not medium-sized enterprises in waiting (Kuczi 2000). They are different not only in size but also in kind. The difference between small and larger enterprises can be traced back to the essential point of the relationship between enterprise and household. In small businesses the household and the enterprise are intermingled. The small business is just one part of a portfolio of strategies aiming not at profit maximization but at the maximization of household consumption. It is household-centered. This is reflected in the legal form most small businesses take. They are not incorporated companies with limited liability, but sole proprietorships, where a single individual and his household carries all the responsibility for the business as the well-being of the household is one with the well-being of the business.

Accumulation is social. What the self-employed save they accumulate in housing and other goods that enhance social status. They also invest in the human capital of their children, sending them to private schools, hiring tutors, and paying for education-related expenses. Because expansion is not the main goal, bank credit on interest is rarely sought. Whatever extra money is needed is borrowed from family and friends. The main assets of the self-employed are their labor and skills. As a result, the two most obvious ways to increase income are to work more, often to the point of self-exploitation, and to upgrade skills. The owner's particular expertise also limits the diversification of business activities.

The post-Fordist approach argues that the small enterprise will not grow because it is not separated from the household. Its budget is a subordinate part of the household budget. The enterprise's natural limits are set by the – often extended – household. When small enterprises hire new workers, they hire from a limited pool of relatives, friends, and acquaintances and not from the anonymous labor market. Small entrepreneurs do not have the organizational skill to command a staff, and they are reluctant to take on the responsibilities of an employer because that means that they would lose flexibility, including the possibility of temporarily closing down. As a result, the size of small enterprises is inelastic. This approach would concur that the small sector can alleviate unemployment—its countercyclicality makes it even more useful in mitigating the effects of recessions. But it would also argue that small enterprises help the unemployed not by hiring more people but by letting the unemployed start their own businesses.

While a real entrepreneur would find business wherever opportunity emerges, the self-employed, tied to their households, are geographically locked into local markets near their residences. As they are most unlikely to step outside the confines of the domestic market, their share in exports is meager. Their spatial inertia is reinforced by the important role of family and close friends in the operation of the enterprise.

This paradigm explains the upsurge of small businesses with a set of factors different from those proposed by its rival. It points to the collapse of universal state employment (Rona-Tas 1997), the transformational recession (Kornai 1994), the weak post-communist state which can enforce tax discipline only for larger companies, and pre-communist traditions of artisanry and petty trade.

Having sketched the ideal types characterizing each approach, advocates of neither paradigm are so foolish as to believe that only their type of small business exists.[2] Those subscribing to the entrepreneurial paradigm will readily admit that there are self-employed people who may never rise above their solitary state. Those in the opposite camp also acknowledge that there are true entrepreneurs in the small private sector. The point of empirical disagreement between the two camps is twofold. On the one hand, they disagree over the relative weight of the two types in the economy. This is a disagreement over the distribution of the types at a given point in time. On the other hand, the two approaches differ in how they expect small businesses to behave over time. The post-Fordist self-employment thesis believes that the small private sector has little growth potential, so that the small will stay small. The entrepreneurial thesis posits that while not all enterprises will grow, many will. Had we found that the vast majority of small enterprises show the characteristics of self-employment, the entrepreneurial approach would still argue that the form of the enterprise is endogenous and it changes as soon as business success requires it to change.

DATA

To evaluate the relative merits of the two paradigms, we will use data from three sources. In studying entrepreneurs and small enterprises, the methodological problems are considerable. Some small businesses operate in the shadow economy and they are fully or partially unobserved. But even what is observed is hard to compare as countries use different rules to register and monitor businesses. Estonia's relatively low number of enterprises is partly due to the fact that their sole proprietors have to register only with the National Tax Board and only if their net annual sales exceed USD 19,200 (OECD, 2002). In Latvia, individual peasants and sole proprietors under a certain income level are not included in central registries (Kuzmina 2003:153–4). In Poland, peasants are not sole proprietors and are excluded from small business statistics.[3]

Our first source is CESTAT, a project initiated by the national statistical institutes of the Czech Republic, Hungary, Poland, and Slovakia in 1991 to harmonize methodology and provide comparative national economic and social indicators. Later other transition countries joined along with Cyprus. The CESTAT data is a census of all enterprises and relies on registry information and the statistical reports businesses must file with their country's statistical office. Despite all efforts, CESTAT cannot correct for unobserved activities and variations in rules of registration.

The second data source is the project sponsored by EUROSTAT, the statistical agency of the European Union. The project originally covered 10 transition countries in East and Central Europe. It is a panel study of small- and medium-sized businesses. Named the Demography Of Small and Medium sized Enterprises (DOSME), the project began in 1995. There were two follow-up surveys, one in 1997 and another in 2001.[4] Each year there was a survey of the newly registered businesses. The survey omitted enterprises in agriculture, forestry, and fisheries and included companies with 250 employees or less.[5] Because the EUROSTAT sampling design depends on national business registries, the problems encountered by CESTAT were reproduced.

Finally, we analyzed data from a survey we conducted in Hungary with the TARKI research institute in 2001 on a representative sample of the adult population, which focused on entrepreneurship.[6] All respondents who reported any private independent economic activity present or past were asked a separate set of questions about their history of self-employment. These types of data avoid the distortions from registration but the veracity of the data on personal income or about illegal and semilegal activities is questionable here as well.

DISCUSSION

Our first observation has to be that registered enterprises do not necessarily engage in economic activity of any kind. In fact, a large proportion of enterprises exist only on paper inflating the real number of businesses. In the Czech Republic and Estonia, only 57 and 59% of the registered companies were active in 2001 (Table 1). Being active is usually measured by whether the registered business filed a tax return that states that it operated the previous year. A business is also considered active if it fills out a statistical form or if it was created that year (and thus was too new to file its tax or statistical papers). This definition of being active, of course, does not imply actual economic activity. Many businesses do file their tax return to be able to write off certain expenses without actually doing much. While in many other countries being off the books is the best way to get tax advantages, in transition countries being registered is the common road to self-supplied tax

Table 1. Registered vs. Active[a] Business, March 2001.

	Number of *Registered* Enterprises per 1,000 Inhabitants	Number of *Active* Enterprises per 1,000 Inhabitants (estimates)	Estimated Rate of Activity (%)
Czech Republic	201.9	116	57
Hungary	110.3	89	81
Poland[b]	81.4	50	61
Slovenia	70.6	55	78
Estonia[c]	42.5	25	59
Slovakia	73.7	N.A.	N.A.

Source: CESTAT Statistical Bulletin 2004/4, 2001; State of Small and Medium Enterprises in Slovakia; Statistical Yearbook of Estonia 2000.
[a]An enterprise is active if it files a tax return, or a statistical form, or if it was created that year.
[b]Without individual peasant farmers.
[c]1999.

relief. Therefore, the rate of activity in the table is likely to overestimate the real percentages.

Why are there so many registered but inactive businesses? Most of the inactive businesses are never closed down and deregistered because the owner would need to show that the books are clean and taxes are paid. Moreover, registration has costs and if there is the slimmest chance of reactivating the business, owners would rather keep it dormant. Leaving the business option open is a strategy of flexibility. Once we adjust for these inactive businesses the overall numbers begin to look less miraculous.

Businesses are registered in various forms. In all transition countries by far the most common type is the sole proprietorship. Sole proprietors such as peasants, small traders, self-employed professionals, and service workers with a few exceptions employ only themselves and occasionally their family members. Their business income is their personal income and the two incomes are accounted for and taxed together. Sole proprietorships are not "legal entities," i.e., they have no legal existence independent of the proprietor. The proprietorship's obligations are those of the proprietor, and in the case of business failure, the proprietors are responsible with their entire wealth. The second most numerous type is the business partnership. A business partnership is not a legal entity either, but in it people can join to work together as fully liable partners (or at least one of them must be fully liable). The organization of a business partnership allows for a little more complexity. While many business partnerships consist of a single individual and the choice between sole proprietorship and partnership hinges on arcane details of the tax code, this form is designed to allow strangers to co-operate in simple business ventures. The third type is the corporate enterprise. Its most common form is the limited liability company. The corporate enterprise is a "legal person," an entity separate from its owner(s). These corporations have their own assets and liabilities and must register a base capital of a certain size to protect creditors in the event the company fails. The corporation's business income is accounted for and taxed separately from its owners' earnings. Again, a corporation can consist of a single-person, and there can be reasons for choosing a corporate form as a form of self-employment. The most important one is the security that comes with limited liability. Whether this security is worth it for someone who wants nothing more than to work on his or her own depends on the size of the required base capital and the form in which it is accepted. In some countries, the owner's expertise or human capital can be appraised and included as part of the base capital. Another cost is the more complex bookkeeping and reporting requirements. Our point is that these types open and close opportunities for the owner, but do not force him or her to exploit them. It is almost impossible to run sole proprietorship over a certain size, and owners who want to grow will have to switch to a corporate form. That does not mean that corporations are always larger or necessarily much different in their operation from sole proprietorships, but they can be.

The comparison of the distribution of businesses in 1995 and 2001 indicates that in the 10 transition countries included in the DOSME study, three-fourth of the businesses were sole proprietorships (Table 2). Again, we find a great variety among the countries. Can we conclude that Estonia or Latvia has a more entrepreneurial private sector than the Czech Republic or Slovakia? We cannot, and it is not just the different ways businesses are enumerated in the region that makes comparisons difficult. While within countries corporations are more likely to be forms of entrepreneurship, the variation across countries is driven to a large extent by the minimum capital requirement every founder must deposit at registration. Because the protection corporations provide against personal impoverishment in case of business failure, limited liability businesses are attractive. In Romania, Estonia, and Latvia, where capital requirements are very low, we find a lower share of sole proprietorships.[7] Among high barrier countries, Hungary and Slovenia seem more entrepreneurial; among low barrier countries Latvia and Lithuania are on the high end and Bulgaria is on the low end.

Because most of the businesses are not corporations, the average enterprise size is very small. The vast majority of the businesses employ no one.[8] In sole proprietorships, most of the employees, if any are hired, are family members. There are 2.3 people working in the average sole proprietorship, including the owner, which means that they employ on the average 1.3 people, down from 1.6 in 1995. The largest figures are from the Baltic countries where sole proprietors on the average hire more than two employees. There is no sign that this form of business is moving away from self-employment. Sole proprietors were not hiring more workers in 2001 than they did 6 years earlier. During the same period, the average size of partnerships and corporations also dropped. In 2001, it was half of what it used to be. This marked decrease is the result of enterprise restructuring and privatization. Large state-owned companies had to shed unnecessary labor and many were broken up into several smaller units, hence some of the increase in their share. If the entrepreneur's distinctive skill is the creation of new business *organizations*, the vast majority of transition country businesses are not in need of entrepreneurship.

Moreover, there is evidence that a large portion of these businesses are pursued part-time. In Hungary, in 2001, Tax Office records showed that

Table 2. The Distribution of Active Non-Agricultural SMEs (with <250 Employees) between January 1995 and September 2001 in 10 Post-Communist Countries by the Legal Type of the Business (%)[a].

Country	2001 September				1995 January				Minimum Capital Requirement for Limited Liability Companies (USD)
	Sole proprietorship		Business partnership and corporate enterprise		Sole proprietorship		Business partnership and corporate enterprise		
	Percent of businesses	Average size	Percent of businesses	Average size	Percent of businesses	Average size	Percent of businesses	Average size	
Bulgaria	78.8	2.6	21.2	12.1	84.1	2.1	15.9	56.9	3,330
Czech Republic	83.4	1.9	16.6	13.7	88.9	2.8	11.1	40.2	6,100
Estonia	27.9	3.6	72.1	9.9	22.6	6.1	77.4	16.0	3,300
Hungary	54.5	1.8	45.5	6.5	66.4	1.9	33.6	13.6	15,000
Latvia	26.6	3.7	73.4	12.1	24.4	4.0	75.6	19.8	3,800
Lithuania	68.2	3.1	31.8	18.5	70.4	3.1	29.6	39.6	3,700
Poland	84.3	2.5	15.7	11.6	82.2	3.0	17.8	30.4	15,015
Romania	46.5	1.5	53.5	6.6	31.6	1.4	68.4	7.4	65
Slovakia	83.5	2.5	16.6	16.1	87.3	3.0	12.7	39.5	4,250
Slovenia	74.2	2.5	25.8	9.1	61.8	2.5	38.2	23.3	14,100
Region	75.0	2.3	25.0	10.0	74.6	2.6	25.4	21.5	Average: 7,407.5

Source: DOSME.
[a]Percentages.

only 56% of sole proprietors worked in their business full-time. Sixteen percent carried their business as pensioners and 28% were employed elsewhere (Laky 2002: 50). These numbers are reproduced by our TARKI survey (Table 3) reasonably well. Owners of business partnerships and corporate enterprise are more likely to devote themselves fully to their business, but even there we find a good number of part-timers, about a quarter and 15%, respectively.[9] Part-time entrepreneurship is not necessarily a contradiction in terms. Some real entrepreneurs do launch their ventures from the security of their main job, becoming full-time entrepreneurs only once their undertaking is off the ground. In certain instances, their employment provides the necessary start up conditions such as business ties, references, office space, and tools. For pensioners, the pension supplies the safety net in case of failure. Yet 15 years into the transition, the high proportion of part-time businesses is another sign that for many, business is more a way of supplementing income than initiating a business empire.

In post-communist businesses, the separation of home and business is absent not only in accounting and legal liability but also in a spatial sense. The majority of businesses operate out of the owner's residence (Table 4). Again, the Baltic states are different, i.e., again, most likely due to the peculiarities of registration and the resulting larger business size in the Baltic sample. Moreover, the home office is now more common than it was 6 years ago in almost all the countries. Not to rent a separate office space saves money but it also means not to be committed to a lease and thus it allows for

Table 3.   Part-Time vs. Full-Time Business Engagement in Hungary 2001[a].

	Type of Business			Total
	Sole Proprietorship	Business Partnership	Corporate Enterprise	
Part-Time Business Employee Elsewhere	18.3	20.0	11.4	17.7
Part-Time Business Inactive	22.8	3.5	3.4	17.2
Full-Time Business	58.9	76.5	85.2	65.1
N	496	115	88	699

Source: TARKI, 2001.
[a]Percentages.

Table 4. Percent Active Non-Agricultural SMEs where the Enterprise is Located in the Owner's Residence, with a Single Facility of Operation and a Single Line of Activity in 1995 and 2001.

	Business in Owner's Residence		Business with a Single Facility		Business with a Single Line of Activity	
	2001	1995	2001	1995	2001	1995
Bulgaria	45.9	42.0	95.1	96.8	94.5	90.0
Czech Republic	64.2	60.1	93.0	94.6	82.8	73.5
Estonia	42.0	26.3	87.9	91.3	84.0	76.4
Hungary	37.5	38.4	91.2	95.1	73.3	78.8
Latvia	24.4	22.0	80.2	85.1	77.6	66.6
Lithuania	21.8	20.6	92.2	93.5	92.7	78.0
Poland	61.3	60.5	94.0	92.9	92.1	80.5
Romania	62.9	45.5	93.6	94.8	90.7	77.7
Slovakia	59.1	59.7	93.5	94.2	75.0	76.0
Slovenia	70.5	65.6	95.1	94.0	83.0	83.7
Total	57.6	52.0	93.8	93.4	87.7	79.3

Source: DOSME.

flexibility. As most businesses reported to have only a single facility, and only 6% claim to have other units located elsewhere, the home office is the only facility most businesses have. The structure of these businesses is simple. Just as owners do not have to co-ordinate between multiple sites, they do not have to co-ordinate between multiple lines of activities. As what they do is much more driven by the particular expertise of the proprietor than the opportunities offered by the market, the vast bulk of businesses focus on a single line of activity. They are highly specialized and not diversified.

Finally, these businesses are not interested in growth. The owners spend most of the money they make on their household consumption and only a little over a quarter put any money back into their enterprise (Table 5). This seems a consistent pattern over time. This low level of capital investment is even more remarkable if we consider that many business investments are actually for consumer durables used both by the business and the household. The automobile is one such investment. Writing it off as a business expense is the only way many people can afford to drive a new car. Other typical investment goods are computers, fax machines, and cell phones, all used at home to benefit both the business and the family. This low investment level also indicates that for most businesses, the main and often only input that matters is labor.

Table 5.   Percent of Active Non-Agricultural SMEs that Carried Out Capital Investment or Development Over 1998–2001.

	2001	1998	1999	2000	Average 1998–2001
Bulgaria	15.1	24.8	10.1	15.0	16.3
Czech Republic	32.7	34.6	32.5	31.6	32.9
Estonia	41.5	45.2	33.8	31.2	37.9
Hungary	27.9	43.9	26.9	28.0	31.7
Latvia	21.8	24.7	15.6	14.9	19.3
Lithuania	32.5	25.2	20.6	29.8	27.0
Poland	26.4	27.3	29.7	22.1	26.4
Romania	23.5	20.2	17.4	14.1	18.8
Slovakia	34.9	26.4	29.3	29.7	30.1
Slovenia	42.1	36.4	45.7	34.3	39.6
Total	27.1	29.2	27.5	23.9	26.9

Source: DOSME.

Data from our Hungarian survey (not presented here) reinforce this point. Most Hungarian business people who start with sole proprietorship end with the same type of business. That is equally true for partnerships and corporations. There is no easy movement among the various business forms. The number of people the business owners work with during their career is similarly constant. Business owners do not start small and grow big. They start small and stay small, or start larger and either stay that size or shrink.[10]

Thus, the overall picture that emerges fits better the post-Fordist paradigm. Businesses tend to be small and are intertwined with the household spatially and in terms of legal liability and accounting. They tend to have a single focus and they are local limiting their operations to the vicinity of the proprietor's home. Investment and growth are not priorities and business owners are often reluctant to commit to their business as a full-time career. Enterprises are mostly individual strategies of self-employment; their main and often only purpose is to maximize income from labor and to increase income for consumption. The typical private business is not so much a venue of entrepreneurship but an instrument of a labor market strategy.

Reasons for Starting a Business

If we shift our focus from the business to the business owners, a similar picture emerges. Using our survey data from Hungary, first we will look at what motivation people have to start a business and how different motivations are associated with different types of businesses. Then we will demonstrate that different business types have different patterns of recruitment, i.e., they attract owners of different kinds. Finally, we will show that the financial reward the owners reap depends on the kind of business they run and thus different businesses affect economic inequalities differently. Motivation for starting an enterprise could be thought as the proximate cause of launching a business while recruitment reveals the deeper structural causes of the choice. Financial rewards are the consequences of that choice. We will first discuss these proximate causes to see how business people themselves see the purpose of their enterprise. When asked about the importance of different reasons for starting a business, owners in Hungary name first and foremost the need to create a job for themselves (Table 6). Over 60% named this as a very important reason and less than a quarter claimed it played no role. The importance of employing oneself is even more apparent once we consider that a sizable proportion of the business people run their business part-time from the security of another job or some other permanent income (e.g. pension, disability or maternity pay). For them, job creation is obviously less pressing. If we look at only those who engage in their business full-time, we find that almost 80% named self-employment as a very important concern in a country where the unemployment rate is not exceptionally high, or more to the point, the proportion of the economically active population is not unusually low compared with the rest of the region.

The second most important motivation is to become independent. The desire for independence is quite understandable after decades of state socialism that employed most people in large bureaucratic organizations. The wish to be one's own boss is an entrepreneurial quality as long as it is directed towards the exploitation of market opportunities. Yet to take advantage of market opportunities comes in only at third place, and just a quarter of the business people declared it as a very important motivation. The next reason is to gain tax advantages, about 20% claimed this was very important. About one in eight reported that a very important influence on their decision was their employer's wish to circumvent payroll taxes. In these cases, the employer makes a continuous job relation contingent on the worker's ability to provide invoice for the employer as opposed to demand wages. Then the worker is paid as a subcontractor. Saving on taxes either for oneself or for the employer was named as very important by 29% of the business people. Given that these practices while legal are not exactly officially endorsed, reporting on them is probably biased against full

Table 6. Reasons Given for Starting one's Enterprise in Hungary[a].

| | To Create a Job for Oneself and Family Members[b] | | | | To be Inde-pendent | To Take Advantage of the Transition to a Market Economy[c] | | | | | | | Tax Advantages | Employer Required it |
| | Total | Part-Time | | Full-Time | Total | Total | Part-Time | | Full-Time | Sole Proprietorship | Business Partnership | Corporate Enterprise | Total | Total |
		Employee	Inactive				Employee	Inactive						
Played No Role	24.5	51.6	36.5	10.1	28.4	44.2	48.1	63.5	38.9	46.7	41.9	23.3	55.9	81.6
Not Too Important	12.6	16.5	10.8	11.1	21.5	29.9	32.6	28.4	28.9	29.7	29.0	27.9	24.0	6.4
Very Important	62.9	31.9	52.7	78.8	50.1	25.9	19.3	8.1	32.2	23.6	29.0	48.8	20.1	12.0
N = 100%	661	182	74	405	661	656	181	74	401	508	93	43	658	657

Source: TARKI, 2001.

[a]Percentage.

[b]For the relationship between part-/full-time form of the business and the importance of creating a job for oneself and family members: χ^2: 141.6; degrees of freedom: 4; Significance: 0.000.

[c]For the relationship between part-/full-time business and the importance of taking advantage of the transition to a market economy: χ^2: 28.2; degrees of freedom: 4; Significance: 0.000. For the relationship between the legal form of the business and the importance of taking advantage of the transition to a market economy: χ^2: 15.1; degrees of freedom: 4; Significance: 0.004.

disclosure and their actual importance is likely to be greater than these numbers suggest.

The truly entrepreneurial motivation of taking advantage of market opportunities is distributed unevenly among the various types of enterprises. Full-time business people are more likely to name this as very important than part-timers. Creating job for oneself and exploiting the market are not mutually exclusive motivations, although the first one, as we have seen, is much more common than the second. Yet, it is clear that corporate business owners are more driven by market opportunities than sole proprietors. Sole proprietors are only half as likely to chose market opportunities as a very important reason than corporate business owners. While not all businesses that are created as independent legal entities are vehicles of entrepreneurial activity, the need to put down a sum as base capital and the subsequent requirements of more sophisticated bookkeeping force would-be entrepreneurs to think about the market forces they want to harness.

Recruitment

The large literature on recruitment into entrepreneurships in transition countries rarely distinguish between the self-employed and real entrepreneurs (Nee 1989, 1991; Zhou et al. 1997; Radaev 1997; Stoyanov 1997; Bolcic 1998; Lengyel 1998; Pistrui et al., 2003; Glas and Drnovsek 2003; Kuzmina 2003).[11] Measuring true entrepreneurship is hard, and even if it can be done it will most probably yield such a small segment of the population that their number would be insufficient in common representative samples.

In the analysis below, we present two simple models predicting the choice of business type and the decision to work in one's own business part- or full-time (Table 7). For our first model, we separated destinations into four categories: no business, sole proprietorships, partnerships without legal entity and corporations and included some of the commonly tested variables from the literature. While we will give a short rationale for each independent variable, our purpose here is not to build the best prediction, not even to test the theories behind the independent variables. Our point is that the various business types can result from recruitment patterns that look similar still masking important differences.

We will start with the interrupted embourgeoisiement thesis that posits that entrepreneurial values survived in the family during the decades of communism (Szelenyi 1988). Parental involvement with autonomous private business activity before – and in the Hungarian case during – the communist era generated a set of values and practices that could be mobilized during the market transition. Our model shows that if parents were self-employed, people are more likely to run their own business, other variables in the model being equal. The strongest effect is for sole proprietorship, but the three coefficients are not significantly different from each other and the coefficient for sole proprietorship and corporate enterprise are especially close. There are two possible mechanisms that are compatible with this finding. It is possible that the values work the same way for both or all three types of businesses. Self-employed parents give something generically useful in any type of venture. But it is also possible that the values handed down by the previous generation are best fitting for sole proprietorship and are the kind that one can obtain easily from sources other than the self-employed forebears. At the same time, corporate enterprise does require certain values that only the proper upbringing can provide, but it needs other things as well. In other words, inheriting these values from parents is sufficient but not necessary for sole proprietorship and necessary but not sufficient for corporate enterprise.

The second thesis focuses on life history as the main explanation of becoming economically independent. It is one's experience under communism that helps with the launching of a business. Here two separate, and to some extent contradictory explanations have been developed. The first focuses on continuity of practices and claims that the private sector under socialism, especially in Hungary where it was large and legal, was the proper training ground for business people. The second stresses the continuity of elites and maintains that it is those who amassed useful social ties, special organizational skills and personal wealth available only to leaders under communism are the best positioned to exploit the new opportunities offered by the market. Our first model shows that the effect of participation in the private sector and having been a boss before the end of communism have a mirrored pattern. The first helps more with becoming an individual or a corporate entrepreneur, and the second is most advantageous for entering business partnerships. The pattern for the effect of authority under communism is unexpected. Privatization, where bosses often had the opportunity to get parts of a firm or the entire company they had worked for would have predicted the strongest positive effect for corporate firms. Nevertheless, on the whole, it is not corporate enterprise but partnerships where top jobs under communism help most. This is probably due to the fact that many of these partnerships are in services and trade where ties and reputation one accumulates in position of authority are great assets.

Table 7. Recruitment into Various Business Forms in Hungary (Multinomial Logit).

	Predicting Business Type									
	No business vs. sole proprietorship		No business vs. business partnership		No business vs. corporate enterprise		Variable constrained to have equal effect across all contrasts		
	Coeff.	Sig.	Coeff.	Sig.	Coeff.	Sig.	Δχ2	Δ df	Sig.
Model 1									
Constant	-6.705	0.000	-11.353	0.000	-10.426	0.000			
Parents Self-Employed	0.629	0.000	0.330	0.189	0.501	0.068	1.342	2	0.512
Participated in Private Sector in 1970–80	2.611	0.000	1.350	0.000	2.092	0.000	16.905	2	0.000
Boss in State Sector in 1970–80	0.207	0.223	0.875	0.001	0.519	0.112	4.905	2	0.086
Years of Schooling	0.095	0.000	0.243	0.000	0.268	0.000	24.839	2	0.000
Size of Town	-0.136	0.066	0.489	0.001	0.492	0.003	24.835	2	0.000
Age/10	1.980	0.000	3.885	0.000	3.203	0.000	26.023	4	0.000
$(Age/10)^2$	-0.237	0.000	-0.489	0.000	-0.415	0.000			
Gender	-0.517	0.000	-1.014	0.000	-0.970	0.000	6.815	2	0.033
Model							133.951	16	0.000

χ^2: 1017.037; d.f.: 24
McFadden's pseudo R^2:0.173
$N = 8330$

Predicting Part-Time and Full-Time Business

	No business vs. part-time business		No business vs. full-time business		Variable constrained to have equal effect across all contrasts		
	Coeff.	Sig.	Coeff.	Sig.	$\Delta \chi^2$	Δ df	Sig.
Model 2							
Constant	-8.402	0.00	-9.790	0.000			
Parents Self-Employed	0.548	0.000	0.600	0.000	0.078	1	0.780
Participated in Private Sector in 1970–80	2.726	0.000	2.239	0.000	5.882	1	0.015
Boss in State Sector in 1970–80	0.259	0.199	0.468	0.007	0.759	1	0.384
Years of Schooling	0.187	0.000	0.127	0.000	3.971	1	0.046
Size of Town	-0.213	0.034	0.154	0.039	9.611	1	0.002
Age/10	1.306	0.000	4.238	0.000	137.920	2	0.000
(Age/10)^2	-0.136	0.000	-0.537	0.000			
Gender	-0.228	0.106	-0.882	0.000	14.616	1	0.000
Model					176.589	8	0.000

χ^2: 1085.572; d.f.: 16
McFadden's pseudo R^2: 0.189
$N = 8343$

Source: TARKI, 2001.

The third thesis is associated with the market transition theory. It posits that markets reward human capital better and therefore the private enterprise will be more attractive for better educated people. Indeed, we find that education has a positive effect for all three types of business ownership, but for sole proprietors this effect is much weaker. In fact, the three coefficients are significantly different and most of the discrepancy is between sole proprietors and the other two groups.

The fourth explanation emphasizes market opportunities. Cities are larger markets and should provide more market opportunities than small towns or villages. Larger markets also make specialization possible. Indeed, the effect of town size is strong for two of the three types. Sole proprietors are different. For them this effect is weak and negative because they include peasants and artisans offering less specialized and sophisticated services. Moreover, if self-employment is primarily a way of coping with unemployment, villages where unemployment is higher should have more self-employed. This finding is in line with the data on motivation, which indicated that sole proprietors care most about creating jobs for themselves and much less exploiting market opportunities.

Finally, we control for age and gender. The non-linear effect of age is the consequence that at younger ages people are still not prepared, at older ages are not able to run their own business. The age when business ownership is most likely is around 40. Sole proprietors are a little older and corporate business people are somewhat younger than partnership members. Age works differently for the three types. Being a woman makes one less likely to engage in any of the three types of business as men dominate throughout but women's disadvantage is least in the simplest business type.

If all we care about is the direction and statistical significance of the effects, we find that given this limited set of independent variables recruitment to the three types is quite similar.[12] But if we care about the size of each coefficient, we see the effect of each independent variable varies. If we test whether these differences are due to sampling error by restricting the coefficients to equality across the contrasts, we find that with two exceptions – the effect of parents' self-employment and having been a boss under socialism – the effects are statistically significantly different. For instance, education has a much stronger effect on partnership and corporate enterprise than for sole proprietorship. The same is true for town size. Private sector experience under socialism is an asset for sole proprietors, less so for corporate businessmen and the least for partnerships.

Our second model shows, that if we distinguish between part- and full-time businesses, parents' self-employment, private sector participation under socialism and education, all have positive effects on both types. Small towns are more conducive to part-time, large cities to full-time businesses. Having been a boss under socialism is an asset in full-time business but not in part-time ventures. Being a woman, is less of a disadvantage for the part-time and more for the full-time self-employed. And finally, the part-time self employed are older. Many of them are retired and pursue part-time business as pensioners. We can see that except for parents' self-employment and position of authority under socialism, all the variables affect the two contrasts differently.[13]

Consequences

If the various forms of business engagements spring from diverse motivations, and recruit differently from the population, their outcomes are also distinctly different. The emphasis in the literature is on monetary rewards and income inequality (Gerber and Hout 1998; Xie and Hannum 1996; Bian and Logan 1996) . Estimating incomes for business owners is very difficult. Business owners underreport their personal income and receive various supplements through the personal use of business property such as cars and mobile phones. Moreover, the tax advantages they enjoy can also be construed as hidden income. Here, however, we will emphasize not the differences between business owners and employees but variation among the different forms of business. In the first model, the base of comparison represented by the constant is the group of the sole proprietors both full- and part-time (Table 8). In the second and third model, it is the part-time sole proprietors who are the base group.

In the first model, the monthly income of sole proprietors is about HUF 51,000 (Hungarian Forints).[14] People without any business make HUF 11,000 less or HUF 41,000. Partnership and corporate business owners, on the other hand make 56,000 and 86,000, respectively.

In the second model, we distinguish between part- and full-time businesses. We can see that part-time business people report about the same income as full-timers except for partnerships where full-time business people make actually less than part-timers do from all their jobs. Partnerships without legal entity are more lucrative if one is employed or pensioned off. The main job gives not just income but aids partnerships in various ways, for instance, by supplying simple capital infrastructure or clients. Pensions provide a financial safety net without requiring work effort.

Table 8. The Effect of Business Type on Personal Income in Hungary, 2001 (Nested OLS regression).

	Model 1			Model 2			Model 3		
	Coefficients	Beta	Sig.	Coefficient	Beta	Sig.	Coefficient	Beta	Sig.
Constant	51318.55		0.000	50411.26		0.000	32227.75		0.000
No Business	−11395.66	−0.118	0.000	−10488.37	−0.109	0.000	−7430.36	−0.077	0.000
Business Partnership	14597.89	0.061	0.000	35799.27	0.150	0.000	23227.04	0.097	0.000
Corporate Business	34799.67	0.128	0.000	26781.47	0.098	0.000	16299.36	0.060	0.012
Δ Full–Time Sole Proprietorship				1696.88	0.011	0.504	183.27	0.001	0.935
Δ Full-Time Partnership				−27434.60	−0.099	0.000	−22236.67	−0.080	0.000
Δ Full-Time Corporate Business				11107.27	0.037	0.161	13890.92	0.046	0.048
Parents Self-Employed							2452.72	0.042	0.000
Participated in Private Sector in 1970–80							−2420.46	−0.020	0.066
Boss in State Sector in 1970–80							2323.34	0.025	0.020
Years of Schooling							3003.36	0.365	0.000
Size of Town							−3914.00	−0.117	0.000
Age							35.69	0.025	0.022
Gender							−8248.79	−0.169	0.000
MODEL	Adjusted R^2: 0.049 $N = 7073$			Adjusted R^2:0.051			Adjusted R^2: 0.258		

Source: TARKI, 2001.

We find essentially the same pattern once we control for the selection effect, by holding constant variables we used to predict recruitment. Now the difference between what a sole proprietor and a full-time partnership member makes vanishes. The premium corporate entrepreneurs get for full-time effort becomes statistically significant.

In sum, the most lucrative type of business is the corporate kind and the least one is sole proprietorship. Which type of business one chooses has financial consequences.

CONCLUSION

We argued that the entrepreneurial boom in post-communism is more modest than it seems and much of it has more to do with the post-Fordist restructuring of the economy and the creation of a more flexible work force than with the entrepreneurial spirit. Most businesses are created as a form of self-employment and not as a business enterprise. Their aim is not the development of a new organization, the domination of a market, the increase in business assets or profit but improvement in the consumption of the owners and their household by finding the best strategy for raising labor income. Based on the Weberian distinction between the household bound and the autonomous business, we drew up two ideal types that imply a long series of distinct and testable hypotheses, only a few of which has been investigated, in this chapter. We further contended that despite serious difficulties in measuring various forms of independent economic activities, one must try not to conflate them. At the beginning of the transition, it was still defensible to lump together the independent newspaper vendor on the urban street corner, the freelance journalist and the owner of the printing shop directing a dozen employees. Since then, the private sector grew and became internally differentiated. Research on private sector development in transition economies must distinguish among the various forms of independent economic activity in the private sector as different forms follow different logics, they operate, recruit and reward differently.

They also have different policy implications. The romanticization of self-employment by projecting the demiurgic world of Steve Jobs, Viktor Kozeny, Jozef Majsky, or Erno Rubik onto the masses of shopkeepers, small farmers, petty traders, free professionals and assorted tax dodgers, not only confers on the self-employed our respect along with an exaggerated aura of heroism and excitement, but also results in important policy biases.

From the entrepreneurial perspective, the main policy instrument to stimulate small enterprises is credit. To make credit available to small businesses policy makers must set up special funds that give loans to small enterprises, guarantee funds that entrepreneurs borrow from banks, or persuade banks through regulation or various financial incentives to offer loans on favorable terms. While credit is useful and important not just for the small minority of entrepreneurs but also for the large majority of the self-employed, for the latter their household centric organization and worldview puts limitation on the amount and kind of credit they can use.

Stimulating the small sector is seen by entrepreneurialists as an instrument for cutting unemployment through the expansion of existing businesses that need to hire more employees, although the majority of the small businesses will not hire employees or would do it only form a pool of family and acquaintances. Most small businesses can alleviate unemployment not through hiring but through adding new individuals to the ranks of the self-employed. Efforts to stimulate export will run into similar difficulties. Because the vast majority of the businesses are structured around the household, it is unlikely that they move outside their local markets.

To generate a balanced size structure, that has a sufficient number of medium and large companies, the policy maker will hope that they will grow out of small businesses, when in fact, most have their medium or large size from the outset. To have more medium sized companies, the policy maker must have special tools for the creation of businesses of that size. While a minority of small businesses are entrepreneurial and will grow, will need credit, will hire and export, careful targeting is crucial. The small businesses are viewed by policies guided by the entrepreneurial paradigm as a major source of taxes, even given the awareness that tax collection is not always easy, however, the growth of self-employment is likely to have no or negative effect on tax receipts.

Taking the post-Fordist approach, the policy instrument to emphasize is not credit but help to upgrade skills and to provide infrastructure that small businesses will not be able to supply themselves because of economies of scale. Since the single most important asset these small businesses have is labor, improving skills helps them the most. Because most businesses remain small they will be aided greatly by infrastructure that they individually cannot provide. By promoting associations, trade fairs, making expenses on professional development tax deductible, supporting trade publications, providing market data, accounting services, internet resources, better road and transportation at a subsidized rate, the policy maker can greatly assist small businesses.

While real entrepreneurs are few their importance far outweighs their numeric proportion. The challenge for both scholarship and for policy making is to understand the internal differentiation of the private sector.

NOTES

1. There is an element of the reductionist fallacy behind the boundless enthusiasm of this approach. Arguing that innovation and success at the entrepreneurial level automatically translates into economic development at the level of the national economy is an unwarranted logical jump, as Baumol pointed out by his famous distinction between good and bad entrepreneurship (Baumol 1990). Nevertheless, few would argue that economic dynamism can come about without entrepreneurial forces.

2. The distinction between the entrepreneur and the self-employed is similar to the difference between the *qiye jia* and the *geti hu* in China. The first refers to the enterprise, the second to the household.

3. Poland has a unique history. Unlike other communist countries, it never managed to collectivize its agriculture and as a result it retained a large peasant class that survives to date.

4. A more detailed description of the project can be found at http://forum.europa.eu.int/irc/dsis/dosme/info/data/en/pages/publications/publicat.htm

5. This design ignores only a small portion of the enterprises, although this portion varies somewhat across countries. The share of agriculture in the number of enterprises is well under 10% in these countries.

6. Matild Sagi was the director of the survey.

7. Until 1995, the minimum capital requirement in Estonia was only USD 25. Moreover, the figures for the proportion of sole proprietorships in Latvia and Estonia are underestimates because, as discussed earlier, the sampling methodology used by DOSME relied on registries biased toward larger companies.

8. For instance, in Hungary 71% in the Czech Republic 83% of sole proprietorships employ nobody (CESTAT Statistical Bulletin, 2000/4).

9. Hungary had a long history of part-time private sector participation dating back to communism, as the Hungarian communist leadership was more tolerant of these activities than leaders in other communist countries.

10. This is also consistent with earlier data from DOSME (Rona-Tas 2001).

11. For counterexamples see Hanley 2000; Rona-Tas 1994.

12. Most researcher focus on sign and significance of coefficients because these are comparable across studies.

13. A test of ordinality with respect to these independent variables show that the three categories of the dependent variable (no, part-time, full-time business) do not yield a progression along a single dimension given the independent variables in the model.

14. Estimating the equation with the logarithm of income gives the same results but one loses the intuitive simplicity of the coefficients. One USD was about HUF 250 at the time of the survey.

REFERENCES

Aldrich, Howard E and Roger Waldinger. 1990. "Ethnicity and entrepreneurship." *Annual Review of Sociology* 16:111–135.

Azudová, L'ubica. 1998. "Význam a podpora malopodnikatel'ského sektora v Európskej únii a v Slovenskej republike z pohl'adu zamestnanosti." *Práca a sociálna politika* 6/4:6–11.

Baumol, William J. 1990. "Entrepreneurship – productive, unproductive, and destructive." *Journal of Political Economy* 98/5:893–921.

Bian, Yanjie and John R Logan. 1996. "Market transition and the persistence of power: The changing stratification system in urban China." *American Sociological Review* 61/5:739–758.

Blanchflower, David G and Andrew J Oswald. 1998. "What makes an entrepreneur?." *Journal of Labor Economics* 16/1:26–60.

Bolcic, Silvano. 1998. "Entrepreneurial inclinations and new entrepreneurs in Serbia in the early 1990s." *International Journal of Sociology* 27/4:3–35.

Brusco, Sebastiano. 1982. "The emilian model: Productive decentralization and social integration Cambridge." *Journal of Economics* 6/2:167–184.

Casson, Mark. 1982. *The entrepreneur: An economic theory*. Oxford: Martin Robertson.

Gábor, István R. 1997. "Too many, too small: Small entrepreneurship in Hungary – ailing or prospering?." Pp. 158–175 in *Restructuring networks in post-socialism. legacies, linkages, and localities*, edited by G. Grabher and D. Stark. Oxford: Oxford University Press.

Gerber, Theodore P and Hout Michael. 1998. "More shock than therapy: Market transition employment, and income in Russia, 1991–1995." *The American Journal of Sociology* 104/1:1–50.

Glas, Miroslav and Drnovsek Mateja. 2003. "Small business in Slovenia: Expectations and accomplishments." Pp. 131–151 in *Small firms and economic development in developed and transition economies: A reader*, edited by D.A. Kirby and A. Watson. Burlington, VT: Ashgate.

Hamilton, Barton H. 2000. "Does entrepreneurship pay? An empirical analysis of the returns of self-employment." *The Journal of Political Economy* 108/3:604–631.

Hanley, Eric. 2000. "Self-employment in post-communist Eastern Europe: A refuge from poverty or road to riches." *Communist & Post-Communist Studies* 33/3:379–402.

Hirst, Paul and Zeitlin Jonathan. 1991. "Flexible specialization versus post-fordism: Theory, evidence, and policy implications." *Economy and Society* 20/1:1–56.

Kent, Calvin A. 1989. "The treatment of entrepreneurship in principles of economics textbooks." *The Journal of Economic Education* 20/2:153–164.

Kirzner, Israel M. 1973. *Competition and entrepreneurship*. Chicago: University of Chicago Press.

——————. 1980. The prime mover of progress: The entrepreneur in capitalism and socialism. London: Institute of Economic Affairs.

Knight, Frank H. 1921/1957. *Risk, uncertainty and profit*. New York: Kelley & Millman.

Kornai, János. 1994. "Transformational recession: The main causes." *The Journal of Comparative Economics* 19/1:39–65.

Kuczi, Tibor. 2000. *Kisvállakozás és társadalmi környezet. (Small enterprise and social environment)*. Budapest: Replika Kör.

Kumar, Krishan. 1995. *From post-industrial to post-modern society*. Oxford: Blackwell.

Kuzmina, Irina. 2003. "Entrepreneurship and small business development in latvia." Pp. 153–163 in *Small firms and economic development in developed and transition economies: A reader*, edited by D.A. Kirby and A. Watson. Burlington, VT: Ashgate.

Laki, Mihály. 1998. *Kisvállalkozás a szocializmus után. (Small Enterprise after Socialism)*. Budapest: Közgazdasági Szemle Alapitvány.

Laky, Teréz. 1994. *Vállalkozások a Start-hitel segitségével. (Enterprises with START credit)*. Budapest: Magyar Vállalkozásfejlesztési Alap.

------. 1998. "A kisvállalkozások növekedésének korlátai. [Limits of growth for small enterprises]." *Szociológia* 1:23–40.

------. 2002. *Main trends in labour demand and supply*. Budapest: Labour Research Institute.

Lengyel, György. 1998. "Entrepreneurial inclination in Hungary 1988–1996." *International Journal of Sociology* 27/4:36–49.

Martinelli, Alberto. 1994. "Entrepreneurship and management." Pp. 476–503 in *Handbook of economic sociology*, edited by N.J. Smelser and R. Swedberg. Princeton, NJ: Princeton University Press.

Národná Agentúrav Pre Rozvoj Malého a Stredného Podnikania. (National Agency for Development of Small and Medium Enterprises) 1997. *Stav Malého a Stredného Podnikania 1997.* (The State of Small and Medium Sized Enterprises 1997.) Bratislava.

Nee, Victor. 1989. "A theory of market transition: From redistribution to markets in state socialism." *American Sociological Review* 54/5:663–681.

------. 1991. "Social inequalities in reforming state socialism: Between redistribution and markets in China." *American Sociological Review* 56/3:267–282.

OECD. 1996. "Small business in transition economies." OECD Working Papers No.4. Paris.

OECD. 2002. "Forum for enterprise development. Baltic Regional Programme: Estonia Country Assessment." May 2002.

Piore, Michael J and Charles F Sabel. 1984. *The second industrial divide. Possibilities for prosperity*. New York: Basic Books.

Pistrui, , David, WelschHarold P, Hans J Pohl, Oliver Wintermantel, and Jianwen Liao. 2003. "Entrepreneurship in the New Germany." Pp. 116–130 in *Small Firms and economic development in developed and transition economies: A reader*, edited by D.A. Kirby and A. Watson. Burlington, VT: Ashgate.

Radaev, Vadim. 1997. "Practicing and potential entrepreneurs in Russia." *International Journal of Sociology* 27/3:15–50.

Rona-Tas, Akos. 1994. "The first shall be last? Entrepreneurship and communist cadres in the transition from socialism." *American Journal of Sociology* 100/1:40–69.

------. 1997. *The great surprise of the small transformation: The demise of communism and the rise of the private sector in Hungary*. Ann Arbor, MI: University of Michigan Press.

------. 2000. "Legacies, institutions and markets: Small entrepreneurship in Hungary, slovakia and the Czech Republic." in *Successful transitions political factors of socio-economic progress in post-socialist countries*, edited by J. Beyer, J. Wielgohs and H. Wiesenthal. Nomos Verlag: Baden-Baden.

------. 2001. "The worm and the caterpillar: The small private sector in the Czech Republic, Hungary and Slovakia." Pp. 39–65 in *The new entrepreneurs of Europe and Asia: Patterns of business development in Russia, Eastern Europe, and China*, edited by V. Bonnell and T. Gold. Armonk, N.Y.: M.E. Sharpe.

Scase, Richard. 2003. "Entrepreneurship and proprietorship in transition. Policy implications for small- and medium-size enterprise SECTOR." Pp. 64–77 in *Small and medium en-*

terprises in transitional economies, edited by R.J. McIntyre and B. Dallago. New York: Palgrave MacMillan.

Schumpeter, Joseph A. 1936. *The theory of economic development; An inquiry into profits, capital, credit, interest, and the business cycle translated from the German by Redvers Opie.* Cambridge, Mass: Harvard University Press.

------. 1947/1989. "The creative response in economic history." Pp. 253–271 in *Essays*, edited by R.V. Clemence. New Brunswick: Transaction Publishers.

------. 1949/1989. "Economic theory and entrepreneurial history." Pp. 253–271 in *Essays*, edited by R.V. Clemence. New Brunswick: Transaction Publishers.

Stoyanov, Alexander. 1997. "Private business and entrepreneurial inclinations." *International Journal of Sociology* 27/3:51–79.

Szelenyi, Ivan. 1988. *Socialist entrepreneurs rural embourgeoisiement in Hungary.* Madison, WI: University of Wisconsin Press.

Thornton, Patricia H. 1999. "The sociology of entrepreneurship." *Annual Review of Sociology* 25:19–46.

Weber, Max. 1921/1978. *Economy and Society: An outline of interpretative sociology.* Edited by Guenther Roth and Claus Wittich. Berkeley, CA: University of California Press.

Xie, Yu and Hannum Emily. 1996. "Regional variation in earnings inequality in reform-era urban China." *The American Journal of Sociology* 101/4:950–992.

Zhou, , Xueguang, Nancy Brandon Tuma, and Phyllis Moen. 1997. "Institutional change and job-shift patterns in urban China 1949 to 1994." *American Sociological Review* 62/3:339–365.

ENTREPRENEURIAL STRATEGIES DURING INSTITUTIONAL TRANSITIONS

Mike W. Peng and Yi Jiang

INTRODUCTION

Since institutions are typically conceptualized as "the rules of the game in a society" (North 1990: 3; Scott 1995), "institutional transitions" are defined as "fundamental and comprehensive changes introduced to the formal and informal rules of the game" (Peng 2003: 275). One of the most dramatic sets of institutional transitions in the last two decades has been the political, economic, and social changes sweeping across Central and Eastern Europe (CEE), the newly independent states (NIS) of the former Soviet Union, and the East Asian countries of China and Vietnam. In fact, these institutional transitions are so profound that these countries, formerly known as the Eastern bloc, have now been collectively labeled "transition economies."

In transition economies, the emergence of a viable private sector has played a central role in the transition from plan to market. The role of entrepreneurs in transition economies has become a crucial area of research (McMillan and Woodruff 2002; Peng 2000, 2001; Puffer and McCarthy 2001; Wright et al. 2005). Although there are numerous country- and region-specific studies, there have been few attempts that shed light on the *overall* development of entrepreneurship throughout these transition

Entrepreneurship
Research in the Sociology of Work, Volume 15, 311–325
Copyright © 2005 by Elsevier Ltd.
All rights of reproduction in any form reserved
ISSN: 0277-2833/doi:10.1016/S0277-2833(05)15012-2

economies spanning from Shanghai to St. Petersburg. Therefore, in this chapter, we focus on the entrepreneurial strategies throughout transition economies and address two questions: How do entrepreneurs, who in this chapter are defined as "founders of a new businesses," strategize during institutional transitions? How do these strategies affect their work as entrepreneurs?

CHANGE OVER TIME

Despite the harsh political conditions, entrepreneurship existed in virtually all of these countries before major transitions took place in the 1980s (Peng 2001). By the 1980s, most socialist governments started to loosen restrictions on the private sector, resulting in an initial wave of entrepreneurship. Legal acts adopted to that end gave the first opportunities to create new legal start-ups (whereas many "businesses" in the former regime were either illegal or in the "gray area"). However, the development of new enterprise forms also brought quite a number of problems. Thus, even as the legal acts gave rather broad opportunities for the development of small state enterprises and cooperatives, further legislation put a number of restrictions on their activities. These included restrictions on specific types of activities, such as obtaining certain raw materials, rising of tax rates, and dictating of price policy.

After a period of slow but steady growth in the 1980s, private entrepreneurship blossomed in the 1990s throughout transition economies. Although the visible hand of the government is still considerably more prevalent in transition economies than in Western Europe and North America, its grip has been relaxed a great deal. The development of entrepreneurship, as exemplified by the growth of small and medium business, seems to be the major success story of the 1990s in CEE, where lackluster state-owned enterprises (SOEs) were often restructuring and downsizing. In the Czech Republic, Hungary, Poland, and Slovakia, the number of self-employed grew from just over 1 million in 1989 to 2.6 million in 1994. In China, it is the growth of smaller, entrepreneurial firms – either privately or collectively owned – that has fueled the strong growth of the economy (Peng 1997).

Entrepreneurship depends a lot on formal institutional frameworks centered on laws and regulations, which are influenced by other reforms, such as the ownership, tax, and administrative reforms (Johnson, McMillan and Woodruff 2002; Peng 2000). Ownership reform is often implemented by privatization which has become a core component of the transition process in CEE and the NIS (and less so in China and Vietnam). Since the mid-1990s, the majority of the GDP has been contributed by the private sector throughout CEE and the NIS (e.g., approximately 80% in Hungary, 75% in the Czech Republic, and 70% in Russia). At the same time, the non-state sector in China has quietly but steadily become the backbone of the economy, contributing nearly 70% of the total industrial output. During the 1990s, in CEE, about 5% of the adult working population attempted to start up a new firm or become self-employed (Mugler 2000), a figure very similar to the percentage of *nascent* entrepreneurs in the United States and Western Europe (Aldrich 1999: 75). In a nutshell, the 1990s was indeed a golden era for entrepreneurial start-ups throughout transition economies.

MAJOR ENTREPRENEURIAL STRATEGIES

In the early years of institutional transitions, the absence of credit markets, courts, and other market-supporting institutions created substantial impediments to entrepreneurs. How did the entrepreneurs succeed in overcoming the lack of effective market-supporting institutions? Recent research focusing on transition economies has highlighted three major entrepreneurial strategies: (1) prospecting, (2) networking, and (3) boundary blurring (Peng 2000, 2001). These strategies are not necessarily unique to transition economies. Prospecting and networking, for example, have been widely practiced by entrepreneurs elsewhere. What is interesting in transition economies is the importance of these strategies.

Prospecting

Prospectors rely on the product and market development to bring change to the environment around them to generate profits. They undertake relatively radical innovations and therefore face a more uncertain environment (Miles and Snow 1978). Prospectors, in contrast to defenders, constantly examine the environment for product and market opportunities. While larger SOEs and recently privatized ex-SOEs tend to be defenders which follow the existing institutional rules, private firms tend to deviate from such taken-for-granted rules, searching for strategic opportunities to enhance self-interest (Peng 2003). The start-ups, which are latecomer underdogs, cannot compete against the larger and more established SOEs head on. But they spend more time on scanning the external environment and evaluating opportunities and threats, which allows them to react quickly to opportunities, and to be the first movers while forcing their competitors to be defenders (Peng, Tan and Tong 2004). Further, start-ups have little inherited organizational baggage from the socialist era, low fixed costs, and the ability to attract the most talented people.

Optimus, Poland's leading computer maker exemplifies such a strategy. Founded in 1988, this start-up held 35% of the Polish PC market by 1995. The owner attributed his success to a "guerilla" strategy that sought first-mover advantages in the PC market when the PC revolution was starting to gain momentum in Poland in the early 1990s. Optimus thrived by always moving ahead of the competitors in terms of products and services. Specifically, while competitors imported models approaching the end of their product life cycle, Optimus provided locally assembled, low-cost PCs equipped with the latest versions of Intel chips, Samsung monitors, and Microsoft operating systems (Peng 2001).

A prospector strategy is not without limitations. Successful start-ups often attract other private firms to follow suit. Since the industries that entrepreneurs enter tend to have relatively low entry barriers and less capital intensity, first movers are often unable to sustain a competitive advantage facing the new entrants. Overall, a prospector strategy may be viable during the initial phase of the transition, but it is not likely to sustain its advantage in the long run when the economy becomes more developed and the market niches are filled (Puffer and McCarthy 2001).

Networking

Networking as a strategy is not the exclusive territory reserved only for entrepreneurial start-ups in transition economies. To some extent, all entrepreneurial firms around the world rely on this strategy (Aldrich 1999). Even in developed economies, a major source of capital for small and medium-sized firms is trade credit from suppliers. The lack of formal financial markets in transition economies means that credit from suppliers is even more important to private sector firms there (McMillan and Woodruff 2002). In the absence of formal credit markets, courts, and other market-supporting institutions, the informal personal networks of entrepreneurs in transition economies are more important and useful in comparison to entrepreneurial networks in developed economies (Peng 2000).

There are two sets of entrepreneurial networks in transition economies (Peng and Luo 2000). One set of networks is with other firms such as suppliers and buyers. Where courts and laws are unreliable for settling disputes, firms trust their customers to pay their bills and their suppliers to deliver quality goods out of the prospects of future business. Investors are willing to entrust their money to managers in their network because of family ties or ethnicity or because these managers are recommended by a trusted third party (Peng and Heath 1996). While some of these informal relationships at larger firms may have been formalized through mechanisms such as cross shareholdings and interlocking directorates (Keister 2000), most of these relationships, called *guanxi* in China and *blat* in Russia, remain informal at smaller, entrepreneurial firms.

The struggles that entrepreneurs heading China's Lucky Transportation, a trucking company servicing the construction industry, went through can serve as a case in point. Several state-owned construction and trucking firms formed an informal enterprise group aiming at internal collaboration and excluding non-members. The entrepreneurs worked hard to be their friends, including taking them out to dinner and occasionally giving them gifts such as "red envelopes" (containing cash).[1] Eventually, Lucky Transportation was accepted as a member of the group, thus enabling the start-up to achieve significant growth (over 500% growth in sales during its first 3-year period, 1992–1995) (Peng 1997).

Another set of networks is with government officials, which may be more important in transition economies, where government officials still control considerable power and resources. Entrepreneurs must go through a variety of procedures such as applying for business licenses, providing proof of their start-up capital, and filing with the tax, labor, and safety authorities. Based on a major World Bank study (Djankov et al. 2002), Table 1 places the difficulties entrepreneurs in transition economies have to go through when starting up new firms in a global context. While there are other developing countries whose entrepreneurs have to deal with worse regulations (for example, Dominican Republic requires 21 procedures and a total cost of 4.63 times of per capita GDP), the difficulties and costs confronting entrepreneurs in transition economies are evident. Hungary and Vietnam (together with Nigeria, Egypt, Indonesia, and Bolivia) require a total cost of more than their per capita GDP to start up a new firm. In Russia, entrepreneurs are required to go through 20 procedures when setting up a new business.[2] The study took place in 1999, approximately one decade after the fall of the Iron Curtain in CEE and the NIS and two decades since the decision to raise the Bamboo Curtain in China – it was hoped that at this time there would be a relatively more entrepreneur-friendly environment. Yet, these data are sobering. For entrepreneurs, the upshot is that good connections

Table 1. The Costs of Starting Up a New Firm in 42 Countries.

Country	No. of Procedures	Time (days)	Direct Costs (% per capita GDP)	Time + Direct Costs (% per capita GDP)	Per capita GDP 1999 ($US)
Canada	2	2	1.45	2.25	19,320
Australia	2	2	2.25	3.05	20,050
New Zealand	3	3	0.53	1.73	13,780
Denmark	3	3	1.00	1.12	32,030
Ireland	3	16	1.16	1.80	19,160
United States	4	4	0.50	1.69	30,600
Norway	4	18	4.72	11.92	32,880
United Kingdom	5	4	1.43	3.03	22,640
Hong Kong	5	15	3.33	9.33	23,520
Mongolia	5	22	3.31	12.11	350
Finland	5	24	1.16	10.76	23,780
Israel	5	32	21.32	34.12	15,860
Sweden	6	13	2.56	7.76	25,040
Zambia	6	29	60.49	72.09	320
Switzerland	7	16	17.24	23.64	38,350
Singapore	7	22	11.91	20.71	29,610
Latvia	7	23	42.34	51.54	2,470
Netherlands	8	31	18.41	30.81	24,320
Taiwan	8	37	6.60	21.40	13,248
Hungary	8	39	85.87	101.47	4,650
South Africa	9	26	8.44	18.84	3,160
Thailand	9	35	6.39	20.39	1,960
Nigeria	9	36	257.00	271.40	310
Chile	10	28	13.08	24.28	4,740
Germany	10	42	15.69	32.49	25,350
Czech Republic	10	65	8.22	34.22	5,060
India	10	77	57.76	88.56	450
Japan	11	26	11.61	22.01	32,230
Egypt	11	51	96.59	116.99	1,400
Poland	11	58	25.46	48.66	3,960
Spain	11	82	17.30	50.10	14,000
Indonesia	11	128	53.79	104.99	580
China	12	92	14.17	50.97	780
South Korea	13	27	16.27	27.07	8,490
Brazil	15	63	20.14	45.34	4,420
Mexico	15	67	56.64	83.44	4,400
Italy	16	62	20.02	44.82	19,710
Vietnam	16	112	133.77	178.57	370
Madagascar	17	152	42.63	103.43	250
Russia	20	57	19.79	42.59	2,270
Bolivia	20	88	265.58	300.78	1,010

Table 1. (*Continued*)

Country	No. of Procedures	Time (days)	Direct Costs (% per capita GDP)	Time + Direct Costs (% per capita GDP)	Per capita GDP 1999 ($US)
Dominican Republic	21	80	463.09	495.09	191
Global Average	10.48	47.49	47.08	65.98	8,226

Note: **Bold typeface** indicates a transition economy.
Source: Adapted from Djankov et al. (2002).
Drawing on a major World Bank study, the table is based on the ascending order of (1) the total number of procedures domestic entrepreneurs must fulfill, (2) the number of days to obtain legal status to start up a firm, and (3) the direct costs, as a percentage of per capita GDP, to do so. The measure, time and direct costs, captures the monetized value of entrepreneurs' time in addition to direct costs. Global average is based on the full sample of 85 countries, and this table reports on 42 of them.

and relationships with government officials can make their lives a little easier and firm performance a little better (Peng and Luo 2000).

Networking has its limitations too. Possessing effective personal networks may be a necessary, but not sufficient, condition for business success (Peng and Luo 2000). Also, previous relationships may turn into "dark resources" that constrain rent-seeking activities of entrepreneurs and negatively affect their sales and other performance indicators (Portes 1998).

Boundary Blurring

In virtually all transition countries, some form of privatization has occurred. Some entrepreneurial start-ups adopt the strategy of blurring the public–private boundaries in the environment which is still institutionally unfriendly to private ownership. In China, while there have been numerous small privatizations, there have been relatively few outright sales of SOEs, thus the overall impact of privatization has been limited. However, informal privatization has been widespread (Peng 2001). Entrepreneurs can bid for long-term leases to control SOEs. Although such lease agreements do not entitle lease-holders to formal property rights, they are widely viewed as de facto property rights. Another form of ownership that blurs the public and private boundary is partial private control of former SOEs. The Chinese Communist Party recently committed a massive privatization program under the slogan "seize the large, release the small," which roughly translates as privatizing all but the largest 300 or so SOEs. The implementation of this plan takes time, which will result in partially privatized SOEs during the process. These public–private mixed firms represent a gradual evolution from public to private ownership. Even when formal discriminatory policies are removed, pure, private firms are still at a great disadvantage in obtaining state-controlled resources such as bank credit. Under the particular circumstances of the transition, a public–private boundary blurring strategy, which results in what Nee (1992) calls "collective hybrids," may lead to the better of the two worlds. Given the general movement toward clearer specification of property rights throughout transition economies, the question becomes: Can such ambiguous property rights be efficient during institutional transitions? The answer is a qualified "yes" (Nee 1992). Overall, the public–private hybrid represents an interesting and previously unencountered phenomenon in global entrepreneurship practice and research, and deserves further attention from practitioners, researchers, and policymakers.

In CEE and the NIS, many entrepreneurs use a strategy of blurring the legal–illegal boundaries. Except for the "shadow economy" which is criminal (drug cartels, for instance), there are another kind of unrecorded value adding activity – "unofficial" activities, which avoid the burden of tax burdens and administrative regulations (licenses, permits, etc.) (Kaufmann and Kaliberda 1996). Many entrepreneurs face the choice of operating officially or unofficially. The choice is made on the basis of cost–benefit considerations. An activity will not operate officially unless its net costs are lower than those of operating unofficially. The profits of operating unofficially increase in a transition economy where the market-based institutions are weak, particularly with regard to a country's legal framework, its enforcement inefficacy, and the degree of corruptibility of the judiciary service. The size of the overall "gray" economy is, of course, very difficult to estimate. Tentative figures in the mid-1990s put the total size of the unofficial "gray" economy to be approximately 11–12% of the GDP in the Czech Republic and Poland, about 30% in Bulgaria and Hungary, 40–50% in Russia and Ukraine, and, in the extreme case, over 60% in Azerbaijian and Georgia (Johnson, Kaufmann and Shleifer 1997).

It is important to note that to acknowledge the blurring of legal–illegal boundaries does not mean to celebrate it. However undesirable, the emergence of these "gray" organizations may be a natural byproduct of economic transitions. In 1995, Russia's privatization program transferred control of the most valuable natural resource firms to a small group of "oligarchs" at very low prices. In the absence of a strong legal and regulatory regime as formal constraints, informal constraints such as rules and regulations imposed by the mafia rise to fill the vacuum as a form of "self government" to provide some "public" goods such as protection from thieves and contract enforcement. Given the high cost of operating officially, it is not surprising that unofficial activities have mushroomed in transition economies. In Ukraine, for instance, the administrative impediments in the trade, exchange rate, and pricing regimes, in addition to the high tax rates implied a very high cost of doing business officially. Doing business unofficially thus has been the strategy for many to reduce the very high cost of operating, and in many instances, of merely surviving (Kaufmann and Kaliberda 1996).

While such a "boundary blurring" strategy may be viable during the initial, chaotic phase of the transition, how sustainable this strategy is in the long run when the "dust settles" remains to be seen. It seems that lawlessness cannot work in the long run. As transition economies establish more legislation and regulations backed by gradually credible law enforcement, these "gray" organizations will have to confront increasing pressures for legitimization. The CEO of Bulgaria's Multigroup perhaps provided the best advice on a future strategy called "tail cutting:" "The lizard survives if it cuts off its tail. It is time for our [illegal] economic groups to cut off their illegal tails" (Peng 2001: 102).

IMPLICATIONS FOR THE WORK OF ENTREPRENEURS IN TRANSITION ECONOMIES

Entrepreneurs are in a very unusual line of work. The nature of entrepreneurship during institutional transitions suggests a number of implications for such work in the future. This section elaborates on these implications.

Take Collective Action to Promote Entrepreneurial Development

Market liberalization and openness directly affect entrepreneurial development in transition economies. Entrepreneurs should mobilize to form industry or business owners' associations in order to lobby the new government, the media, as well as the public about the wealth creation role they play in the economy, and the importance of economic reform. Of course, similar to lizards cutting their tails, "gray" organizations with a criminal or dubious background may have to cut off their illegal tails, as advised by the CEO of Bulgaria's Multigroup, in order to advance their legitimate interests.

Foreign entrepreneurs also need to take collective action to facilitate entry into transition economies. Recently, industry and trade associations exclusively representing foreign business interests in transition economies, such as the U.S.–China Business Council and the Working Committee on Eastern Europe of the European Council for Small Business, have become increasingly visible. For example, facing the Chinese government's bans on direct marketing and Internet investment in 1998 and 1999, respectively, American direct marketing companies and Internet venture capital firms pressed their cases through U.S. trade negotiators in China's World Trade Organization talks, and eventually obtained significant concessions from the Chinese side.

Establish Alliances With Larger, More Legitimate Players

This is the heart of networking and boundary-blurring strategies discussed earlier. After decades of reform, the market institutions in transition economies are still inadequate, although improving. The turbulent environment and inadequate institutions add to the general uncertainty to entrepreneurial start-ups, thus raising barriers to entry. Forming alliances with large SOEs can lower this barrier, and blurring the public–private boundary can make it easier for entrepreneurs to get credit from the bank in an environment unfriendly to private ownership. Forming alliances with large enterprises can also help entrepreneurs to get access to a larger pool of suppliers and customers in the existing networks, which would have cost a lot more if they try to set up the network from scratch. China's Lucky Transportation's efforts to register as a "collective" firm and join an enterprise group serve as a case in point here. For the same reason, many private Internet start-ups in China have investment from government-run Internet service providers.

Partners in these alliances can include not only established domestic firms, but also foreign entrants. Foreign entrepreneurs and managers interested in investing in transition economies can benefit from forming alliances with large local firms. When encountering extensive software piracy in China, Microsoft, through its wholly owned subsidiary, chose to collaborate with the Ministry of Electronics to develop new software, instead of challenging the government head-on. Microsoft figured that once the government has a stake in the sales of legitimate Microsoft products, it may also have a strong interest in using its clout to crack down on sales of counterfeit software.

Build Dynamic Core Competencies

A telling measure of the success or failure of entrepreneurial firms is the time path of entrants' profits. Fig. 1 shows the path of non-state firms' profits in the five years following the start of institutional transitions in three major transition economies: China (1979–1984), Poland (1990–1995), and Russia (1990–1995). Robust entry in China (Naughton 1995) and Poland (Konings, Lehmann and Schaffer 1996) brought plummeting profits of new entrants. In Russia, the entry rate was slow (Djankov and Nenova 2001) and profits remained high. The high profits earned by new entrepreneurial firms initially was because of a heavily distorted economy with unfilled market niches. Firms that were able to overcome the impediments to doing business were

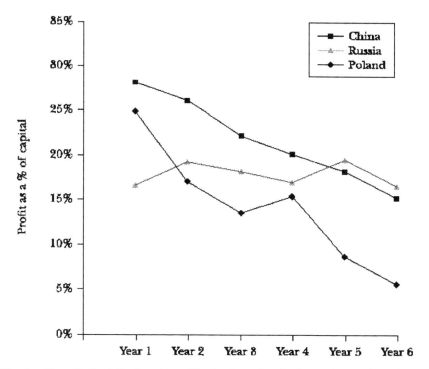

Fig. 1. Time Path of Profits. *Note*: The horizontal axis shows the number of years into reform. For China, year 1 means 1979 and year 6 means 1984. For Poland and Russia, year 1 means 1990 and year 6 means 1995. *Source*: China: Naughton (1995); Poland and Russia: Johnson, McMillan and Woodruff (2002).

very profitable. However, the competition engendered by rapid entry eventually caused the fall in profits.

With little exaggeration, we can suggest that most early entrepreneurial strategies in transition economies are highly opportunistic, making the first move to fill many unfilled gaps. This is precisely the heart of a prospector or guerilla strategy. While entrepreneurs might operate without a clearly articulated strategy at the early stage of institutional transitions, developing entrepreneurial capability and an explicit, long-term strategic vision becomes more critical as transitions deepen and competition becomes more saturated. The days when entrepreneurs could "hit and run" in the early stages of the transition seem to be passing. The new competition requires sustained investment in core competencies-based strongholds which can be defended and strengthened, thus often leading to a "deep niching" strategy for many entrepreneurial firms. Moreover, these core competencies have to be dynamic, that is, they should be continuously updated and extended. It is necessary for the entrepreneurs to keep the spirit of prospectors and examine the environment for product and market opportunities (Peng et al. 2004). Facing gigantic multinationals targeting these economies, the built-in flexibility of the entrepreneurial firms, due to their small size and informal structure, may be especially helpful (Dawar and Frost 1999). Poland's Optimus Computer can serve as a vivid case in point here.

CONCLUSION

"By pursuing his own interest," Adam Smith notably wrote of the merchant, "he frequently promotes that of society more effectually than when he really intends to promote it." The entrepreneurs in transition economies exemplify Smith's dictum. In pursuit of economic profits, these entrepreneurs can hardly care less about political ideologies. Yet, as a group, these entrepreneurs have collectively and effectively undermined the foundation of the socialist economy and helped promote the emergence of a market economy. Indeed, much of the task of devising the new ways of doing business in transition economies has been taken on by entrepreneurs. How do entrepreneurs create wealth in the environments traditionally hostile to entrepreneurship? A short answer is that they accomplish this through aggressive prospector and guerilla strategies, extensive networking, and active boundary blurring. These strategies have a significant bearing on the work of entrepreneurs who try to navigate and survive the treacherous waters of institutional transitions in these countries.

In contrast to the voluminous country- and region-specific publications, this article has sketched the broad contours of entrepreneurial strategies during institutional transitions through a generalization approach. While the lessons are derived from a multinational triangulation process based on the experience of practitioners throughout these countries, the advice from officials and advisors guiding the transitions, and the findings of scholars around the world, it is important to caution against over-generalization. Obviously, every transition economy is different in its own right. The lessons for relatively more developed economies (e.g., Poland), while insightful, are not likely to be of equal importance to less developed economies (e.g., Vietnam) and some "submerging" economies in the NIS (e.g., Belarus). For large countries such as China and Russia, regional differences within a country are enormous, thus making over-generalization dangerous. The history of economic transitions in the past two decades suggests that what transition economies need is not a set of standard lessons, recipes, or packages (e.g., "big bang" or "shock therapy"), but rather institutional and organizational experimentation to allow for the evolutionary emergence of wealth-creating and value-adding entrepreneurship.

NOTES

1. Most entrepreneurs such as those running Lucky Transportation resent having to resort to bribery to get things done. However, they face a competitive dilemma: If they refuse to pay while competitors do, then entrepreneurs who do not pay bribes may be disadvantaged in terms of market opportunities and resources. This dilemma is similar to the one confronting many U.S. firms abroad, which are constrained by the Foreign Corrupt Practice Act which forbids them from making "corrupt" payments. Their global competitors, however, are not similarly constrained. German law, until the late 1990s, permitted bribery expenses abroad to be deducted from German corporate taxes. See Peng (2006).

2. In contrast, governments in developed economies impose fewer procedures (as low as two procedures and two days in Canada and Australia) and a lower total cost (less than 2% of per capita GDP in New Zealand, Denmark, Ireland, and the United States).

ACKNOWLEDGMENTS

This research was supported in part by a National Science Foundation Faculty Career Grant (SES 0238820). We thank Lisa Keister for her encouragement.

REFERENCES

Aldrich, Howard A. 1999. *Organizations Evolving*. London: Sage.

Dawar, N. and T. Frost. 1999. "Competing with Giants: Survival Strategies for Local Companies in Emerging Markets." *Harvard Business Review* March–April:119–129.

Djankov, S., and T. Nenova. 2001. "Constraints to Entrepreneurship in Kazakhstan." Working paper, World Bank.

Djankov, S., R. La Porta, F. Lopez-de-Silanes, and A. Shleifer. 2002. "The Regulation of Entry." *Quarterly Journal of Economies* 117(1):1–37.

Johnson, S., D. Kaufmann, and A. Shleifer. 1997. "The Unofficial Economy in Transition." *Brooking Papers on Economic Activity* 2:159–238.

Johnson, S., J. McMillan, and C. Woodruff. 2002. "Property Rights and Finance." *American Economic Review* 92(5):1335–1356.

Kaufmann, D., and A. Kaliberda. 1996. "Integrating the unofficial Economy into the Dynamics of Post-socialist Economies." Working paper, World Bank.

Keister, L. 2000. *Chinese Business Groups*. New York: Oxford University Press.

Konings, J., H. Lehmann, and M.E. Schaffer. 1996. "Job Creation and Job Destruction in a Transition Economy: Ownership, Firm Size and Gross Job Flows in Polish Manufacturing." *Labour Economics* 3(2):299–317.

McMillan, J. and C. Woodruff. 2002. "The Central Role of Entrepreneurs in Transition Economies." *Journal of Economic Perspectives* 16(3):153–170.

Miles, R. and C. Snow. 1978. *Organizational Strategy, Structure, and Process*. New York: McGraw-Hill.

Mugler, J. 2000. "The Climate for Entrepreneurship in European Countries in Transition." in *The Blackwell Handbook of Entrepreneurship*, edited by D. Sexton and H. Landstrom. Oxford, UK: Blackwell.

Naughton, B. 1995. *Growing Out of the Plan*. New York: Cambridge University Press.

Nee, V. 1992. "Organizational Dynamics of Market Transition: Hybrid Forms, Property Rights, and Mixed Economy in China." *Administrative Science Quarterly* 37:1–27.

North, D.C. 1990. *Institutions, Institutional Change, and Economic Performance*. Cambridge, England: Cambridge University Press.

Peng, M.W. 1997. "Firm Growth in Transition Economies: Three Longitudinal Cases from China, 1989–1996." *Organization Studies* 18(3):385–413.

------. 2000. *Business Strategies in Transition Economies*. Thousand Oaks, CA: Sage.

------. 2001. "How Entrepreneurs Create Wealth in Transition Economies." *Academy of Management Executive* 15(1):95–108.

------. 2003. "Institutional Transitions and Strategic Choices." *Academy of Management Review* 28(2):275–296.

------. 2006. *Global Strategy*. Cincinnati: Thomson South–Western.

Peng, M.W. and P. Heath. 1996. "The Growth of the Firm in Planned Economies in Transition: Institutions, Organizations, and Strategic Choices." *Academy of Management Review* 21(2):492–528.

Peng, M.W. and Y. Luo. 2000. "Managerial Ties and Firm Performance in a Transition Economy: The Nature of a macro-micro link." *Academy of Management Journal* 43(3):486–501.

Peng, M.W., J. Tan, and T. Tong. 2004. "Ownership Types and Strategic Groups in an Emerging Economy." *Journal of Management Studies* 41(7):1105–1129.

Portes, A. 1998. "Social Capital: Its Origin and Applications in Modern Sociology." *Annual Review of Sociology* 24:1–24.

Puffer, S. and D. McCarthy. 2001. "Navigator the Hostile Maze: A Framework for Russian Entrepreneurship." *Academy of Management Executive* 15:24–36.

Scott, W.R. 1995. *Institutions and Organizations.* Thousand Oaks, CA: Sage.

Wright, M., I. Filatotchev, R. Hoskisson, and M.W. Peng. 2005. "Strategy Research in Emerging Economies: Challenging the Conventional Wisdom." *Journal of Management Studies* 42(1):1–33.

LINEAGE NETWORKS, RURAL ENTREPRENEURS, AND MAX WEBER

Yusheng Peng

ABSTRACT

Nearly a century ago, Max Weber studied Chinese lineage system and argued that the power of the patriarchal sib impeded the emergence of industrial capitalism in China. Recently, Martin Whyte re-evaluated Weber's thesis on the basis of development studies and argued that, rather than an obstacle, Chinese family pattern and lineage ties may have facilitated the economic growth in China since the 1980s. This paper empirically tests the competing hypotheses by focusing on the relationship between lineage networks and the development of rural enterprises. Analyses of village-level data show that lineage networks, measured by proportion of most common surnames, have large positive effects on the count of entrepreneurs and total workforce size of private enterprises in rural China.

INTRODUCTION

At the beginning of the 20th century, in an attempt to support his analyses of the relationship between rationalization and the rise of modern capitalism

Entrepreneurship
Research in the Sociology of Work, Volume 15, 327–355
Copyright © 2005 by Elsevier Ltd.
All rights of reproduction in any form reserved
ISSN: 0277-2833/doi:10.1016/S0277-2833(05)15013-4

in the West, Max Weber systematically examined Chinese society because he perceived China together with India as farthest removed from the western civilization. In *The Religion of China* ([1916]1951), Weber identified a number of features in Chinese society as inhibiting factors to the rise of capitalism. These factors include: Confucian ideology that glorified humanistic culturing and office-seeking and belittled commercial pursuit; patrimonial characteristics of the state bureaucracy that limited administrative rationalization;[1] a prebendal officialdom and tax-quota system that bred systematic corruption;[2] a highly arbitrary legal system that resembled "khadi" justice;[3] and a strong patriarchal "sib organization" (lineage) that dominated the rural society.

In recent years many of Weber's original observations have been brought under critical scrutiny. First of all, a number of scholars began to challenge Weber's negative view of Confucianism either by reflecting on the success of the East Asian tigers (Berger 1988; Rozman 1991) or arguing that the New-Confucianism since the Song era is quite conducive to entrepreneurial spirits (Yu [1985]2004; Metzger 1986). Secondly, the patrimonial beauracracy in imperial China was characterized as a variety of its own and different from the western ideal type (Hamilton 1984, 1990); and patrimonial authority is shown to be adaptable to modern large corporations (Biggart 1997). Thirdly, fiscal decentralization (tax-quota system) was singled out as an important system promoting local economic growth (Oi 1999; Walder 1995). Fourthly, new evidence reveals that the legal system of Qing China was much less arbitrary than Weber assumed (Huang 1996) and, if not fitting the definition of formally rational law based on pure legal reasoning, should be classified as "substantively rational"(Marsh 2000). Last but not the least, Martin Whyte (1995, 1996) calls for a re-evaluation of the relationship between economic growth and Chinese family and kinship structures. It is the kinship aspect of Weber's observations that I will focus on in this paper, using a village level data set on lineage networks and entrepreneurial activities in rural China.

Weber's understanding and misunderstanding of China have been criticized on both methodological and conceptual grounds. Methodologically, Weber was relying on second-hand materials, often with gross mistakes in translation, and tended to disregard the chronological sequence of events (Van Der Sprenkel 1964). Theoretically, because Weber was using China as a negative case to support his general theses and ideal-types about western societies, his interpretation of Chinese history was "more based upon logical coherence than factual accuracy" and "through the typological filter provided by *Economy and Society*, Weber blocked out the distinctiveness of Chinese civilization" (Hamilton 1984:401).

Given all the methodological flaws and factual inaccuracies, however, no one suggested that we should brush aside Weber's work on China as irrelevant. This is because "even Weber's mistakes are apt to be more stimulating, and open up more fertile lines of inquiry, than most other people's target-centered truths" (Van Der Sprenkel 1964:349). Every social scientist interested in China study should read *The Religion of China*, I think, not only because Weber's profound insights and penetrating analysis shine through the passage of time and shed light on our present-day understanding of Chinese history, but more importantly because his arguments about China are closely related to his theory about the rise of western capitalism and any confirmation or disconfirmation of the former bear on the latter. In this spirit, I will revisit Weber's thesis about sib organization as an obstacle to capitalism in China and place it in the context of his general theory about the role of rationalization in the rise of western capitalism.

Rural industrialization in China provides an ideal platform for examining the relationship between lineage networks, normally found in rural settings, and industrial enterprises, usually located in urban areas. The mushrooming of entrepreneurial activities in Chinese villages since the 1980s has brought the two ill-assorted phenomena in the same locale. Using village-level data collected in 1993–1994, I will first show that lineage networks have played a large role in promoting entrepreneurial activities in rural China and then discuss the implications of this finding for Weber's general theses about the link between rationalism, formalism and capitalism.

LINEAGE NETWORKS: OBSTACLE OR ENGINE?

Rationalization is the central theme, "a master concept," in Weber's theory about the rise of modern capitalism. The patriarchal clan is a traditionalistic and therefore irrational social structure and its elimination is a precondition for the rise of capitalism. According to Weber, the task of eliminating the clan in the West was completed during the Middle Ages. Two rationalizing forces, the Christian church and the bureaucratic state, contributed to the disintegration of the clan and thus cleared the path for the rise of modern capitalism. Religious prophets built up their community of followers that ignored and cut across clan boundaries; the royal power feared the clan and replaced "lineage charisma" with bureaucratic authority (Weber 1927/1981:44–45).

While being driven to extinction in the west, the clan organization was completely preserved in China and developed to an extent unknown elsewhere in the world (Weber 1951:86). Even today, lineage still figures prominently in the social and economic life of Chinese peasanttry. Weber characterized the state bureaucracy in imperial China, with its free and open official examination system,[4] as highly rational (i.e. favorable to capitalism), but at the same time "unmistakably" patrimonial (i.e. unfavorable to capitalism). The patrimonial bureaucracy was geographically thinned out over the large empire and had never grown strong enough to penetrate below the county (*xian*) level. Consequently the power of the clans remained unbroken and dominated rural society:

> The rationalism of the bureaucracy was confronted with a resolute and traditionalistic power which, on the whole and in the long run, was stronger because it operated continuously and was supported by the most intimate personal associations...Economic organizations which went beyond the scope of the individual establishment rested almost wholly upon actual or imitated personal sib relationships....This sib organization [*tsung-tsu*] owned, in addition to the ancestral temple and the school building, sib houses for provisions and implements for the processing of rice, for the preparation of conserves, for weaving, and other domestic industries. Possibly a manager was employed. Apart from that, the *tsung-tsu* supported its members in need through mutual aid and free or cheap credit. (1951:95–96)

Weber depicted the unbroken power of the clan as "sib fetters" that strangled capitalist development. Because the clan provided so many of the individual's social and economic needs, it fostered individual dependence, suffocated individual initiatives, and stifled individual freedom. The clan developed extensive auxiliary industries for self-consumption and thus slowed down the growth of profit-oriented capitalist enterprises. The power of the sib elders implied a steadfast adherence to tradition and rejection of any sort of innovation. Partly due to these "sib fetters," even the primitive form of capitalistic enterprises that matured in the west during the Middle Ages had failed to emerge in China (Weber 1951:100).

Accurate or not in his description of the Chinese lineage system, Weber's theoretical logic is clear. The concept of formal rationality is key to his overall theory of capitalism and is defined in the case of economic actions as the degree to which the provision of needs "is capable of being expressed in numerical, calculable terms, and is so expressed" (Weber 1968:85). Economic rationality achieves its highest form in capital accounting, i.e. systematic and meticulous book-keeping and the striking of a balance. Capitalism is as old as history; capital accounting distinguishes modern industrial capitalism from primitive types. The "maximum formal rationality of capital accounting" depends, however, on a set of presuppositions

(p. 161). Four of these presuppositions are relevant to the current analysis and are listed below (see Weber 1927, 1968; Collins 1980):

(1) The appropriation of all physical means of production (land, machines, etc.) by autonomous private enterprises. This implies that productive assets will be used for profit-making purposes.
(2) Expropriation of all means of production from workers so that the workers are free and compelled to sell his labor under the whip of hunger. This "commodification of labor" (in Marxian term) allows the calculation of labor productivity.
(3) A market system that is free from irrational limitations.[5]
(4) Calculable formal laws and rational administration that guarantee property rights and contractual rights and ensure the calculability of the market exchange process.

With its patriarchal authority structure, the lineage system is distinctively traditionalistic and personalistic and hence contradicts these presuppositions of maximum formal rationality. First, corporate ownership of farmland and auxiliary industries may hamper the appropriation of productive assets by private enterprises. Second, kin obligation and personal loyalty may interfere with free selection of workers and its welfare aspects soften work disciplines. Third, the in-group solidarity and cohesion of the lineage pose barriers to free trade because of "ethical dualism," i.e. double business practices for insiders and outsiders.[6] Fourth, its strong power may impede the full bureaucratization and rationalization of the state administration and thus deprive capitalism of calculable law and rational administration. Thus, a strong lineage would presumably inhibit the rise of capitalism.

Weber's analysis about rationalization and the rise of capitalism has engendered an intellectual legacy that has shaped sociological discourse for generations and his work on China has made a similar impact on sinological discourse. American sociologists (e.g. Parsons 1937; Bendix 1962) elaborated the Weberian thesis and developed the dichotomy of universalism vis-à-vis particularism as the contrasting organizing principles of modern vis-à-vis traditional societies. Modernization theorists (e.g. Inkeles 1966; Kerr et al. 1964) embraced this dichotomy and prescribed that the task of modernization for the underdeveloped countries is to adopt (or wholesale import) the legal-rational institutions and value system of the western style.

Sinologists, e.g. Marion Levy (1949) and Albert Feuerwerker (1958) extended Weber's "sib fetters" argument to the study of Chinese familism. In *The Family Revolution in Modern China*, Levy (1949) argued that one prerequisite of modern industry is institutionalized universalism, but the "traditional" Chinese family was a highly particularistic structure. "Wide spread particularism as much as any other factor is a major obstacle to the spread of modern industry" (p. 354). Particularism "enormously complicates" the operation of modern enterprises in two major ways. One is pervasive nepotism in employment decisions where the first consideration was not competence and qualification but closeness in personal connection such as family members, relatives, friends, and localistic ties and so on. As a result the Chinese family firms tend to be staffed with incompetent family members whereas the talented outsiders are driven away. This kind of practices may be good for the family members but apparently bad for efficiency.[7]

The second dysfunctional manifestation of particularism is the difficulty in maintaining business relationship across organizations. Business transactions are not carried out efficiently in rational and impersonal manners, but often have to be smoothed with personal *guanxi*. Cultivating *guanxi* networks takes a large amount of time and energy and brew graft and corruption. Thus, Levy (1949) suggested that China should rely on the national government to invest in and operate large industrial establishments in order to achieve rapid industrialization because "there is a long tradition of universalism in this sphere"(p. 361).

During the past two decades, this negative view of Chinese family and kinship has come under fire, mostly from development studies. The economic success of Asian NICs, particularly, Taiwan, Hong Kong and Singapore, suggests that Chinese family structure, rather than being an obstacle, may actually be an engine of modern industrial development (Berger 1988; Wong 1985, 1988; Greenhalgh 1988). I summarize their arguments into three points.

First, instead of being dysfunction, family loyalty and obligations foster a hard working ethics. Chinese people work hard, live frugally, and exercise self-denial like the English Puritans. They work hard not for salvation or self-enjoyment, but for the welfare of their family, sons and daughters, and future offspring (Harrell 1985). Familism provides organizational loyalty and stable authority. In small family operated enterprises, family members and kinfolk are willing to work long hours and for low pay. They have natural loyalty to their family firm. They are likely to stay with the firm and help the firm to survive hard times (Niehoff 1987).

Second, a widespread critique of Chinese family businesses is that their growth is confined within the boundaries of the family core and close kin and that they tend to disintegrate by the second generation. Greenhalgh (1988) observes that family enterprises in Taiwan use family members to staff key decision-making positions and rely heavily on kin and friends for pooling capital, recruiting labor, and collecting information. However, Greenhalgh views this practice in a favorable light as successful family enterprises may divisionalize among sons and daughters to form a group of related firms (*qiye jituan*). She describes the Taiwanese family enterprise as "the package of individual incentives and group insurance that promotes the emergence of highly motivated, risk-taking entrepreneurs" (pp. 233–234). Taiwan's economic miracle attests to the effectiveness of this organizational form.

Third, reliance on kinship and personal networks is also more advantageous than problematic because it can reduce transaction costs by lowering the likelihood of commercial and legal disputes and providing trustworthy access to opportunities and resources in unstable political and economic environments. Furthermore, imitated kinship relations (*guanxi* networks) can grow beyond the boundaries of kinship groups and operate in ever widening circles. Wong actually played down the importance of kinship networks in Hong Kong's textile industry. "In Chinese economic conduct the crucial distinction is not that of kin and non-kin, but personal and impersonal." "While the kin circle is finite and bound, the personalized economic network used by the Chinese can reach widely...; family ties only serve as the nucleus from which a Chinese can spin a web of ever-widening social circles" (Wong 1988:136–137).

Thus, Wong (1988) argued that by pinning his hope for modernization on the rationalizing effect of the Chinese state, Levy has totally misread the economic potential of Chinese families and "has bet on the wrong horse" (p. 146). The great economic potential of the Chinese family has been constrained by the state preoccupied with "coordination and integration." Once these constraints are removed, the Chinese family could "fuel the engine of development"(p. 146).

Comparing the main points of both engine and obstacle arguments, Whyte (1996) proposes that both sides are oversimplified. "Chinese families do not have the immutable qualities that conflict with modern economic activity, or for that matter that can fuel growth under all circumstances" (p. 20). He points out that the Communist Revolution in China has transformed the Chinese family patterns, such as the shift from extended to nuclear family, the phasing out of pre-arranged marriage, the softening of the power of the elders, etc. But the collective farms distributed harvests to peasant families as a whole and allowed the families to keep private plots and engaged in some side line production. As a result, some features of Chinese familism persisted, such as family loyalty and obligations to the larger kinship network, sacrifice by members for the sake of the family, and the power of the kin relationships upon individual behavior. It is these persistent patterns that provide favorable conditions for economic development during the reform era. "The continued strength of family loyalties provided a resource that could be used to mobilize family economic efforts under changed conditions while the softening of the parental authority helped to ensure that these efforts would take innovative and productive direction" (Whyte 1995:1007). However, this entrepreneurial potential of the new Chinese family patterns had been pent-up by the socialist command economy. Return to family farming and market-oriented liberalization since 1978 unleashed its potential.

Clanism (*zongzu zhuyi*) is an extreme but logical extension of familism (*jiazu zhuyi*). To the extent both operate on particularistic principles and reply on personal ties, arguments about why Chinese family patterns should foster entrepreneurial capitalism are applicable to kinship structure as well (Whyte 1995). In keeping with Whyte's analysis, I propose that Chinese lineage system has also gone through a transformation and has become conducive to entrepreneurial activities during the reform era, a hypothesis to be developed in the next section.

LINEAGE NETWORKS AND RURAL ENTREPRENEURS

Clan organization in Chinese history has gone through a vicissitude of evolution and changes. Contrary to Weber's belief that the lineage system in China has been preserved intact and static from antiquity to the present, the primitive agnatic political organizations that were closely enmeshed with feudal prerogatives survived only to the period of the Warring States some two millennia ago. The Qin Emperor, in his process of building an empire and state bureaucracy, did strategically break the powerful clans, especially those of the conquered states. The lineage organizations that sinologists observed today were actually reconstructed by the Song imperial state under the influence of New-Confucianists (Ebrey 1986; Qian 1994; Chang 2000). The New-Confucian manderins and scholars perceived an affinity between ancestor worship and the central Confucian concept of filial piety (*xiao*) and decided to encourage lineage activities among the plebeians. Weber was correct in describing the lineage as the "only corporate actor" in the Chinese countryside, because it did own communal land, which were rented to its members on preferential terms, built ancestral halls, maintained schools, sometimes operated handy-craft industries, extended cheap credit to its members (Freedman 1958; Qian 1994).[8] As the head of the corporate actor, the lineage elder used to wield great power over lineage members, included carrying out death penalties such as the caning or drowning of serious offenders of clan codes. Weber was incorrect, however, in overstating the conflict and tension between the lineage and the state bureaucracy because the lineage normally worked with rather than against the state in mediating conflicts, administering justice, protecting the property and lives of its members, and even collecting taxes for the state (Zhong 2000; Huang 1993; Wang 1991). Historically, the clan power did not confront or counterbalance the power of the state bureaucracy. Rather, the bureaucratic state chose to let the clan power grow due to exhaustion of administrative resources and overstretching of central control.

The lineage system was to face the most serious and unprecedented challenges posed by the Communist Revolution. Since the 1950s the Communist Party waged deliberate assaults on the lineage organizations. It confiscated clan communal land and properties, deprived clan elders of their power, repealed clan codes, and injected the ideology of class consciousness and class struggle to diffuse clan identity (Wang 1991). Consequently, the economic foundation and organizational structure of the lineage system were systematically dismantled and replaced with collective farms and grassroots administration. During the collectivization campaign and the Cultural Revolution, ancestral halls, the shrine where ancestors are consecrated, were turned into offices, schools, or storage rooms, if not destroyed; genealogy books were burned as feudalistic remnants; and of course, the *fengshui* of ancestral burial sites was disturbed. Lineage seemed being reduced to a subterranean cultural phenomenon, a lingering mentality.

In 1978, Deng Xiaoping launched China on a long and arduous march toward capitalism. Collective farms were dismantled and households, again, became the basic units of economic activities. With the more liberal atmosphere following the market reform, ancestral halls were rebuilt, genealogy recompiled, and annual pilgrimage to the ancestral burial cites reactivated, usually with the ardent support of clan members. The ghosts of dead forefathers were revived, not to reinstitute the patriarchal power of the elders, but to create solidarity and identity among off-springs, which can be used for new purposes. Without economic resources, the authority of clan leaders is mostly symbolic and ritualistic, based primarily on personal charisma, seniority, and ability. Their duties include presiding over marriage ceremonies and burial rituals, mediating conflicts within the clan, organizing collective activities, and occasionally making clan-related decisions (Wang 1991).

Instead of being a hierarchically organized corporate actor, the revived lineage today is a collective actor, i.e. an agnatic community with a common identity. To use Coleman's (1990) distinction, a community is the group of natural persons who may bind themselves together through collective action to pursue their common interests. "But in a corporation a new entity has been created, whose interests and resources are distinct from those who brought it into being" (p. 539). Obviously, lineage in contemporary Chinese villages fits the definition of a community – the locus of collective action and normative control. All its structural features spell social capital benefits. Strong ties provide the bonds and obligations; cultural identity generalizes bilateral bonds and obligations into group loyalty; leadership and density help mobilizing these resources into capacities for collective action and normative control. In other words, lineage becomes a network resource (social capital) that the rational actors (families, individuals or both) decide to use or not use and how to use it. Ironically, the revived strength of lineage is most clearly demonstrated in the village elections that have been instituted all over China in the 1990s. Political scientists and government officials have become quite concerned with the swaying of village elections by powerful lineage groups (Xiao 2001; Liu 2005).

The normative control capacities of lineage networks manifest two aspects: bounded solidarity and enforceable trust.[9] Lineage solidarity protects the collective and individual interests of lineage members against perceived or real outside threats. Kin trust promotes trustworthy and cooperative behavior between lineage members. In a parallel paper (Peng 2004), I argue that during the early stage of China's transition from planning to market, lineage solidarity and kin trust promoted rural entrepreneurship by protecting entrepreneur's property and contractual rights when the formal legal framework was ineffective. The following paragraphs recount my argument.

Rural industrialization in China has attracted much academic limelight, because it has been the locomotive of China's economic growth for the past two decades and has played a crucial role in China's successful transition from a planed economy to a market economy (Peng 1999; Oi 1999). It is also a sector with the most vibrant entrepreneurial activities. In official language, rural enterprises are called *xiangzhen qiye*, translated as township–village enterprises or TVEs, which actually include both collective and private enterprises. The ownership configuration of this sector has given rise to heated debates among scholars (Rawski 1999; Woo 1999; Peng 1992, 2001, 2004; Walder 1995; Nee 1992). According to national statistics (Fig. 1), from

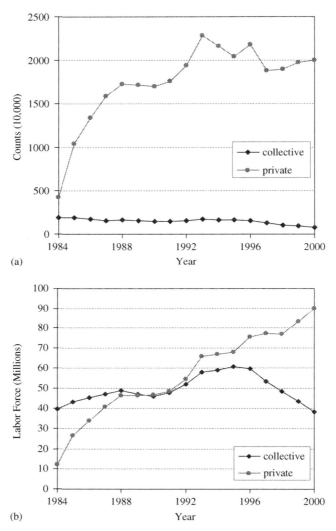

Fig. 1. Growth of Rural Enterprises by Ownership between 1984 and 2000. (a) Count of Rural Enterprises by Ownership, (b) Rural Enterprise Employment by Ownership. Data from various years of The *Statistical Yearbook of Township and Village Enterprises* (China Ministry of Agriculture 1997–2001). Note that the 1994 count and employment data for private enterprises are the averages of 1993 and 1995 data because the original data are obviously wrong.

1984 to the mid-1990s while the number of collective TVEs stagnated between 1.8 and 1.6 millions, the number of registered private entrepreneurs,
with or without employees, mushroomed from about 4 millions to over 20
millions. Although the collective sector maintained a healthy growth in terms
of employment and output, the private sector was growing at a faster rate
and surpassed the collective sector in the mid-1990s. After the mid-1990s, the
collective sector started shrinking due to a privatization campaign.

The changing ownership configuration reflected the changing legal environment regarding private entrepreneurs. Generally speaking, the evolution
of formal government policies is a process in which the central state yielded,
step by step, to the preferences of economic actors for private ownership
while abandoning gradually its adherence to the socialist orthodox of collective ownership. Before the 1980s, private entrepreneurial activities were
strictly forbidden. Throughout the 1980s and up until the mid-1990s, the
central government insisted on the "dominant role" of public ownership.
Enforcement of the constitutional rights of private entrepreneurs was
ineffective at best. Specific legal codes to protect private property rights are
still being incubated today. On the one hand, new constitutions carved out a
general platform for private entrepreneurial initiatives. On the other, the
vague wording of the constitution, ambivalent attitudes of the center, and
the vacillating political ideology gave local actors much leeway to interpret
and improvise. After 30 years of socialist indoctrination, the idea of
respecting the property and contractual rights of private entrepreneurs took
time to sink in. With some exceptions, local cadres tended to suppress,
harass, and prey on private entrepreneurs, sometimes out of ideological
bias, and more often out of more rational reasons: their bonuses and benefits were pegged to these "extra-budgetary" revenues. Private entrepreneurs
faced discrimination in dealing with the state sector (such as banks and
SOEs) and had to endure harassment and extortion by local officials, tax
collectors, and a myriad of other government agencies at different levels.
Prior to the mid-1990s, cadre predation and political discrimination were
probably the biggest obstacle to the development of private entrepreneurship. When their rights were violated, private entrepreneurs did not have
any specific legal codes to turn to for help. They had to seek shelter in
informal norms and social networks.

A lineage group may help its entrepreneurs via three possible mechanisms.
Firstly, lineage solidarity may help protecting private property rights in the
absence of effective formal property rights law. Historically, lineage organizations functioned to protect the lives and property of kin members, as well
as to mediate conflicts and administer informal justice. The protection of

property was particularly relevant for private entrepreneurs during the reform era because they needed the shelter from predatory cadres. The intrinsic solidarity of the lineage group may provide such protection. If the village cadre is non-kin, then he would not want to take on the power of the whole clan. If the cadre is kin, then he is bound by kinship obligations to protect and support fellow kin. If the cadre does not honor his obligation to support his kin and preys on them instead, he may face collective sanction such as ostracism. This is not to say that predatory behavior never occurs among kinsmen, but that it may occur less frequently and less blatantly than among non-kin. Chinese peasants may not have the concept of universal rights, but they do have a deep-rooted sense of kin obligations.

Secondly, kin trust may facilitate economic transaction and cooperation such as inter-personal loans and pooling of funds. Because official financial institutions discriminated against private entrepreneurs, informal rotary credit associations (*biaohui*) that rely on kinship and social networks have played an important role providing start-up capital and emergency cash to private entrepreneurs (Tsai 2000).

Thirdly, lineage network may provide useful bridging ties (see Burt 1992 for definition). During partial reform, *guanxi* ties were very important for both obtaining plan-allocated goods and for channeling market information, especially for private entrepreneurs who were excluded from plan allocation (Nee 1992; Wank 1999; Xin and Pearce 1996). But I doubt this is very important mechanism because kin ties are mostly nonbridging ties, which are not useful for start-up entrepreneurs (Renzulli, Aldrich and Moody 2000).

DATA, MEASUREMENT AND METHOD

The administrative village is my unit of analysis. I use two sample data sets collected by sociologists at the Chinese Academy of Social Sciences in 1993 and 1994. The 1993 sample consists of 259 villages from 15 counties and the 1994 sample consists of 119 villages from 7 counties.[10] The 22 counties were selected by "experts" with an eye to representativeness, and the villages in each county were randomly sampled on a proportional basis (for a description of the survey, see Shen, Chen and Gao 2000). After deleting 12 villages from the two samples with missing or outlying values on key variables, 366 valid cases were retained.[11]

To give an idea of an administrative village, there are on average 439 households in the sample villages, with a mean population of less than 2000.

Table 1.   Descriptive Statistics of Chinese Villages (1993/1994; $N = 366$ villages).

	Minimum	1st Quartile	Median	Mean	3rd Quartile	Maximum
Population	194	1,098	1,587	1,844	2,405	9,663
Number of households	53	254	388	439	565	1,650
Number of private enterprises	0	0	0	3.4	1	96
Workforce of private enterprises	0	5	16	45	48	1,178
% the largest lineage group	0	0	14.9	21.8	29.3	100
% top three lineage groups	0	0	37.2	39.9	64.4	100
% finished junior high school	2.2	13.3	20.4	22.2	28.3	86.6
Farmland per laborer (mu)	0.3	1.5	2.2	3.5	4.1	19.3
Collective savings 1976 (yuan)	0	4,915	6,003	24,550	19,540	6,86,900

The largest village in the sample has a population close to 10,000, and the smallest village 194 people (Table 1).

Measurement

Nearly identical questionnaires were used in both surveys, and they included questions regarding the number of rural enterprises in the village and the number of households belonging to each lineage group. The key variables are defined in the following, and basic statistics are reported in Table 1.

Private enterprises refer to the count of rural enterprises in a village owned by single households or multiple households in partnership.[12] This measure does not include small-scale family operations, that is, self-employed individuals. Only 29% of the sample villages reported any private enterprises. On average there are three and a half private enterprises in the sample.[13]

The rural enterprise employment is the total labor force working in rural enterprises, including both employees and employers. Because the growth of rural enterprises in China is primarily through size expansion, employment data should serves as a good alternative measure of rural industrial development.[14] Private enterprise employment includes employers and employees in all private enterprises (*siying qiye*) in an administrative village. Private sector employment includes private enterprise employment and all self-employed individuals (*getihu*) and their employees, often family members, in an administrative village.

Lineage networks are measured by the proportion of households that belong to the top three lineage groups in the whole village. In the current sample of 366 administrative villages, on the one extreme five villages uniformly share the same surname (i.e. the whole village descends from the same ancestors) and another 10 have over 90% of the households belonging to the same lineage group; on the other extreme about a quarter of the sample villages (95 cases) do not have any lineage groups and therefore report zero on this variable. On average, 22% of the households belong to the largest lineage group and 40% belong to the top three groups.[15] As lineage system is patrilineal and patriarchal, it excludes marital ties of wives and daughters, which are another important source of social capital in rural China.

The following defines control variables that are relevant for rural industrialization but not key for the current analysis.

Total rural labor force is the number of all able-bodied laborers who are registered residents in the administrative villages.

Human capital stock is measured as the proportion of people with at least junior high school or equivalent education in the village labor force. On an average, 22% of the village labor force had completed junior high school. Nee (1992) argues that the market transition should enhance the return to human capital in rural China. In the research based on county level data, Peng (1999) finds that human capital stock has a much stronger impact on rural industrial growth than on agricultural growth, which suggests that enhanced return to education was probably due to rural industrialization through which a large proportion of the rural population shifted off farm.

Urban distancce is measured by the log distance between the village and the nearest city. Naughton (1995) observes that during the early stage of economic reform, rural reform was more successful than urban reform, resulting in the expansionary force of urban industries spilled over into the surrounding countryside. Peng (1999) finds that proximity to cities is an important explanatory factor of rural nonagricultural growth. Therefore, log distance should have a negative effect on rural entrepreneurship.

Land–labor ratio is the total amount of farmland divided by the total rural labor force. This is the inverse measure of a village's surplus labor. Entrepreneurship provides an alternative livelihood for idle farmers short on farmland. Alleviating unemployment pressure is one of the motives and effects of rural industrialization. Land–labor ratios vary greatly from village to village. In an average village, each peasant has slightly more than half an acre of farmland (1 acre = 6 *mu*), with a minimum of 1/20th of an acre per peasant and a maximum of nearly 3 acres per peasant. This variable should have a negative coefficient on rural entrepreneurial development.

Initial collective accumulation is measured as the village collective savings in 1976. As log income data proximate normality, I reassigned normal random numbers below the mean to 22 cases reporting zeros on this variable. Another 112 missing values were replaced with the sample mean. This variable should have a positive coefficient in the regression.

Southern Provinces include Guangdong, Yunnan, Fujian, Jianxi, Zhejian, Jiangsu, Hunan, Hubei. Northern provinces include Anhui, Jilin, Liaoning, Heilongjiang, Shaaxi, Ningxia, and Xinjiang. Lineage culture is strong in south China and relatively weak in north China, due to more frequent large-scale migrations in history.

Coastal region refers to villages in coastal provinces (Guangdong, Fujian, Zhejiang, Jiangsu, Shandong, and Liaoning). Coastal provinces had an early start in economic reform and lead the country in economic growth.

Statistical Model

Two indicators of rural entrepreneurial development will be analyzed: the numerical counts and employment sizes of rural enterprises. Count data are usually estimated with either a Poisson model or a negative binomial model. Poisson distribution is more restrictive than negative binomial distribution because it assumes that the variance equals the mean. As the count of rural enterprises and their total employment size in Chinese villages are highly skewed (with many zeros) and therefore may be overdispersed, I assume negative binomial distribution. Because the villages are sampled from 21 counties, standard errors are adjusted for possible clustering within counties. The negative binomial regression model is specified as

$$\ln \hat{Y} = \alpha + \beta K + \gamma \mathbf{X}$$

in which $\hat{Y}$ stands for predicted counts or employment size of rural enterprises; and K for the proportion of households belonging to the largest lineage group in the village, $\mathbf{X}$ is a vector of controlled variables including log collective savings in 1976, log number of villagers with at least junior high schooling, log distance from the nearest city, log farmland per laborer, log current labor force size, and dummy variables for southern provinces, coastal provinces and 1993 sample. Negative binomial models are estimated in STATA 8 (both data and the Stata program codes will be available upon request).

RESULTS

The results of regression analyses are presented in Table 2. Regressions of both enterprise counts and enterprise employment yield quite consistent results. Briefly, lineage networks in Chinese villages have large positive

Table 2. Negative Binomial Regression of Enterprise Count and Employment in Chinese Villages (1993/1994, $N = 366$ villages).

	Count of Entrepreneurs (1)	Workforce in Private Sector (including *getihu*) (2)	Workforce in Private Enterprises (3)
Intercept	−13.33***	−4.485***	−11.16***
	(7.09)[a]	(4.04)	(5.39)
% top three lineage group (× 10)	0.185**	0.068**	0.201***
	(3.69)	(2.84)	(4.41)
Log % junior high or above schooling	0.815*	0.395***	1.085***
	(2.34)	(3.49)	(3.91)
Log distance from city	−0.115	−0.095	−0.105
	(0.94)	(1.10)	(0.85)
Log collective savings 1976	0.399**	0.044	0.121
	(3.15)	(0.62)	(0.84)
Log land–labor ratio	−0.204	−0.191	−0.159
	(0.86)	(1.39)	(0.68)
Log total village labor force	0.903***	0.993***	1.334***
	(4.80)	(8.76)	(5.69)
Southern provinces	0.678	−0.572**	−1.001***
	(1.55)	(3.17)	(3.61)
Coastal provinces	0.003	0.706**	0.565
	(0.01)	(3.34)	(1.13)
1993 Sample	1.027**	−0.195	−0.423
	(2.51)	(1.15)	(1.21)
Wald log pseudo-likelihood ratio χ^2	118.31	150.76	176.25
Degrees of freedom	9	9	9

*, **, and *** indicate significance at $p < 0.05$, 0.01, and 0.001, two-tailed.
[a]Figures in parentheses are the absolute values of z-ratios.

effects on the development of private enterprises. The following examines the findings in more detail.

Lineage networks exert very strong and consistent effects both on the count of private enterprises and on their employment sizes. Eqs. (1) and (3) in Table 2 show that a 10% increase in the proportion of households belonging to the top three lineage groups is expected to increase the count of private entrepreneurs (not including self-employed individuals) in the village by 20% ($\approx e^{.185} - 1$) and to increase their workforce size by 22% ($\approx e^{.201} - 1$). To put the effects of lineage networks in perspective: the average proportion of households belonging to the top three lineage groups in the sample villages roughly doubles [$\approx e^{0.185 \times 4} - 1$] the number of private entrepreneurs and increases their workforce by 220%, *ceteris paribus*. That is to say, without kinship networks, the total number of private enterprises in Chinese villages in the early 1990s would have been sliced by half.

If we take self-employed individuals into the picture (Eq. (2) in Table 2), the corresponding effect is smaller but still significant: a 10% increase in the proportion of households belonging to the largest lineage group is expected to increase the total employment in the private sector by 7%. Apparently, kin support is more important for owners of private enterprises (*siying qiye*) than for self-employed individuals (*getihu*). This may suggest that kin networks not only helped private entrepreneurs to start up as self-employed but also helped them greatly to grow into an "enterprise," albeit still small in scale. Private entrepreneurs needed kin support even more as they grew beyond the scale of family operations, testing more political restrictions and attracting more cadre predation.

All control variables have correct signs even though some are insignificant. For instance, the number of people with at least a junior high school education has a large and significant effect on the count of private enterprises, in line with the common wisdom that schooling brews entrepreneurial skills. Distance from cities has consistently negative coefficients for all regressions, even though not always significant.

CONCLUSION

The above results show unequivocally that lineage networks have promoted rural entrepreneurship in Chinese villages. This evidence should conclude the long debate between the Weberian "sib fetters" line of argument and Whyte's engine argument regarding the relationship between kinship networks and entrepreneurial development. Lineage networks may have facilitated private entrepreneurship via three possible mechanisms: the informal enforcement of property rights (solidarity), the pooling of funds (enforceable trust), and "network resources" via external bridging ties. I proposed a normative control argument emphasizing that it is the lineage solidarity and kin trust that produced the large effects on entrepreneurship whereas the benefit of external bridging ties is probably limited, if any. During the process of partial reform, China's property rights and market institutions are vaguely formulated and ineffectively enforced. Governmental support for private entrepreneurs was tinted with ambivalences and inconsistencies. In such historical contexts, lineage solidarity functioned to enforce informal property rights by protecting private entrepreneurs within each lineage group. Kin trust and bridging ties functioned to substitute ineffective contract laws and sluggish market mechanisms. When formal institutions are ineffective, informal substitution can be effective to a large degree.

Where had Weber erred about Chinese lineage? First of all, we should note that we are not here dealing with exactly the same question that Weber was asking. Weber was primarily concerned with the genesis of capitalism and asked: why did capitalism emerge in the Occident and did not in the Orient? The theoretical relevance of the current analysis probably should be reposed as: Can the traditional culture and social structures of China, such as Confucianism and lineage system, adapt to capitalist development? Weber himself seemed to hint an affirmative prediction to the latter question:

> The Chinese in all probability would be quite capable, probably more capable than the Japanese, of assimilating capitalism which has technically and economically been fully developed in the modern culture area. It is obviously not a question of deeming the Chinese "naturally ungifted" for the demands of capitalism (1951:248).

It would be absurd to blame Weber for having failed to ask the question of assimilation and adaptability and to reveal to the future generations what factors would deter or encourage the assimilation of capitalism. Present-day researchers (e.g. Peter Berger, Martin Whyte, and Gary Hamilton) are dialoguing with the ghost of Weber and deducing what he would say if he were alive. Weber's analyses of the rise of capitalism are broad and have logical ramifications for questions of compatibility and adaptability. He complicated the picture by mixing functional analysis and causal argument. The factors that Weber emphasized, such as private ownership of productive assets, free labor, free market, are logical "presuppositions" of capitalism as much as its causal antecedents. Pre-existing social structures that are congruent with these logical presuppositions (or functional imperatives) should be conducive to the rise or assimilation of capitalism and those incongruent structures may pose obstacles.

Indeed, after the Industrial Revolution first happened in England, by chance or by fate, all other countries were assimilating and adapting to industrial capitalism voluntarily or involuntarily. Native cultural settings may speed up or deter the process of assimilation. Cultural ideas are inert to the extent that vested interests will try to resist change. Upon the impact of western gunship in the mid-19th century, the Qing officials and literati did tenaciously hold onto the Confucian orthodoxy that they embodied and steadfastly resisted assimilation and change – until they were swept away by the Kuomintang Nationalist Revolution in 1911. Lineage elders probably resisted changes, too, and the Socialist Revolution deprived them of their power and prerogatives. Cultural ideas are malleable to the extent that there is affinity between the old and the new. Confucian rationalism can be reconstructed into economic rationalism and family obligations into hardworking ethics, just as Calvinist asceticism were used by the ascending bourgeois to justify the pursuit of money. Whereas Protestants seek salvation, Chinese seek glorification of their ancestors. Calvinist Puritans work hard, live frugally, and accumulate wealth in order to prove their virtues before God, lineage members were enjoined to glorify their ancestors through education and becoming an official. Now, they are encouraged to glorify their ancestor through multiplication to perpetuate the patrilineal blood line and accumulation of wealth to ensue the future prosperity of off-springs.

Secondly, the lineage networks studied here are not the same "corporate actor" that Weber observed. The Communist Revolution transformed lineage from a well-organized hierarchical social, economic and political organization into, at best, a closely knit network group with high level of solidarity and personal trust. The lineage no longer owns much economic resources (such as land or factory) to provide welfare to its member. The new lineage head, with much weakened authority and less traditionalistic orientation, is probably quite open to entrepreneurial ventures and business investment. Kin obligations are quite limited now and may at most attenuate but not stifle entrepreneurial incentives. Lineage is best described as a form of group-level social capital that useful for collective actions and normative control.

Corporate actor or collective actor, however, lineage would definitely not be on Weber's list of cultural items favorable or adaptable to capitalism. Lineage epitomizes the cultural accent of personal (blood) ties rather than impersonal rules and formal procedures. What he perceived as favorable to capitalism in Chinese society were probably the "sober" and rational elements in Confucianism and the bureaucratic elements in the imperial state. He was obviously counting on the latter to grow strong enough to shake off patrimonial prebendalism and break the patriarchal power of the clan. Ironically, when the Communist state bureaucracy penetrated deep down into the rural society, broke the power of the clan, and achieved a high degree of fiscal centralization, it also wiped out all capitalist entrepreneurial activities. It was the revived lineage solidarity, the receding state penetration, and fiscal decentralization (tax farming) during the reform era that fostered capitalist entrepreneurship in Chinese villages. Weber was betting on the wrong horse, too. He was wrong in the sense that formalism is not as essential as he had us to believe. Centralized bureaucratic administration is not necessarily conducive to capitalism; informal and personal organizations such as the lineage are not always inimical to capitalist entrepreneurs.

What does Weber's misinterpretation of the China case imply for his general theory of capitalism? When Weber chose China as a negative case in his comparative scheme, he was probably expecting to find high level of irrationalism, in congruence with his general thesis about the relationship between rationalization and capitalism. What he did find in Confucian ideology and the bureaucratic organization of the imperial state, however, was not so much an absence of rationalism as was a lack of formalism. This may have led him to an excessive and exclusive emphasis on formal rationality at the expense of informal norms and interpersonal relationship.

For Weber, formalism is no less important than rationalism per se because it underwrites rational calculation and calculability. Capital accounting is too sensitive to uncertainties and unpredictability associated with personal whims and caprices. Throughout the pages of *Economy and Society*, *The Religion of China*, and *General Economic History* Weber repeatedly used the expression of "calculable law" and rational administration that "work like machine."

Calculability is a key concept in modern economic theory as well. The question is if formal procedure and formal law are the only means to achieve "the maximum formal rationality of capital accounting." Weber's discussion of the appropriation of material means of production by private owners would accord well with present-day property rights theory (e.g. Demsetz 1967). As Williamson (1985) points out, human rationality is bounded due to limited cognitive ability, imperfect information, and opportunistic behaviors of self-interested individuals. Institutions function to economize on bounded rationality. Institutions refer to all man-made rules and norms, both formal and informal, that regulate human behaviors and human interactions. Institutions are important for economic performance because they structure incentives, transform uncertainties into calculable risks, and reduce transaction costs.

But contemporary institutional theorists recognize the importance of both formal institutions and informal norms. Formal institutions, such as property rights laws and contract laws, are purposively constructed and enforced by the state or formal organizations and are impersonal and universalistic. Informal institutions refer to cultural norms and customs that are supported by social networks and interpersonal ties. Coleman (1993) depicted the modernization process as a transformation from primordial social organizations based on blood and personal ties to purposively constructed organizations. But informal norms and social networks have important roles to play as well. Economists (North 1994), legal scholars (Macaulay 1963; Ellickson 1991; Posner 2000), and of course sociologists are paying more and more attention to the functions and evolution of informal norms and social networks (e.g. Hechter and Opp 2001) and the interaction between the formal and informal (e.g. Nee & Ingram 1998). The advantages of formal institutions are that they can effectively handle high-volume and high-stake economic transactions and social exchanges. The downside is its high costs. Informal institutions, such as customs and norms, are supported by social networks and are therefore personal and particularistic. The advantage of informal institutions is its low costs because its enforcement is absorbed into daily lives and everyday interaction. The downside lies in its limited scope and volume, and low "calculability" (Guseva and Rona-Tas 2001). Informal networks and informal norms should be healthy to economic growth to the extent they are compatible with rationally constructed formal institutions. They are dysfunctional to the extent they conflict with and interrupt the normal operation of the rationally constructed formal institutions.

In their critique of the methodological individualism of economists, Hamilton and Biggart (1988) pointed out that social networks play an important role in the social and economic life of Asian countries. Actually social networks are important for both western and Asian economic life, as suggested by Granovetter (1985). Granovetter uses the image of social embeddedness to launch a critique on the atomistic and individualistic assumption of neoclassical economics. From Granovetter's idea of social embeddedness to economists' institutional environment, the consensus is that even in the western "self-regulated" market system, social relations between the rational and self-interested individuals are important and inevitable. For instance, formal organizations always are enmeshed in or countered by informal networks and cliques (Homans 1961; Dalton 1959); a mix of arm's-length and embedded personal ties with banks and contractors enables a firm to obtain bank loan at a lower interest rate and increases its chances for survival (Uzzi 1999,1996); even competing firms brew and benefit from personal friendship ties among managers (Ingram 2000). Amidst the surging academic interests in "social capital," we hear voices hailing the coming of a network society (Castells 1996).

If we recast Weber's rationalization thesis in institutional theory, it is obvious that he focused exclusively on the rationally constructed formal institutions. Weber apparently posed a false dichotomy between the formal and informal, the rational and affective, just as Parsons did with the dichotomy between universalism and particularism. Weber had obviously overstated both upside of the formal and rational and the downside of the informal and personal. He was too optimistic about the capability of the legal-rational institutions, no matter how ingeniously designed, to reduce uncertainty and achieve calculability. Future contingencies are impossible to predict and human opportunistic behaviors hard to calculate. Furthermore, formal law and rational administration are quite costly to operate even if they are in place and in effect.

Weber's pessimism about the informal, personal, and emotional is understandable because when Weber wrote *Economy and Society* and did his comparative study of nonwestern religions, capitalism and bourgeois were faced with old cultural legacies that were hostile to or incompatible with the newly constructed capitalist institutions. But informal norms and informal social structures (such as personal networks) evolve and adapt, even though their transformation may not always be purposively engineered. Weber's doomed vision of the inevitable entrapment of human race in the "iron cage" of formal rationality has not come true even in the western world. Bureaucratization and formalization have not crowded out the informal, personal and emotional. While our public and private lives are increasingly shaped by rationally constructed institutions (Coleman 1993), a large part of our social life remains informal and personal. As Elster (1999) and Lawler (2001) point out, in today's postindustrial age emotionality remains an important aspect of our social life, if not more so, and constitute a crucial ingredient in our rational choice of actions. So long as emotionality is a fact of life, personal relations and informal networks will stay and have a role to play.

Historically Chinese people were never used to impersonal administration and formal procedures and are much more comfortable with the personal and informal. Therefore, they may fare well with an institutional mix that tips toward the personal and informal, especially when formal institutions do not work very well yet, or are interfered and emasculated by the personal *guanxi* networks anyway.

As an ending remark, I do not intend to paint too rosy a picture of lineage networks. Cultural norms and social networks, because they are informal and personal, are more susceptible to sinister manipulation than rational designing. Old and powerful people tend to have accumulated more social capital and are more likely to support status quo. Thus, social networks tend to serve vested interests and status quo. As Coleman put it

> [Normative systems] operate more via constraints and coercion than via incentives and rewards. They are inegalitarian, giving those with most power in the community free-doms that are denied others. They discriminate, particularly against the young, enforcing norms that are in the interests of elders; they inhibit innovation and creativity; they bring a greyness to life that dampens hope and aspiration. (1993:10)

NOTES

1. Patriarchy refers to the authority structure of the extended household or agna-tic group in which the founding father wields great personal power over its members. Patriarchal domination is based "not on obedience to abstract norms, but on a strict personal loyalty" and the master's power is only limited by tradition (Weber 1968:1006). Patrimonialism can be understood as the extension of patriarchal au-thority in state affairs. The similarity is best illustrated by the analogy that a pat-rimonial king can execute his officials at will, just as a patriarchal father can murder his son with immunity.

2. It seemed that Weber (1968) distinguished three types of state structure: feudal estates, prebendal officialdom, and legal-rational bureaucracy. Both feudalism and prebendal officialdom are patrimonial in nature, but feudal fiefs are hereditary whereas prebendal benefices are not. Weber used the term "patrimonial bureauc-racy" for prebendal officialdom because it signifies a half-way house between feu-dalism and legal-rational bureaucracy. Patrimonial bureaucracy falls short of full bureauractization in that the private and official spheres are not separated. On the one hand, a prebendal official receives a "salary" that is supposed to cover both his personal and official expenditures (including staff salary) but not nearly enough. On the other hand, he pays a fixed-quota tax to his emperor or superior and derives most of his private income from taxation in his jurisdiction. Obviously, prebendalism leads to what we today call "institutionalized corruption." Chinese history evolved from feudalism of the Zhou Dynasty to patrimonial bureaucracy of the Qin Empire during the third century B.C.

3. The khadi is a judge in the Moslem *sharia* court who gave out judgments in a purely arbitrary and capricious fashion. Khadi justice symbolizes Weber's ideal type of "substantively irrational" legal system (see Marsh 2000).

4. The official examination system in imperial China was a merit-based system to select officials from the most talented. In the sense that it was open to all, regardless of family class background, this is quite universalistic. Unfortunately, the content of

the examination was mainly Confucian ideology and literature. Therefore, the imperial bureaucratic office was staffed by a scholar who, "but not in the least degree trained for administration; he knows no jurisprudence but is a fine writer, can make verses, knows the age-old literature of the Chinese and can interpret it" (Weber 1927:338). Justin Lin (1995) proposed an interesting hypothesis regarding the official examination: Had its contents been on scientific subjects, such as mathematics, rather than humanistic literature, China might have been the first to industrialize."

5. Weber, too, believed that the security of property and contractual rights is crucial for capitalism. He described its ambiguity: "In China it may happen that a man who has sold a house to another may later come to him and ask to be taken in because in the meantime he has been impoverished. If the purchaser refuses to heed the ancient Chinese command to help a brother, the spirits will be disturbed; hence the impoverished seller comes into the house as a renter who pays no rent. Capitalism cannot operate on the basis of a law so constituted. What it requires is law which can be counted upon, like a machine; ritualistic-religious and magical consideration must be excluded" (Weber 1981:342–343).

6. Collins (1980) interprets "ethical dualism" in the following paragraph: "In virtually all premodern societies there are two sharply divergent sets of ethical beliefs and practices. Within a social group, economic transactions are strictly controlled by rules of fairness, status, and tradition.... The prohibition on usury reflected this internal ethic, requiring an ethic of charity and the avoidance of calculation of gain from loans within the community... In regard to outsiders, however, economic ethics were at the opposite extreme: cheating, price gouging, and loans at exorbitant interest were the rule. Both forms of ethic were obstacle to rational, large-scale capitalism: the internal ethic because it prevented the commercialization of economic life, the external ethic because it made trading relations too episodic and distrustful. The lifting of this barrier and the overcoming of this ethical dualism were crucial for the development of any extensive capitalism" (p. 931)

7. This argument is actually not that old and echoed in a recent book titled *Trust* by Fukuyama (1995), which portraits China as a low-trust society. In a low-trust society, transaction costs are very high in such societies because trust and loyalty are limited to a small circle of family members, relatives, and friends and impersonal and "generalized trust" could not develop.

8. Freedman (1958) argued that because the clan tended to rent its communal land its members on preferential terms, clan members tended to stay in the village rather than trying their luck elsewhere.

9. The concepts of bounded solidarity and enforceable trust are borrowed from studies of immigrant ethnic entrepreneurship (Portes and Zhou 1992). Lineage groups share certain similarities with immigrant ethnic groups. Both are normative communities.

10. The 22 counties are Zhangwu, Haicheng (Liaoning); Huichun (Jilin); Anda (Heilongjiang); Zhangjiagang (Jiangsu); Tianchang (Anhui); Tongxiang (Zhejiang); Xingguo, Gaoan, Xunwu (Jiangxi); Sangzhi, Yizhang (Hunan); Yichang (Hubei); Xinhui, Xingnin, Meixian (Guangdong); Xichang (Sichuan); Lunan (Yunnan); Tongguan (Shaanxi); Wuzhong, Guyuan (Ningxia); and Huocheng (Xinjiang).

11. I excluded the 1991 sample of the same survey because it did not distinguish the ownership types of rural enterprises.

12. Four villages reported one or two firms that were wholly or partially funded by overseas investment (*sanzi qiye*). I did not count these firms as rural enterprises.

13. There are two cases in which the number of private enterprises is larger than 100, and 10 cases in which the number of private enterprise managers is larger than 200. As these outliers do not overlap, I recalibrated them according to regressions of each variable on the other. As a result, the largest count of private enterprises is now 96, which is credible.

14. These measures are taken from questions regarding the occupational classification of the village labor force and are separate from questions about the number of private entrepreneurs in the village. Thus, there are some minor discrepancies in measurement. For instance, the workforce of collective enterprises may include some commuters who work in township-owned enterprises. Such discrepancies serve as a good robustness check of the regression results against measurement errors.

15. It is rare for a single lineage group to dominate a whole administrative village. During a field trip to Jiangxi, I found that administrative villages often consist of 2, 3, 4 lineage groups, each dominating one or two natural villages. Freedman (1958) reported the same observation.

ACKNOWLEDGMENT

I wish to thank the Asia-Pacific Research Center at Stanford University for providing access to its wonderful facilities. For helpful comments, I acknowledge Mranda Brown, Lucie Cheng, Liser Keister, Chingkuan Lee, James Lee, Thomas Gold, Philip Huang, Xueguan Zhou, Min Zhou, Deborah Davis, and Andrew Walder.

REFERENCES

Bendix, Reinhard. 1962. *Max Weber: An Intellectual Portrait.* New York: Anchor Books.

Berger, Peter L. 1988. "An East Asian Development Model?." Pp. 3–11 in *Search of an East Asian Development Model*, edited by P. Berger and H.H. Michael Hsiao. New Brunswick, NJ: Transaction Books.

Biggart, Nicole Woolsey. 1997. "Institutionalized Patrimonialism in Korean Business." Pp. 215–236 in *The Economic Organization of East Asian Capitalism*, edited by M. Orru, N.W. Biggart and G. Hamilton. Thousand Oaks, CA: Sage.

Burt, Ronald. 1992. *Structural Holes.* Cambridge, MA: Harvard University Press.

Castells, Manuel. 1996. *The Rise of the Network Society.* Oxford: Blackwell Publishers.

Chang, Jiahua. 2000. "Zongzu zhidu de lishi guiji (The Historical Trajectory of the Lineage System)." Pp. 293–335 in *Zhongguo Shehuishilun (A Social History of China)*, edited by Z. Jiming and S. Dejin. Hubei, China: Hubei jiaoyu chubanshe.

China Ministry of Agriculture 1997–2001. *Zhongguo Xiangzhen Qiye Nianjian (Chinese Township and Village Enterprise Yearbook)*. Beijing: China Agricultural Publishing House.

Coleman, James S. 1990. *Foundations of Social Theory*. Cambridge, MA: The Belknap Press of Harvard University Press.
------. 1993. "Rational Reconstruction of Society: 1992 Presidential Address." *American Sociological Review* 58:1–15.
Collins, Randall. 1980. "Weber's last theory of capitalism: A systematization." *American Sociological Review* 45:925–942.
Demsetz, Harold. 1967. "Toward a Theory of Property Rights." *American Economic Review* 57(2):347–359.
Ebrey, Patricia B. 1986. "The Early Stages in the Development of Descent Group Organization." Pp. 16–61 in *Kinship Organization in Late Imperial China 1000–1940*, edited by P.B. Ebrey and J.L. Watson. Berkeley, CA: University of California Press.
Ellickson, Robert C. 1991. *Order Without Law: How Neighbors Settle Disputes*. Cambridge, Massachusetts: Harvard University Press.
Elster, Jon. 1999. *Alchemies of the Mind: Rationality and Emotions*. Cambridge, UK: Cambridge University Press.
Feuerwerker, Albert. 1958. *China's Early Industrialization: Sheng Hsuan-Huai and Manderin Enterprise*. Cambridge, MA: Harvard University Press.
Freedman, Maurice. 1958. *Lineage Organization in Southeastern China*. London: The Athlone Press.
Fukuyama, Francis. 1995. *Trust: The Social Virtues and The Creation of Prosperity*. London: Penguin Books.
Granovetter, Mark. 1985. "Economic Action and Social Structure: The Problem of Embeddedness." *American Journal Sociology* 91(3):481–510.
Greenhalgh, Susan. 1988. "Families and Networks in Tawan's Economic Development." Pp. 225–245 in *Contending Approaches to the Political Economy of Taiwan*, edited by E.A. Winckler and S. Greenhalgh. Armonk, NY: M. E. Sharpe, Inc.
Guseva, Alya and Akos Rona-Tas. 2001. "Uncertainty, Risk, and Trust: Russian and American Credit Markets Compared." *American Sociological Review* 66(5):623–646.
Hamilton, Gary. 1984. "Patriarchalism in Imperial China and Western Europe: A Revision of Weber's Sociology of Domination." *Theory and Society* 13(3):393–425.
------. 1990. "Patriarchy, Patrimonialism, and Filial Piety: A Comparison of China and Western Europe." *British Journal of Sociology* 41:77–104.
Hamilton, Gary and Nicole Woosley Biggart. 1988. "Market, Culture, and Authority: Analysis of Management and Organization in the Far East." *American Journal of Sociology* 94(Supp.):S52–S94.
Harrell, Stevan. 1985. "Why Do the Chinese Work So Hard: Reflections on an Entrepreneurial Ethic?." *Modern China* 11(2):203–226.
Hechter, Micheal and Karl-Dieter Opp, eds. 2001. *Social Norms*. New York: Russell Sage Foundation.
Homans, George C. 1961. *Social Behavior: Its Elementary Form*. New York: Harcourt Brace Jovanovich.
Huang, Philip C.C. 1996. "Between Informal Mediation and Formal Adjudication: The Third Realm of Qing Civil Justice." *Modern China* 19(3):251–298.
------. 1996. *Civil Justice in China*. Stanford, CA: Stanford University Press.
Ingram, Paul. 2000. "Friendship Among Competitors in the Sydney Hotel Industry." *American Journal of Sociology* 106:387–432.

Inkeles, Alex. 1966. "The Modernization of Man." Pp. 138–150 in *Modernization*, edited by Myron Weiner. New York: Basic Books.

Kerr, Clark, Dunlop John, Frediric Harbison, and Charles Meyers. 1964. *Industrialism and Industrial Man*. New York: Oxford University Press.

Lawler, Edward. 2001. "An Affect Theory of Social Exchange." *American Journal of Sociology* 107(2):321–352.

Levy, S. and J. Marion. 1949. *The Family Revolution in Modern China*. New York: Atheneum.

Lin, Justin Y. 1995. "The Needham Puzzle: Why the Industrial Revolution Did Not Originate in China?." *Economic Development and Cultural Change* 43(2):269–292.

Liu Liangqun. 2005. "Zonzu dui nongcunshequ gonggongquanli de yingxiang" (The Influence of Lineage on the Administrative Power of Rural Communities). *Zhongguo Xiangcun Yanjiu Studies of Rural China*, Vol. 3. Beijing: Shangwu Yinshuguan.

Macaulay, Stewart. 1963. "Non-contractual Relations in Business: A Preliminary Study." *American Sociological Review* 28:55–67.

Marsh, Robert. 2000. "Weber's Misunderstanding of Chinese Law." *American Journal of Sociology* 106(2):281–302.

Metzger, Thomas A. 1986. *Escape from Predicament*. New York: Columbia University Press.

Naughton, Barry. 1995. *Growing Out of the Plan*. Cambridge, UK: Cambridge University Press.

Nee, Victor. 1992. "Organizational Dynamics of Market Transition: Hybrid Forms, Property Rights, and Mixed Economy in China." *Administrative Science Quarterly* 37(1):1–27.

Nee, Vector and Ingram Paul. 1998. "Embeddedness and Beyond." Pp. 19–45 in *The New Institutionalism in Sociology*, edited by M. Brinton and V. Nee. New York: Russell Sage Foundation.

Niehoff, Justin. 1987. "The Villager as Industrialist: Ideologies of Household Manufacturing." *Modern China* 13(3):278–309.

North, Douglass C. 1994. "Economic Performance through Time." *American Economic Review* 84(3):359–368.

Oi, Jean. 1999. *Rural China Takes Off: Institutional Foundations of Economic Reform*. Berkeley: University of California Press.

Parsons, Talcott. 1937. *The Structure of Social Action*. New York: McMgraw-Hill Book Company.

Peng, Yusheng. 1992. "Wage Determination in Rural and Urban China: A Comparison of Public and Private Industrial Sectors." *American Sociological Review* 57:198–213.

------. 1999. "Agricultural and Nonagricultural Growth and Inter-county Inequality in China, 1985–1991." *Modern China* 25(3):235–263.

------. 2001. "Chinese Townships and Villages as Industrial Corporations: Ownership, Governance, and Productivity." *American Journal of Sociology* 106(5):1338–1370.

------. 2004. "Kinship Networks and Entrepreneurs in China's Transitional Economy." *American Journal of Sociology* 109(5):1045–1074.

Portes, Alejandro and Min Zhou. 1992. "Gaining the Upper Hand: Economic Mobility among Immigrant and Domestic Minorities." *Ethnic and Racial Studies* 15(4):491–522.

Posner, Eric A. 2000. *Law and Social Norms*. Cambridge, MA: Harvard University Press.

Qian Hang, 1994. *Zhongguo Zongzu Zhidu Xintan (Exploring the Lineage System in China)*. Hong Kong: Zhonghua Shuju.

Rawski, Tomas G. 1999. "Reforming China's Economy: What Have we Learned?." *The China Journal* 41:139–149.

Renzulli, Linda A., Howard Aldrich, and James Moody. 2000. "Family Matters: Gender, Networks, and Entrepreneurial Outcomes." *Social Forces* 79(2):523–546.

Rozman, Gilbert, eds. 1991. *The East Asian Region: Confucian Heritage and Its Modern Adaptation.* Princeton: Princeton University Press.

Shen, Chonglin, Yingying Chan, and Yong Gao. 2000. *Zhongguo Baixian Diaocha: Diaocha Baogao he Ziliao Huibian (Survey of 100 Counties in China: Reports and Data Compilation).* Beijing: China Encyclopedia Press.

Tsai, Kellee S. (2000). "Banquet Banking: Gender and Rotating Savings and Credit Associations in South China." *The China Quarterly*, Vol. 161, Pp. 142–170.

Uzzi, Brian. 1996. "The Sources and Consequences of Embeddedness for the Economic Performance of Organizations: the Network Effect." *American Sociological Review* 61(4):674–698.

------. 1999. "Social Relations and Networks in the Making of Financial Capital." *American Sociological Review* 64(4):481–505.

Van Der Sprenkel, Otto B. 1964. "Max Weber on China." *History and Theory* 3(3):348–370.

Walder, Andrew. 1995. "Local Governments as Industrial Firms." *American Journal of Sociology* 101(2):263–301.

Wang, Huning. 1991. *Dandai Zhongguo Cunluo Jiazu Wenhua (Lineage Culture in Contemporary China).* Shanghai: Shanghai Renmin Chubanshe.

Wank, David L. 1999. *Commodifying Communism.* Cambridge: Cambridge University Press.

Weber, Max. 1951[1916]. *The Religion of China.* New York: Free Press.

------. 1968. *Economy and Society.* New York: Bedminster Press.

------. 1927/1981. *General Economic History.* New Brunswick, NJ: Transaction Books.

Whyte, Martin K. 1995. "The Social Roots of China's Economic Development." *The China Quarterly* 144:999–1019.

------. 1996. "The Chinese Family and Economic Development: Obstacle or Engine?." *Economic Development and Cultural Change* 45(1):1–30.

Williamson, Olive. 1985. *The Economic Institutions of Capitalism.* New York: The Free Press.

Wong, Siu-lun. 1985. "The Chinese Family Firm: A Model." *The British Journal of Sociology* 36(1):58–72.

------. 1988. "The Applicability of Asian Family Values to Other Sociocultural Settings." Pp. 134–146 in *Search of an East Asian Development Model*, edited by P. Berger and H.H. Michael Hsiao. New Brunswick, NJ: Transaction Books.

Woo, Wing Thye. 1999. "The Real Reasons for China's Growth." *The China Journal* 41:115–137.

Xiao, Tangbiao. 2001. *Cunzhi Zhong De Zongzu (Lineage Organization and Village Administration).* Shanghai: Shanghai shudian chubanshe.

Xin, Katherine R. and Jone L. Pearce. 1996. "Guanxi: Connections as Substitutes for Formal Institutional Support." *Academy of Management Journal* 39(6):1641–1658.

Yu, Ying-Shih. 2004[1985]. *Rujialunli Yu Shangren Jingshen (Confucian Ethics and Business Spirits).* Guangxi, China: Guangxi shifandaxue chubanshe.

Zhong Nian. 2000. "Zhongguo xiangcun shehui kongzhi de bianqian" (The Evolution of Social Control in Rural China). Pp. 293–335 in *Zhongguo Shehuishilun (A Social History of China)*, edited by Zhou Jiming, and Song Dejin. Hubei, China: Hubei jiaoyu chubanshe.